EMOTIONAL INTELLIGENCE

The 10th Anniversary Edition

Also by Daniel Goleman

THE MEDITATIVE MIND

VITAL LIES, SIMPLE TRUTHS

WORKING WITH EMOTIONAL INTELLIGENCE

PRIMAL LEADERSHIP (Coauthor)

DESTRUCTIVE EMOTIONS (Narrator)

SOCIAL INTELLIGENCE

EMOTIONAL INTELLIGENCE

The 10th Anniversary Edition

DANIEL GOLEMAN

Bantam Books

New York   Toronto   London   Sydney   Auckland

EMOTIONAL INTELLIGENCE
A Bantam Book

PUBLISHING HISTORY
Bantam hardcover edition published October 1995
Bantam trade paperback edition published July 1997
Bantam 10th anniversary trade paperback edition published October 2005
Bantam 10th anniversary hardcover edition / October 2006

Published by
Bantam Dell
A Division of Random House, Inc.
New York, New York

Illustration of brain on page 19 is adapted from "Emotional
Memory and the Brain" by Joseph E. LeDoux.
Copyright © 1994 by Scientific American, Inc.
All rights reserved.
Artist: Roberto Osti

Book design by Irving Perkins Associates

Library of Congress Catalog Card Number: 95-16685

ISBN-13: 978-0-553-80491-1
ISBN-10: 0-553-80491-X

Printed in the United States of America
Published simultaneously in Canada

www.bantamdell.com

BVG 10 9 8 7 6 5

For Tara, wellspring of emotional wisdom

Contents

PART FIVE
EMOTIONAL LITERACY

Introduction

Tenth Anniversary Edition of **Emotional Intelligence**

In 1990, in my role as a science reporter at *The New York Times,* I chanced upon an article in a small academic journal by two psychologists, John Mayer, now at the University of New Hampshire, and Yale's Peter Salovey. Mayer and Salovey offered the first formulation of a concept they called "emotional intelligence."

Those were days when the preeminence of IQ as the standard of excellence in life was unquestioned; a debate raged over whether it was set in our genes or due to experience. But here, suddenly, was a new way of thinking about the ingredients of life success. I was electrified by the notion, which I made the title of this book in 1995. Like Mayer and Salovey, I used the phrase to synthesize a broad range of scientific findings, drawing together what had been separate strands of research—reviewing not only their theory but a wide variety of other exciting scientific developments, such as the first fruits of the nascent field of affective neuroscience, which explores how emotions are regulated in the brain.

I remember having the thought, just before this book was published ten years ago, that if one day I overheard a conversation in which two strangers used the phrase *emotional intelligence* and both understood what it meant, I would have succeeded in spreading the concept more widely into the culture. Little did I know.

The phrase *emotional intelligence,* or its casual shorthand *EQ,* has become ubiquitous, showing up in settings as unlikely as the cartoon strips *Dilbert* and *Zippy the Pinhead* and in Roz Chast's sequential art in *The New Yorker.* I've seen boxes of toys that claim to boost a child's EQ; lovelorn personal ads sometimes trumpet it in those seeking prospective mates. I once found a quip about EQ printed on a shampoo bottle in my hotel room.

And the concept has spread to the far corners of our planet. *EQ* has become a word recognized, I'm told, in languages as diverse as German and Portuguese, Chinese, Korean, and Malay. (Even so, I prefer *EI* as the English abbreviation for *emotional intelligence.*) My e-mail inbox often contains queries from, for example, a doctoral student in Bulgaria, a schoolteacher in Poland, a college student in Indonesia, a business consultant in South Africa, a management expert in the Sultanate of Oman, an executive in Shanghai. Business students in India read about EI and leadership; a CEO in Argentina recommends the book I later wrote on that topic. I've also heard from religious scholars within Christianity, Judaism, Islam, Hinduism, and Buddhism that the concept of EI resonates with outlooks in their own faith.

Most gratifying for me has been how ardently the concept has been embraced by educators, in the form of programs in "social and emotional learning," or SEL. Back in 1995 I was able to find only a handful of such programs teaching emotional intelligence skills to children. Now, a decade later, tens of thousands of schools worldwide offer children SEL. In the United States many districts and even entire states currently make SEL a curriculum requirement, mandating that just as students must attain a certain level of competence in math and language, so too should they master these essential skills for living.

In Illinois, for instance, specific learning standards in SEL abilities have been established for every grade from kindergarten through the last year of high school. To give just one example of a remarkably detailed and comprehensive curriculum, in the early elementary years students should learn to recognize and accurately label their emotions and how they lead them to act. By the late elementary years lessons in empathy should make children able to identify the nonverbal clues to how someone else feels; in junior high they should be able to analyze what creates stress for them or what motivates their best performance. And in high school the SEL skills include listening and talking in ways that resolve conflicts instead of escalating them, and negotiating for win-win solutions.

Around the world Singapore has undertaken an active initiative in SEL, as have some schools in Malaysia, Hong Kong, Japan, and Korea. In Europe the U.K. has led the way, but more than a dozen other countries have schools that embrace EI, as do Australia and New Zealand, and here and there countries in Latin America and Africa. In 2002 UNESCO began a worldwide initiative to promote SEL, sending a statement of ten basic principles for implementing SEL to the ministries of education in 140 countries.

In some states and nations SEL has become the organizing umbrella under which are gathered programs in character education, violence prevention, antibullying, drug prevention, and school discipline. The goal is not just to reduce these problems among schoolchildren but to enhance the school climate and, ultimately, students' academic performance.

In 1995 I outlined the preliminary evidence suggesting that SEL was the active ingredient in programs that enhance children's learning while preventing problems such as violence. Now the case can be made scientifically: helping children improve their self-awareness and confidence, manage their disturbing emotions and impulses, and increase their empathy pays off not just in improved behavior but in measurable academic achievement.

This is the big news contained in a recently completed meta-analysis of 668 evaluation studies of SEL programs for children from preschoolers through high school.[1] The massive survey was conducted by Roger Weissberg, who directs the Collaborative for Academic, Social and Emotional Learning at the University of Illinois at Chicago—the organization that has led the way in bringing SEL into schools worldwide.

The data show that SEL programs yielded a strong benefit in academic accomplishment, as demonstrated in achievement test results and grade-point averages. In participating schools, up to 50 percent of children showed improved achievement scores, and up to 38 percent improved their grade-point averages. SEL programs also made schools safer: incidents of misbehavior dropped by an average of 28 percent; suspensions by 44 percent; and other disciplinary actions by 27 percent. At the same time, attendance rates rose, while 63 percent of students demonstrated significantly more positive behavior. In the world of social science research, these are remarkable results for any program promoting behavioral change. SEL has delivered on its promise.

In 1995 I also proposed that a good part of the effectiveness of SEL came from its impact in shaping children's developing neural circuitry, particularly the executive functions of the prefrontal cortex, which manage working memory—what we hold in mind as we learn—and inhibit disruptive emotional impulses. Now the first preliminary scientific evidence for that notion has arrived. Mark Greenberg of Pennsylvania State University, a codeveloper of the PATHS curriculum in SEL, reports not only that this program for elementary school students boosts academic achievement but, even more significantly, that much of the increased learning can be attributed to improvements in attention and working memory, key functions of the prefrontal cortex.[2] This strongly suggests that neuroplasticity, the shaping of the brain through repeated experiences, plays a key role in the benefits from SEL.

Perhaps the biggest surprise for me has been the impact of EI in the world of business, particularly in the areas of leadership and employee development (a form of adult education). The *Harvard Business Review* has hailed emotional intelligence as "a ground-breaking, paradigm-shattering idea," one of the most influential business ideas of the decade.

Such claims in the business world too often prove to be fads, with no real underlying substance. But here a far-flung network of researchers has been at work, ensuring that the application of EI will be grounded in solid data. The Rutgers University–based Consortium for Research on Emotional Intelligence in Organizations (CREIO) has led the way in catalyzing this scientific work, collaborating with organizations that range from the Office of Personnel Management in the federal government to American Express.

Today companies worldwide routinely look through the lens of EI in hiring, promoting, and developing their employees. For instance, Johnson & Johnson (another CREIO member) found that in divisions around the world, those identified at midcareer as having high leadership potential were far stronger in EI competencies than were their less-promising peers. CREIO continues to foster such research, which can offer evidence-based guidelines for organizations seeking to enhance their ability to achieve their business goals or fulfill a mission.

When Salovey and Mayer published their seminal article in 1990, no one could have envisioned how the scholarly field they founded would be thriving just fifteen years later. Research has blossomed in this area; while in 1995 there was virtually nothing in the scientific literature on EI, today the field has legions of researchers. A search of the database for doctoral dissertations investigating aspects of emotional intelligence yields more than seven hundred completed to date, with many more in the pipeline— not to mention studies done by professors and others not counted in that database.[3]

The growth of this area of scholarship owes much to Mayer and Salovey, who, along with their colleague David Caruso, a business consultant, have worked tirelessly on behalf of the scientific acceptance of emotional intelligence. By formulating a scientifically defensible theory of emotional intelligence and providing a rigorous measure of this capacity for effective living, they have set an impeccable research standard for the field.

Another major source of the burgeoning academic findings about EI has been Reuven Bar-On, now at the University of Texas Medical Branch in Houston, whose own theory of EI—and high-energy enthusiasm—have inspired many studies using a measure he devised. Bar-On has also been instrumental in developing and editing academic books that have helped give the field a critical mass, including *The Handbook of Emotional Intelligence.*

The growing EI field of study has met some entrenched opposition within the insular world of scholars of intelligence, particularly those who embrace IQ as the sole acceptable measure of human aptitudes. Nevertheless, the field has emerged as a vibrant paradigm. Any important theoretical model, observed the philosopher of science Thomas Kuhn, should become progressively revised and refined as more stringent tests of its premises are made. That process seems well under way for EI.

There are by now three main models of EI, with dozens of variations. Each represents a different perspective. That of Salovey and Mayer rests firmly in the tradition of intelligence shaped by the original work on IQ a century ago. The model put forth by Reuven Bar-On is based on his research on well-being. And my own model focuses on performance at work and organizational leadership, melding EI theory with decades of research on modeling the competencies that set star performers apart from average.

Unfortunately, misreadings of this book have spawned some myths, which I would like to clear up here and now. One is the bizarre—though widely repeated—fallacy that "EQ accounts for 80 percent of success." This claim is preposterous.

The misinterpretation stems from data suggesting IQ accounts for about 20 percent of career success. Because that estimate—and it is only an estimate—leaves a large portion of success unaccounted for, we must seek other factors to explain the rest. It does *not* mean, however, that emotional intelligence represents the rest of the factors in success: they certainly include a very wide range of forces—from the wealth and education of the family we are born into, to temperament, to blind luck and the like—in addition to emotional intelligence.

As John Mayer and his associates point out: "To the unsophisticated reader, bringing up the '80 percent unaccounted for variance' suggests that there may indeed be a heretofore overlooked variable that truly can predict huge portions of life success. Although that is desirable, no variable studied in a century of psychology has made such a huge contribution."[4]

Another common misconception takes the form of recklessly applying this book's subtitle—"Why it can matter more than IQ"—to domains like academic achievement, where it does not apply without careful qualification. The extreme form of this misconception is the myth that EI "matters more than IQ" in all pursuits.

Emotional intelligence trumps IQ primarily in those "soft" domains where intellect is relatively less relevant for success—where, for example, emotional self-regulation and empathy may be more salient skills than purely cognitive abilities.

As it happens, some of these circumscribed realms are of major importance in our lives. One that comes to mind is health (as detailed in Chapter 11), to the extent that disturbing emotions and toxic relationships have been identified as risk factors in disease. Those who can manage their emotional lives with more calm and self-awareness seem to have a distinct and measurable health advantage, as has now been confirmed by many studies.

Another such domain is romantic love and personal relationships (see Chapter 9), where, as we all know, very smart people can do very dumb things. A third—though I have not written about it here—occurs at the top levels of competitive endeavors such as world-class sports. At that level, as I was told by a sports psychologist who coaches U.S. Olympic teams, everyone has put in the requisite ten thousand–plus hours of practice, so success hinges on the athlete's mental game.

Research findings about leadership in business and the professions paint a more complex picture (Chapter 10). IQ scores predict extremely well whether we can handle the cognitive challenges that a given position demands. Hundreds, perhaps thousands, of studies have shown that IQ predicts which career rungs a person can manage. No question there.

But IQ washes out when it comes to predicting who, among a talented pool of candidates *within* an intellectually demanding profession, will become the strongest leader. In part this is because of the "floor effect": everyone at the top echelons of a given profession, or at the top levels of a large organization, has already been sifted for intellect and expertise. At those lofty levels a high IQ becomes a "threshold" ability, one needed just to get into and stay in the game.

As I proposed in my 1998 book *Working with Emotional Intelligence,* EI abilities rather than IQ or technical skills emerge as the "discriminating" competency that best predicts who among a group of very smart people will lead most ably. If you scan the competencies that organizations around the world have independently determined identify their star leaders, you discover that indicators of IQ and technical skill drop toward the bottom of the list the higher the position. (IQ and technical expertise are much stronger predictors of excellence in lower-rung jobs.)

That point was developed more fully in my 2002 book *Primal Leadership: Learning to Lead with Emotional Intelligence* (coauthored with Richard Boyatzis and Annie McKee). At the very highest levels, competence models for leadership typically consist of anywhere from 80 to 100 percent EI-based abilities. As the head of research at a global executive search firm put it, "CEOs are hired for their intellect and business expertise—and fired for a lack of emotional intelligence."

When I wrote *Emotional Intelligence,* I saw my role as that of a science journalist, reporting on a significant new trend in psychology, particularly the merging of neuroscience with the study of emotions. But as my involvement in the field deepened, I stepped back into my old role as psychologist to offer my insights into models of EI. As a result, my formulation of emotional intelligence has progressed since I wrote these pages.

In *Working with Emotional Intelligence* I proposed an expanded framework that reflects how the fundamentals of EI—self-awareness, self-management, social awareness, and the ability to manage relationships—translate into on-the-job success. In doing so, I borrowed a concept from David McClelland, the Harvard psychologist who had been my mentor in graduate school: *competency.*

While our emotional *intelligence* determines our potential for learning the fundamentals of self-mastery and the like, our emotional *competence* shows how much of that potential we have mastered in ways that translate into on-the-job capabilities. To be adept at an emotional competence like customer service or teamwork requires an underlying ability in EI fundamentals, specifically social awareness and relationship management. But emotional competencies are learned abilities: having social awareness or skill at managing relationships does not guarantee that one has mastered the additional learning required to handle a customer adeptly or to resolve a conflict. One simply has the potential to *become* skilled at these competencies.

Again, an underlying EI ability is necessary, though not sufficient, to manifest a given competency or job skill. A cognitive analog would be the student who has excellent spatial abilities yet never learns geometry, let alone becomes an architect. So, too, can one be highly empathic yet poor at handling customers—without having learned the competency for customer service. (For those ultradedicated souls wanting to understand how my current model nests twenty or so emotional competencies within the four EI clusters, see the appendix to *Primal Leadership*.)

In 1995 I reported data from a nationwide, demographically representative sample of more than three thousand children aged seven to sixteen, rated by their parents and teachers, showing that over the decade or so between the mid-1970s and mid-1980s, indicators of emotional well-being among America's kids underwent a marked decline. These children were more troubled and had more problems, ranging from loneliness and anxiety to disobedience and whining. (Of course, there are always individual exceptions—children who grow up to be outstanding human beings—whatever the overall numbers show.)

But a later group of children, rated in 1999, seem to have improved markedly, rating far better than those in the late 1980s, though they were not quite restored to the levels recorded in the mid-1970s.[5] True, parents are still likely to complain in general about their kids, still concerned that their children are hanging out with "bad influences," and whining seems worse than ever. But the trend is clearly upward.

Frankly, I'm puzzled. I had conjectured that today's children are unintended victims of economic and technological progress, deskilled in EI because their parents spend more time at work than in previous generations, because increased mobility has cut ties to extended family, and because "free" time has become so structured and overorganized. After all, emotional intelligence has traditionally been passed on in the midst of everyday life—with parents and relatives, and in the rough-and-tumble of free play—opportunities that are now being lost to the young.

Then there's the technological factor. Today's children spend more time alone than ever before in human history, staring at a video monitor. That amounts to a natural experiment on an unprecedented scale. Will these tech-savvy children become adults who are as comfortable with other people as they are with their computers? I suspected, rather, that a childhood spent relating to a virtual world would deskill our young people when it came to relating person to person.

So went my arguments. Nothing has happened in the last decade or so to reverse these trends. Yet children, thankfully, seem to be faring better.

Thomas Achenbach, the University of Vermont psychologist who has done these studies, hypothesizes that the economic boom of the 1990s lifted children as well as adults; more jobs and less crime meant better child-rearing. Should there be another major economic recession, he suggests, we would see another decline in this measure of children's skills for life. That may well be; only time will tell.

The hyperspeed at which EI has become a topic of importance in a wide array of fields makes prediction difficult, but let me offer some thoughts on what I hope for the field in the near future.

Many of the benefits that accrue from developing emotional intelligence capabilities have gone to the privileged, such as high-level business executives and children in private schools. Of course, many children in impoverished neighborhoods have also benefited—for instance, if their schools implemented SEL. But I encourage a further democratization of this variety of human skill development, reaching into often-neglected pools, like families in poverty (where children so often suffer emotional wounds that compound their plight) and to prisons (particularly for young offenders who could benefit enormously from strengthening skills like anger management, self-awareness, and empathy). Given the right help with these abilities, their lives would improve, and their communities would be safer.

I'd also like to see the scope of thinking about emotional intelligence itself expand, leaping from a focus on capacities within the individual to a focus on what emerges when people interact, whether one on one or in larger groups. Some research, notably the University of New Hampshire psychologist Vanessa Druskat's work on how teams can become emotionally intelligent, has seamlessly made this leap already. But much more could be done.

Finally, I envision a day when emotional intelligence will have become so widely understood that we need not mention it because it has melded with our lives. In such a future, SEL would have become standard practice in schools everywhere. Likewise, EI qualities such as self-awareness, managing destructive emotions, and empathy would be givens in the workplace, "must-haves" for being hired and promoted, and most especially for leadership. If EI were to become as widespread as IQ has become, and as ingrained in society as a measure of human qualities, then, I believe, our families, schools, jobs, and communities would be all the more humane and nourishing.

Aristotle's Challenge

Anyone can become angry—that is easy. But to be angry with the right person, to the right degree, at the right time, for the right purpose, and in the right way—that is not easy.

ARISTOTLE, *The Nichomachean Ethics*

It was an unbearably steamy August afternoon in New York City, the kind of sweaty day that makes people sullen with discomfort. I was heading back to a hotel, and as I stepped onto a bus up Madison Avenue I was startled by the driver, a middle-aged black man with an enthusiastic smile, who welcomed me with a friendly, "Hi! How you doing?" as I got on, a greeting he proffered to everyone else who entered as the bus wormed through the thick midtown traffic. Each passenger was as startled as I, and, locked into the morose mood of the day, few returned his greeting.

But as the bus crawled uptown through the gridlock, a slow, rather magical transformation occurred. The driver gave a running monologue for our benefit, a lively commentary on the passing scene around us: there was a terrific sale at that store, a wonderful exhibit at this museum, did you hear about the new movie that just opened at that cinema down the block? His delight in the rich possibilities the city offered was infectious. By the time people got off the bus, each in turn had shaken off the sullen shell they had entered with, and when the driver shouted out a "So long, have a great day!" each gave a smiling response.

The memory of that encounter has stayed with me for close to twenty years. When I rode that Madison Avenue bus, I had just finished my own doctorate in psychology—but there was scant attention paid in the psychology of the day to just how such a transformation could happen. Psychological science knew little or nothing of the mechanics of emotion. And yet, imagining the spreading virus of good feeling that must have rippled through the city, starting from passengers on his bus, I saw that this bus driver was an urban peacemaker of sorts, wizardlike in his power to transmute the sullen irritability that seethed in his passengers, to soften and open their hearts a bit.

In stark contrast, some items from this week's paper:

• At a local school, a nine-year-old goes on a rampage, pouring paint over school desks, computers, and printers, and vandalizing a car in the school parking lot. The reason: some third-grade classmates called him a "baby" and he wanted to impress them.

• Eight youngsters are wounded when an inadvertent bump in a crowd of teenagers milling outside a Manhattan rap club leads to a shoving match, which ends when one of those affronted starts shooting a .38 caliber automatic handgun into the crowd. The report notes that such shootings over seemingly minor slights, which are perceived as acts of disrespect, have become increasingly common around the country in recent years.

• For murder victims under twelve, says a report, 57 percent of the murderers are their parents or stepparents. In almost half the cases, the parents say they were "merely trying to discipline the child." The fatal beatings were prompted by "infractions" such as the child blocking the TV, crying, or soiling diapers.

• A German youth is on trial for murdering five Turkish women and girls in a fire he set while they slept. Part of a neo-Nazi group, he tells of failing to hold jobs, of drinking, of blaming his hard luck on foreigners. In a barely audible voice, he pleads, "I can't stop being sorry for what we've done, and I am infinitely ashamed."

Each day's news comes to us rife with such reports of the disintegration of civility and safety, an onslaught of mean-spirited impulse running amok. But the news simply reflects back to us on a larger scale a creeping sense of emotions out of control in our own lives and in those of the people around us. No one is insulated from this erratic tide of outburst and regret; it reaches into all of our lives in one way or another.

The last decade has seen a steady drumroll of reports like these, portraying an uptick in emotional ineptitude, desperation, and recklessness in our families, our communities, and our collective lives. These years have chronicled surging rage and despair, whether in the quiet loneliness of latchkey kids left with a TV for a babysitter, or in the pain of children abandoned, neglected, or abused, or in the ugly intimacy of marital violence. A spreading emotional malaise can be read in numbers showing a jump in depression around the world, and in the reminders of a surging tide of aggression—teens with guns in schools, freeway mishaps ending in shootings, disgruntled ex-employees massacring former fellow workers. *Emotional abuse, drive-by shooting,* and *post-traumatic stress* all entered the common lexicon over the last decade, as the slogan of the hour shifted from the cheery "Have a nice day" to the testiness of "Make my day."

This book is a guide to making sense of the senselessness. As a psychologist, and for the last decade as a journalist for *The New York Times,* I have been tracking the progress of our scientific understanding of the realm of the irrational. From that perch I have been struck by two opposing trends, one portraying a growing calamity in our shared emotional life, the other offering some hopeful remedies.

WHY THIS EXPLORATION NOW

The last decade, despite its bad news, has also seen an unparalleled burst of scientific studies of emotion. Most dramatic are the glimpses of the brain at work, made possible by innovative methods such as new brain-imaging technologies. They have made visible for the first time in human history what has always been a source of deep mystery: exactly how this intricate mass of cells operates while we think and feel, imagine and dream. This flood of neurobiological data lets us understand more clearly than ever how the brain's centers for emotion move us to rage or to tears, and how more ancient parts of the brain, which stir us to make war as well as love, are channeled for better or worse. This unprecedented clarity on the workings of emotions and their failings brings into focus some fresh remedies for our collective emotional crisis.

I have had to wait till now before the scientific harvest was full enough to write this book. These insights are so late in coming largely because the place of feeling in mental life has been surprisingly slighted by research over the years, leaving the emotions a largely unexplored continent for scientific psychology. Into this void has rushed a welter of self-help books, well-intentioned advice based at best on clinical opinion but lacking much, if any, scientific basis. Now science is finally able to speak with authority to these urgent and perplexing questions of the psyche at its most irrational, to map with some precision the human heart.

This mapping offers a challenge to those who subscribe to a narrow view of intelligence, arguing that IQ is a genetic given that cannot be changed by life experience, and that our destiny in life is largely fixed by these aptitudes. That argument ignores the more challenging question: What *can* we change that will help our children fare better in life? What factors are at play, for example, when people of high IQ flounder and those of modest IQ do surprisingly well? I would argue that the difference quite often lies in the abilities called here *emotional intelligence*, which include self-control, zeal and persistence, and the ability to motivate oneself. And these skills, as we shall see, can be taught to children, giving them a better chance to use whatever intellectual potential the genetic lottery may have given them.

Beyond this possibility looms a pressing moral imperative. These are times when the fabric of society seems to unravel at ever-greater speed, when selfishness, violence, and a meanness of spirit seem to be rotting the goodness of our communal lives. Here the argument for the importance of emotional intelligence hinges on the link between sentiment, character, and moral instincts. There is growing evidence that fundamental ethical stances in life stem from underlying emotional capacities. For one, impulse is the medium of emotion; the seed of all impulse is a feeling bursting to express itself in action. Those who are at the mercy of impulse—who lack self-control—suffer a moral deficiency: The ability to control impulse is the base of will and character. By the same token, the root of altruism lies in empathy, the ability to read emotions in others; lacking a sense of another's need or despair, there is no caring. And if there are any two moral stances that our times call for, they are precisely these, self-restraint and compassion.

OUR JOURNEY

In this book I serve as a guide in a journey through these scientific insights into the emotions, a voyage aimed at bringing greater understanding to some of the most perplexing moments in our own lives and in the world around us. The journey's end is to understand what it means—and how— to bring intelligence to emotion. This understanding itself can help to some degree; bringing cognizance to the realm of feeling has an effect something like the impact of an observer at the quantum level in physics, altering what is being observed.

Our journey begins in Part One with new discoveries about the brain's emotional architecture that offer an explanation of those most baffling moments in our lives when feeling overwhelms all rationality. Understanding the interplay of brain structures that rule our moments of rage and fear—or passion and joy—reveals much about how we learn the emotional habits that can undermine our best intentions, as well as what we can do to subdue our more destructive or self-defeating emotional impulses. Most important, the neurological data suggest a window of opportunity for shaping our children's emotional habits.

The next major stop on our journey, Part Two of this book, is in seeing how neurological givens play out in the basic flair for living called *emotional intelligence:* being able, for example, to rein in emotional impulse; to read another's innermost feelings; to handle relationships smoothly—as Aristotle put it, the rare skill "to be angry with the right person, to the right degree, at the right time, for the right purpose, and in the right way." (Readers who are not drawn to neurological detail may want to proceed directly to this section.)

This expanded model of what it means to be "intelligent" puts emotions at the center of aptitudes for living. Part Three examines some key differences this aptitude makes: how these abilities can preserve our most prized relationships, or their lack corrode them; how the market forces that are reshaping our worklife are putting an unprecedented premium on emotional intelligence for on-the-job success; and how toxic emotions put our physical health at as much risk as does chain-smoking, even as emotional balance can help protect our health and well-being.

Our genetic heritage endows each of us with a series of emotional setpoints that determines our temperament. But the brain circuitry involved is extraordinarily malleable; temperament is not destiny. As Part Four shows, the emotional lessons we learn as children at home and at school shape the emotional circuits, making us more adept—or inept—at the basics of emotional intelligence. This means that childhood and adolescence are critical windows of opportunity for setting down the essential emotional habits that will govern our lives.

Part Five explores what hazards await those who, in growing to maturity, fail to master the emotional realm—how deficiencies in emotional intelligence heighten a spectrum of risks, from depression or a life of violence to eating disorders and drug abuse. And it documents how pioneering schools are teaching children the emotional and social skills they need to keep their lives on track.

Perhaps the most disturbing single piece of data in this book comes from a massive survey of parents and teachers and shows a worldwide trend for the present generation of children to be more troubled emotionally than the last: more lonely and depressed, more angry and unruly, more nervous and prone to worry, more impulsive and aggressive.

If there is a remedy, I feel it must lie in how we prepare our young for life. At present we leave the emotional education of our children to chance, with ever more disastrous results. One solution is a new vision of what schools can do to educate the whole student, bringing together mind and heart in the classroom. Our journey ends with visits to innovative classes that aim to give children a grounding in the basics of emotional intelligence. I can foresee a day when education will routinely include inculcating essential human competencies such as self-awareness, self-control, and empathy, and the arts of listening, resolving conflicts, and cooperation.

In *The Nichomachean Ethics,* Aristotle's philosophical enquiry into virtue, character, and the good life, his challenge is to manage our emotional life with intelligence. Our passions, when well exercised, have wisdom; they guide our thinking, our values, our survival. But they can easily go awry, and do so all too often. As Aristotle saw, the problem is not with emotionality, but with the *appropriateness* of emotion and its expression. The question is, how can we bring intelligence to our emotions—and civility to our streets and caring to our communal life?

PART ONE

THE EMOTIONAL BRAIN

1

What Are Emotions For?

It is with the heart that one sees rightly; what is essential is invisible to the eye.

ANTOINE DE SAINT-EXUPÉRY,
The Little Prince

Ponder the last moments of Gary and Mary Jane Chauncey, a couple completely devoted to their eleven-year-old daughter Andrea, who was confined to a wheelchair by cerebral palsy. The Chauncey family were passengers on an Amtrak train that crashed into a river after a barge hit and weakened a railroad bridge in Louisiana's bayou country. Thinking first of their daughter, the couple tried their best to save Andrea as water rushed into the sinking train; somehow they managed to push Andrea through a window to rescuers. Then, as the car sank beneath the water, they perished.[1]

Andrea's story, of parents whose last heroic act is to ensure their child's survival, captures a moment of almost mythic courage. Without doubt such incidents of parental sacrifice for their progeny have been repeated countless times in human history and prehistory, and countless more in the larger course of evolution of our species.[2] Seen from the perspective of evolutionary biologists, such parental self-sacrifice is in the service of "reproductive success" in passing on one's genes to future generations. But from the perspective of a parent making a desperate decision in a moment of crisis, it is about nothing other than love.

As an insight into the purpose and potency of emotions, this exemplary act of parental heroism testifies to the role of altruistic love—and every other emotion we feel—in human life.[3] It suggests that our deepest feelings, our passions and longings, are essential guides, and that our species owes much of its existence to their power in human affairs. That power is extraordinary: Only a potent love—the urgency of saving a cherished child—could lead a parent to override the impulse for personal survival. Seen from the intellect, their self-sacrifice was arguably irrational; seen from the heart, it was the only choice to make.

Sociobiologists point to the preeminence of heart over head at such crucial moments when they conjecture about why evolution has given emotion such a central role in the human psyche. Our emotions, they say, guide us in facing predicaments and tasks too important to leave to intellect alone—danger, painful loss, persisting toward a goal despite frustrations, bonding with a mate, building a family. Each emotion offers a distinctive readiness to act; each points us in a direction that has worked well to handle the recurring challenges of human life.[4] As these eternal situations were repeated and repeated over our evolutionary history, the survival value of our emotional repertoire was attested to by its becoming imprinted in our nerves as innate, automatic tendencies of the human heart.

A view of human nature that ignores the power of emotions is sadly shortsighted. The very name *Homo sapiens,* the thinking species, is misleading in light of the new appreciation and vision of the place of emotions in our lives that science now offers. As we all know from experience, when it comes to shaping our decisions and our actions, feeling counts every bit as much—and often more—than thought. We have gone too far in emphasizing the value and import of the purely rational—of what IQ measures— in human life. For better or worse, intelligence can come to nothing when the emotions hold sway.

WHEN PASSIONS OVERWHELM REASON

It was a tragedy of errors. Fourteen-year-old Matilda Crabtree was just playing a practical joke on her father: she jumped out of a closet and yelled "Boo!" as her parents came home at one in the morning from visiting friends.

But Bobby Crabtree and his wife thought Matilda was staying with friends that night. Hearing noises as he entered the house, Crabtree reached for his .357 caliber pistol and went into Matilda's bedroom to investigate. When his daughter jumped from the closet, Crabtree shot her in the neck. Matilda Crabtree died twelve hours later.[5]

One emotional legacy of evolution is the fear that mobilizes us to protect our family from danger; that impulse impelled Bobby Crabtree to get his gun and search his house for the intruder he thought was prowling there. Fear primed Crabtree to shoot before he could fully register what he was shooting at, even before he could recognize his daughter's voice. Automatic reactions of this sort have become etched in our nervous system, evolutionary biologists presume, because for a long and crucial period in human prehistory they made the difference between survival and death. Even more important, they mattered for the main task of evolution: being able to bear progeny who would carry on these very genetic predispositions—a sad irony, given the tragedy at the Crabtree household.

But while our emotions have been wise guides in the evolutionary long run, the new realities civilization presents have arisen with such rapidity that the slow march of evolution cannot keep up. Indeed, the first laws and proclamations of ethics—the Code of Hammurabi, the Ten Commandments of the Hebrews, the Edicts of Emperor Ashoka—can be read as attempts to harness, subdue, and domesticate emotional life. As Freud described in *Civilization and Its Discontents,* society has had to enforce from without rules meant to subdue tides of emotional excess that surge too freely within.

Despite these social constraints, passions overwhelm reason time and again. This given of human nature arises from the basic architecture of mental life. In terms of biological design for the basic neural circuitry of emotion, what we are born with is what worked best for the last 50,000 human generations, not the last 500 generations—and certainly not the last five. The slow, deliberate forces of evolution that have shaped our emotions have done their work over the course of a million years; the last 10,000 years—despite having witnessed the rapid rise of human civilization and the explosion of the human population from five million to five billion—have left little imprint on our biological templates for emotional life.

For better or for worse, our appraisal of every personal encounter and our responses to it are shaped not just by our rational judgments or our personal history, but also by our distant ancestral past. This leaves us with sometimes tragic propensities, as witness the sad events at the Crabtree household. In short, we too often confront postmodern dilemmas with an emotional repertoire tailored to the urgencies of the Pleistocene. That predicament is at the heart of my subject.

Impulses to Action

One early spring day I was driving along a highway over a mountain pass in Colorado, when a snow flurry suddenly blotted out the car a few lengths ahead of me. As I peered ahead I couldn't make out anything; the swirling snow was now a blinding whiteness. Pressing my foot on the brake, I could feel anxiety flood my body and hear the thumping of my heart.

The anxiety built to full fear: I pulled over to the side of the road, waiting for the flurry to pass. A half hour later the snow stopped, visibility returned, and I continued on my way—only to be stopped a few hundred yards down the road, where an ambulance crew was helping a passenger in a car that had rear-ended a slower car in front; the collision blocked the highway. If I had continued driving in the blinding snow, I probably would have hit them.

The caution fear forced on me that day may have saved my life. Like a rabbit frozen in terror at the hint of a passing fox—or a protomammal hiding from a marauding dinosaur—I was overtaken by an internal state that compelled me to stop, pay attention, and take heed of a coming danger.

All emotions are, in essence, impulses to act, the instant plans for handling life that evolution has instilled in us. The very root of the word *emotion* is *motere*, the Latin verb "to move," plus the prefix "e-" to connote "move away," suggesting that a tendency to act is implicit in every emotion. That emotions lead to actions is most obvious in watching animals or children; it is only in "civilized" adults we so often find the great anomaly in the animal kingdom, emotions—root impulses to act—divorced from obvious reaction.[6]

In our emotional repertoire each emotion plays a unique role, as revealed by their distinctive biological signatures (see Appendix A for details on "basic" emotions). With new methods to peer into the body and brain, researchers are discovering more physiological details of how each emotion prepares the body for a very different kind of response:[7]

• With *anger* blood flows to the hands, making it easier to grasp a weapon or strike at a foe; heart rate increases, and a rush of hormones such as adrenaline generates a pulse of energy strong enough for vigorous action.

• With *fear* blood goes to the large skeletal muscles, such as in the legs, making it easier to flee—and making the face blanch as blood is shunted away from it (creating the feeling that the blood "runs cold"). At the same time, the body freezes, if only for a moment, perhaps allowing time to gauge whether hiding might be a better reaction. Circuits in the brain's emotional centers trigger a flood of hormones that put the body on general alert, making it edgy and ready for action, and attention fixates on the threat at hand, the better to evaluate what response to make.

• Among the main biological changes in *happiness* is an increased activity in a brain center that inhibits negative feelings and fosters an increase in available energy, and a quieting of those that generate worrisome thought. But there is no particular shift in physiology save a quiescence, which makes the body recover more quickly from the biological arousal of upsetting emotions. This configuration offers the body a general rest, as well as readiness and enthusiasm for whatever task is at hand and for striving toward a great variety of goals.

• *Love*, tender feelings, and sexual satisfaction entail parasympathetic arousal—the physiological opposite of the "fight-or-flight" mobilization shared by fear and anger. The parasympathetic pattern, dubbed the "relaxation response," is a bodywide set of reactions that generates a general state of calm and contentment, facilitating cooperation.

• The lifting of the eyebrows in *surprise* allows the taking in of a larger visual sweep and also permits more light to strike the retina. This offers more information about the unexpected event, making it easier to figure out exactly what is going on and concoct the best plan for action.

• Around the world an expression of *disgust* looks the same, and sends the identical message: something is offensive in taste or smell, or metaphorically so. The facial expression of disgust—the upper lip curled to the side as the nose wrinkles slightly—suggests a primordial attempt, as Darwin observed, to close the nostrils against a noxious odor or to spit out a poisonous food.

• A main function for *sadness* is to help adjust to a significant loss, such as the death of someone close or a major disappointment. Sadness brings a drop in energy and enthusiasm for life's activities, particularly diversions and pleasures, and, as it deepens and approaches depression, slows the body's metabolism. This introspective withdrawal creates the opportunity to mourn a loss or frustrated hope, grasp its consequences for one's life, and, as energy returns, plan new beginnings. This loss of energy may well have kept saddened—and vulnerable—early humans close to home, where they were safer.

These biological propensities to act are shaped further by our life experience and our culture. For instance, universally the loss of a loved one elicits sadness and grief. But how we show our grieving—how emotions are displayed or held back for private moments—is molded by culture, as are which particular people in our lives fall into the category of "loved ones" to be mourned.

The protracted period of evolution when these emotional responses were hammered into shape was certainly a harsher reality than most humans endured as a species after the dawn of recorded history. It was a time when few infants survived to childhood and few adults to thirty years, when predators could strike at any moment, when the vagaries of droughts and floods meant the difference between starvation and survival. But with the coming of agriculture and even the most rudimentary human societies, the odds for survival began to change dramatically. In the last ten thousand years, when these advances took hold throughout the world, the ferocious pressures that had held the human population in check eased steadily.

Those same pressures had made our emotional responses so valuable for survival; as they waned, so did the goodness of fit of parts of our emotional repertoire. While in the ancient past a hair-trigger anger may have offered a crucial edge for survival, the availability of automatic weaponry to thirteen-year-olds has made it too often a disastrous reaction.[8]

Our Two Minds

A friend was telling me about her divorce, a painful separation. Her husband had fallen in love with a younger woman at work, and suddenly announced he was leaving to live with the other woman. Months of bitter wrangling over house, money, and custody of the children followed. Now, some months later, she was saying that her independence was appealing to her, that she was happy to be on her own. "I just don't think about him anymore—I really don't care," she said. But as she said it, her eyes momentarily welled up with tears.

That moment of teary eyes could easily pass unnoted. But the empathic understanding that someone's watering eyes means she is sad despite her words to the contrary is an act of comprehending just as surely as is distilling meaning from words on a printed page. One is an act of the emotional mind, the other of the rational mind. In a very real sense we have two minds, one that thinks and one that feels.

These two fundamentally different ways of knowing interact to construct our mental life. One, the rational mind, is the mode of comprehension we are typically conscious of: more prominent in awareness, thoughtful, able to ponder and reflect. But alongside that there is another system of knowing: impulsive and powerful, if sometimes illogical—the emotional mind. (For a more detailed description of the characteristics of the emotional mind, see Appendix B.)

The emotional/rational dichotomy approximates the folk distinction between "heart" and "head"; knowing something is right "in your heart" is a different order of conviction—somehow a deeper kind of certainty—than thinking so with your rational mind. There is a steady gradient in the ratio of rational-to-emotional control over the mind; the more intense the feeling, the more dominant the emotional mind becomes—and the more ineffectual the rational. This is an arrangement that seems to stem from eons of evolutionary advantage to having emotions and intuitions guide our instantaneous response in situations where our lives are in peril—and where pausing to think over what to do could cost us our lives.

These two minds, the emotional and the rational, operate in tight harmony for the most part, intertwining their very different ways of knowing to guide us through the world. Ordinarily there is a balance between emotional and rational minds, with emotion feeding into and informing the operations of the rational mind, and the rational mind refining and sometimes vetoing the inputs of the emotions. Still, the emotional and rational minds are semi-independent faculties, each, as we shall see, reflecting the operation of distinct, but interconnected, circuitry in the brain.

In many or most moments these minds are exquisitely coordinated; feelings are essential to thought, thought to feeling. But when passions surge the balance tips: it is the emotional mind that captures the upper hand, swamping the rational mind. The sixteenth-century humanist Erasmus of Rotterdam wrote in a satirical vein of this perennial tension between reason and emotion:[9]

> Jupiter has bestowed far more passion than reason—you could calculate the ratio as 24 to one. He set up two raging tyrants in opposition to Reason's solitary power: anger and lust. How far Reason can prevail against the combined forces of these two the common life of man makes quite clear. Reason does the only thing she can and shouts herself hoarse, repeating formulas of virtue, while the other two bid her go hang herself, and are increasingly noisy and offensive, until at last their Ruler is exhausted, gives up, and surrenders.

HOW THE BRAIN GREW

To better grasp the potent hold of the emotions on the thinking mind—and why feeling and reason are so readily at war—consider how the brain evolved. Human brains, with their three pounds or so of cells and neural juices, are about triple the size of those in our nearest cousins in evolution, the nonhuman primates. Over millions of years of evolution, the brain has grown from the bottom up, with its higher centers developing as elaborations of lower, more ancient parts. (The growth of the brain in the human embryo roughly retraces this evolutionary course.)

The most primitive part of the brain, shared with all species that have more than a minimal nervous system, is the brainstem surrounding the top of the spinal cord. This root brain regulates basic life functions like breathing and the metabolism of the body's other organs, as well as controlling stereotyped reactions and movements. This primitive brain cannot be said to think or learn; rather it is a set of preprogrammed regulators that keep the body running as it should and reacting in a way that ensures survival. This brain reigned supreme in the Age of the Reptiles: Picture a snake hissing to signal the threat of an attack.

From the most primitive root, the brainstem, emerged the emotional centers. Millions of years later in evolution, from these emotional areas evolved the thinking brain or "neocortex," the great bulb of convoluted tissues that make up the top layers. The fact that the thinking brain grew from the emotional reveals much about the relationship of thought to feeling; there was an emotional brain long before there was a rational one.

The most ancient root of our emotional life is in the sense of smell, or, more precisely, in the olfactory lobe, the cells that take in and analyze smell. Every living entity, be it nutritious, poisonous, sexual partner, predator or prey, has a distinctive molecular signature that can be carried in the wind. In those primitive times smell commended itself as a paramount sense for survival.

From the olfactory lobe the ancient centers for emotion began to evolve, eventually growing large enough to encircle the top of the brainstem. In its rudimentary stages, the olfactory center was composed of little more than thin layers of neurons gathered to analyze smell. One layer of cells took in what was smelled and sorted it out into the relevant categories: edible or toxic, sexually available, enemy or meal. A second layer of cells sent reflexive messages throughout the nervous system telling the body what to do: bite, spit, approach, flee, chase.[10]

With the arrival of the first mammals came new, key layers of the emotional brain. These, surrounding the brainstem, look roughly like a bagel with a bite taken out at the bottom where the brainstem nestles into them. Because this part of the brain rings and borders the brainstem, it was called the "limbic" system, from "limbus," the Latin word for "ring." This new neural territory added emotions proper to the brain's repertoire.[11] When we are in the grip of craving or fury, head-over-heels in love or recoiling in dread, it is the limbic system that has us in its grip.

As it evolved, the limbic system refined two powerful tools: learning and memory. These revolutionary advances allowed an animal to be much smarter in its choices for survival, and to fine-tune its responses to adapt to changing demands rather than having invariable and automatic reactions. If a food led to sickness, it could be avoided next time. Decisions like knowing what to eat and what to spurn were still determined largely through smell; the connections between the olfactory bulb and the limbic system now took on the tasks of making distinctions among smells and recognizing them, comparing a present smell with past ones, and so discriminating good from bad. This was done by the "rhinencephalon," literally, the "nose brain," a part of the limbic wiring, and the rudimentary basis of the neocortex, the thinking brain.

About 100 million years ago the brain in mammals took a great growth spurt. Piled on top of the thin two-layered cortex—the regions that plan, comprehend what is sensed, coordinate movement—several new layers of brain cells were added to form the neocortex. In contrast to the ancient brain's two-layered cortex, the neocortex offered an extraordinary intellectual edge.

The *Homo sapiens* neocortex, so much larger than in any other species, has added all that is distinctly human. The neocortex is the seat of thought; it contains the centers that put together and comprehend what the senses perceive. It adds to a feeling what we think about it—and allows us to have feelings about ideas, art, symbols, imaginings.

In evolution the neocortex allowed a judicious fine-tuning that no doubt has made enormous advantages in an organism's ability to survive adversity, making it more likely that its progeny would in turn pass on the genes that contain that same neural circuitry. The survival edge is due to the neocortex's talent for strategizing, long-term planning, and other mental wiles. Beyond that, the triumphs of art, of civilization and culture, are all fruits of the neocortex.

This new addition to the brain allowed the addition of nuance to emotional life. Take love. Limbic structures generate feelings of pleasure and sexual desire—the emotions that feed sexual passion. But the addition of the neocortex and its connections to the limbic system allowed for the mother-child bond that is the basis of the family unit and the long-term commitment to childrearing that makes human development possible. (Species that have no neocortex, such as reptiles, lack maternal affection; when their young hatch, the newborns must hide to avoid being cannibalized.) In humans the protective bond between parent and child allows much of maturation to go on over the course of a long childhood—during which the brain continues to develop.

As we proceed up the phylogenetic scale from reptile to rhesus to human, the sheer mass of the neocortex increases; with that increase comes a geometric rise in the interconnections in brain circuitry. The larger the number of such connections, the greater the range of possible responses. The neocortex allows for the subtlety and complexity of emotional life, such as the ability to have feelings *about* our feelings. There is more neocortex-to-limbic system in primates than in other species—and vastly more in humans—suggesting why we are able to display a far greater range of reactions to our emotions, and more nuance. While a rabbit or rhesus has a restricted set of typical responses to fear, the larger human neocortex allows a far more nimble repertoire—including calling 911. The more complex the social system, the more essential is such flexibility—and there is no more complex social world than our own.[12]

But these higher centers do not govern all of emotional life; in crucial matters of the heart—and most especially in emotional emergencies—they can be said to defer to the limbic system. Because so many of the brain's higher centers sprouted from or extended the scope of the limbic area, the emotional brain plays a crucial role in neural architecture. As the root from which the newer brain grew, the emotional areas are intertwined via myriad connecting circuits to all parts of the neocortex. This gives the emotional centers immense power to influence the functioning of the rest of the brain—including its centers for thought.

2

Anatomy of an Emotional Hijacking

Life is a comedy for those who think and a tragedy for those who feel.

HORACE WALPOLE

It was a hot August afternoon in 1963, the same day that the Rev. Martin Luther King, Jr., gave his "I Have a Dream" speech to a civil rights march on Washington. On that day Richard Robles, a seasoned burglar who had just been paroled from a three-year sentence for the more than one hundred break-ins he had pulled to support a heroin habit, decided to do one more. He wanted to renounce crime, Robles later claimed, but he desperately needed money for his girlfriend and their three-year-old daughter.

The apartment he broke into that day belonged to two young women, twenty-one-year-old Janice Wylie, a researcher at *Newsweek* magazine, and twenty-three-year-old Emily Hoffert, a grade-school teacher. Though Robles chose the apartment on New York's swanky Upper East Side to burglarize because he thought no one would be there, Wylie was home. Threatening her with a knife, Robles tied her up. As he was leaving, Hoffert came home. To make good his escape, Robles began to tie her up, too.

As Robles tells the tale years later, while he was tying up Hoffert, Janice Wylie warned him he would not get away with this crime: She would remember his face and help the police track him down. Robles, who had promised himself this was to have been his last burglary, panicked at that, completely losing control. In a frenzy, he grabbed a soda bottle and clubbed

13

the women until they were unconscious, then, awash in rage and fear, he slashed and stabbed them over and over with a kitchen knife. Looking back on that moment some twenty-five years later, Robles lamented, "I just went bananas. My head just exploded."

To this day Robles has lots of time to regret those few minutes of rage unleashed. At this writing he is still in prison, some three decades later, for what became known as the "Career Girl Murders."

Such emotional explosions are neural hijackings. At those moments, evidence suggests, a center in the limbic brain proclaims an emergency, recruiting the rest of the brain to its urgent agenda. The hijacking occurs in an instant, triggering this reaction crucial moments before the neocortex, the thinking brain, has had a chance to glimpse fully what is happening, let alone decide if it is a good idea. The hallmark of such a hijack is that once the moment passes, those so possessed have the sense of not knowing what came over them.

These hijacks are by no means isolated, horrific incidents that lead to brutal crimes like the Career Girl Murders. In less catastrophic form—but not necessarily less intense—they happen to us with fair frequency. Think back to the last time you "lost it," blowing up at someone—your spouse or child, or perhaps the driver of another car—to a degree that later, with some reflection and hindsight, seemed uncalled for. In all probability, that, too, was such a hijacking, a neural takeover which, as we shall see, originates in the amygdala, a center in the limbic brain.

Not all limbic hijackings are distressing. When a joke strikes someone as so uproarious that their laughter is almost explosive, that, too, is a limbic response. It is at work also in moments of intense joy: When Dan Jansen, after several heartbreaking failures to capture an Olympic Gold Medal for speed skating (which he had vowed to do for his dying sister), finally won the Gold in the 1,000-meter race in the 1994 Winter Olympics in Norway, his wife was so overcome by the excitement and happiness that she had to be rushed to emergency physicians at rinkside.

THE SEAT OF ALL PASSION

In humans the amygdala (from the Greek word for "almond") is an almond-shaped cluster of interconnected structures perched above the brainstem, near the bottom of the limbic ring. There are two amygdalas, one on each side of the brain, nestled toward the side of the head. The human amygdala is relatively large compared to that in any of our closest evolutionary cousins, the primates.

The hippocampus and the amygdala were the two key parts of the primitive "nose brain" that, in evolution, gave rise to the cortex and then the neocortex. To this day these limbic structures do much or most of the brain's learning and remembering; the amygdala is the specialist for emotional matters. If the amygdala is severed from the rest of the brain, the result is a striking inability to gauge the emotional significance of events; this condition is sometimes called "affective blindness."

Lacking emotional weight, encounters lose their hold. One young man whose amygdala had been surgically removed to control severe seizures became completely uninterested in people, preferring to sit in isolation with no human contact. While he was perfectly capable of conversation, he no longer recognized close friends, relatives, or even his mother, and remained impassive in the face of their anguish at his indifference. Without an amygdala he seemed to have lost all recognition of feeling, as well as any feeling about feelings.[1] The amygdala acts as a storehouse of emotional memory, and thus of significance itself; life without the amygdala is a life stripped of personal meanings.

More than affection is tied to the amygdala; all passion depends on it. Animals that have their amygdala removed or severed lack fear and rage, lose the urge to compete or cooperate, and no longer have any sense of their place in their kind's social order; emotion is blunted or absent. Tears, an emotional signal unique to humans, are triggered by the amygdala and a nearby structure, the cingulate gyrus; being held, stroked, or otherwise comforted soothes these same brain regions, stopping the sobs. Without an amygdala, there are no tears of sorrow to soothe.

Joseph LeDoux, a neuroscientist at the Center for Neural Science at New York University, was the first to discover the key role of the amygdala in the emotional brain.[2] LeDoux is part of a fresh breed of neuroscientists who draw on innovative methods and technologies that bring a previously unknown level of precision to mapping the brain at work, and so can lay bare mysteries of mind that earlier generations of scientists have found impenetrable. His findings on the circuitry of the emotional brain overthrow a long-standing notion about the limbic system, putting the amygdala at the center of the action and placing other limbic structures in very different roles.[3]

LeDoux's research explains how the amygdala can take control over what we do even as the thinking brain, the neocortex, is still coming to a decision.

As we shall see, the workings of the amygdala and its interplay with the neocortex are at the heart of emotional intelligence.

THE NEURAL TRIPWIRE

Most intriguing for understanding the power of emotions in mental life are those moments of impassioned action that we later regret, once the dust has settled; the question is how we so easily become so irrational. Take, for example, a young woman who drove two hours to Boston to have brunch and spend the day with her boyfriend. During brunch he gave her a present she'd been wanting for months, a hard-to-find art print brought back from Spain. But her delight dissolved the moment she suggested that after brunch they go to a matinee of a movie she'd been wanting to see and her friend stunned her by saying he couldn't spend the day with her because he had softball practice. Hurt and incredulous, she got up in tears, left the cafe, and, on impulse, threw the print in a garbage can. Months later, recounting the incident, it's not walking out she regrets, but the loss of the print.

It is in moments such as these—when impulsive feeling overrides the rational—that the newly discovered role for the amygdala is pivotal. Incoming signals from the senses let the amygdala scan every experience for trouble. This puts the amygdala in a powerful post in mental life, something like a psychological sentinel, challenging every situation, every perception, with but one kind of question in mind, the most primitive: "Is this something I hate? That hurts me? Something I fear?" If so—if the moment at hand somehow draws a "Yes"—the amygdala reacts instantaneously, like a neural tripwire, telegraphing a message of crisis to all parts of the brain.

In the brain's architecture, the amygdala is poised something like an alarm company where operators stand ready to send out emergency calls to the fire department, police, and a neighbor whenever a home security system signals trouble.

When it sounds an alarm of, say, fear, it sends urgent messages to every major part of the brain: it triggers the secretion of the body's fight-or-flight hormones, mobilizes the centers for movement, and activates the cardiovascular system, the muscles, and the gut.[4] Other circuits from the amygdala signal the secretion of emergency dollops of the hormone norepinephrine to heighten the reactivity of key brain areas, including those that make the senses more alert, in effect setting the brain on edge. Additional signals from the amygdala tell the brainstem to fix the face in a fearful expression, freeze unrelated movements the muscles had underway, speed heart rate and raise blood pressure, slow breathing. Others rivet attention on the source of the fear, and prepare the muscles to react accordingly. Simultaneously, cortical memory systems are shuffled to retrieve any knowledge relevant to the emergency at hand, taking precedence over other strands of thought.

And these are just part of a carefully coordinated array of changes the amygdala orchestrates as it commandeers areas throughout the brain (for a more detailed account, see Appendix C). The amygdala's extensive web of neural connections allows it, during an emotional emergency, to capture and drive much of the rest of the brain—including the rational mind.

THE EMOTIONAL SENTINEL

A friend tells of having been on vacation in England, and eating brunch at a canalside cafe. Taking a stroll afterward along the stone steps down to the canal, he suddenly saw a girl gazing at the water, her face frozen in fear. Before he knew quite why, he had jumped in the water—in his coat and tie. Only once he was in the water did he realize that the girl was staring in shock at a toddler who had fallen in—whom he was able to rescue.

What made him jump in the water before he knew why? The answer, very likely, was his amygdala.

In one of the most telling discoveries about emotions of the last decade, LeDoux's work revealed how the architecture of the brain gives the amygdala a privileged position as an emotional sentinel, able to hijack the brain.[5] His research has shown that sensory signals from eye or ear travel first in the brain to the thalamus, and then—across a single synapse—to the amygdala; a second signal from the thalamus is routed to the neocortex—the thinking brain. This branching allows the amygdala to begin to respond *before* the neocortex, which mulls information through several levels of brain circuits before it fully perceives and finally initiates its more finely tailored response.

LeDoux's research is revolutionary for understanding emotional life because it is the first to work out neural pathways for feelings that bypass the neocortex. Those feelings that take the direct route through the amygdala include our most primitive and potent; this circuit does much to explain the power of emotion to overwhelm rationality.

The conventional view in neuroscience had been that the eye, ear, and other sensory organs transmit signals to the thalamus, and from there to sensory processing areas of the neocortex, where the signals are put together into objects as we perceive them. The signals are sorted for meanings so that the brain recognizes what each object is and what its presence means. From the neocortex, the old theory held, the signals are sent to the limbic brain, and from there the appropriate response radiates out through the brain and the rest of the body. That is the way it works much or most of the time—but LeDoux discovered a smaller bundle of neurons that leads directly from the thalamus to the amygdala, in addition to those going through the larger path of neurons to the cortex. This smaller and shorter pathway—something like a neural back alley—allows the amygdala to receive some direct inputs from the senses and start a response *before* they are fully registered by the neocortex.

This discovery overthrows the notion that the amygdala must depend entirely on signals from the neocortex to formulate its emotional reactions. The amygdala can trigger an emotional response via this emergency route even as a parallel reverberating circuit begins between the amygdala and neocortex. The amygdala can have us spring to action while the slightly slower—but more fully informed—neocortex unfolds its more refined plan for reaction.

LeDoux overturned the prevailing wisdom about the pathways traveled by emotions through his research on fear in animals. In a crucial experiment he destroyed the auditory cortex of rats, then exposed them to a tone paired with an electric shock. The rats quickly learned to fear the tone, even though the sound of the tone could not register in their neocortex. Instead, the sound took the direct route from ear to thalamus to amygdala, skipping all higher avenues. In short, the rats had learned an emotional reaction without any higher cortical involvement: The amygdala perceived, remembered, and orchestrated their fear independently.

"Anatomically the emotional system can act independently of the neocortex," LeDoux told me. "Some emotional reactions and emotional memories can be formed without any conscious, cognitive participation at all." The amygdala can house memories and response repertoires that we enact without quite realizing why we do so because the shortcut from thalamus to amygdala completely bypasses the neocortex. This bypass seems to allow the amygdala to be a repository for emotional impressions and memories that we have never known about in full awareness. LeDoux proposes that it is the amygdala's subterranean role in memory that explains, for example, a startling experiment in which people acquired a preference for oddly shaped

FIGHT OR FLIGHT RESPONSE:
*Heart rate and blood pressure
increase. Large muscles prepare for
quick action.*

*A visual signal first goes from the retina to the thalamus, where it is
translated into the language of the brain. Most of the message then
goes to the visual cortex, where it is analyzed and assessed for
meaning and appropriate response; if that response is emotional, a
signal goes to the amygdala to activate the emotional centers. But a
smaller portion of the original signal goes straight from the thalamus
to the amygdala in a quicker transmission, allowing a faster (though
less precise) response. Thus the amygdala can trigger an emotional
response before the cortical centers have fully understood what is
happening.*

geometric figures that had been flashed at them so quickly that they had no conscious awareness of having seen them at all![6]

Other research has shown that in the first few milliseconds of our perceiving something we not only unconsciously comprehend what it is, but decide whether we like it or not; the "cognitive unconscious" presents our awareness with not just the identity of what we see, but an opinion about it.[7] Our emotions have a mind of their own, one which can hold views quite independently of our rational mind.

THE SPECIALIST IN EMOTIONAL MEMORY

Those unconscious opinions are emotional memories; their storehouse is the amygdala. Research by LeDoux and other neuroscientists now seems to suggest that the hippocampus, which has long been considered the key structure of the limbic system, is more involved in registering and making sense of perceptual patterns than with emotional reactions. The hippocampus's main input is in providing a keen memory of context, vital for emotional meaning; it is the hippocampus that recognizes the differing significance of, say, a bear in the zoo versus one in your backyard.

While the hippocampus remembers the dry facts, the amygdala retains the emotional flavor that goes with those facts. If we try to pass a car on a two-lane highway and narrowly miss having a head-on collision, the hippocampus retains the specifics of the incident, like what stretch of road we were on, who was with us, what the other car looked like. But it is the amygdala that everafter will send a surge of anxiety through us whenever we try to pass a car in similar circumstances. As LeDoux put it to me, "The hippocampus is crucial in recognizing a face as that of your cousin. But it is the amygdala that adds you don't really like her."

The brain uses a simple but cunning method to make emotional memories register with special potency: the very same neurochemical alerting systems that prime the body to react to life-threatening emergencies by fighting or fleeing also stamp the moment in memory with vividness.[8] Under stress (or anxiety, or presumably even the intense excitement of joy) a nerve running from the brain to the adrenal glands atop the kidneys triggers a secretion of the hormones epinephrine and norepinephrine, which surge through the body priming it for an emergency. These hormones activate receptors on the vagus nerve; while the vagus nerve carries messages from the brain to regulate the heart, it also carries signals back into the brain, triggered by epinephrine and norepinephrine. The amygdala is the main site in the brain where these signals go; they activate neurons within the amygdala to signal other brain regions to strengthen memory for what is happening.

This amygdala arousal seems to imprint in memory most moments of emotional arousal with an added degree of strength—that's why we are more likely, for example, to remember where we went on a first date, or what we were doing when we heard the news that the space shuttle *Challenger* had exploded. The more intense the amygdala arousal, the stronger the imprint; the experiences that scare or thrill us the most in life are among our most indelible memories. This means that, in effect, the brain has two memory systems, one for ordinary facts and one for emotionally charged ones. A special system for emotional memories makes excellent sense in evolution, of course, ensuring that animals would have particularly vivid memories of what threatens or pleases them. But emotional memories can be faulty guides to the present.

OUT-OF-DATE NEURAL ALARMS

One drawback of such neural alarms is that the urgent message the amygdala sends is sometimes, if not often, out-of-date—especially in the fluid social world we humans inhabit. As the repository for emotional memory, the amygdala scans experience, comparing what is happening now with what happened in the past. Its method of comparison is associative: when one key element of a present situation is similar to the past, it can call it a "match"—which is why this circuit is sloppy: it acts before there is full confirmation. It frantically commands that we react to the present in ways that were imprinted long ago, with thoughts, emotions, reactions learned in response to events perhaps only dimly similar, but close enough to alarm the amygdala.

Thus a former army nurse, traumatized by the relentless flood of ghastly wounds she once tended in wartime, is suddenly swept with a mix of dread, loathing, and panic—a repeat of her battlefield reaction triggered once again, years later, by the stench when she opens a closet door to find her toddler had stashed a stinking diaper there. A few spare elements of the situation is all that need seem similar to some past danger for the amygdala to trigger its emergency proclamation. The trouble is that along with the emotionally charged memories that have the power to trigger this crisis response can come equally outdated ways of responding to it.

The emotional brain's imprecision in such moments is added to by the fact that many potent emotional memories date from the first few years of life, in the relationship between an infant and its caretakers. This is especially true for traumatic events, like beatings or outright neglect. During this early period of life other brain structures, particularly the hippocampus, which is crucial for narrative memories, and the neocortex, seat of rational thought, have yet to become fully developed. In memory, the amygdala and hippocampus work hand-in-hand; each stores and retrieves its special information independently. While the hippocampus retrieves information, the amygdala determines if that information has any emotional valence. But the amygdala, which matures very quickly in the infant's brain, is much closer to fully formed at birth.

LeDoux turns to the role of the amygdala in childhood to support what has long been a basic tenet of psychoanalytic thought: that the interactions of life's earliest years lay down a set of emotional lessons based on the attunement and upsets in the contacts between infant and caretakers.[9] These emotional lessons are so potent and yet so difficult to understand from the vantage point of adult life because, believes LeDoux, they are stored in the amygdala as rough, wordless blueprints for emotional life. Since these earliest emotional memories are established at a time before infants have words for their experience, when these emotional memories are triggered in later life there is no matching set of articulated thoughts about the response that takes us over. One reason we can be so baffled by our emotional outbursts, then, is that they often date from a time early in our lives when things were bewildering and we did not yet have words for comprehending events. We may have the chaotic feelings, but not the words for the memories that formed them.

WHEN EMOTIONS ARE FAST AND SLOPPY

It was somewhere around three in the morning when a huge object came crashing through the ceiling in a far corner of my bedroom, spilling the contents of the attic into the room. In a second I leapt out of bed and ran out of the room, terrified the entire ceiling would cave in. Then, realizing I was safe, I cautiously peered back in the bedroom to see what had caused all the damage—only to discover that the sound I had taken to be the ceiling caving in was actually the fall of a tall pile of boxes my wife had stacked in the corner the day before while she sorted out her closet. Nothing had fallen from the attic: there was no attic. The ceiling was intact, and so was I.

My leap from bed while half-asleep—which might have saved me from injury had it truly been the ceiling falling—illustrates the power of the amygdala to propel us to action in emergencies, vital moments before the neocortex has time to fully register what is actually going on. The emergency route from eye or ear to thalamus to amygdala is crucial: it saves time in an emergency, when an instantaneous response is required. But this circuit from thalamus to amygdala carries only a small portion of sensory messages, with the majority taking the main route up to the neocortex. So what registers in the amygdala via this express route is, at best, a rough signal, just enough for a warning. As LeDoux points out, "You don't need to know exactly what something is to know that it may be dangerous."[10]

The direct route has a vast advantage in brain time, which is reckoned in thousandths of a second. The amygdala in a rat can begin a response to a perception in as little as twelve milliseconds—twelve thousandths of a second. The route from thalamus to neocortex to amygdala takes about twice as long. Similar measurements have yet to be made in the human brain, but the rough ratio would likely hold.

In evolutionary terms, the survival value of this direct route would have been great, allowing a quick-response option that shaves a few critical milliseconds in reaction time to dangers. Those milliseconds could well have saved the lives of our protomammalian ancestors in such numbers that this arrangement is now featured in every mammalian brain, including yours and mine. In fact, while this circuit may play a relatively limited role in human mental life, largely restricted to emotional crises, much of the mental life of birds, fish, and reptiles revolves around it, since their very survival depends on constantly scanning for predators or prey. "This primitive, minor brain system in mammals is the main brain system in non-mammals," says LeDoux. "It offers a very rapid way to turn on emotions. But it's a quick-and-dirty process; the cells are fast, but not very precise."

Such imprecision in, say, a squirrel, is fine, since it leads to erring on the side of safety, springing away at the first sign of anything that might signal a looming enemy, or springing toward a hint of something edible. But in human emotional life that imprecision can have disastrous consequences for our relationships, since it means, figuratively speaking, we can spring at or away from the wrong thing—or person. (Consider, for example, the waitress who dropped a tray of six dinners when she glimpsed a woman with a huge, curly mane of red hair—exactly like the woman her ex-husband had left her for.)

Such inchoate emotional mistakes are based on feeling prior to thought. LeDoux calls it "precognitive emotion," a reaction based on neural bits and pieces of sensory information that have not been fully sorted out and integrated into a recognizable object. It's a very raw form of sensory information, something like a neural *Name That Tune,* where, instead of snap judgments of melody being made on the basis of just a few notes, a whole perception is grasped on the basis of the first few tentative parts. If the amygdala senses a sensory pattern of import emerging, it jumps to a conclusion, triggering its reactions before there is full confirming evidence—or any confirmation at all.

Small wonder we can have so little insight into the murk of our more explosive emotions, especially while they still hold us in thrall. The amygdala can react in a delirium of rage or fear before the cortex knows what is going on because such raw emotion is triggered independent of, and prior to, thought.

THE EMOTIONAL MANAGER

A friend's six-year-old daughter Jessica was spending her first night ever sleeping over at a playmate's, and it was unclear who was more nervous about it, mother or daughter. While the mother tried not to let Jessica see the intense anxiety she felt, her tension peaked near midnight that night, as she was getting ready for bed and heard the phone ring. Dropping her toothbrush, she raced to the phone, her heart pounding, images of Jessica in terrible distress racing through her mind.

The mother snatched the receiver, and blurted, "Jessica!" into the phone—only to hear a woman's voice say, "Oh, I think this must be a wrong number. . . ."

At that, the mother recovered her composure, and in a polite, measured tone, asked, "What number were you calling?"

While the amygdala is at work in priming an anxious, impulsive reaction, another part of the emotional brain allows for a more fitting, corrective response. The brain's damper switch for the amygdala's surges appears to lie at the other end of a major circuit to the neocortex, in the prefrontal lobes just behind the forehead. The prefrontal cortex seems to be at work when someone is fearful or enraged, but stifles or controls the feeling in order to deal more effectively with the situation at hand, or when a reappraisal calls for a completely different response, as with the worried mother on the phone. This neocortical area of the brain brings a more analytic or appropriate response to our emotional impulses, modulating the amygdala and other limbic areas.

Ordinarily the prefrontal areas govern our emotional reactions from the start. The largest projection of sensory information from the thalamus, remember, goes not to the amygdala, but to the neocortex and its many centers for taking in and making sense of what is being perceived; that information and our response to it is coordinated by the prefrontal lobes, the seat of planning and organizing actions toward a goal, including emotional ones. In the neocortex a cascading series of circuits registers and analyzes that information, comprehends it, and, through the prefrontal lobes, orchestrates a reaction. If in the process an emotional response is called for, the prefrontal lobes dictate it, working hand-in-hand with the amygdala and other circuits in the emotional brain.

This progression, which allows for discernment in emotional response, is the standard arrangement, with the significant exception of emotional emergencies. When an emotion triggers, within moments the prefrontal lobes perform what amounts to a risk/benefit ratio of myriad possible reactions, and bet that one of them is best.[11] For animals, when to attack, when to run. And for we humans . . . when to attack, when to run—and also, when to placate, persuade, seek sympathy, stonewall, provoke guilt, whine, put on a facade of bravado, be contemptuous—and so on, through the whole repertoire of emotional wiles.

The neocortical response is slower in brain time than the hijack mechanism because it involves more circuitry. It can also be more judicious and considered, since more thought precedes feeling. When we register a loss and become sad, or feel happy after a triumph, or mull over something someone has said or done and then get hurt or angry, the neocortex is at work.

Just as with the amygdala, absent the workings of the prefrontal lobes, much of emotional life would fall away; lacking an understanding that something merits an emotional response, none comes. This role of the prefrontal lobes in emotions has been suspected by neurologists since the advent in the 1940s of that rather desperate—and sadly misguided—surgical "cure" for mental illness: the prefrontal lobotomy, which (often sloppily) removed part of the prefrontal lobes or otherwise cut connections between the prefrontal cortex and the lower brain. In the days before any effective medications for mental illness, the lobotomy was hailed as the answer to grave emotional distress—sever the links between the prefrontal lobes and the rest of the brain, and patients' distress was "relieved." Unfortunately, the cost was that most of patients' emotional lives seemed to vanish, too. The key circuitry had been destroyed.

Emotional hijackings presumably involve two dynamics: triggering of the amygdala and a failure to activate the neocortical processes that usually keep emotional response in balance—or a recruitment of the neocortical zones to the emotional urgency.[12] At these moments the rational mind is swamped by the emotional. One way the prefrontal cortex acts as an efficient manager of emotion—weighing reactions before acting—is by dampening the signals for activation sent out by the amygdala and other limbic centers—something like a parent who stops an impulsive child from grabbing and tells the child to ask properly (or wait) for what it wants instead.[13]

The key "off" switch for distressing emotion seems to be the left prefrontal lobe. Neuropsychologists studying moods in patients with injuries to parts of the frontal lobes have determined that one of the tasks of the left frontal lobe is to act as a neural thermostat, regulating unpleasant emotions. The right prefrontal lobes are a seat of negative feelings like fear and aggression, while the left lobes keep those raw emotions in check, probably by inhibiting the right lobe.[14] In one group of stroke patients, for example, those whose lesions were in the left prefrontal cortex were prone to catastrophic worries and fears; those with lesions on the right were "unduly cheerful"; during neurological exams they joked around and were so laid back they clearly did not care how well they did.[15] And then there was the case of the happy husband: a man whose right prefrontal lobe had been partially removed in surgery for a brain malformation. His wife told physicians that after the operation he underwent a dramatic personality change, becoming less easily upset and, she was happy to say, more affectionate.[16]

The left prefrontal lobe, in short, seems to be part of a neural circuit that can switch off, or at least dampen down, all but the strongest negative surges of emotion. If the amygdala often acts as an emergency trigger, the left prefrontal lobe appears to be part of the brain's "off" switch for disturbing emotion: the amygdala proposes, the prefrontal lobe disposes. These prefrontal-limbic connections are crucial in mental life far beyond fine-tuning emotion; they are essential for navigating us through the decisions that matter most in life.

HARMONIZING EMOTION AND THOUGHT

The connections between the amygdala (and related limbic structures) and the neocortex are the hub of the battles or cooperative treaties struck between head and heart, thought and feeling. This circuitry explains why emotion is so crucial to effective thought, both in making wise decisions and in simply allowing us to think clearly.

Take the power of emotions to disrupt thinking itself. Neuroscientists use the term "working memory" for the capacity of attention that holds in mind the facts essential for completing a given task or problem, whether it be the ideal features one seeks in a house while touring several prospects, or the elements of a reasoning problem on a test. The prefrontal cortex is the brain region responsible for working memory.[17] But circuits from the limbic brain to the prefrontal lobes mean that the signals of strong emotion—anxiety, anger, and the like—can create neural static, sabotaging the ability of the prefrontal lobe to maintain working memory. That is why when we are emotionally upset we say we "just can't think straight"—and why continual emotional distress can create deficits in a child's intellectual abilities, crippling the capacity to learn.

These deficits, if more subtle, are not always tapped by IQ testing, though they show up through more targeted neuropsychological measures, as well as in a child's continual agitation and impulsivity. In one study, for example, primary school boys who had above-average IQ scores but nevertheless were doing poorly in school were found via these neuropsychological tests to have impaired frontal cortex functioning.[18] They also were impulsive and anxious, often disruptive and in trouble—suggesting faulty prefrontal control over their limbic urges. Despite their intellectual potential, these are the children at highest risk for problems like academic failure, alcoholism, and criminality—not because their intellect is deficient, but because their control over their emotional life is impaired. The emotional brain, quite separate from those cortical areas tapped by IQ tests, controls rage and compassion alike. These emotional circuits are sculpted by experience throughout childhood—and we leave those experiences utterly to chance at our peril.

Consider, too, the role of emotions in even the most "rational" decision-making. In work with far-reaching implications for understanding mental life, Dr. Antonio Damasio, a neurologist at the University of Iowa College of Medicine, has made careful studies of just what is impaired in patients with damage to the prefrontal-amygdala circuit.[19] Their decision-making is terribly flawed—and yet they show no deterioration at all in IQ or any cognitive ability. Despite their intact intelligence, they make disastrous choices in business and their personal lives, and can even obsess endlessly over a decision so simple as when to make an appointment.

Dr. Damasio argues that their decisions are so bad because they have lost access to their *emotional* learning. As the meeting point between thought and emotion, the prefrontal-amygdala circuit is a crucial doorway to the repository for the likes and dislikes we acquire over the course of a lifetime. Cut off from emotional memory in the amygdala, whatever the neocortex mulls over no longer triggers the emotional reactions that have been associated with it in the past—everything takes on a gray neutrality. A stimulus, be it a favorite pet or a detested acquaintance, no longer triggers either attraction or aversion; these patients have "forgotten" all such emotional lessons because they no longer have access to where they are stored in the amygdala.

Evidence like this leads Dr. Damasio to the counter-intuitive position that feelings are typically *indispensable* for rational decisions; they point us in the proper direction, where dry logic can then be of best use. While the world often confronts us with an unwieldy array of choices (How should you invest your retirement savings? Whom should you marry?), the emotional learning that life has given us (such as the memory of a disastrous investment or a painful breakup) sends signals that streamline the decision by eliminating some options and highlighting others at the outset. In this way, Dr. Damasio argues, the emotional brain is as involved in reasoning as is the thinking brain.

The emotions, then, matter for rationality. In the dance of feeling and thought the emotional faculty guides our moment-to-moment decisions, working hand-in-hand with the rational mind, enabling—or disabling—thought itself. Likewise, the thinking brain plays an executive role in our emotions—except in those moments when emotions surge out of control and the emotional brain runs rampant.

In a sense we have two brains, two minds—and two different kinds of intelligence: rational and emotional. How we do in life is determined by both—it is not just IQ, but *emotional* intelligence that matters. Indeed, intellect cannot work at its best without emotional intelligence. Ordinarily the complementarity of limbic system and neocortex, amygdala and prefrontal lobes, means each is a full partner in mental life. When these partners interact well, emotional intelligence rises—as does intellectual ability.

This turns the old understanding of the tension between reason and feeling on its head: it is not that we want to do away with emotion and put reason in its place, as Erasmus had it, but instead find the intelligent balance of the two. The old paradigm held an ideal of reason freed of the pull of emotion. The new paradigm urges us to harmonize head and heart. To do that well in our lives means we must first understand more exactly what it means to use emotion intelligently.

PART TWO

THE NATURE OF EMOTIONAL INTELLIGENCE

3

When Smart Is Dumb

Exactly why David Pologruto, a high-school physics teacher, was stabbed with a kitchen knife by one of his star students is still debatable. But the facts as widely reported are these:

Jason H., a sophomore and straight-A student at a Coral Springs, Florida, high school, was fixated on getting into medical school. Not just any medical school—he dreamt of Harvard. But Pologruto, his physics teacher, had given Jason an 80 on a quiz. Believing the grade—a mere B—put his dream in jeopardy, Jason took a butcher knife to school and, in a confrontation with Pologruto in the physics lab, stabbed his teacher in the collarbone before being subdued in a struggle.

A judge found Jason innocent, temporarily insane during the incident—a panel of four psychologists and psychiatrists swore he was psychotic during the fight. Jason claimed he had been planning to commit suicide because of the test score, and had gone to Pologruto to tell him he was killing himself because of the bad grade. Pologruto told a different story: "I think he tried to completely do me in with the knife" because he was infuriated over the bad grade.

After transferring to a private school, Jason graduated two years later at the top of his class. A perfect grade in regular classes would have given him a straight-A, 4.0 average, but Jason had taken enough advanced courses to raise his grade-point average to 4.614—way beyond A+. Even as Jason graduated with highest honors, his old physics teacher, David Pologruto, complained that Jason had never apologized or even taken responsibility for the attack.[1]

The question is, how could someone of such obvious intelligence do something so irrational—so downright dumb? The answer: Academic intelligence has little to do with emotional life. The brightest among us can founder on the shoals of unbridled passions and unruly impulses; people with high IQs can be stunningly poor pilots of their private lives.

One of psychology's open secrets is the relative inability of grades, IQ, or SAT scores, despite their popular mystique, to predict unerringly who will succeed in life. To be sure, there is a relationship between IQ and life circumstances for large groups as a whole: many people with very low IQs end up in menial jobs, and those with high IQs tend to become well-paid—but by no means always.

There are widespread exceptions to the rule that IQ predicts success—many (or more) exceptions than cases that fit the rule. At best, IQ contributes about 20 percent to the factors that determine life success, which leaves 80 percent to other forces.[2] As one observer notes, "The vast majority of one's ultimate niche in society is determined by non-IQ factors, ranging from social class to luck."

Even Richard Herrnstein and Charles Murray, whose book *The Bell Curve* imputes a primary importance to IQ, acknowledge this; as they point out, "Perhaps a freshman with an SAT math score of 500 had better not have his heart set on being a mathematician, but if instead he wants to run his own business, become a U.S. Senator or make a million dollars, he should not put aside his dreams. . . . The link between test scores and those achievements is dwarfed by the totality of other characteristics that he brings to life."[3]

My concern is with a key set of these "other characteristics," *emotional intelligence:* abilities such as being able to motivate oneself and persist in the face of frustrations; to control impulse and delay gratification; to regulate one's moods and keep distress from swamping the ability to think; to empathize and to hope. Unlike IQ, with its nearly one-hundred-year history of research with hundreds of thousands of people, emotional intelligence is a new concept. No one can yet say exactly how much of the variability from person to person in life's course it accounts for. But what data exist suggest it can be as powerful, and at times more powerful, than IQ. And while there are those who argue that IQ cannot be changed much by experience or education, I will show in Part Five that the crucial emotional competencies can indeed be learned and improved upon by children—if we bother to teach them.

EMOTIONAL INTELLIGENCE AND DESTINY

I remember the fellow in my own class at Amherst College who had attained five perfect 800 scores on the SAT and other achievement tests he took before entering. Despite his formidable intellectual abilities, he spent most of his time hanging out, staying up late, and missing classes by sleeping until noon. It took him almost ten years to finally get his degree.

IQ offers little to explain the different destinies of people with roughly equal promises, schooling, and opportunity. When ninety-five Harvard students from the classes of the 1940s—a time when people with a wider spread of IQ were at Ivy League schools than is presently the case—were followed into middle age, the men with the highest test scores in college were not particularly successful compared to their lower-scoring peers in terms of salary, productivity, or status in their field. Nor did they have the greatest life satisfaction, nor the most happiness with friendships, family, and romantic relationships.[4]

A similar follow-up in middle age was done with 450 boys, most sons of immigrants, two thirds from families on welfare, who grew up in Somerville, Massachusetts, at the time a "blighted slum" a few blocks from Harvard. A third had IQs below 90. But again IQ had little relationship to how well they had done at work or in the rest of their lives; for instance, 7 percent of men with IQs under 80 were unemployed for ten or more years, but so were 7 percent of men with IQs over 100. To be sure, there was a general link (as there always is) between IQ and socioeconomic level at age forty-seven. But childhood abilities such as being able to handle frustrations, control emotions, and get on with other people made the greater difference.[5]

Consider also data from an ongoing study of eighty-one valedictorians and salutatorians from the 1981 class in Illinois high schools. All, of course, had the highest grade-point averages in their schools. But while they continued to achieve well in college, getting excellent grades, by their late twenties they had climbed to only average levels of success. Ten years after graduating from high school, only one in four were at the highest level of young people of comparable age in their chosen profession, and many were doing much less well.

Karen Arnold, professor of education at Boston University, one of the researchers tracking the valedictorians, explains, "I think we've discovered the 'dutiful'—people who know how to achieve in the system. But valedictorians struggle as surely as we all do. To know that a person is a valedictorian is to know only that he or she is exceedingly good at achievement as measured by grades. It tells you nothing about how they react to the vicissitudes of life."[6]

And that is the problem: academic intelligence offers virtually no preparation for the turmoil—or opportunity—life's vicissitudes bring. Yet even though a high IQ is no guarantee of prosperity, prestige, or happiness in life, our schools and our culture fixate on academic abilities, ignoring *emotional* intelligence, a set of traits—some might call it character—that also matters immensely for our personal destiny. Emotional life is a domain that, as surely as math or reading, can be handled with greater or lesser skill, and requires its unique set of competencies. And how adept a person is at those is crucial to understanding why one person thrives in life while another, of equal intellect, dead-ends: emotional aptitude is a *meta-ability,* determining how well we can use whatever other skills we have, including raw intellect.

Of course, there are many paths to success in life, and many domains in which other aptitudes are rewarded. In our increasingly knowledge-based society, technical skill is certainly one. There is a children's joke: "What do you call a nerd fifteen years from now?" The answer: "Boss." But even among "nerds" emotional intelligence offers an added edge in the workplace, as we shall see in Part Three. Much evidence testifies that people who are emotionally adept—who know and manage their own feelings well, and who read and deal effectively with other people's feelings—are at an advantage in any domain of life, whether romance and intimate relationships or picking up the unspoken rules that govern success in organizational politics. People with well-developed emotional skills are also more likely to be content and effective in their lives, mastering the habits of mind that foster their own productivity; people who cannot marshal some control over their emotional life fight inner battles that sabotage their ability for focused work and clear thought.

A DIFFERENT KIND OF INTELLIGENCE

To the casual observer, four-year-old Judy might seem a wallflower among her more gregarious playmates. She hangs back from the action at playtime, staying on the margins of games rather than plunging into the center. But Judy is actually a keen observer of the social politics of her preschool classroom, perhaps the most sophisticated of her playmates in her insights into the tides of feeling within the others.

Her sophistication is not apparent until Judy's teacher gathers the four-year-olds around to play what they call the Classroom Game. The Classroom Game—a dollhouse replica of Judy's own preschool classroom, with stick figures who have for heads small photos of the students and teachers—is a test of social perceptiveness. When Judy's teacher asks her to put each girl and boy in the part of the room they like to play in most—the art corner, the blocks corner, and so on—Judy does so with complete accuracy. And when asked to put each boy and girl with the children they like to play with most, Judy shows she can match best friends for the entire class.

Judy's accuracy reveals that she has a perfect social map of her class, a level of perceptiveness exceptional for a four-year-old. These are the skills that, in later life, might allow Judy to blossom into a star in any of the fields where "people skills" count, from sales and management to diplomacy.

That Judy's social brilliance was spotted at all, let alone this early, was due to her being a student at the Eliot-Pearson Preschool on the campus of Tufts University, where Project Spectrum, a curriculum that intentionally cultivates a variety of kinds of intelligence, was then being developed. Project Spectrum recognizes that the human repertoire of abilities goes far beyond the three R's, the narrow band of word-and-number skills that schools traditionally focus on. It acknowledges that capacities such as Judy's social perceptiveness are talents that an education can nurture rather than ignore or even frustrate. By encouraging children to develop a full range of the abilities that they will actually draw on to succeed, or use simply to be fulfilled in what they do, school becomes an education in life skills.

The guiding visionary behind Project Spectrum is Howard Gardner, a psychologist at the Harvard School of Education.[7] "The time has come," Gardner told me, "to broaden our notion of the spectrum of talents. The single most important contribution education can make to a child's development is to help him toward a field where his talents best suit him, where he will be satisfied and competent. We've completely lost sight of that. Instead we subject everyone to an education where, if you succeed, you will be best suited to be a college professor. And we evaluate everyone along the way according to whether they meet that narrow standard of success. We should spend less time ranking children and more time helping them to identify their natural competencies and gifts, and cultivate those. There are hundreds and hundreds of ways to succeed, and many, many different abilities that will help you get there."[8]

If anyone sees the limits of the old ways of thinking about intelligence, it is Gardner. He points out that the glory days of the IQ tests began during World War I, when two million American men were sorted out through the first mass paper-and-pencil form of the IQ test, freshly developed by Lewis Terman, a psychologist at Stanford. This led to decades of what Gardner calls the "IQ way of thinking": "that people are either smart or not, are born that way, that there's nothing much you can do about it, and that tests can tell you if you are one of the smart ones or not. The SAT test for college admissions is based on the same notion of a single kind of aptitude that determines your future. This way of thinking permeates society."

Gardner's influential 1983 book *Frames of Mind* was a manifesto refuting the IQ view; it proposed that there was not just one, monolithic kind of intelligence that was crucial for life success, but rather a wide spectrum of intelligences, with seven key varieties. His list includes the two standard academic kinds, verbal and mathematical-logical alacrity, but it goes on to include the spatial capacity seen in, say, an outstanding artist or architect; the kinesthetic genius displayed in the physical fluidity and grace of a Martha Graham or Magic Johnson; and the musical gifts of a Mozart or YoYo Ma. Rounding out the list are two faces of what Gardner calls "the personal intelligences": interpersonal skills, like those of a great therapist such as Carl Rogers or a world-class leader such as Martin Luther King, Jr., and the "intrapsychic" capacity that could emerge, on the one hand, in the brilliant insights of Sigmund Freud, or, with less fanfare, in the inner contentment that arises from attuning one's life to be in keeping with one's true feelings.

The operative word in this view of intelligences is *multiple:* Gardner's model pushes way beyond the standard concept of IQ as a single, immutable factor. It recognizes that the tests that tyrannized us as we went through school—from the achievement tests that sorted us out into those who would be shunted toward technical schools and those destined for college, to the SATs that determined what, if any, college we would be allowed to attend— are based on a limited notion of intelligence, one out of touch with the true range of skills and abilities that matter for life over and beyond IQ.

Gardner acknowledges that seven is an arbitrary figure for the variety of intelligences; there is no magic number to the multiplicity of human talents. At one point, Gardner and his research colleagues had stretched these seven to a list of twenty different varieties of intelligence. Interpersonal intelligence, for example, broke down into four distinct abilities: leadership, the ability to nurture relationships and keep friends, the ability to resolve conflicts, and skill at the kind of social analysis that four-year-old Judy excels at.

This multifaceted view of intelligence offers a richer picture of a child's ability and potential for success than the standard IQ. When Spectrum students were evaluated on the Stanford-Binet Intelligence Scale—once the gold standard of IQ tests—and again by a battery designed to measure Gardner's spectrum of intelligences, there was no significant relationship between children's scores on the two tests.[9] The five children with the highest IQs (from 125 to 133) showed a variety of profiles on the ten strengths measured by the Spectrum test. For example, of the five "smartest" children according to the IQ tests, one was strong in three areas, three had strengths in two areas, and one "smart" child had just one Spectrum strength. Those strengths were scattered: four of these children's strengths were in music, two in the visual arts, one in social understanding, one in logic, two in language. None of the five high-IQ kids were strong in movement, numbers, or mechanics; movement and numbers were actually weak spots for two of these five.

Gardner's conclusion was that "the Stanford-Binet Intelligence Scale did not predict successful performance across or on a consistent subset of Spectrum activities." On the other hand, the Spectrum scores give parents and teachers clear guidance about the realms that these children will take a spontaneous interest in, and where they will do well enough to develop the passions that could one day lead beyond proficiency to mastery.

Gardner's thinking about the multiplicity of intelligence continues to evolve. Some ten years after he first published his theory, Gardner gave these nutshell summaries of the personal intelligences:

> *Inter*personal intelligence is the ability to understand other people: what motivates them, how they work, how to work cooperatively with them. Successful salespeople, politicians, teachers, clinicians, and religious leaders are all likely to be individuals with high degrees of interpersonal intelligence. *Intra*personal intelligence . . . is a correlative ability, turned inward. It is a capacity to form an accurate, veridical model of oneself and to be able to use that model to operate effectively in life.[10]

In another rendering, Gardner noted that the core of interpersonal intelligence includes the "capacities to discern and respond appropriately to the moods, temperaments, motivations, and desires of other people." In intrapersonal intelligence, the key to self-knowledge, he included "access to one's own feelings and the ability to discriminate among them and draw upon them to guide behavior."[11]

SPOCK VS. DATA: WHEN COGNITION IS NOT ENOUGH

There is one dimension of personal intelligence that is broadly pointed to, but little explored, in Gardner's elaborations: the role of emotions. Perhaps this is so because, as Gardner suggested to me, his work is so strongly informed by a cognitive-science model of mind. Thus his view of these intelligences emphasizes cognition—the *understanding* of oneself and of others in motives, in habits of working, and in putting that insight into use in conducting one's own life and getting along with others. But like the kinesthetic realm, where physical brilliance manifests itself nonverbally, the realm of the emotions extends, too, beyond the reach of language and cognition.

While there is ample room in Gardner's descriptions of the personal intelligences for insight into the play of emotions and mastery in managing them, Gardner and those who work with him have not pursued in great detail the role of *feeling* in these intelligences, focusing more on cognitions *about* feeling. This focus, perhaps unintentionally, leaves unexplored the rich sea of emotions that makes the inner life and relationships so complex, so compelling, and so often puzzling. And it leaves yet to be plumbed both the sense in which there is intelligence *in* the emotions and the sense in which intelligence can be brought *to* emotions.

Gardner's emphasis on the cognitive elements in the personal intelligences reflects the zeitgeist of psychology that has shaped his views. Psychology's overemphasis on cognition even in the realm of emotion is, in part, due to a quirk in the history of that science. During the middle decades of this century academic psychology was dominated by behaviorists in the mold of B. F. Skinner, who felt that only behavior that could be seen objectively, from the outside, could be studied with scientific accuracy. The behaviorists ruled all inner life, including emotions, out-of-bounds for science.

Then, with the coming in the late 1960s of the "cognitive revolution," the focus of psychological science turned to how the mind registers and stores information, and the nature of intelligence. But emotions were still off-limits. Conventional wisdom among cognitive scientists held that intelligence entails a cold, hard-nosed processing of fact. It is hyperrational, rather like *Star Trek*'s Mr. Spock, the archetype of dry information bytes unmuddied by feeling, embodying the idea that emotions have no place in intelligence and only muddle our picture of mental life.

The cognitive scientists who embraced this view have been seduced by the computer as the operative model of mind, forgetting that, in reality, the brain's wetware is awash in a messy, pulsating puddle of neurochemicals, nothing like the sanitized, orderly silicon that has spawned the guiding metaphor for mind. The predominant models among cognitive scientists of how the mind processes information have lacked an acknowledgment that rationality is guided by—and can be swamped by—feeling. The cognitive model is, in this regard, an impoverished view of the mind, one that fails to explain the Sturm und Drang of feelings that brings flavor to the intellect. In order to persist in this view, cognitive scientists themselves have had to ignore the relevance for their models of mind of their personal hopes and fears, their marital squabbles and professional jealousies—the wash of feeling that gives life its flavor and its urgencies, and which in every moment biases exactly how (and how well or poorly) information is processed.

The lopsided scientific vision of an emotionally flat mental life—which has guided the last eighty years of research on intelligence—is gradually changing as psychology has begun to recognize the essential role of feeling in thinking. Rather like the Spockish character Data in *Star Trek: The Next Generation,* psychology is coming to appreciate the power and virtues of emotions in mental life, as well as their dangers. After all, as Data sees (to his own dismay, could he feel dismay), his cool logic fails to bring the right *human* solution. Our humanity is most evident in our feelings; Data seeks to feel, knowing that something essential is missing. He wants friendship, loyalty; like the Tin Man in *The Wizard of Oz,* he lacks a heart. Lacking the lyrical sense that feeling brings, Data can play music or write poetry with technical virtuosity, but not feel its passion. The lesson of Data's yearning for yearning itself is that the higher values of the human heart—faith, hope, devotion, love—are missing entirely from the coldly cognitive view. Emotions enrich; a model of mind that leaves them out is impoverished.

When I asked Gardner about his emphasis on thoughts about feelings, or metacognition, more than on emotions themselves, he acknowledged that he tended to view intelligence in a cognitive way, but told me, "When I first wrote about the personal intelligences, I *was* talking about emotion, especially in my notion of intrapersonal intelligence—one component is emotionally tuning in to yourself. It's the visceral-feeling signals you get that are essential for interpersonal intelligence. But as it has developed in practice, the theory of multiple intelligence has evolved to focus more on metacognition"—that is, awareness of one's mental processes—"rather than on the full range of emotional abilities."

Even so, Gardner appreciates how crucial these emotional and relationship abilities are in the rough-and-tumble of life. He points out that "many people with IQs of 160 work for people with IQs of 100, if the former have poor intrapersonal intelligence and the latter have a high one. And in the day-to-day world no intelligence is more important than the interpersonal. If you don't have it, you'll make poor choices about who to marry, what job to take, and so on. We need to train children in the personal intelligences in school."

CAN EMOTIONS BE INTELLIGENT?

To get a fuller understanding of just what such training might be like, we must turn to other theorists who agree with Gardner's view—most notably psychologists Peter Salovey and John Mayer. They have mapped in great detail the ways in which we can bring intelligence to our emotions.[12] This endeavor is not new; over the years even the most ardent theorists of IQ have occasionally tried to bring emotions within the domain of intelligence, rather than seeing "emotion" and "intelligence" as an inherent contradiction in terms. Thus E. L. Thorndike, an eminent psychologist who was also influential in popularizing the notion of IQ in the 1920s and 1930s, proposed in a *Harper's Magazine* article that one aspect of emotional intelligence, "social" intelligence—the ability to understand others and "act wisely in human relations"—was itself an aspect of a person's IQ. Other psychologists of the time took a more cynical view of social intelligence, seeing it in terms of skills for manipulating other people—getting them to do what you want, whether they want to or not. But neither of these formulations of social intelligence held much sway with theorists of IQ, and by 1960 an influential textbook on intelligence tests pronounced social intelligence a "useless" concept.

But personal intelligence would not be ignored, mainly because it makes both intuitive and common sense. For example, when Yale psychologist Robert Sternberg asked people to describe an "intelligent person," practical people skills were among the main traits listed. More systematic research by Sternberg led him back to Thorndike's conclusion: that social intelligence is both distinct from academic abilities and a key part of what makes people do well in the practicalities of life. Among the practical intelligences that are, for instance, so highly valued in the workplace is the kind of sensitivity that allows effective managers to pick up tacit messages.[13]

In recent years a growing group of psychologists has come to similar conclusions, agreeing with Gardner that the old concepts of IQ revolved around a narrow band of linguistic and math skills, and that doing well on IQ tests was most directly a predictor of success in the classroom or as a professor but less and less so as life's paths diverged from academe. These psychologists—Sternberg and Salovey among them—have taken a wider view of intelligence, trying to reinvent it in terms of what it takes to lead life successfully. And that line of enquiry leads back to an appreciation of just how crucial "personal" or emotional intelligence is.

Salovey, with his colleague John Mayer, offered an elaborated definition of emotional intelligence, expanding these abilities into five main domains:[14]

1. *Knowing one's emotions.* Self-awareness—recognizing a feeling *as it happens*—is the keystone of emotional intelligence. As we will see in Chapter 4, the ability to monitor feelings from moment to moment is crucial to psychological insight and self-understanding. An inability to notice our true feelings leaves us at their mercy. People with greater certainty about their feelings are better pilots of their lives, having a surer sense of how they really feel about personal decisions from whom to marry to what job to take.

2. *Managing emotions.* Handling feelings so they are appropriate is an ability that builds on self-awareness. Chapter 5 will examine the capacity to soothe oneself, to shake off rampant anxiety, gloom, or irritability—and the consequences of failure at this basic emotional skill. People who are poor in this ability are constantly battling feelings of distress, while those who excel in it can bounce back far more quickly from life's setbacks and upsets.

3. *Motivating oneself.* As Chapter 6 will show, marshaling emotions in the service of a goal is essential for paying attention, for self-motivation and mastery, and for creativity. Emotional self-control—delaying gratification and stifling impulsiveness—underlies accomplishment of every sort. And being able to get into the "flow" state enables outstanding performance of all kinds. People who have this skill tend to be more highly productive and effective in whatever they undertake.

4. *Recognizing emotions in others.* Empathy, another ability that builds on emotional self-awareness, is the fundamental "people skill." Chapter 7 will investigate the roots of empathy, the social cost of being emotionally tone-deaf, and the reason empathy kindles altruism. People who are empathic are more attuned to the subtle social signals that indicate what others need or want. This makes them better at callings such as the caring professions, teaching, sales, and management.

5. *Handling relationships.* The art of relationships is, in large part, skill in managing emotions in others. Chapter 8 looks at social competence and incompetence, and the specific skills involved. These are the abilities that undergird popularity, leadership, and interpersonal effectiveness. People

who excel in these skills do well at anything that relies on interacting smoothly with others; they are social stars.

Of course, people differ in their abilities in each of these domains; some of us may be quite adept at handling, say, our own anxiety, but relatively inept at soothing someone else's upsets. The underlying basis for our level of ability is, no doubt, neural, but as we will see, the brain is remarkably plastic, constantly learning. Lapses in emotional skills can be remedied: to a great extent each of these domains represents a body of habit and response that, with the right effort, can be improved on.

IQ AND EMOTIONAL INTELLIGENCE: PURE TYPES

IQ and emotional intelligence are not opposing competencies, but rather separate ones. We all mix intellect and emotional acuity; people with a high IQ but low emotional intelligence (or low IQ and high emotional intelligence) are, despite the stereotypes, relatively rare. Indeed, there is a slight correlation between IQ and some aspects of emotional intelligence—though small enough to make clear these are largely independent entities.

Unlike the familiar tests for IQ, there is, as yet, no single paper-and-pencil test that yields an "emotional intelligence score" and there may never be one. Although there is ample research on each of its components, some of them, such as empathy, are best tested by sampling a person's actual ability at the task—for example, by having them read a person's feelings from a video of their facial expressions. Still, using a measure for what he calls "ego resilience" which is quite similar to emotional intelligence (it includes the main social and emotional competences), Jack Block, a psychologist at the University of California at Berkeley, has made a comparison of two theoretical pure types: people high in IQ versus people high in emotional aptitudes.[15] The differences are telling.

The high-IQ pure type (that is, setting aside emotional intelligence) is almost a caricature of the intellectual, adept in the realm of mind but inept in the personal world. The profiles differ slightly for men and women. The high-IQ male is typified—no surprise—by a wide range of intellectual interests and abilities. He is ambitious and productive, predictable and dogged, and untroubled by concerns about himself. He also tends to be critical and condescending, fastidious and inhibited, uneasy with sexuality and sensual experience, unexpressive and detached, and emotionally bland and cold.

By contrast, men who are high in emotional intelligence are socially poised, outgoing and cheerful, not prone to fearfulness or worried rumination. They have a notable capacity for commitment to people or causes, for taking responsibility, and for having an ethical outlook; they are sympathetic and caring in their relationships. Their emotional life is rich, but appropriate; they are comfortable with themselves, others, and the social universe they live in.

Purely high-IQ women have the expected intellectual confidence, are fluent in expressing their thoughts, value intellectual matters, and have a wide range of intellectual and aesthetic interests. They also tend to be introspective, prone to anxiety, rumination, and guilt, and hesitate to express their anger openly (though they do so indirectly).

Emotionally intelligent women, by contrast, tend to be assertive and express their feelings directly, and to feel positive about themselves; life holds meaning for them. Like the men, they are outgoing and gregarious, and express their feelings appropriately (rather than, say, in outbursts they later regret); they adapt well to stress. Their social poise lets them easily reach out to new people; they are comfortable enough with themselves to be playful, spontaneous, and open to sensual experience. Unlike the women purely high in IQ, they rarely feel anxious or guilty, or sink into rumination.

These portraits, of course, are extremes—all of us mix IQ and emotional intelligence in varying degrees. But they offer an instructive look at what each of these dimensions adds separately to a person's qualities. To the degree a person has both cognitive and emotional intelligence, these pictures merge. Still, of the two, emotional intelligence adds far more of the qualities that make us more fully human.

4

Know Thyself

A belligerent samurai, an old Japanese tale goes, once challenged a Zen master to explain the concept of heaven and hell. But the monk replied with scorn, "You're nothing but a lout—I can't waste my time with the likes of you!"

His very honor attacked, the samurai flew into a rage and, pulling his sword from its scabbard, yelled, "I could kill you for your impertinence."

"That," the monk calmly replied, "is hell."

Startled at seeing the truth in what the master pointed out about the fury that had him in its grip, the samurai calmed down, sheathed his sword, and bowed, thanking the monk for the insight.

"And that," said the monk, "is heaven."

The sudden awakening of the samurai to his own agitated state illustrates the crucial difference between being caught up in a feeling and becoming aware that you are being swept away by it. Socrates's injunction "Know thyself" speaks to this keystone of emotional intelligence: awareness of one's own feelings as they occur.

It might seem at first glance that our feelings are obvious; more thoughtful reflection reminds us of times we have been all too oblivious to what we really felt about something, or awoke to these feelings late in the game. Psychologists use the rather ponderous term *metacognition* to refer to an awareness of thought process, and *metamood* to mean awareness of one's own emotions. I prefer the term *self-awareness,* in the sense of an ongoing attention to one's internal states.[1] In this self-reflexive awareness mind observes and investigates experience itself, including the emotions.[2]

This quality of awareness is akin to what Freud described as an "evenly hovering attention," and which he commended to those who would do psychoanalysis. Such attention takes in whatever passes through awareness with impartiality, as an interested yet unreactive witness. Some psychoanalysts call it the "observing ego," the capacity of self-awareness that allows the analyst to monitor his own reactions to what the patient is saying, and which the process of free association nurtures in the patient.[3]

Such self-awareness would seem to require an activated neocortex, particularly the language areas, attuned to identify and name the emotions being aroused. Self-awareness is not an attention that gets carried away by emotions, overreacting and amplifying what is perceived. Rather, it is a neutral mode that maintains self-reflectiveness even amidst turbulent emotions. William Styron seems to be describing something like this faculty of mind in writing of his deep depression, telling of a sense "of being accompanied by a second self— a wraithlike observer who, not sharing the dementia of his double, is able to watch with dispassionate curiosity as his companion struggles."[4]

At its best, self-observation allows just such an equanimous awareness of passionate or turbulent feelings. At a minimum, it manifests itself simply as a slight stepping-back from experience, a parallel stream of consciousness that is "meta": hovering above or beside the main flow, aware of what is happening rather than being immersed and lost in it. It is the difference between, for example, being murderously enraged at someone and having the self-reflexive thought "This is anger I'm feeling" even as you are enraged. In terms of the neural mechanics of awareness, this subtle shift in mental activity presumably signals that neocortical circuits are actively monitoring the emotion, a first step in gaining some control. This awareness of emotions is the fundamental emotional competence on which others, such as emotional self-control, build.

Self-awareness, in short, means being "aware of both our mood and our thoughts about that mood," in the words of John Mayer, a University of New Hampshire psychologist who, with Yale's Peter Salovey, is a coformulator of the theory of emotional intelligence.[5] Self-awareness can be a nonreactive, nonjudgmental attention to inner states. But Mayer finds that this sensibility also can be less equanimous; typical thoughts bespeaking emotional self-awareness include "I shouldn't feel this way," "I'm thinking good things to cheer up," and, for a more restricted self-awareness, the fleeting thought "Don't think about it" in reaction to something highly upsetting.

Although there is a logical distinction between being aware of feelings and acting to change them, Mayer finds that for all practical purposes the two usually go hand-in-hand: to recognize a foul mood is to want to get out of it. This recognition, however, is distinct from the efforts we make to keep from acting on an emotional impulse. When we say "Stop that!" to a child whose anger has led him to hit a playmate, we may stop the hitting, but the anger still simmers. The child's thoughts are still fixated on the trigger for the anger—"But he stole my toy!"—and the anger continues unabated. Self-awareness has a more powerful effect on strong, aversive feelings: the realization "This is anger I'm feeling" offers a greater degree of freedom—not just the option not to act on it, but the added option to try to let go of it.

Mayer finds that people tend to fall into distinctive styles for attending to and dealing with their emotions:[6]

• *Self-aware.* Aware of their moods as they are having them, these people understandably have some sophistication about their emotional lives. Their clarity about emotions may undergird other personality traits: they are autonomous and sure of their own boundaries, are in good psychological health, and tend to have a positive outlook on life. When they get into a bad mood, they don't ruminate and obsess about it, and are able to get out of it sooner. In short, their mindfulness helps them manage their emotions.

• *Engulfed.* These are people who often feel swamped by their emotions and helpless to escape them, as though their moods have taken charge. They are mercurial and not very aware of their feelings, so that they are lost in them rather than having some perspective. As a result, they do little to try to escape bad moods, feeling that they have no control over their emotional life. They often feel overwhelmed and emotionally out of control.

• *Accepting.* While these people are often clear about what they are feeling, they also tend to be accepting of their moods, and so don't try to change them. There seem to be two branches of the accepting type: those who are usually in good moods and so have little motivation to change them, and people who, despite their clarity about their moods, are susceptible to bad ones but accept them with a laissez-faire attitude, doing nothing to change them despite their distress—a pattern found among, say, depressed people who are resigned to their despair.

THE PASSIONATE AND THE INDIFFERENT

Imagine for a moment that you're on an airplane flying from New York to San Francisco. It's been a smooth flight, but as you approach the Rockies the pilot's voice comes over the plane intercom. "Ladies and gentlemen, there's some turbulence ahead. Please return to your seats and fasten your seatbelts." And then the plane hits the turbulence, which is rougher than you've ever endured—the airplane is tossed up and down and side to side like a beach ball in the waves.

The question is, what do you do? Are you the kind of person who buries yourself in your book or magazine, or continues watching the movie, tuning out the turbulence? Or are you likely to take out the emergency card and review the precautions, or watch the flight attendants to see if they show signs of panic, or strain to hear the engines to see if there's anything worrisome?

Which of these responses comes more naturally to us is a sign of our favored attentional stance under duress. The airplane scenario itself is an item from a psychological test developed by Suzanne Miller, a psychologist at Temple University, to assess whether people tend to be vigilant, attending carefully to every detail of a distressing predicament, or, in contrast, deal with such anxious moments by trying to distract themselves. These two attentional stances toward distress have very different consequences for how people experience their own emotional reactions. Those who tune in under duress can, by the very act of attending so carefully, unwittingly amplify the magnitude of their own reactions—especially if their tuning in is devoid of the equanimity of self-awareness. The result is that their emotions seem all the more intense. Those who tune out, who distract themselves, notice less about their own reactions, and so minimize the experience of their emotional response, if not the size of the response itself.

At the extremes, this means that for some people emotional awareness is overwhelming, while for others it barely exists. Consider the college student who, one evening, spotted a fire that had broken out in his dorm, went to get a fire extinguisher, and put the fire out. Nothing unusual—except that on his way to get the extinguisher and then on the way back to the fire, he walked instead of running. The reason? He didn't feel there was any urgency.

This story was told to me by Edward Diener, a University of Illinois at Urbana psychologist who has been studying the *intensity* with which people experience their emotions.[7] The college student stood out in his collection of case studies as one of the least intense Diener had ever encountered. He was, essentially, a man without passions, someone who goes through life feeling little or nothing, even about an emergency like a fire.

By contrast, consider a woman at the opposite end of Diener's spectrum. When she once lost her favorite pen, she was distraught for days. Another time she was so thrilled on seeing an ad for a big sale on women's shoes at an expensive store that she dropped what she was doing, hopped in her car, and drove three hours to the store in Chicago.

Diener finds that women, in general, feel both positive and negative emotions more strongly than do men. And, sex differences aside, emotional life is richer for those who notice more. For one thing, this enhanced emotional sensitivity means that for such people the least provocation unleashes emotional storms, whether heavenly or hellish, while those at the other extreme barely experience any feeling even under the most dire circumstances.

THE MAN WITHOUT FEELINGS

Gary infuriated his fiancée, Ellen, because even though he was intelligent, thoughtful, and a successful surgeon, Gary was emotionally flat, completely unresponsive to any and all shows of feeling. While Gary could speak brilliantly of science and art, when it came to his feelings—even for Ellen—he fell silent. Try as she might to elicit some passion from him, Gary was impassive, oblivious. "I don't naturally express my feelings," Gary told the therapist he saw at Ellen's insistence. When it came to emotional life, he added, "I don't know what to talk about; I have no strong feelings, either positive or negative."

Ellen was not alone in being frustrated by Gary's aloofness; as he confided to his therapist, he was unable to speak openly about his feelings with anyone in his life. The reason: He did not know what he felt in the first place. So far as he could tell, he had no angers, no sadnesses, no joys.[8]

As his own therapist observes, this emotional blankness makes Gary and others like him colorless, bland: "They bore everybody. That's why their wives send them into treatment." Gary's emotional flatness exemplifies what psychiatrists call *alexithymia*, from the Greek *a-* for "lack," *lexis* for "word," and *thymos* for "emotion." Such people lack words for their feelings. Indeed, they seem to lack feelings altogether, although this may actually be because of their inability to *express* emotion rather than from an absence of emotion altogether. Such people were first noticed by psychoanalysts puzzled by a class of patients who were untreatable by that method because they reported no feelings, no fantasies, and colorless dreams—in short, no inner emotional life to talk about at all.[9] The clinical features that mark alexithymics include having difficulty describing feelings—their own or anyone else's—and a sharply limited emotional vocabulary.[10] What's more, they have trouble discriminating among emotions as well as between emotion and bodily sensation, so that they might tell of having butterflies in the stomach, palpitations, sweating, and dizziness—but they would not know they are feeling anxious.

"They give the impression of being different, alien beings, having come from an entirely different world, living in the midst of a society which is dominated by feelings," is the description given by Dr. Peter Sifneos, the Harvard psychiatrist who in 1972 coined the term *alexithymia*.[11] Alexithymics rarely cry, for example, but if they do their tears are copious. Still, they are bewildered if asked what the tears are all about. One patient with alexithymia was so upset after seeing a movie about a woman with eight children who was dying of cancer that she cried herself to sleep. When her therapist suggested that perhaps she was upset because the movie reminded her of her own mother, who was in actuality dying of cancer, the woman sat motionless, bewildered and silent. When her therapist then asked her how she felt at that moment, she said she felt "awful," but couldn't clarify her feelings beyond that. And, she added, from time to time she found herself crying, but never knew exactly what she was crying about.[12]

And that is the nub of the problem. It is not that alexithymics never feel, but that they are unable to know—and especially unable to put into words—precisely what their feelings are. They are utterly lacking in the fundamental skill of emotional intelligence, self-awareness—knowing what we are feeling as emotions roil within us. Alexithymics belie the common-sense notion that it is perfectly self-evident what we are feeling: they haven't a clue. When something—or more likely, someone—does move them to feeling, they find the experience baffling and overwhelming, something to avoid at all costs. Feelings come to them, when they come at all, as a befuddling bundle of distress; as the patient who cried at the movie put it, they feel "awful," but can't say exactly which *kind* of awful it is they feel.

This basic confusion about feelings often seems to lead them to complain of vague medical problems when they are actually experiencing emotional distress—a phenomenon known in psychiatry as *somaticizing,* mistaking an emotional ache for a physical one (and different from a psychosomatic disease, in which emotional problems cause genuine medical ones). Indeed, much of the psychiatric interest in alexithymics is in weeding them out from among those who come to doctors seeking help, for they are prone to lengthy—and fruitless—pursuit of a medical diagnosis and treatment for what is actually an emotional problem.

While no one can as yet say for sure what causes alexithymia, Dr. Sifneos proposes a disconnection between the limbic system and the neocortex, particularly its verbal centers, which fits well with what we are learning about the emotional brain. Patients with severe seizures who had that connection surgically severed to relieve their symptoms, notes Sifneos, became emotionally flat, like people with alexithymia, unable to put their feelings into words and suddenly devoid of fantasy life. In short, though the circuits of the emotional brain may react with feelings, the neocortex is not able to sort out these feelings and add the nuance of language to them. As Henry Roth observed in his novel *Call It Sleep* about this power of language, "If you could put words to what you felt, it was yours." The corollary, of course, is the alexithymic's dilemma: having no words for feelings means not making the feelings your own.

IN PRAISE OF GUT FEELING

Elliot's tumor, growing just behind his forehead, was the size of a small orange; surgery removed it completely. Although the surgery was declared a success, afterward people who knew him well said that Elliot was no longer Elliot—he had undergone a drastic personality change. Once a successful corporate lawyer, Elliot could no longer hold a job. His wife left him. Squandering his savings in fruitless investments, he was reduced to living in a spare bedroom at his brother's home.

There was a puzzling pattern to Elliot's problem. Intellectually he was as bright as ever, but he used his time terribly, getting lost in minor details; he seemed to have lost all sense of priority. Reprimands made no difference; he was fired from a succession of legal jobs. Though extensive intellectual tests found nothing wrong with Elliot's mental faculties, he went to see a neurologist anyway, hoping that discovery of a neurological problem might get him the disability benefits to which he felt he was entitled. Otherwise the conclusion seemed to be that he was just a malingerer.

Antonio Damasio, the neurologist Elliot consulted, was struck by one element missing from Elliot's mental repertoire: though nothing was wrong with his logic, memory, attention, or any other cognitive ability, Elliot was virtually oblivious to his feelings about what had happened to him.[13] Most strikingly, Elliot could narrate the tragic events of his life with complete dispassion, as though he were an onlooker to the losses and failures of his past—without a note of regret or sadness, frustration or anger at life's unfairness. His own tragedy brought him no pain; Damasio felt more upset by Elliot's story than did Elliot himself.

The source of this emotional unawareness, Damasio concluded, was the removal, along with the brain tumor, of part of Elliot's prefrontal lobes. In effect, the surgery had severed ties between the lower centers of the emotional brain, especially the amygdala and related circuits, and the thinking abilities of the neocortex. Elliot's thinking had become computerlike, able to make every step in the calculus of a decision, but unable to assign *values* to differing possibilities. Every option was neutral. And that overly dispassionate reasoning, suspected Damasio, was the core of Elliot's problem: too little awareness of his own feelings about things made Elliot's reasoning faulty.

The handicap showed up even in mundane decisions. When Damasio tried to choose a time and date for the next appointment with Elliot, the result was a muddle of indecisiveness: Elliot could find arguments for and against every date and time that Damasio proposed, but could not choose among them. At the rational level, there were perfectly good reasons for objecting to or accepting virtually every possible time for the appointment. But Elliot lacked any sense of how he *felt* about any of the times. Lacking that awareness of his own feelings, he had no preferences at all.

One lesson from Elliot's indecisiveness is the crucial role of feeling in navigating the endless stream of life's personal decisions. While strong feelings can create havoc in reasoning, the *lack* of awareness of feeling can also be ruinous, especially in weighing the decisions on which our destiny largely depends: what career to pursue, whether to stay with a secure job or switch to one that is riskier but more interesting, whom to date or marry, where to live, which apartment to rent or house to buy—and on and on through life. Such decisions cannot be made well through sheer rationality; they require gut feeling, and the emotional wisdom garnered through past experiences. Formal logic alone can never work as the basis for deciding whom to marry or trust or even what job to take; these are realms where reason without feeling is blind.

The intuitive signals that guide us in these moments come in the form of limbic-driven surges from the viscera that Damasio calls "somatic markers"—literally, gut feelings. The somatic marker is a kind of automatic alarm, typically calling attention to a potential danger from a given course of action. More often than not these markers steer us *away* from some choice that experience warns us against, though they can also alert us to a golden opportunity. We usually do not, at that moment, recall what specific experiences formed this negative feeling; all we need is the signal that a given potential course of action could be disastrous. Whenever such a gut feeling rises up, we can immediately drop or pursue that avenue of consideration with greater confidence, and so pare down our array of choices to a more manageable decision matrix. The key to sounder personal decision-making, in short: being attuned to our feelings.

PLUMBING THE UNCONSCIOUS

Elliot's emotional vacuity suggests that there may be a spectrum of people's ability to sense their emotions as they have them. By the logic of neuroscience, if the absence of a neural circuit leads to a deficit in an ability, then the relative strength or weakness of that same circuit in people whose brains are intact should lead to comparable levels of competence in that same ability. In terms of the role of prefrontal circuits in emotional attunement, this suggests that for neurological reasons some of us may more easily detect the stirring of fear or joy than do others, and so be more emotionally self-aware.

It may be that a talent for psychological introspection hinges on this same circuitry. Some of us are naturally more attuned to the emotional mind's special symbolic modes: metaphor and simile, along with poetry, song, and fable, are all cast in the language of the heart. So too are dreams and myths, in which loose associations determine the flow of narrative, abiding by the logic of the emotional mind. Those who have a natural attunement to their own heart's voice—the language of emotion—are sure to be more adept at articulating its messages, whether as a novelist, songwriter, or psychotherapist. This inner attunement should make them more gifted in giving voice to the "wisdom of the unconscious"—the felt meanings of our dreams and fantasies, the symbols that embody our deepest wishes.

Self-awareness is fundamental to psychological insight; this is the faculty that much of psychotherapy means to strengthen. Indeed, Howard Gardner's model for intrapsychic intelligence is Sigmund Freud, the great mapper of the psyche's secret dynamics. As Freud made clear, much of emotional life is unconscious; feelings that stir within us do not always cross the threshold into awareness. Empirical verification of this psychological axiom comes, for instance, from experiments on unconscious emotions, such as the remarkable finding that people form definite likings for things they do not even realize they have seen before. Any emotion can be—and often is— unconscious.

The physiological beginnings of an emotion typically occur before a person is consciously aware of the feeling itself. For example, when people who fear snakes are shown pictures of snakes, sensors on their skin will detect sweat breaking out, a sign of anxiety, though they say they do not feel any fear. The sweat shows up in such people even when the picture of a snake is presented so rapidly that they have no conscious idea of what, exactly, they just saw, let alone that they are beginning to get anxious. As such pre-conscious emotional stirrings continue to build, they eventually become strong enough to break into awareness. Thus there are two levels of emotion, conscious and unconscious. The moment of an emotion coming into awareness marks its registering as such in the frontal cortex.[14]

Emotions that simmer beneath the threshold of awareness can have a powerful impact on how we perceive and react, even though we have no idea they are at work. Take someone who is annoyed by a rude encounter early in the day, and then is peevish for hours afterward, taking affront where none is intended and snapping at people for no real reason. He may well be oblivious to his continuing irritability and will be surprised if someone calls attention to it, though it stews just out of his awareness and dictates his curt replies. But once that reaction is brought into awareness—once it registers in the cortex—he can evaluate things anew, decide to shrug off the feelings left earlier in the day, and change his outlook and mood. In this way emotional self-awareness is the building block of the next fundamental of emotional intelligence: being able to shake off a bad mood.

5

Passion's Slaves

Thou hast been . . .
A man that Fortune's buffets and rewards
Has taken with equal thanks. . . . Give me that man
That is not passion's slave, and I will wear him
In my heart's core, aye, in my heart of hearts
As I do thee. . . .

—HAMLET TO HIS FRIEND HORATIO

A sense of self-mastery, of being able to withstand the emotional storms that the buffeting of Fortune brings rather than being "passion's slave," has been praised as a virtue since the time of Plato. The ancient Greek word for it was *sophrosyne,* "care and intelligence in conducting one's life; a tempered balance and wisdom," as Page DuBois, a Greek scholar, translates it. The Romans and the early Christian church called it *temperantia,* temperance, the restraining of emotional excess. The goal is balance, not emotional suppression: every feeling has its value and significance. A life without passion would be a dull wasteland of neutrality, cut off and isolated from the richness of life itself. But, as Aristotle observed, what is wanted is *appropriate* emotion, feeling proportionate to circumstance. When emotions are too muted they create dullness and distance; when out of control, too extreme and persistent, they become pathological, as in immobilizing depression, overwhelming anxiety, raging anger, manic agitation.

Indeed, keeping our distressing emotions in check is the key to emotional well-being; extremes—emotions that wax too intensely or for too long—undermine our stability. Of course, it is not that we should feel only one kind of emotion; being happy all the time somehow suggests the blandness of those smiley-face badges that had a faddish moment in the 1970s. There is much to be said for the constructive contribution of suffering to creative and spiritual life; suffering can temper the soul.

Downs as well as ups spice life, but need to be in balance. In the calculus of the heart it is the ratio of positive to negative emotions that determines the sense of well-being—at least that is the verdict from studies of mood in which hundreds of men and women have carried beepers that reminded them at random times to record their emotions at that moment.[1] It is not that people need to avoid unpleasant feelings to feel content, but rather that stormy feelings not go unchecked, displacing all pleasant moods. People who have strong episodes of anger or depression can still feel a sense of well-being if they have a countervailing set of equally joyous or happy times. These studies also affirm the independence of emotional from academic intelligence, finding little or no relationship between grades or IQ and people's emotional well-being.

Just as there is a steady murmur of background thoughts in the mind, there is a constant emotional hum; beep someone at six A.M. or seven P.M. and he will always be in some mood or other. Of course, on any two mornings someone can have very different moods; but when people's moods are averaged over weeks or months, they tend to reflect that person's overall sense of well-being. It turns out that for most people, extremely intense feelings are relatively rare; most of us fall into the gray middle range, with mild bumps in our emotional roller coaster.

Still, managing our emotions is something of a full-time job: much of what we do—especially in our free time—is an attempt to manage mood. Everything from reading a novel or watching television to the activities and companions we choose can be a way to make ourselves feel better. The art of soothing ourselves is a fundamental life skill; some psychoanalytic thinkers, such as John Bowlby and D. W. Winnicott, see this as one of the most essential of all psychic tools. The theory holds that emotionally sound infants learn to soothe themselves by treating themselves as their caretakers have treated them, leaving them less vulnerable to the upheavals of the emotional brain.

As we have seen, the design of the brain means that we very often have little or no control over *when* we are swept by emotion, nor over *what* emotion it will be. But we can have some say in *how long* an emotion will last. The issue arises not with garden-variety sadness, worry, or anger; normally such moods pass with time and patience. But when these emotions are of great intensity and linger past an appropriate point, they shade over into their distressing extremes—chronic anxiety, uncontrollable rage, depression. And, at their most severe and intractable, medication, psychotherapy, or both may be needed to lift them.

In these times, one sign of the capacity for emotional self-regulation may be recognizing when chronic agitation of the emotional brain is too strong to be overcome without pharmacologic help. For example, two thirds of those who suffer from manic-depression have never been treated for the disorder. But lithium or newer medications can thwart the characteristic cycle of paralyzing depression alternating with manic episodes that mix chaotic elation and grandiosity with irritation and rage. One problem with manic-depression is that while people are in the throes of mania they often feel so overly confident that they see no need for help of any kind despite the disastrous decisions they are making. In such severe emotional disorders psychiatric medication offers a tool for managing life better.

But when it comes to vanquishing the more usual range of bad moods, we are left to our own devices. Unfortunately, those devices are not always effective—at least such is the conclusion reached by Diane Tice, a psychologist at Case Western Reserve University, who asked more than four hundred men and women about the strategies they used to escape foul moods, and how successful those tactics were for them.[2]

Not everyone agrees with the philosophical premise that bad moods should be changed; there are, Tice found, "mood purists," the 5 percent or so of people who said they never try to change a mood since, in their view, all emotions are "natural" and should be experienced just as they present themselves, no matter how dispiriting. And then there were those who regularly sought to get into unpleasant moods for pragmatic reasons: physicians who needed to be somber to give patients bad news; social activists who nurtured their outrage at injustice so as to be more effective in battling it; even a young man who told of working up his anger to help his little brother with playground bullies. And some people were positively Machiavellian about manipulating moods—witness the bill collectors who purposely worked themselves into a rage in order to be all the firmer with deadbeats.[3] But these rare purposive cultivations of unpleasantness aside, most everyone complained of being at the mercy of their moods. People's track records at shaking bad moods were decidedly mixed.

THE ANATOMY OF RAGE

Say someone in another car cuts dangerously close to you as you are driving on the freeway. If your reflexive thought is "That son of a bitch!" it matters immensely for the trajectory of rage whether that thought is followed by more thoughts of outrage and revenge: "He could have hit me! That bastard—I can't let him get away with that!" Your knuckles whiten as you tighten your hold on the steering wheel, a surrogate for strangling his throat. Your body mobilizes to fight, not run—leaving you trembling, beads of sweat on your forehead, your heart pounding, the muscles in your face locked in a scowl. You want to kill the guy. Then, should a car behind you honk because you have slowed down after the close call, you are apt to explode in rage at that driver too. Such is the stuff of hypertension, reckless driving, even freeway shootings.

Contrast that sequence of building rage with a more charitable line of thought toward the driver who cut you off: "Maybe he didn't see me, or maybe he had some good reason for driving so carelessly, such as a medical emergency." That line of possibility tempers anger with mercy, or at least an open mind, short-circuiting the buildup of rage. The problem, as Aristotle's challenge to have only *appropriate* anger reminds us, is that more often than not our anger surges out of control. Benjamin Franklin put it well: "Anger is never without a reason, but seldom a good one."

There are, of course, different kinds of anger. The amygdala may well be a main source of the sudden spark of rage we feel at the driver whose carelessness endangers us. But the other end of the emotional circuitry, the neocortex, most likely foments more calculated angers, such as cool-headed revenge or outrage at unfairness or injustice. Such thoughtful angers are those most likely, as Franklin put it, to "have good reasons" or seem to.

Of all the moods that people want to escape, rage seems to be the most intransigent; Tice found anger is the mood people are worst at controlling. Indeed, anger is the most seductive of the negative emotions; the self-righteous inner monologue that propels it along fills the mind with the most convincing arguments for venting rage. Unlike sadness, anger is energizing, even exhilarating. Anger's seductive, persuasive power may in itself explain why some views about it are so common: that anger is uncontrollable, or that, at any rate, it *should not* be controlled, and that venting anger in "catharsis" is all to the good. A contrasting view, perhaps a reaction against the bleak picture of these other two, holds that anger can be prevented entirely. But a careful reading of research findings suggests that all these common attitudes toward anger are misguided, if not outright myths.[4]

The train of angry thoughts that stokes anger is also potentially the key to one of the most powerful ways to defuse anger: undermining the convictions that are fueling the anger in the first place. The longer we ruminate about what has made us angry, the more "good reasons" and self-justifications for being angry we can invent. Brooding fuels anger's flames. But seeing things differently douses those flames. Tice found that reframing a situation more positively was one of the most potent ways to put anger to rest.

The Rage ''Rush''

That finding squares well with the conclusions of University of Alabama psychologist Dolf Zillmann, who, in a lengthy series of careful experiments, has taken precise measure of anger and the anatomy of rage.[5] Given the roots of anger in the fight wing of the fight-or-flight response, it is no surprise that Zillmann finds that a universal trigger for anger is the sense of being endangered. Endangerment can be signaled not just by an outright physical threat but also, as is more often the case, by a symbolic threat to self-esteem or dignity: being treated unjustly or rudely, being insulted or demeaned, being frustrated in pursuing an important goal. These perceptions act as the instigating trigger for a limbic surge that has a dual effect on the brain. One part of that surge is a release of catecholamines, which generate a quick, episodic rush of energy, enough for "one course of vigorous action," as Zillmann puts it, "such as in fight or flight." This energy surge lasts for minutes, during which it readies the body for a good fight or a quick flight, depending on how the emotional brain sizes up the opposition.

Meanwhile, another amygdala-driven ripple through the adrenocortical branch of the nervous system creates a general tonic background of action readiness, which lasts much longer than the catecholamine energy surge. This generalized adrenal and cortical excitation can last for hours and even days, keeping the emotional brain in special readiness for arousal, and becoming a foundation on which subsequent reactions can build with particular quickness. In general, the hair-trigger condition created by adrenocortical arousal explains why people are so much more prone to anger if they have already been provoked or slightly irritated by something else. Stress of all sorts creates adrenocortical arousal, lowering the threshold for what provokes anger. Thus someone who has had a hard day at work is especially vulnerable to becoming enraged later at home by something—the kids being too noisy or messy, say—that under other circumstances would not be powerful enough to trigger an emotional hijacking.

Zillmann comes to these insights on anger through careful experimentation. In a typical study, for example, he had a confederate provoke men and women who had volunteered by making snide remarks about them. The volunteers then watched a pleasant or upsetting film. Later the volunteers were given the chance to retaliate against the confederate by giving an evaluation they thought would be used in a decision whether or not to hire him. The intensity of their retaliation was directly proportional to how aroused they had gotten from the film they had just watched; they were angrier after seeing the unpleasant film, and gave the worst ratings.

Anger Builds on Anger

Zillmann's studies seem to explain the dynamic at work in a familiar domestic drama I witnessed one day while shopping. Down the supermarket aisle drifted the emphatic, measured tones of a young mother to her son, about three: "Put . . . it . . . back!"

"But I *want* it!" he whined, clinging more tightly to a Ninja Turtles cereal box.

"Put it back!" Louder, her anger taking over.

At that moment the baby in her shopping cart seat dropped the jar of jelly she had been mouthing. When it shattered on the floor the mother yelled, "That's it!" and, in a fury, slapped the baby, grabbed the three-year-old's box and slammed it onto the nearest shelf, scooped him up by the waist, and rushed down the aisle, the shopping cart careening perilously in front, the baby now crying, her son, his legs dangling, protesting, "Put me *down,* put me *down!*"

Zillmann has found that when the body is already in a state of edginess, like the mother's, and something triggers an emotional hijacking, the subsequent emotion, whether anger or anxiety, is of especially great intensity. This dynamic is at work when someone becomes enraged. Zillmann sees escalating anger as "a sequence of provocations, each triggering an excitatory reaction that dissipates slowly." In this sequence every successive anger-provoking thought or perception becomes a minitrigger for amygdala-driven surges of catecholamines, each building on the hormonal momentum of those that went before. A second comes before the first has subsided, and a third on top of those, and so on; each wave rides the tails of those before, quickly escalating the body's level of physiological arousal. A thought that comes later in this buildup triggers a far greater intensity of anger than one that comes at the beginning. Anger builds on anger; the emotional brain heats up. By then rage, unhampered by reason, easily erupts in violence.

At this point people are unforgiving and beyond being reasoned with; their thoughts revolve around revenge and reprisal, oblivious to what the consequences may be. This high level of excitation, Zillmann says, "fosters an illusion of power and invulnerability that may inspire and facilitate aggression" as the enraged person, "failing cognitive guidance," falls back on the most primitive of responses. The limbic urge is ascendant; the rawest lessons of life's brutality become guides to action.

Balm for Anger

Given this analysis of the anatomy of rage, Zillmann sees two main ways of intervening. One way of defusing anger is to seize on and challenge the thoughts that trigger the surges of anger, since it is the original appraisal of an interaction that confirms and encourages the first burst of anger, and the subsequent reappraisals that fan the flames. Timing matters; the earlier in the anger cycle the more effective. Indeed, anger can be completely short-circuited if the mitigating information comes before the anger is acted on.

The power of understanding to deflate anger is clear from another of Zillmann's experiments, in which a rude assistant (a confederate) insulted and provoked volunteers who were riding an exercise bike. When the volunteers were given the chance to retaliate against the rude experimenter (again, by giving a bad evaluation they thought would be used in weighing his candidacy for a job) they did so with an angry glee. But in one version of the experiment another confederate entered after the volunteers had been provoked, and just before the chance to retaliate; she told the provocative experimenter he had a phone call down the hall. As he left he made a snide remark to her too. But she took it in good spirits, explaining after he left that he was under terrible pressures, upset about his upcoming graduate orals. After that the irate volunteers, when offered the chance to retaliate against the rude fellow, chose not to; instead they expressed compassion for his plight.

Such mitigating information allows a reappraisal of the anger-provoking events. But there is a specific window of opportunity for this de-escalation. Zillmann finds it works well at moderate levels of anger; at high levels of rage it makes no difference because of what he calls "cognitive incapacitation"—in other words, people can no longer think straight. When people were already highly enraged, they dismissed the mitigating information with "That's just too bad!" or "the strongest vulgarities the English language has to offer," as Zillmann put it with delicacy.

Cooling Down

> Once when I was about 13, in an angry fit, I walked out of the house vowing I would never return. It was a beautiful summer day, and I walked far along lovely lanes, till gradually the stillness and beauty calmed and soothed me, and after some hours I returned repentant and almost melted. Since then when I am angry, I do this if I can, and find it the best cure.

The account is by a subject in one of the very first scientific studies of anger, done in 1899.[6] It still stands as a model of the second way of de-escalating anger: cooling off physiologically by waiting out the adrenal surge in a setting where there are not likely to be further triggers for rage. In an argument, for instance, that means getting away from the other person for the time being. During the cooling-off period, the angered person can put the brakes on the cycle of escalating hostile thought by seeking out distractions. Distraction, Zillmann finds, is a highly powerful mood-altering device, for a simple reason: It's hard to stay angry when we're having a pleasant time. The trick, of course, is to get anger to cool to the point where someone can *have* a pleasant time in the first place.

Zillmann's analysis of the ways anger escalates and de-escalates explains many of Diane Tice's findings about the strategies people commonly say they use to ease anger. One such fairly effective strategy is going off to be alone while cooling down. A large proportion of men translate this into going for a drive—a finding that gives one pause when driving (and, Tice told me, inspired her to drive more defensively). Perhaps a safer alternative is going for a long walk; active exercise also helps with anger. So do relaxation methods such as deep breathing and muscle relaxation, perhaps because they change the body's physiology from the high arousal of anger to a low-arousal state, and perhaps too because they distract from whatever triggered the anger. Active exercise may cool anger for something of the same reason: after high levels of physiological activation during the exercise, the body rebounds to a low level once it stops.

But a cooling-down period will not work if that time is used to pursue the train of anger-inducing thought, since each such thought is in itself a minor trigger for more cascades of anger. The power of distraction is that it stops that angry train of thought. In her survey of people's strategies for handling anger, Tice found that distractions by and large help calm anger: TV, movies, reading, and the like all interfere with the angry thoughts that stoke rage. But,

Tice found, indulging in treats such as shopping for oneself and eating do not have much effect; it is all too easy to continue with an indignant train of thought while cruising a shopping mall or devouring a piece of chocolate cake.

To these strategies add those developed by Redford Williams, a psychiatrist at Duke University who sought to help hostile people, who are at higher risk for heart disease, to control their irritability.[7] One of his recommendations is to use self-awareness to catch cynical or hostile thoughts as they arise, and write them down. Once angry thoughts are captured this way, they can be challenged and reappraised, though, as Zillmann found, this approach works better before anger has escalated to rage.

The Ventilation Fallacy

As I settle into a New York City cab, a young man crossing the street stops in front of the cab to wait for traffic to clear. The driver, impatient to start, honks, motioning for the young man to move out of the way. The reply is a scowl and an obscene gesture.

"You son of a bitch!" the driver yells, making threatening lunges with the cab by hitting the accelerator and brake at the same time. At this lethal threat, the young man sullenly moves aside, barely, and smacks his fist against the cab as it inches by into traffic. At this, the driver shouts a foul litany of expletives at the man.

As we move along the driver, still visibly agitated, tells me, "You can't take any shit from anyone. You gotta yell back—at least it makes you feel better!"

Catharsis—giving vent to rage—is sometimes extolled as a way of handling anger. The popular theory holds that "it makes you feel better." But, as Zillmann's findings suggest, there is an argument against catharsis. It has been made since the 1950s, when psychologists started to test the effects of catharsis experimentally and, time after time, found that giving vent to anger did little or nothing to dispel it (though, because of the seductive nature of anger, it may *feel* satisfying).[8] There may be some specific conditions under which lashing out in anger does work: when it is expressed directly to the person who is its target, when it restores a sense of control or rights an injustice, or when it inflicts "appropriate harm" on the other person and gets him to change some grievous activity without retaliating. But because of the incendiary nature of anger, this may be easier to say than to do.[9]

Tice found that ventilating anger is one of the worst ways to cool down: outbursts of rage typically pump up the emotional brain's arousal, leaving people feeling more angry, not less. Tice found that when people told of times they had taken their rage out on the person who provoked it, the net effect was to prolong the mood rather than end it. Far more effective was when people first cooled down, and then, in a more constructive or assertive manner, confronted the person to settle their dispute. As I once heard Chogyam Trungpa, a Tibetan teacher, reply when asked how best to handle anger: "Don't suppress it. But don't act on it."

SOOTHING ANXIETY: WHAT, ME WORRY?

Oh, no! The muffler sounds bad. . . . What if I have to take it to the shop? . . . I can't afford the expense. . . . I'd have to draw the money from Jamie's college fund. . . . What if I can't afford his tuition? . . . That bad school report last week. . . . What if his grades go down and he can't get into college? . . . Muffler sounds bad. . . .

And so the worrying mind spins on in an endless loop of low-grade melodrama, one set of concerns leading on to the next and back again. The above specimen is offered by Lizabeth Roemer and Thomas Borkovec, Pennsylvania State University psychologists, whose research on worrying—the heart of all anxiety—has raised the topic from neurotic's art to science.[10] There is, of course, no hitch when worry works; by mulling over a problem—that is, employing constructive reflection, which can look like worrying—a solution can appear. Indeed, the reaction that underlies worry is the vigilance for potential danger that has, no doubt, been essential for survival over the course of evolution. When fear triggers the emotional brain, part of the resulting anxiety fixates attention on the threat at hand, forcing the mind to obsess about how to handle it and ignore anything else for the time being. Worry is, in a sense, a rehearsal of what might go wrong and how to deal with it; the task of worrying is to come up with positive solutions for life's perils by anticipating dangers before they arise.

The difficulty is with chronic, repetitive worries, the kind that recycle on and on and never get any nearer a positive solution. A close analysis of chronic worry suggests that it has all the attributes of a low-grade emotional hijacking: the worries seem to come from nowhere, are uncontrollable, generate a steady hum of anxiety, are impervious to reason, and lock the worrier into a single, inflexible view of the worrisome topic. When this same cycle of worry intensifies and persists, it shades over the line into full-blown neural hijackings, the anxiety disorders: phobias, obsessions and compulsions, panic attacks. In each of these disorders worry fixates in a distinct fashion; for the phobic, anxieties rivet on the feared situation; for the obsessive, they fixate on preventing some feared calamity; in panic attacks, the worries can focus on a fear of dying or on the prospect of having the attack itself.

In all these conditions the common denominator is worry run amok. For example, a woman being treated for obsessive-compulsive disorder had a series of rituals that took most of her waking hours: forty-five-minute showers several times daily, washing her hands for five minutes twenty or more times a day. She would not sit down unless she first swabbed the seat with rubbing alcohol to sterilize it. Nor would she touch a child or an animal—both were "too dirty." All these compulsions were stirred by her underlying morbid fear of germs; she worried constantly that without her washing and sterilizing she would catch a disease and die.[11]

A woman being treated for "generalized anxiety disorder"—the psychiatric nomenclature for being a constant worrier—responded to the request to worry aloud for one minute this way:

> I might not do this right. This may be so artificial that it won't be an indication of the real thing and we need to get at the real thing. . . . Because if we don't get at the real thing, I won't get well. And if I don't get well I'll never be happy.[12]

In this virtuoso display of worrying about worrying, the very request to worry for one minute had, within a few short seconds, escalated to contemplation of a lifelong catastrophe: "I'll never be happy." Worries typically follow such lines, a narrative to oneself that jumps from concern to concern and more often than not includes catastrophizing, imagining some terrible tragedy. Worries are almost always expressed in the mind's ear, not its eye—that is, in words, not images—a fact that has significance for controlling worry.

Borkovec and his colleagues began to study worrying per se when they were trying to come up with a treatment for insomnia. Anxiety, other researchers have observed, comes in two forms: *cognitive,* or worrisome thoughts, and *somatic,* the physiological symptoms of anxiety, such as sweating, a racing heart, or muscle tension. The main trouble with insomniacs, Borkovec found, was not the somatic arousal. What kept them up were intrusive thoughts. They were chronic worriers, and could not stop worrying, no matter how sleepy they were. The one thing that worked in helping them get to sleep was getting their minds off their worries, focusing instead on the sensations produced by a relaxation method. In short, the worries could be stopped by shifting attention away.

Most worriers, however, can't seem to do this. The reason, Borkovec believes, has to do with a partial payoff from worrying that is highly reinforcing to the habit. There is, it seems, something positive in worries: worries are ways to deal with potential threats, with dangers that may come one's way. The work of worrying—when it succeeds—is to rehearse what those dangers are, and to reflect on ways to deal with them. But worry doesn't work all that well. New solutions and fresh ways of seeing a problem do not typically come from worrying, especially chronic worry. Instead of coming up with solutions to these potential problems, worriers typically simply ruminate on the danger itself, immersing themselves in a low-key way in the dread associated with it while staying in the same rut of thought. Chronic worriers worry about a wide range of things, most of which have almost no chance of happening; they read dangers into life's journey that others never notice.

Yet chronic worriers tell Borkovec that worrying helps them, and that their worries are self-perpetuating, an endless loop of angst-ridden thought. Why should worry become what seems to amount to a mental addiction? Oddly, as Borkovec points out, the worry habit is reinforcing in the same sense that superstitions are. Since people worry about many things that have a very low probability of actually occurring—a loved one dying in a plane crash, going bankrupt, and the like—there is, to the primitive limbic brain at least, something magical about it. Like an amulet that wards off some anticipated evil, the worry psychologically gets the credit for preventing the danger it obsesses about.

The Work of Worrying

She had moved to Los Angeles from the Midwest, lured by a job with a publisher. But the publisher was bought by another soon after, and she was left without a job. Turning to freelance writing, an erratic marketplace, she found herself either swamped with work or unable to pay her rent. She often had to ration phone calls, and for the first time was without health insurance. This lack of coverage was particularly distressing: she found herself catastrophizing about her health, sure every headache signaled a brain tumor, picturing herself in an accident whenever she had to drive somewhere. She often found herself lost in a long reverie of worry, a medley of distress. But, she said, she found her worries almost addictive.

Borkovec discovered another unexpected benefit to worrying. While people are immersed in their worried thoughts, they do not seem to notice the subjective sensations of the anxiety those worries stir—the speedy heartbeat, the beads of sweat, the shakiness—and as the worry proceeds it actually seems to suppress some of that anxiety, at least as reflected in heart rate. The sequence presumably goes something like this: The worrier notices something that triggers the image of some potential threat or danger; that imagined catastrophe in turn triggers a mild attack of anxiety. The worrier then plunges into a long series of distressed thoughts, each of which primes yet another topic for worry; as attention continues to be carried along by this train of worry, focusing on these very thoughts takes the mind off the original catastrophic image that triggered the anxiety. Images, Borkovec found, are more powerful triggers for physiological anxiety than are thoughts, so immersion in thoughts, to the exclusion of catastrophic images, partially alleviates the experience of being anxious. And, to that extent, the worry is also reinforced, as a halfway antidote to the very anxiety it evoked.

But chronic worries are self-defeating too in that they take the form of stereotyped, rigid ideas, not creative breakthroughs that actually move toward solving the problem. This rigidity shows up not just in the manifest content of worried thought, which simply repeats more or less the same ideas over and over. But at a neurological level there seems to be a cortical rigidity, a deficit in the emotional brain's ability to respond flexibly to changing circumstance. In short, chronic worry works in some ways, but not in other, more consequential ones: it eases some anxiety, but never solves the problem.

The one thing that chronic worriers cannot do is follow the advice they are most often given: "Just stop worrying" (or, worse, "Don't worry—be happy"). Since chronic worries seem to be low-grade amygdala episodes, they come unbidden. And, by their very nature, they persist once they arise in the mind. But after much experimentation, Borkovec discovered some simple steps that can help even the most chronic worrier control the habit.

The first step is self-awareness, catching the worrisome episodes as near their beginning as possible—ideally, as soon as or just after the fleeting catastrophic image triggers the worry-anxiety cycle. Borkovec trains people in this approach by first teaching them to monitor cues for anxiety, especially learning to identify situations that trigger worry, or the fleeting thoughts and images that initiate the worry, as well as the accompanying sensations of anxiety in the body. With practice, people can identify the worries at an earlier and earlier point in the anxiety spiral. People also learn relaxation methods that they can apply at the moment they recognize the worry beginning, and practice the relaxation method daily so they will be able to use it on the spot, when they need it the most.

The relaxation method, though, is not enough in itself. Worriers also need to actively challenge the worrisome thoughts; failing this, the worry spiral will keep coming back. So the next step is to take a critical stance toward their assumptions: Is it very probable that the dreaded event will occur? Is it necessarily the case that there is only one or no alternative to letting it happen? Are there constructive steps to be taken? Does it really help to run through these same anxious thoughts over and over?

This combination of mindfulness and healthy skepticism would, presumably, act as a brake on the neural activation that underlies low-grade anxiety. Actively generating such thoughts may prime the circuitry that can inhibit the limbic driving of worry; at the same time, actively inducing a relaxed state counters the signals for anxiety the emotional brain is sending throughout the body.

Indeed, Borkovec points out, these strategies establish a train of mental activity that is incompatible with worry. When a worry is allowed to repeat over and over unchallenged, it gains in persuasive power; challenging it by contemplating a range of equally plausible points of view keeps the one worried thought from being naively taken as true. Even some people whose worrying is serious enough to qualify for a psychiatric diagnosis have been relieved of the worrying habit this way.

On the other hand, for people with worries so severe they have flowered into phobia, obsessive-compulsive disorder, or panic disorder, it may be prudent—indeed, a sign of self-awareness—to turn to medication to interrupt the cycle. A retraining of the emotional circuitry through therapy is still called for, however, in order to lessen the likelihood that anxiety disorders will recur when medication is stopped.[13]

MANAGING MELANCHOLY

The single mood people generally put most effort into shaking is sadness; Diane Tice found that people are most inventive when it comes to trying to escape the blues. Of course, not all sadness should be escaped; melancholy, like every other mood, has its benefits. The sadness that a loss brings has certain invariable effects: it closes down our interest in diversions and pleasures, fixes attention on what has been lost, and saps our energy for starting new endeavors—at least for the time being. In short, it enforces a kind of reflective retreat from life's busy pursuits, and leaves us in a suspended state to mourn the loss, mull over its meaning, and, finally, make the psychological adjustments and new plans that will allow our lives to continue.

Bereavement is useful; full-blown depression is not. William Styron renders an eloquent description of "the many dreadful manifestations of the disease," among them self-hatred, a sense of worthlessness, a "dank joylessness" with "gloom crowding in on me, a sense of dread and alienation and, above all, a stifling anxiety."[14] Then there are the intellectual marks: "confusion, failure of mental focus and lapse of memories," and, at a later stage, his mind "dominated by anarchic distortions," and "a sense that my thought processes were engulfed by a toxic and unnameable tide that obliterated any enjoyable response to the living world." There are the physical effects: sleeplessness, feeling as listless as a zombie, "a kind of numbness, an enervation, but more particularly an odd fragility," along with a "fidgety restlessness." Then there is the loss of pleasure: "Food, like everything else within the scope of sensation, was utterly without savor." Finally, there was the vanishing of hope as the "gray drizzle of horror" took on a despair so palpable it was like physical pain, a pain so unendurable that suicide seemed a solution.

In such major depression, life is paralyzed; no new beginnings emerge. The very symptoms of depression bespeak a life on hold. For Styron, no medication or therapy helped; it was the passing of time and the refuge of a hospital that finally cleared away the despondency. But for most people, especially those with less severe cases, psychotherapy can help, as can medication—Prozac is the treatment of the hour, but there are more than a dozen other compounds offering some help, especially for major depression.

My focus here is the far more common sadness that at its upper limits becomes, technically speaking, a "subclinical depression"—that is, ordinary melancholy. This is a range of despondency that people can handle on their own, if they have the internal resources. Unfortunately, some of the strategies most often resorted to can backfire, leaving people feeling worse than before. One such strategy is simply staying alone, which is often appealing when people are feeling down; more often than not, however, it only adds a sense of loneliness and isolation to the sadness. That may partly explain why Tice found the most popular tactic for battling depression is socializing—going out to eat, to a ballgame or movie; in short, doing something with friends or family. That works well if the net effect is to get the person's mind off his sadness. But it simply prolongs the mood if he uses the occasion just to mull over what put him in the funk.

Indeed, one of the main determinants of whether a depressed mood will persist or lift is the degree to which people ruminate. Worrying about what's depressing us, it seems, makes the depression all the more intense and prolonged. In depression, worry takes several forms, all focusing on some aspect of the depression itself—how tired we feel, how little energy or motivation we have, for instance, or how little work we're getting done. Typically none of this reflection is accompanied by any concrete course of action that might alleviate the problem. Other common worries include "isolating yourself and thinking about how terrible you feel, worrying that your spouse might reject you because you are depressed, and wondering whether you are going to have another sleepless night," says Stanford psychologist Susan Nolen-Hoeksma, who has studied rumination in depressed people.[15]

Depressed people sometimes justify this kind of rumination by saying they are trying to "understand themselves better"; in fact, they are priming the feelings of sadness without taking any steps that might actually lift their mood. Thus in therapy it might be perfectly helpful to reflect deeply on the causes of a depression, if that leads to insights or actions that will change the conditions that cause it. But a passive immersion in the sadness simply makes it worse.

Rumination can also make the depression stronger by creating conditions that are, well, more depressing. Nolen-Hoeksma gives the example of a saleswoman who gets depressed and spends so many hours worrying about it that she doesn't get around to important sales calls. Her sales then decline, making her feel like a failure, which feeds her depression. But if she reacted to depression by trying to distract herself, she might well plunge into the sales calls as a way to get her mind off the sadness. Sales would be less likely to decline, and the very experience of making a sale might bolster her self-confidence, lessening the depression somewhat.

Women, Nolen-Hoeksma finds, are far more prone to ruminate when they are depressed than are men. This, she proposes, may at least partly explain the fact that women are diagnosed with depression twice as often as are men. Of course, other factors may come into play, such as women being more open to disclosing their distress or having more in their lives to be depressed about. And men may drown their depression in alcoholism, for which their rate is about twice that of women.

Cognitive therapy aimed at changing these thought patterns has been found in some studies to be on a par with medication for treating mild clinical depression, and superior to medication in preventing the return of mild depression. Two strategies are particularly effective in the battle.[16] One is to learn to challenge the thoughts at the center of rumination—to question their validity and think of more positive alternatives. The other is to purposely schedule pleasant, distracting events.

One reason distraction works is that depressing thoughts are automatic, intruding on one's state of mind unbidden. Even when depressed people try to suppress their depressing thoughts, they often cannot come up with better alternatives; once the depressive tide of thought has started, it has a powerful magnetic effect on the train of association. For example, when depressed people were asked to unscramble jumbled six-word sentences, they were much better at figuring out the depressing messages ("The future looks very dismal") than the upbeat ones ("The future looks very bright").[17]

The tendency for depression to perpetuate itself shades even the kinds of distractions people choose. When depressed people were given a list of upbeat or ponderous ways to get their minds off something sad, such as the funeral of a friend, they picked more of the melancholy activities. Richard Wenzlaff, the University of Texas psychologist who did these studies, concludes that people who are already depressed need to make a special effort to get their attention on something that is completely upbeat, being careful not to inadvertently choose something—a tearjerker movie, a tragic novel— that will drag their mood down again.

Mood-lifters

Imagine that you're driving on an unfamiliar, steep, and winding road through fog. Suddenly a car pulls out of a driveway only a few feet in front of you, too close for you to stop in time. Your foot slams the brake to the floor and you go into a skid, your car sliding into the side of the other one. You see that the car is full of youngsters, a carpool on the way to preschool—just before the explosion of glass shattering and metal bending into metal. Then, out of the sudden silence after the collision, you hear a chorus of crying. You manage to run to the other car, and see that one of the children is lying motionless. You are flooded with remorse and sadness over this tragedy. . . .

Such heart-wrenching scenarios were used to get volunteers upset in one of Wenzlaff's experiments. The volunteers then tried to keep the scene out of their minds while they jotted notes about the stream of their thoughts for nine minutes. Each time the thought of the disturbing scene intruded into their minds, they made a check mark as they wrote. While most people thought about the upsetting scene less and less as time went on, those volunteers who were more depressed actually showed a pronounced *increase* in intruding thoughts of the scene as time passed, and even made oblique references to it in the thoughts that were supposed to be distractions from it.

What's more, the depression-prone volunteers used other distressing thoughts to distract themselves. As Wenzlaff told me, "Thoughts are associated in the mind not just by content, but by mood. People have what amounts to a set of bad-mood thoughts that come to mind more readily when they are feeling down. People who get depressed easily tend to create very strong networks of association between these thoughts, so that it is harder to suppress them once some kind of bad mood is evoked. Ironically, depressed people seem to use one depressing topic to get their minds off another, which only stirs more negative emotions."

Crying, one theory holds, may be nature's way of lowering levels of the brain chemicals that prime distress. While crying can sometimes break a spell of sadness, it can also leave the person still obsessing about the reasons for despair. The idea of a "good cry" is misleading: crying that reinforces rumination only prolongs the misery. Distractions break the chain of sadness-maintaining thinking; one of the leading theories of why electroconvulsive therapy is effective for the most severe depressions is that it causes a loss of short-term memory—patients feel better because they can't remember why they were so sad. At any rate, to shake garden-variety sadness, Diane Tice found, many people reported turning to distractions such as reading, TV and movies, video games and puzzles, sleeping, and daydreams such as planning a fantasy vacation. Wenzlaff would add that the most effective distractions are ones that will shift your mood—an exciting sporting event, a funny movie, an uplifting book. (A note of caution here: Some distractors in themselves can perpetuate depression. Studies of heavy TV watchers have found that, after watching TV, they are generally more depressed than before they started!)

Aerobic exercise, Tice found, is one of the more effective tactics for lifting mild depression, as well as other bad moods. But the caveat here is that the mood-lifting benefits of exercise work best for the lazy, those who usually do not work out very much. For those with a daily exercise routine, whatever mood-changing benefits it offers were probably strongest when they first took up the exercise habit. In fact, for habitual exercisers there is a reverse effect on mood: they start to feel bad on those days when they skip their workout. Exercise seems to work well because it changes the physiological state the mood evokes: depression is a low-arousal state, and aerobics pitches the body into high arousal. By the same token, relaxation techniques, which put the body into a low-arousal state, work well for anxiety, a high-arousal state, but not so well for depression. Each of these approaches seems to work to break the cycle of depression or anxiety because it pitches the brain into a level of activity incompatible with the emotional state that has had it in its grip.

Cheering oneself up through treats and sensual pleasures was another fairly popular antidote to the blues. Common ways people soothed themselves when depressed ranged from taking hot baths or eating favorite foods, to listening to music or having sex. Buying oneself a gift or treat to get out of a bad mood was particularly popular among women, as was shopping in general, even if only window-shopping. Among those in college, Tice found that eating was three times as common a strategy for soothing sadness among women than men; men, on the other hand, were five times as likely to turn to drinking or drugs when they felt down. The trouble with overeating or alcohol as antidotes, of course, is that they can easily backfire: eating to excess brings regret; alcohol is a central nervous system depressant, and so only adds to the effects of depression itself.

A more constructive approach to mood-lifting, Tice reports, is engineering a small triumph or easy success: tackling some long-delayed chore around the house or getting to some other duty they've been wanting to clear up. By the same token, lifts to self-image also were cheering, even if only in the form of getting dressed up or putting on makeup.

One of the most potent—and, outside therapy, little used—antidotes to depression is seeing things differently, or *cognitive reframing*. It is natural to bemoan the end of a relationship and to wallow in self-pitying thoughts such as the conviction that "this means I'll always be alone," but it's sure to thicken the sense of despair. However, stepping back and thinking about the ways the relationship wasn't so great, and ways you and your partner were mismatched—in other words, seeing the loss differently, in a more positive light—is an antidote to the sadness. By the same token, cancer patients, no matter how serious their condition, were in better moods if they were able to bring to mind another patient who was in even worse shape ("I'm not so bad off—at least I can walk"); those who compared themselves to healthy people were the most depressed.[18] Such downward comparisons are surprisingly cheering: suddenly what had seemed quite dispiriting doesn't look all that bad.

Another effective depression-lifter is helping others in need. Since depression feeds on ruminations and preoccupations with the self, helping others lifts us out of those preoccupations as we empathize with people in pain of their own. Throwing oneself into volunteer work—coaching Little League, being a Big Brother, feeding the homeless—was one of the most powerful mood-changers in Tice's study. But it was also one of the rarest.

Finally, at least some people are able to find relief from their melancholy in turning to a transcendent power. Tice told me, "Praying, if you're very religious, works for all moods, especially depression."

REPRESSORS: UPBEAT DENIAL

"He kicked his roommate in the stomach . . ." the sentence begins. It ends, ". . . but he meant to turn on the light."

That transformation of an act of aggression into an innocent, if slightly implausible, mistake is repression captured *in vivo*. It was composed by a college student who had volunteered for a study of *repressors,* people who habitually and automatically seem to blot emotional disturbance from their awareness. The beginning fragment "He kicked his roommate in the stomach . . ." was given to this student as part of a sentence-completion test. Other tests showed that this small act of mental avoidance was part of a larger pattern in his life, a pattern of tuning out most emotional upset.[19] While at first researchers saw repressors as a prime example of the inability to feel emotion—cousins of alexithymics, perhaps—current thinking sees them as quite proficient in regulating emotion. They have become so adept at buffering themselves against negative feelings, it seems, that they are not even aware of the negativity. Rather than calling them repressors, as has been the custom among researchers, a more apt term might be *unflappables.*

Much of this research, done principally by Daniel Weinberger, a psychologist now at Case Western Reserve University, shows that while such people may seem calm and imperturbable, they can sometimes seethe with physiological upsets they are oblivious to. During the sentence-completion test, volunteers were also being monitored for their level of physiological arousal. The repressors' veneer of calm was belied by the agitation of their bodies: when faced with the sentence about the violent roommate and others like it, they gave all the signs of anxiety, such as a racing heart, sweating, and climbing blood pressure. Yet when asked, they said they felt perfectly calm.

This continual tuning-out of emotions such as anger and anxiety is not uncommon: about one person in six shows the pattern, according to Wein-berger. In theory, children might learn to become unflappable in any of several ways. One might be as a strategy for surviving a troubling situation such as having an alcoholic parent in a family where the problem itself is denied. Another might be having a parent or parents who are themselves repressors and so pass on the example of perennial cheerfulness or a stiff upper lip in the face of disturbing feelings. Or the trait may simply be inherited temperament. While no one can say as yet just how such a pattern begins in life, by the time repressors reach adulthood they are cool and collected under duress.

The question remains, of course, as to just how calm and cool they actually are. Can they really be unaware of the physical signs of distressing emotions, or are they simply feigning calm? The answer to that has come from clever research by Richard Davidson, a University of Wisconsin psychologist and an early collaborator with Weinberger. Davidson had people with the unflappable pattern free-associate to a list of words, most neutral, but several with hostile or sexual meanings that stir anxiety in almost everyone. And, as their bodily reactions revealed, they had all the physiological signs of distress in response to the loaded words, even though the words they associated to almost always showed an attempt to sanitize the upsetting words by linking them to an innocent one. If the first word was "hate," the response might be "love."

Davidson's study took advantage of the fact that (in right-handed people) a key center for processing negative emotion is in the right half of the brain, while the center for speaking is in the left. Once the right hemisphere recognizes that a word is upsetting, it transmits that information across the corpus callosum, the great divide between the brain's halves, to the speech center, and a word is spoken in response. Using an intricate arrangement of lenses, Davidson was able to display a word so that it was seen in only half of the visual field. Because of the neural wiring of the visual system, if the display was to the left half of the visual field, it was recognized first by the right half of the brain, with its sensitivity to distress. If the display was to the right half of the visual field, the signal went to the left side of the brain without being assessed for upset.

When the words were presented to the right hemisphere, there was a lag in the time it took the unflappables to utter a response—but only if the word they were responding to was one of the upsetting ones. They had *no* time lag in the speed of their associations to *neutral* words. The lag showed up *only* when the words were presented to the right hemisphere, not to the left. In short, their unflappableness seems due to a neural mechanism that slows or interferes with the transfer of upsetting information. The implication is that they are *not* faking their lack of awareness about how upset they are; their brain is keeping that information from them. More precisely, the layer of mellow feeling that covers over such disturbing perceptions may well be due to the workings of the left prefrontal lobe. To his surprise, when Davidson measured activity levels in their prefrontal lobes, they had a decided predominance of activity on the left—the center for good feeling—and less on the right, the center for negativity.

These people "present themselves in a positive light, with an upbeat mood," Davidson told me. "They deny that stress is upsetting them and show a pattern of left frontal activation while just sitting at rest that is associated with positive feelings. This brain activity may be the key to their positive claims, despite the underlying physiological arousal that looks like distress." Davidson's theory is that, in terms of brain activity, it is energy-demanding work to experience distressing realities in a positive light. The increased physiological arousal may be due to the sustained attempt by the neural circuitry to maintain positive feelings or to suppress or inhibit any negative ones.

In short, unflappableness is a kind of upbeat denial, a positive dissociation—and, possibly, a clue to neural mechanisms at play in the more severe dissociative states that can occur in, say, post-traumatic stress disorder. When it is simply involved in equanimity, says Davidson, "it seems to be a successful strategy for emotional self-regulation" though with an unknown cost to self-awareness.

6

The Master Aptitude

Just once in my life have I been paralyzed by fear. The occasion was a calculus exam during my freshman year in college for which I somehow had managed not to study. I still remember the room I marched to that spring morning with feelings of doom and foreboding heavy in my heart. I had been in that lecture hall for many classes. This morning, though, I noticed nothing through the windows and did not see the hall at all. My gaze shrank to the patch of floor directly in front of me as I made my way to a seat near the door. As I opened the blue cover of my exam book, there was the thump in my ears of heartbeat, there was the taste of anxiety in the pit of my stomach.

I looked at the exam questions once, quickly. Hopeless. For an hour I stared at that page, my mind racing over the consequences I would suffer. The same thoughts repeated themselves over and over, a tape loop of fear and trembling. I sat motionless, like an animal frozen in mid-move by curare. What strikes me most about that dreadful moment was how constricted my mind became. I did not spend the hour in a desperate attempt to patch together some semblance of answers to the test. I did not daydream. I simply sat fixated on my terror, waiting for the ordeal to finish.[1]

That narrative of an ordeal by terror is my own; it is to this day for me the most convincing evidence of the devastating impact of emotional distress on mental clarity. I now see that my ordeal was most likely a testament to the power of the emotional brain to overpower, even paralyze, the thinking brain.

The extent to which emotional upsets can interfere with mental life is no news to teachers. Students who are anxious, angry, or depressed don't learn; people who are caught in these states do not take in information efficiently or deal with it well. As we saw in Chapter 5, powerful negative emotions twist attention toward their own preoccupations, interfering with the attempt to focus elsewhere. Indeed, one of the signs that feelings have veered over the line into the pathological is that they are so intrusive they overwhelm all other thought, continually sabotaging attempts to pay attention to whatever other task is at hand. For the person going through an upsetting divorce—or the child whose parents are—the mind does not stay long on the comparatively trivial routines of the work or school day; for the clinically depressed, thoughts of self-pity and despair, hopelessness and helplessness, override all others.

When emotions overwhelm concentration, what is being swamped is the mental capacity cognitive scientists call "working memory," the ability to hold in mind all information relevant to the task at hand. What occupies working memory can be as mundane as the digits that compose a telephone number or as complicated as the intricate plot lines a novelist is trying to weave together. Working memory is an executive function par excellence in mental life, making possible all other intellectual efforts, from speaking a sentence to tackling a knotty logical proposition.[2] The prefrontal cortex executes working memory—and, remember, is where feelings and emotions meet.[3] When the limbic circuitry that converges on the prefrontal cortex is in the thrall of emotional distress, one cost is in the effectiveness of working memory: we can't think straight, as I discovered during that dread calculus exam.

On the other hand, consider the role of positive motivation—the marshaling of feelings like enthusiasm and confidence to enhance achievement. Studies of Olympic athletes, world-class musicians, and chess grand masters find their unifying trait is the ability to motivate themselves to pursue relentless training routines.[4] And, with a steady rise in the degree of excellence required to be a world-class performer, these rigorous training routines now increasingly must begin in childhood. At the 1992 Olympics, twelve-year-old members of the Chinese diving team had put in as many total lifetime practice dives as had members of the American team in their early twenties—the Chinese divers started their rigorous training at age four. Likewise, the best violin virtuosos of the twentieth century began studying their instrument at around age five; international chess champions started on the game at an average age of seven, while those who rose only to national prominence started at ten. Starting earlier offers a lifetime edge: the top violin students at the best music academy in Berlin, all in their early twenties, had put in ten thousand total hours' lifetime practice, while the second-tier students averaged around seventy-five hundred hours.

What seems to set apart those at the very top of competitive pursuits from others of roughly equal ability is the degree to which, beginning early in life, they can pursue an arduous practice routine for years and years. And that doggedness depends on emotional traits—enthusiasm and persistence in the face of setbacks—above all else.

The added payoff for life success from motivation, apart from other innate abilities, can be seen in the remarkable performance of Asian students in American schools and professions. One thorough review of the evidence suggests that Asian-American children may have an average IQ advantage over whites of just two or three points.[5] Yet on the basis of the professions, such as law and medicine, that many Asian-Americans end up in, as a group they behave as though their IQ were much higher—the equivalent of an IQ of 110 for Japanese-Americans and of 120 for Chinese-Americans.[6] The reason seems to be that from the earliest years of school, Asian children work harder than whites. Sanford Dorenbusch, a Stanford sociologist who studied more than ten thousand high-school students, found that Asian-Americans spent 40 percent more time doing homework than did other students. "While most American parents are willing to accept a child's weak areas and emphasize the strengths, for Asians, the attitude is that if you're not doing well, the answer is to study later at night, and if you still don't do well, to get up and study earlier in the morning. They believe that anyone can do well in school with the right effort." In short, a strong cultural work ethic translates into higher motivation, zeal, and persistence—an emotional edge.

To the degree that our emotions get in the way of or enhance our ability to think and plan, to pursue training for a distant goal, to solve problems and the like, they define the limits of our capacity to use our innate mental abilities, and so determine how we do in life. And to the degree to which we are motivated by feelings of enthusiasm and pleasure in what we do— or even by an optimal degree of anxiety—they propel us to accomplishment. It is in this sense that emotional intelligence is a master aptitude, a capacity that profoundly affects all other abilities, either facilitating or interfering with them.

IMPULSE CONTROL: THE MARSHMALLOW TEST

Just imagine you're four years old, and someone makes the following proposal: If you'll wait until after he runs an errand, you can have two marshmallows for a treat. If you can't wait until then, you can have only one—but you can have it right now. It is a challenge sure to try the soul of any four-year-old, a microcosm of the eternal battle between impulse and restraint, id and ego, desire and self-control, gratification and delay. Which of these choices a child makes is a telling test; it offers a quick reading not just of character, but of the trajectory that child will probably take through life.

There is perhaps no psychological skill more fundamental than resisting impulse. It is the root of all emotional self-control, since all emotions, by their very nature, lead to one or another impulse to act. The root meaning of the word *emotion,* remember, is "to move." The capacity to resist that impulse to act, to squelch the incipient movement, most likely translates at the level of brain function into inhibition of limbic signals to the motor cortex, though such an interpretation must remain speculative for now.

At any rate, a remarkable study in which the marshmallow challenge was posed to four-year-olds shows just how fundamental is the ability to restrain the emotions and so delay impulse. Begun by psychologist Walter Mischel during the 1960s at a preschool on the Stanford University campus and involving mainly children of Stanford faculty, graduate students, and other employees, the study tracked down the four-year-olds as they were graduating from high school.[7]

Some four-year-olds were able to wait what must surely have seemed an endless fifteen to twenty minutes for the experimenter to return. To sustain themselves in their struggle they covered their eyes so they wouldn't have to stare at temptation, or rested their heads in their arms, talked to themselves, sang, played games with their hands and feet, even tried to go to sleep. These plucky preschoolers got the two-marshmallow reward. But others, more impulsive, grabbed the one marshmallow, almost always within seconds of the experimenter's leaving the room on his "errand."

The diagnostic power of how this moment of impulse was handled became clear some twelve to fourteen years later, when these same children were tracked down as adolescents. The emotional and social difference between the grab-the-marshmallow preschoolers and their gratification-delaying peers was dramatic. Those who had resisted temptation at four were now, as adolescents, more socially competent: personally effective, self-assertive, and better able to cope with the frustrations of life. They were less likely to go to pieces, freeze, or regress under stress, or become rattled and disorganized when pressured; they embraced challenges and pursued them instead of giving up even in the face of difficulties; they were self-reliant and confident, trustworthy and dependable; and they took initiative and plunged into projects. And, more than a decade later, they were still able to delay gratification in pursuit of their goals.

The third or so who grabbed for the marshmallow, however, tended to have fewer of these qualities, and shared instead a relatively more troubled psychological portrait. In adolescence they were more likely to be seen as shying away from social contacts; to be stubborn and indecisive; to be easily upset by frustrations; to think of themselves as "bad" or unworthy; to regress or become immobilized by stress; to be mistrustful and resentful about not "getting enough"; to be prone to jealousy and envy; to overreact to irritations with a sharp temper, so provoking arguments and fights. And, after all those years, they still were unable to put off gratification.

What shows up in a small way early in life blossoms into a wide range of social and emotional competences as life goes on. The capacity to impose a delay on impulse is at the root of a plethora of efforts, from staying on a diet to pursuing a medical degree. Some children, even at four, had mastered the basics: they were able to read the social situation as one where delay was beneficial, to pry their attention from focusing on the temptation at hand, and to distract themselves while maintaining the necessary perseverance toward their goal—the two marshmallows.

Even more surprising, when the tested children were evaluated again as they were finishing high school, those who had waited patiently at four were far superior *as students* to those who had acted on whim. According to their parents' evaluations, they were more academically competent: better able to put their ideas into words, to use and respond to reason, to concentrate, to make plans and follow through on them, and more eager to learn. Most astonishingly, they had dramatically higher scores on their SAT tests. The third of children who at four grabbed for the marshmallow most eagerly had an average verbal score of 524 and quantitative (or "math") score of 528; the third who waited longest had average scores of 610 and 652, respectively—a 210-point difference in total score.[8]

At age four, how children do on this test of delay of gratification is twice as powerful a predictor of what their SAT scores will be as is IQ at age four; IQ becomes a stronger predictor of SAT only after children learn to read.[9] This suggests that the ability to delay gratification contributes powerfully to intellectual potential quite apart from IQ itself. (Poor impulse control in childhood is also a powerful predictor of later delinquency, again more so than IQ.[10]) As we shall see in Part Five, while some argue that IQ cannot be changed and so represents an unbendable limitation on a child's life potential, there is ample evidence that emotional skills such as impulse control and accurately reading a social situation *can* be learned.

What Walter Mischel, who did the study, describes with the rather infelicitous phrase "goal-directed self-imposed delay of gratification" is perhaps the essence of emotional self-regulation: the ability to deny impulse in the service of a goal, whether it be building a business, solving an algebraic equation, or pursuing the Stanley Cup. His finding underscores the role of emotional intelligence as a meta-ability, determining how well or how poorly people are able to use their other mental capacities.

FOUL MOODS, FOULED THINKING

I worry about my son. He just started playing on the varsity football team, so he's bound to get an injury sometime. It's so nerve-wracking to watch him play that I've stopped going to his games. I'm sure my son must be disappointed that I'm not watching him play, but it's simply too much for me to take.

The speaker is in therapy for anxiety; she realizes that her worry is interfering with leading the kind of life she would like.[11] But when it comes time to make a simple decision, such as whether to watch her son play football, her mind floods with thoughts of disaster. She is not free to choose; her worries overwhelm her reason.

As we have seen, worry is the nub of anxiety's damaging effect on mental performance of all kind. Worry, of course, is in one sense a useful response gone awry—an overly zealous mental preparation for an anticipated threat. But such mental rehearsal is disastrous cognitive static when it becomes trapped in a stale routine that captures attention, intruding on all other attempts to focus elsewhere.

Anxiety undermines the intellect. In a complex, intellectually demanding, and high-pressure task such as that of air traffic controllers, for example, having chronically high anxiety is an almost sure predictor that a person will eventually fail in training or in the field. The anxious are more likely to fail even given superior scores on intelligence tests, as a study of 1,790 students in training for air traffic control posts discovered.[12] Anxiety also sabotages academic performance of all kinds: 126 different studies of more than 36,000 people found that the more prone to worries a person is, the poorer their academic performance, no matter how measured—grades on tests, grade-point average, or achievement tests.[13]

When people who are prone to worry are asked to perform a cognitive task such as sorting ambiguous objects into one of two categories, and narrate what is going through their mind as they do so, it is the negative thoughts—"I won't be able to do this," "I'm just no good at this kind of test," and the like—that are found to most directly disrupt their decision-making. Indeed, when a comparison group of nonworriers was asked to worry on purpose for fifteen minutes, their ability to do the same task deteriorated sharply. And when the worriers were given a fifteen-minute relaxation session—which reduced their level of worrying—before trying the task, they had no problem with it.[14]

Test anxiety was first studied scientifically in the 1960s by Richard Alpert, who confessed to me that his interest was piqued because as a student his nerves often made him do poorly on tests, while his colleague, Ralph Haber, found that the pressure before an exam actually helped him to do better.[15] Their research, among other studies, showed that there are two kinds of anxious students: those whose anxiety undoes their academic performance, and those who are able to do well despite the stress—or, perhaps, because of it.[16] The irony of test anxiety is that the very apprehension about doing well on the test that, ideally, can motivate students like Haber to study hard in preparation and so do well can sabotage success in others. For people who are too anxious, like Alpert, the pretest apprehension interferes with the clear thinking and memory necessary to study effectively, while during the test it disrupts the mental clarity essential for doing well.

The number of worries that people report while taking a test directly predicts how poorly they will do on it.[17] The mental resources expended on one cognitive task—the worrying—simply detract from the resources available for processing other information; if we are preoccupied by worries that we're going to flunk the test we're taking, we have that much less attention to expend on figuring out the answers. Our worries become self-fulfilling prophecies, propelling us toward the very disaster they predict.

People who are adept at harnessing their emotions, on the other hand, can use anticipatory anxiety—about an upcoming speech or test, say—to motivate themselves to prepare well for it, thereby doing well. The classical literature in psychology describes the relationship between anxiety and performance, including mental performance, in terms of an upside-down U. At the peak of the inverted U is the optimal relationship between anxiety and performance, with a modicum of nerves propelling outstanding achievement. But too little anxiety—the first side of the U—brings about apathy or too little motivation to try hard enough to do well, while too much anxiety—the other side of the U—sabotages any attempt to do well.

A mildly elated state—*hypomania,* as it is technically called—seems optimal for writers and others in creative callings that demand fluidity and imaginative diversity of thought; it is somewhere toward the peak of that inverted U. But let that euphoria get out of control to become outright mania, as in the mood swings of manic-depressives, and the agitation undermines the ability to think cohesively enough to write well, even though ideas flow freely—indeed, much too freely to pursue any one of them far enough to produce a finished product.

Good moods, while they last, enhance the ability to think flexibly and with more complexity, thus making it easier to find solutions to problems, whether intellectual or interpersonal. This suggests that one way to help someone think through a problem is to tell them a joke. Laughing, like elation, seems to help people think more broadly and associate more freely, noticing relationships that might have eluded them otherwise—a mental skill important not just in creativity, but in recognizing complex relationships and foreseeing the consequences of a given decision.

The intellectual benefits of a good laugh are most striking when it comes to solving a problem that demands a creative solution. One study found that people who had just watched a video of television bloopers were better at solving a puzzle long used by psychologists to test creative thinking.[18] In the test people are given a candle, matches, and a box of tacks and asked to attach the candle to a corkboard wall so it will burn without dripping wax on the floor. Most people given this problem fall into "functional fixedness," thinking about using the objects in the most conventional ways. But those who had just watched the funny film, compared to others who had watched a film on math or who exercised, were more likely to see an alternative use for the box holding the tacks, and so come up with the creative solution: tack the box to the wall and use it as a candleholder.

Even mild mood changes can sway thinking. In making plans or decisions people in good moods have a perceptual bias that leads them to be more expansive and positive in their thinking. This is partly because memory is state-specific, so that while in a good mood we remember more positive events; as we think over the pros and cons of a course of action while feeling pleasant, memory biases our weighing of evidence in a positive direction, making us more likely to do something slightly adventurous or risky, for example.

By the same token, being in a foul mood biases memory in a negative direction, making us more likely to contract into a fearful, overly cautious decision. Emotions out of control impede the intellect. But, as we saw in Chapter 5, we can bring out-of-control emotions back into line; this emotional competence is the master aptitude, facilitating all other kinds of intelligence. Consider some cases in point: the benefits of hope and optimism, and those soaring moments when people outdo themselves.

PANDORA'S BOX AND POLLYANNA: THE POWER OF POSITIVE THINKING

College students were posed the following hypothetical situation:

> Although you set your goal of getting a B, when your first exam score, worth 30% of your final grade is returned, you have received a D. It is now one week after you have learned about the D grade. What do you do?[19]

Hope made all the difference. The response by students with high levels of hope was to work harder and think of a range of things they might try that could bolster their final grade. Students with moderate levels of hope thought of several ways they might up their grade, but had far less determination to pursue them. And, understandably, students with low levels of hope gave up on both counts, demoralized.

The question is not just theoretical, however. When C. R. Snyder, the University of Kansas psychologist who did this study, compared the actual academic achievement of freshman students high and low on hope, he discovered that hope was a better predictor of their first-semester grades than were their scores on the SAT, a test supposedly able to predict how students will fare in college (and highly correlated with IQ). Again, given roughly the same range of intellectual abilities, emotional aptitudes make the critical difference.

Snyder's explanation: "Students with high hope set themselves higher goals and know how to work hard to attain them. When you compare students of equivalent intellectual aptitude on their academic achievements, what sets them apart is hope."[20]

As the familiar legend has it, Pandora, a princess of ancient Greece, was given a gift, a mysterious box, by gods jealous of her beauty. She was told she must never open the gift. But one day, overcome by curiosity and temptation,

Pandora lifted the lid to peek in, letting loose in the world the grand afflictions—disease, malaise, madness. But a compassionate god let her close the box just in time to capture the one antidote that makes life's misery bearable: hope.

Hope, modern researchers are finding, does more than offer a bit of solace amid affliction; it plays a surprisingly potent role in life, offering an advantage in realms as diverse as school achievement and bearing up in onerous jobs. Hope, in a technical sense, is more than the sunny view that everything will turn out all right. Snyder defines it with more specificity as "believing you have both the will and the way to accomplish your goals, whatever they may be."

People tend to differ in the general degree to which they have hope in this sense. Some typically think of themselves as able to get out of a jam or find ways to solve problems, while others simply do not see themselves as having the energy, ability, or means to accomplish their goals. People with high levels of hope, Snyder finds, share certain traits, among them being able to motivate themselves, feeling resourceful enough to find ways to accomplish their objectives, reassuring themselves when in a tight spot that things will get better, being flexible enough to find different ways to get to their goals or to switch goals if one becomes impossible, and having the sense to break down a formidable task into smaller, manageable pieces.

From the perspective of emotional intelligence, having hope means that one will not give in to overwhelming anxiety, a defeatist attitude, or depression in the face of difficult challenges or setbacks. Indeed, people who are hopeful evidence less depression than others as they maneuver through life in pursuit of their goals, are less anxious in general, and have fewer emotional distresses.

OPTIMISM: THE GREAT MOTIVATOR

Americans who follow swimming had high hopes for Matt Biondi, a member of the U.S. Olympic Team in 1988. Some sportswriters were touting Biondi as likely to match Mark Spitz's 1972 feat of taking seven gold medals. But Biondi finished a heartbreaking third in his first event, the 200-meter freestyle. In his next event, the 100-meter butterfly, Biondi was inched out for the gold by another swimmer who made a greater effort in the last meter.

Sportscasters speculated that the defeats would dispirit Biondi in his successive events. But Biondi rebounded from defeat and took a gold medal in his next five events. One viewer who was not surprised by Biondi's come-back was Martin Seligman, a psychologist at the University of Pennsylvania, who had tested Biondi for optimism earlier that year. In an experiment done with Seligman, the swimming coach told Biondi during a special event meant to showcase Biondi's best performance that he had a worse time than was actually the case. Despite the downbeat feedback, when Biondi was asked to rest and try again, his performance—actually already very good—was even better. But when other team members who were given a false bad time—and whose test scores showed they were pessimistic—tried again, they did even worse the second time.[21]

Optimism, like hope, means having a strong expectation that, in general, things will turn out all right in life, despite setbacks and frustrations. From the standpoint of emotional intelligence, optimism is an attitude that buffers people against falling into apathy, hopelessness, or depression in the face of tough going. And, as with hope, its near cousin, optimism pays dividends in life (providing, of course, it is a realistic optimism; a too-naive optimism can be disastrous).[22]

Seligman defines optimism in terms of how people explain to themselves their successes and failures. People who are optimistic see a failure as due to something that can be changed so that they can succeed next time around, while pessimists take the blame for failure, ascribing it to some lasting characteristic they are helpless to change. These differing explanations have profound implications for how people respond to life. For example, in reaction to a disappointment such as being turned down for a job, optimists tend to respond actively and hopefully, by formulating a plan of action, say, or seeking out help and advice; they see the setback as something that can be remedied. Pessimists, by contrast, react to such setbacks by assuming there is nothing they can do to make things go better the next time, and so do nothing about the problem; they see the setback as due to some personal deficit that will always plague them.

As with hope, optimism predicts academic success. In a study of five hundred members of the incoming freshman class of 1984 at the University of Pennsylvania, the students' scores on a test of optimism were a better predic-tor of their actual grades freshman year than were their SAT scores or their high-school grades. Said Seligman, who studied them, "College entrance exams measure talent, while explanatory style tells you who gives up. It is the combination of reasonable talent and the ability to keep going in the face of defeat that leads to success. What's missing in tests of ability is motivation. What you need to know about someone is whether they will keep going when things get frustrating. My hunch is that for a given level of intelligence, your actual achievement is a function not just of talent, but also of the capacity to stand defeat."[23]

One of the most telling demonstrations of the power of optimism to motivate people is a study Seligman did of insurance salesmen with the MetLife company. Being able to take a rejection with grace is essential in sales of all kinds, especially with a product like insurance, where the ratio of noes to yeses can be so discouragingly high. For this reason, about three quarters of insurance salesmen quit in their first three years. Seligman found that new salesmen who were by nature optimists sold 37 percent more insurance in their first two years on the job than did pessimists. And during the first year the pessimists quit at twice the rate of the optimists.

What's more, Seligman persuaded MetLife to hire a special group of applicants who scored high on a test for optimism but failed the normal screening tests (which compared a range of their attitudes to a standard profile based on answers from agents who have been successful). This special group outsold the pessimists by 21 percent in their first year, and 57 percent in the second.

Just why optimism makes such a difference in sales success speaks to the sense in which it is an emotionally intelligent attitude. Each no a salesperson gets is a small defeat. The emotional reaction to that defeat is crucial to the ability to marshal enough motivation to continue. As the noes mount up, morale can deteriorate, making it harder and harder to pick up the phone for the next call. Such rejection is especially hard to take for a pessimist, who interprets it as meaning, "I'm a failure at this; I'll never make a sale"—an interpretation that is sure to trigger apathy and defeatism, if not depression. Optimists, on the other hand, tell themselves, "I'm using the wrong approach," or "That last person was just in a bad mood." By seeing not themselves but something in the situation as the reason for their failure, they can change their approach in the next call. While the pessimist's mental set leads to despair, the optimist's spawns hope.

One source of a positive or negative outlook may well be inborn temperament; some people by nature tend one way or the other. But as we shall also see in Chapter 14, temperament can be tempered by experience. Optimism and hope—like helplessness and despair—can be learned. Underlying both is an outlook psychologists call *self-efficacy,* the belief that one has mastery over the events of one's life and can meet challenges as they come up. Developing a competency of any kind strengthens the sense of self-efficacy, making a person more willing to take risks and seek out more demanding challenges. And surmounting those challenges in turn increases the sense of self-efficacy. This attitude makes people more likely to make the best use of whatever skills they may have—or to do what it takes to develop them.

Albert Bandura, a Stanford psychologist who has done much of the research on self-efficacy, sums it up well: "People's beliefs about their abilities have a profound effect on those abilities. Ability is not a fixed property; there is a huge variability in how you perform. People who have a sense of self-efficacy bounce back from failures; they approach things in terms of how to handle them rather than worrying about what can go wrong."[24]

FLOW: THE NEUROBIOLOGY OF EXCELLENCE

A composer describes those moments when his work is at its best:

> You yourself are in an ecstatic state to such a point that you feel as though you almost don't exist. I've experienced this time and again. My hand seems devoid of myself, and I have nothing to do with what is happening. I just sit there watching in a state of awe and wonderment. And it just flows out by itself.[25]

His description is remarkably similar to those of hundreds of diverse men and women—rock climbers, chess champions, surgeons, basketball players, engineers, managers, even filing clerks—when they tell of a time they outdid themselves in some favored activity. The state they describe is called "flow" by Mihaly Csikszentmihalyi, the University of Chicago psychologist who has collected such accounts of peak performance during two decades of research.[26] Athletes know this state of grace as "the zone," where excellence becomes effortless, crowd and competitors disappearing into a blissful, steady absorption in the moment. Diane Roffe-Steinrotter, who captured a gold medal in skiing at the 1994 Winter Olympics, said after she finished her turn at ski racing that she remembered nothing about it but being immersed in relaxation: "I felt like a waterfall."[27]

Being able to enter flow is emotional intelligence at its best; flow represents perhaps the ultimate in harnessing the emotions in the service of performance and learning. In flow the emotions are not just contained and channeled, but positive, energized, and aligned with the task at hand. To be caught in the ennui of depression or the agitation of anxiety is to be barred from flow. Yet flow (or a milder microflow) is an experience almost everyone enters from time to time, particularly when performing at their peak or stretching beyond their former limits. It is perhaps best captured by ecstatic lovemaking, the merging of two into a fluidly harmonious one.

That experience is a glorious one: the hallmark of flow is a feeling of spontaneous joy, even rapture. Because flow feels so good, it is intrinsically rewarding. It is a state in which people become utterly absorbed in what they are doing, paying undivided attention to the task, their awareness merged with their actions. Indeed, it interrupts flow to reflect too much on what is happening—the very thought "I'm doing this wonderfully" can break the feeling of flow. Attention becomes so focused that people are aware only of the narrow range of perception related to the immediate task, losing track of time and space. A surgeon, for example, recalled a challenging operation during which he was in flow; when he completed the surgery he noticed some rubble on the floor of the operating room and asked what had happened. He was amazed to hear that while he was so intent on the surgery part of the ceiling had caved in—he hadn't noticed at all.

Flow is a state of self-forgetfulness, the opposite of rumination and worry: instead of being lost in nervous preoccupation, people in flow are so absorbed in the task at hand that they lose all self-consciousness, dropping the small preoccupations—health, bills, even doing well—of daily life. In this sense moments of flow are egoless. Paradoxically, people in flow exhibit a masterly control of what they are doing, their responses perfectly attuned to the changing demands of the task. And although people perform at their peak while in flow, they are unconcerned with how they are doing, with thoughts of success or failure—the sheer pleasure of the act itself is what motivates them.

There are several ways to enter flow. One is to intentionally focus a sharp attention on the task at hand; a highly concentrated state is the essence of flow. There seems to be a feedback loop at the gateway to this zone: it can require considerable effort to get calm and focused enough to begin the task—this first step takes some discipline. But once focus starts to lock in, it takes on a force of its own, both offering relief from emotional turbulence and making the task effortless.

Entry to this zone can also occur when people find a task they are skilled at, and engage in it at a level that slightly taxes their ability. As Csikszentmihalyi told me, "People seem to concentrate best when the demands on them are a bit greater than usual, and they are able to give more than usual. If there is too little demand on them, people are bored. If there is too much for them to handle, they get anxious. Flow occurs in that delicate zone between boredom and anxiety."[28]

The spontaneous pleasure, grace, and effectiveness that characterize flow are incompatible with emotional hijackings, in which limbic surges capture the rest of the brain. The quality of attention in flow is relaxed yet highly focused. It is a concentration very different from straining to pay attention when we are tired or bored, or when our focus is under siege from intrusive feelings such as anxiety or anger.

Flow is a state devoid of emotional static, save for a compelling, highly motivating feeling of mild ecstasy. That ecstasy seems to be a by-product of the attentional focus that is a prerequisite of flow. Indeed, the classic literature of contemplative traditions describes states of absorption that are experienced as pure bliss: flow induced by nothing more than intense concentration.

Watching someone in flow gives the impression that the difficult is easy; peak performance appears natural and ordinary. This impression parallels what is going on within the brain, where a similar paradox is repeated: the most challenging tasks are done with a minimum expenditure of mental energy. In flow the brain is in a "cool" state, its arousal and inhibition of neural circuitry attuned to the demand of the moment. When people are engaged in activities that effortlessly capture and hold their attention, their brain "quiets down" in the sense that there is a lessening of cortical arousal.[29] That discovery is remarkable, given that flow allows people to tackle the most challenging tasks in a given domain, whether playing against a chess master or solving a complex mathematical problem. The expectation would be that such challenging tasks would require *more* cortical activity, not less. But a key to flow is that it occurs only within reach of the summit of ability, where skills are well-rehearsed and neural circuits are most efficient.

A strained concentration—a focus fueled by worry—produces increased cortical activation. But the zone of flow and optimal performance seems to be an oasis of cortical efficiency, with a bare minimum of mental energy expended. That makes sense, perhaps, in terms of the skilled practice that allows people to get into flow: having mastered the moves of a task, whether a physical one such as rock climbing or a mental one such as computer programming, means that the brain can be more efficient in performing them. Well-practiced moves require much less brain effort than do ones just being learned, or those that are still too hard. Likewise, when the brain is working less efficiently because of fatigue or nervousness, as happens at the end of a long, stressful day, there is a blurring of the precision of cortical effort, with too many superfluous areas being activated—a neural state experienced as being highly distracted.[30] The same happens in boredom. But when the brain is operating at peak efficiency, as in flow, there is a precise relation between the active areas and the demands of the task. In this state even hard work can seem refreshing or replenishing rather than draining.

LEARNING AND FLOW: A NEW MODEL FOR EDUCATION

Because flow emerges in the zone in which an activity challenges people to the fullest of their capacities, as their skills increase it takes a heightened challenge to get into flow. If a task is too simple, it is boring; if too challenging, the result is anxiety rather than flow. It can be argued that mastery in a craft or skill is spurred on by the experience of flow—that the motivation to get better and better at something, be it playing the violin, dancing, or gene-splicing, is at least in part to stay in flow while doing it. Indeed, in a study of two hundred artists eighteen years after they left art school, Csikszentmihalyi found that it was those who in their student days had savored the sheer joy of painting itself who had become serious painters. Those who had been motivated in art school by dreams of fame and wealth for the most part drifted away from art after graduating.

Csikszentmihalyi concludes: "Painters must want to paint above all else. If the artist in front of the canvas begins to wonder how much he will sell it for, or what the critics will think of it, he won't be able to pursue original avenues. Creative achievements depend on single-minded immersion."[31]

Just as flow is a prerequisite for mastery in a craft, profession, or art, so too with learning. Students who get into flow as they study do better, quite apart from their potential as measured by achievement tests. Students in a special Chicago high school for the sciences—all of whom had scored in the top 5 percent on a test of math proficiency—were rated by their math teachers as high or low achievers. Then the way these students spent their time was monitored, each student carrying a beeper that signaled them at random times during the day to write down what they were doing and what their mood was. Not surprisingly, the low achievers spent only about fifteen hours a week studying at home, much less than the twenty-seven hours a week of homework done by their high-achieving peers. The low achievers spent most of the hours during which they were not studying in socializing, hanging out with friends and family.

When their moods were analyzed, a telling finding emerged. Both the high and low achievers spent a great deal of time during the week being bored by activities, such as TV watching, that posed no challenge to their abilities. Such, after all, is the lot of teenagers. But the key difference was in their experience of studying. For the high achievers, studying gave them the pleasing, absorbing challenge of flow 40 percent of the hours they spent at it. But for the low achievers, studying produced flow only 16 percent of the time; more often than not, it yielded anxiety, with the demands outreaching their abilities. The low achievers found pleasure and flow in socializing, not in studying. In short, students who achieve up to the level of their academic potential and beyond are more often drawn to study because it puts them in flow. Sadly, the low achievers, by failing to hone the skills that would get them in flow, both forfeit the enjoyment of study and run the risk of limiting the level of intellectual tasks that will be enjoyable to them in the future.[32]

Howard Gardner, the Harvard psychologist who developed the theory of multiple intelligences, sees flow, and the positive states that typify it, as part of the healthiest way to teach children, motivating them from inside rather than by threat or promise of reward. "We should use kids' positive states to draw them into learning in the domains where they can develop competencies," Gardner proposed to me. "Flow is an internal state that signifies a kid is engaged in a task that's right. You have to find something you like and stick to it. It's when kids get bored in school that they fight and act up, and when they're overwhelmed by a challenge that they get anxious about their schoolwork. But you learn at your best when you have something you care about and you can get pleasure from being engaged in."

The strategy used in many of the schools that are putting Gardner's model of multiple intelligences into practice revolves around identifying a child's profile of natural competencies and playing to the strengths as well as trying to shore up the weaknesses. A child who is naturally talented in music or movement, for example, will enter flow more easily in that domain than in those where she is less able. Knowing a child's profile can help a teacher fine-tune the way a topic is presented to a child and offer lessons at the level—from remedial to highly advanced—that is most likely to provide an optimal challenge. Doing this makes learning more pleasurable, neither fearsome nor a bore. "The hope is that when kids gain flow from learning, they will be emboldened to take on challenges in new areas," says Gardner, adding that experience suggests this is the case.

More generally, the flow model suggests that achieving mastery of any skill or body of knowledge should ideally happen naturally, as the child is drawn to the areas that spontaneously engage her—that, in essence, she loves. That initial passion can be the seed for high levels of attainment, as the child comes to realize that pursuing the field—whether it be dance, math, or music—is a source of the joy of flow. And since it takes pushing the limits of one's ability to sustain flow, that becomes a prime motivator for getting better and better; it makes the child happy. This, of course, is a more positive model of learning and education than most of us encountered in school. Who does not recall school at least in part as endless dreary hours of boredom punctuated by moments of high anxiety? Pursuing flow through learning is a more humane, natural, and very likely more effective way to marshal emotions in the service of education.

That speaks to the more general sense in which channeling emotions toward a productive end is a master aptitude. Whether it be in controlling impulse and putting off gratification, regulating our moods so they facilitate rather than impede thinking, motivating ourselves to persist and try, try again in the face of setbacks, or finding ways to enter flow and so perform more effectively—all bespeak the power of emotion to guide effective effort.

7

The Roots of Empathy

Back to Gary, the brilliant but alexithymic surgeon who so distressed his fiancée, Ellen, by being oblivious not only to his own feelings but to hers as well. Like most alexithymics, he lacked empathy as well as insight. If Ellen spoke of feeling down, Gary failed to sympathize; if she spoke of love, he changed the subject. Gary would make "helpful" critiques of things Ellen did, not realizing these criticisms made her feel attacked, not helped.

Empathy builds on self-awareness; the more open we are to our own emotions, the more skilled we will be in reading feelings.[1] Alexithymics like Gary, who have no idea what they feel themselves, are at a complete loss when it comes to knowing what anyone else around them is feeling. They are emotionally tone-deaf. The emotional notes and chords that weave through people's words and actions—the telling tone of voice or shift in posture, the eloquent silence or telltale tremble—go by unnoted.

Confused about their own feelings, alexithymics are equally bewildered when other people express their feelings to them. This failure to register another's feelings is a major deficit in emotional intelligence, and a tragic failing in what it means to be human. For all rapport, the root of caring, stems from emotional attunement, from the capacity for empathy.

That capacity—the ability to know how another feels—comes into play in a vast array of life arenas, from sales and management to romance and parenting, to compassion and political action. The absence of empathy is also telling. Its lack is seen in criminal psychopaths, rapists, and child molesters.

People's emotions are rarely put into words; far more often they are expressed through other cues. The key to intuiting another's feelings is in the ability to read nonverbal channels: tone of voice, gesture, facial expression, and the like. Perhaps the largest body of research on people's ability to read such nonverbal messages is by Robert Rosenthal, a Harvard psychologist, and his students. Rosenthal devised a test of empathy, the PONS (Profile of Nonverbal Sensitivity), a series of videotapes of a young woman expressing feelings ranging from loathing to motherly love.[2] The scenes span the spectrum from a jealous rage to asking forgiveness, from a show of gratitude to a seduction. The video has been edited so that in each portrayal one or more channels of nonverbal communication are systematically blanked out; in addition to having the words muffled, for example, in some scenes all other cues but the facial expression are blocked. In others, only the body movements are shown, and so on, through the main nonverbal channels of communication, so that viewers have to detect emotion from one or another specific nonverbal cue.

In tests with over seven thousand people in the United States and eighteen other countries, the benefits of being able to read feelings from nonverbal cues included being better adjusted emotionally, more popular, more outgoing, and—perhaps not surprisingly—more sensitive. In general, women are better than men at this kind of empathy. And people whose performance improved over the course of the forty-five-minute test—a sign that they have a talent for picking up empathy skills—also had better relationships with the opposite sex. Empathy, it should be no surprise to learn, helps with romantic life.

In keeping with findings about other elements of emotional intelligence, there was only an incidental relationship between scores on this measure of empathic acuity and SAT or IQ scores or school achievement tests. Empathy's independence from academic intelligence has been found too in testing with a version of the PONS designed for children. In tests with 1,011 children, those who showed an aptitude for reading feelings nonverbally were among the most popular in their schools, the most emotionally stable.[3] They also did better in school, even though, on average, their IQs were not higher than those of children who were less skilled at reading nonverbal messages—suggesting that mastering this empathic ability smooths the way for classroom effectiveness (or simply makes teachers like them more).

Just as the mode of the rational mind is words, the mode of the emotions is nonverbal. Indeed, when a person's words disagree with what is conveyed via his tone of voice, gesture, or other nonverbal channel, the emotional truth is in *how* he says something rather than in *what* he says. One rule of thumb used in communications research is that 90 percent or more of an emotional message is nonverbal. And such messages—anxiety in someone's tone of voice, irritation in the quickness of a gesture—are almost always taken in unconsciously, without paying specific attention to the nature of the message, but simply tacitly receiving it and responding. The skills that allow us to do this well or poorly are also, for the most part, learned tacitly.

HOW EMPATHY UNFOLDS

The moment Hope, just nine months old, saw another baby fall, tears welled up in her own eyes and she crawled off to be comforted by her mother, as though it were she who had been hurt. And fifteen-month-old Michael went to get his own teddy bear for his crying friend Paul; when Paul kept crying, Michael retrieved Paul's security blanket for him. Both these small acts of sympathy and caring were observed by mothers trained to record such incidents of empathy in action.[4] The results of the study suggest that the roots of empathy can be traced to infancy. Virtually from the day they are born infants are upset when they hear another infant crying—a response some see as the earliest precursor of empathy.[5]

Developmental psychologists have found that infants feel sympathetic distress even before they fully realize that they exist apart from other people. Even a few months after birth, infants react to a disturbance in those around them as though it were their own, crying when they see another child's tears. By one year or so, they start to realize the misery is not their own but someone else's, though they still seem confused over what to do about it. In research by Martin L. Hoffman at New York University, for example, a one-year-old brought his own mother over to comfort a crying friend, ignoring the friend's mother, who was also in the room. This confusion is seen too when one-year-olds imitate the distress of someone else, possibly to better comprehend what they are feeling; for example, if another baby hurts her fingers, a one-year-old might put her own fingers in her mouth to see if she hurts, too. On seeing his mother cry, one baby wiped his own eyes, though they had no tears.

Such *motor mimicry*, as it is called, is the original technical sense of the word *empathy* as it was first used in the 1920s by E. B. Titchener, an American psychologist. This sense is slightly different from its original introduction into English from the Greek *empatheia*, "feeling into," a term used initially by theoreticians of aesthetics for the ability to perceive the subjective experience of another person. Titchener's theory was that empathy stemmed from a sort of physical imitation of the distress of another, which then evokes the same feelings in oneself. He sought a word that would be distinct from *sympathy,* which can be felt for the general plight of another with no sharing whatever of what that other person is feeling.

Motor mimicry fades from toddlers' repertoire at around two and a half years, at which point they realize that someone else's pain is different from their own, and are better able to comfort them. A typical incident, from a mother's diary:

> A neighbor's baby cries . . . and Jenny approaches and tries to give him some cookies. She follows him around and begins to whimper to herself. She then tries to stroke his hair, but he pulls away. . . . He calms down, but Jenny still looks worried. She continues to bring him toys and to pat his head and shoulders.[6]

At this point in their development toddlers begin to diverge from one another in their overall sensitivity to other people's emotional upsets, with some, like Jenny, keenly aware and others tuning out. A series of studies by Marian Radke-Yarrow and Carolyn Zahn-Waxler at the National Institute of Mental Health showed that a large part of this difference in empathic concern had to do with how parents disciplined their children. Children, they found, were more empathic when the discipline included calling strong attention to the distress their misbehavior caused someone else: "Look how sad you've made her feel" instead of "That was naughty." They found too that children's empathy is also shaped by seeing how others react when someone else is distressed; by imitating what they see, children develop a repertoire of empathic response, especially in helping other people who are distressed.

THE WELL-ATTUNED CHILD

Sarah was twenty-five when she gave birth to twin boys, Mark and Fred. Mark, she felt, was more like herself; Fred was more like his father. That perception may have been the seed of a telling but subtle difference in how she treated each boy. When the boys were just three months old, Sarah would often try to catch Fred's gaze, and when he would avert his face, she would try to catch his eye again; Fred would respond by turning away more emphatically. Once she would look away, Fred would look back at her, and the cycle of pursuit and aversion would begin again—often leaving Fred in tears. But with Mark, Sarah virtually never tried to impose eye contact as she did with Fred. Instead Mark could break off eye contact whenever he wanted, and she would not pursue.

A small act, but telling. A year later, Fred was noticeably more fearful and dependent than Mark; one way he showed his fearfulness was by breaking off eye contact with other people, as he had done with his mother at three months, turning his face down and away. Mark, on the other hand, looked people straight in the eye; when he wanted to break off contact, he'd turn his head slightly upward and to the side, with a winning smile.

The twins and their mother were observed so minutely when they took part in research by Daniel Stern, a psychiatrist then at Cornell University School of Medicine.[7] Stern is fascinated by the small, repeated exchanges that take place between parent and child; he believes that the most basic lessons of emotional life are laid down in these intimate moments. Of all such moments, the most critical are those that let the child know her emotions are met with empathy, accepted, and reciprocated, in a process Stern calls *attunement*. The twins' mother was attuned with Mark, but out of emotional synch with Fred. Stern contends that the countlessly repeated moments of attunement or misattunement between parent and child shape the emotional expectations adults bring to their close relationships—perhaps far more than the more dramatic events of childhood.

Attunement occurs tacitly, as part of the rhythm of relationship. Stern has studied it with microscopic precision through videotaping hours of mothers with their infants. He finds that through attunement mothers let their infants know they have a sense of what the infant is feeling. A baby squeals with delight, for example, and the mother affirms that delight by giving the baby a gentle shake, cooing, or matching the pitch of her voice to the baby's squeal. Or a baby shakes his rattle, and she gives him a quick shimmy in response. In such an interaction the affirming message is in the mother more or less matching the baby's level of excitement. Such small attunements give an infant the reassuring feeling of being emotionally connected, a message that Stern finds mothers send about once a minute when they interact with their babies.

Attunement is very different from simple imitation. "If you just imitate a baby," Stern told me, "that only shows you know what he did, not how he felt. To let him know you sense how he feels, you have to play back his inner feelings in another way. Then the baby knows he is understood."

Making love is perhaps the closest approximation in adult life to this intimate attunement between infant and mother. Lovemaking, Stern writes, "involves the experience of sensing the other's subjective state: shared desire, aligned intentions, and mutual states of simultaneously shifting arousal," with lovers responding to each other in a synchrony that gives the tacit sense of deep rapport.[8] Lovemaking is, at its best, an act of mutual empathy; at its worst it lacks any such emotional mutuality.

THE COSTS OF MISATTUNEMENT

Stern holds that from repeated attunements an infant begins to develop a sense that other people can and will share in her feelings. This sense seems to emerge at around eight months, when infants begin to realize they are separate from others, and continues to be shaped by intimate relationships throughout life. When parents are misattuned to a child it is deeply upsetting. In one experiment, Stern had mothers deliberately over- or underrespond to their infants, rather than matching them in an attuned way; the infants responded with immediate dismay and distress.

Prolonged absence of attunement between parent and child takes a tremendous emotional toll on the child. When a parent consistently fails to show any empathy with a particular range of emotion in the child—joys, tears, needing to cuddle—the child begins to avoid expressing, and perhaps even feeling, those same emotions. In this way, presumably, entire ranges of emotion can begin to be obliterated from the repertoire for intimate relations, especially if through childhood those feelings continue to be covertly or overtly discouraged.

By the same token, children can come to favor an unfortunate range of emotion, depending on which moods are reciprocated. Even infants "catch" moods: Three-month-old babies of depressed mothers, for example, mirrored their mothers' moods while playing with them, displaying more feelings of anger and sadness, and much less spontaneous curiosity and interest, compared to infants whose mothers were not depressed.[9]

One mother in Stern's study consistently underreacted to her baby's level of activity; eventually her baby learned to be passive. "An infant treated that way learns, when I get excited I can't get my mother to be equally excited, so I may as well not try at all," Stern contends. But there is hope in "reparative" relationships: "Relationships throughout life—with friends or relatives, for example, or in psychotherapy—continually reshape your working model of relationships. An imbalance at one point can be corrected later; it's an ongoing, lifelong process."

Indeed, several theories of psychoanalysis see the therapeutic relationship as providing just such an emotional corrective, a reparative experience of attunement. *Mirroring* is the term used by some psychoanalytic thinkers for the therapist's reflecting back to the client an understanding of his inner state, just as an attuned mother does with her infant. The emotional synchrony is unstated and outside conscious awareness, though a patient may bask in the sense of being deeply acknowledged and understood.

The lifetime emotional costs of lack of attunement in childhood can be great—and not just for the child. A study of criminals who committed the cruelest and most violent crimes found that the one characteristic of their early lives that set them apart from other criminals was that they had been shuttled from foster home to foster home, or raised in orphanages—life histories that suggest emotional neglect and little opportunity for attunement.[10]

While emotional neglect seems to dull empathy, there is a paradoxical result from intense, sustained emotional abuse, including cruel, sadistic threats, humiliations, and plain meanness. Children who endure such abuse can become hyperalert to the emotions of those around them, in what amounts to a post-traumatic vigilance to cues that have signaled threat. Such an obsessive preoccupation with the feelings of others is typical of psychologically abused children who in adulthood suffer the mercurial, intense emotional ups and downs that are sometimes diagnosed as "borderline personality disorder." Many such people are gifted at sensing what others around them are feeling, and it is quite common for them to report having suffered emotional abuse in childhood.[11]

THE NEUROLOGY OF EMPATHY

As is so often the case in neurology, reports of quirky and bizarre cases were among the early clues to the brain basis of empathy. A 1975 report, for instance, reviewed several cases in which patients with certain lesions in the right area of the frontal lobes had a curious deficit: they were unable to understand the emotional message in people's tone of voice, though they were perfectly able to understand their words. A sarcastic "Thanks," a grateful "Thanks," and an angry "Thanks" all had the same neutral meaning for them. By contrast, a 1979 report spoke of patients with injuries in other parts of the right hemisphere who had a very different gap in their emotional perception. These patients were unable to express their own emotions through their tone of voice or by gesture. They knew what they felt, but they simply could not convey it. All these cortical brain regions, the various authors noted, had strong connections to the limbic system.

These studies were reviewed as background to a seminal paper by Leslie

Brothers, a psychiatrist at the California Institute of Technology, on the biology of empathy.[12] Reviewing both neurological findings and comparative studies with animals, Brothers points to the amygdala and its connections to the association area of the visual cortex as part of the key brain circuitry underlying empathy.

Much of the relevant neurological research is from work with animals, especially nonhuman primates. That such primates display empathy—or "emotional communication," as Brothers prefers to say—is clear not just from anecdotal accounts, but also from studies such as the following: Rhesus monkeys were trained first to fear a certain tone by hearing it while they received an electric shock. Then they learned to avoid the electric shock by pushing a lever whenever they heard the tone. Next, pairs of these monkeys were put in separate cages, their only communication being through closed-circuit TV, which allowed them to see pictures of the face of the other monkey. The first monkey, but not the second, then heard the dreaded tone sound, which brought a look of fear to its face. At that moment, the second monkey, seeing fear on the face of the first, pushed the lever that prevented the shock—an act of empathy, if not of altruism.

Having established that nonhuman primates do indeed read emotions from the faces of their peers, researchers gently inserted long, fine-tipped electrodes into the brains of monkeys. These electrodes allowed the recording of activity in a single neuron. Electrodes tapping neurons in the visual cortex and in the amygdala showed that when one monkey saw the face of another, that information led to a neuron firing first in the visual cortex, then in the amygdala. This pathway, of course, is a standard route for information that is emotionally arousing. But what is surprising about results from such studies is that they have also identified neurons in the visual cortex that seem to fire *only* in response to specific facial expressions or gestures, such as a threatening opening of the mouth, a fearful grimace, or a docile crouch. These neurons are distinct from others in the same region that recognize familiar faces. This would seem to mean that the brain is designed from the beginning to respond to specific emotional expressions—that is, empathy is a given of biology.

Another line of evidence for the key role of the amygdala-cortical pathway in reading and responding to emotions, Brothers suggests, is research in which monkeys in the wild had the connections to and from the amygdala and cortex severed. When they were released back to their troops, these monkeys were able to contend with ordinary tasks such as feeding themselves and climbing trees. But the unfortunate monkeys had lost all sense of how to respond emotionally to other monkeys in their band. Even when one made a friendly approach, they would run away, and eventually lived as isolates, shunning contact with their own troop.

The very regions of the cortex where the emotion-specific neurons concentrate are also, Brothers notes, those with the heaviest connection to the amygdala; reading emotion involves the amygdala-cortical circuitry, which has a key role in orchestrating the appropriate responses. "The survival value of such a system is obvious" for nonhuman primates, notes Brothers. "The perception of another individual's approach should give rise to a specific pattern of [physiological response]—and very quickly—tailored to whether the intent is to bite, to have a quiet grooming session, or to copulate."[13]

A similar physiological basis for empathy in us humans is suggested in research by Robert Levenson, a University of California at Berkeley psychologist who has studied married couples trying to guess what their partner is feeling during a heated discussion.[14] His method is simple: the couple is videotaped and their physiological responses measured while talking over some troubling issue in their marriage—how to discipline the kids, spending habits, and the like. Each partner reviews the tape and narrates what he or she was feeling from moment to moment. Then the partner reviews the tape a second time, now trying to read the *other's* feelings.

The most empathic accuracy occurred in those husbands and wives *whose own physiology tracked that of the spouse* they were watching. That is, when their partner had an elevated sweat response, so did they; when their partner had a drop in heart rate, their heart slowed. In short, their body mimicked the subtle, moment-to-moment physical reactions of their spouse. If the viewer's physiological patterns simply repeated their own during the original interaction, they were very poor at surmising what their partner was feeling. Only when their bodies were in synch was there empathy.

This suggests that when the emotional brain is driving the body with a strong reaction—the heat of anger, say—there can be little or no empathy. Empathy requires enough calm and receptivity so that the subtle signals of feeling from another person can be received and mimicked by one's own emotional brain.

EMPATHY AND ETHICS: THE ROOTS OF ALTRUISM

"Never send to know for whom the bell tolls; it tolls for thee" is one of the most famous lines in English literature. John Donne's sentiment speaks to the heart of the link between empathy and caring: another's pain is one's own. To feel with another is to care. In this sense, the opposite of *empathy* is *antipathy*. The empathic attitude is engaged again and again in moral judgments, for moral dilemmas involve potential victims: Should you lie to keep from hurting a friend's feelings? Should you keep a promise to visit a sick friend or accept a last-minute invitation to a dinner party instead? When should a life-support system be kept going for someone who would otherwise die?

These moral questions are posed by the empathy researcher Martin Hoffman, who argues that the roots of morality are to be found in empathy, since it is empathizing with the potential victims—someone in pain, danger, or deprivation, say—and so sharing their distress that moves people to act to help them.[15] Beyond this immediate link between empathy and altruism in personal encounters, Hoffman proposes that the same capacity for empathic affect, for putting oneself in another's place, leads people to follow certain moral principles.

Hoffman sees a natural progression in empathy from infancy onward. As we have seen, at one year of age a child feels in distress herself when she sees another fall and start to cry; her rapport is so strong and immediate that she puts her thumb in her mouth and buries her head in her mother's lap, as if she herself were hurt. After the first year, when infants become more aware that they are distinct from others, they actively try to soothe another crying infant, offering them their teddy bears, for example. As early as the age of two, children begin to realize that someone else's feelings differ from their own, and so they become more sensitive to cues revealing what another actually feels; at this point they might, for example, recognize that another child's pride might mean that the best way to help them deal with their tears is not to call undue attention to them.

By late childhood the most advanced level of empathy emerges, as children are able to understand distress beyond the immediate situation, and to see that someone's condition or station in life may be a source of chronic distress. At this point they can feel for the plight of an entire group, such as the poor, the oppressed, the outcast. That understanding, in adolescence, can buttress moral convictions centered on wanting to alleviate misfortune and injustice.

Empathy underlies many facets of moral judgment and action. One is "empathic anger," which John Stuart Mill described as "the natural feeling of retaliation ... rendered by intellect and sympathy applicable to ... those hurts which wound us through wounding others"; Mill dubbed this the "guardian of justice." Another instance in which empathy leads to moral action is when a bystander is moved to intervene on behalf of a victim; the research shows that the more empathy a bystander feels for the victim, the more likely it is that she will intervene. There is some evidence that the level of empathy people feel shades their moral judgments as well. For example, studies in Germany and the United States found that the more empathic people are, the more they favor the moral principle that resources should be allocated according to people's need.[16]

LIFE WITHOUT EMPATHY: THE MIND OF THE MOLESTER, THE MORALS OF THE SOCIOPATH

Eric Eckardt was involved in an infamous crime: the bodyguard of skater Tonya Harding, Eckardt had arranged to have thugs attack Nancy Kerrigan, Harding's archrival for the 1994 women's Olympic figure skating gold medal. In the attack, Kerrigan's knee was battered, sidelining her during crucial training months. But when Eckardt saw the image of a sobbing Kerrigan on television, he had a sudden rush of remorse, and sought out a friend to bare his secret, beginning the sequence that led to the arrest of the attackers. Such is the power of empathy.

But it is typically, and tragically, lacking in those who commit the most mean-spirited of crimes. A psychological fault line is common to rapists, child molesters, and many perpetrators of family violence alike: they are incapable of empathy. This inability to feel their victims' pain allows them to tell themselves lies that encourage their crime. For rapists, the lies include "Women really want to be raped" or "If she resists, she's just playing hard to get"; for molesters, "I'm not hurting the child, just showing love" or "This is just another form of affection"; for physically abusive parents, "This is just good discipline." These self-justifications are all collected from what people being treated for these problems say they have told themselves as they were brutalizing their victims, or preparing to do so.

The blotting out of empathy as these people inflict damage on victims is almost always part of an emotional cycle that precipitates their cruel acts. Witness the emotional sequence that typically leads to a sex crime such as child molestation.[17] The cycle begins with the molester feeling upset: angry, depressed, lonely. These sentiments might be triggered by, say, watching happy couples on TV, and then feeling depressed about being alone. The molester then seeks solace in a favored fantasy, typically about a warm friendship with a child; the fantasy becomes sexual and ends in masturbation. Afterward, the molester feels a temporary relief from the sadness, but the relief is short-lived; the depression and loneliness return even more strongly. The molester begins to think about acting out the fantasy, telling himself justifications like "I'm not doing any real harm if the child is not physically hurt" and "If a child really didn't want to have sex with me, she could stop it."

At this point the molester is seeing the child through the lens of the perverted fantasy, not with empathy for what a real child would feel in the situation. That emotional detachment characterizes everything that follows, from the ensuing plan to get a child alone, to the careful rehearsal of what will happen, and then the execution of the plan. All of it is pursued as though the child involved had no feelings of her own; instead the molester projects on her the cooperative attitude of the child in his fantasy. Her feelings—revulsion, fear, disgust—do not register. If they did, it would "ruin" things for the molester.

This utter lack of empathy for their victims is one of the main focuses of new treatments being devised for child molesters and other such offenders. In one of the most promising treatment programs, the offenders read heart-wrenching accounts of crimes like their own, told from the victim's perspective. They also watch videotapes of victims tearfully telling what it was like to be molested. The offenders then write about their own offense from the victim's point of view, imagining what the victim felt. They read this account to a therapy group, and try to answer questions about the assault from the victim's perspective. Finally, the offender goes through a simulated reenactment of the crime, this time playing the role of the victim.

William Pithers, the Vermont prison psychologist who developed this perspective-taking therapy, told me, "Empathy with the victim shifts perception so that the denial of pain, even in one's fantasies, is difficult" and so strengthens the men's motivation to fight their perverse sexual urges. Sex offenders who have been through the program in prison had only half the rate of subsequent offenses after release compared to those who had no such treatment. Without this initial empathy-inspired motivation, none of the rest of treatment will work.

While there may be some small hope for instilling a sense of empathy in offenders such as child molesters, there is much less for another criminal type, the psychopath (more recently called the *sociopath* as a psychiatric diagnosis). Psychopaths are notorious for being both charming and completely without remorse for even the most cruel and heartless acts. Psychopathy, the incapacity to feel empathy or compassion of any sort, or the least twinge of conscience, is one of the more perplexing of emotional defects. The heart of the psychopath's coldness seems to lie in an inability to make anything more than the shallowest of emotional connections. The cruelest of criminals, such as sadistic serial killers who delight in the suffering of their victims before they die, are the epitome of psychopathy.[18]

Psychopaths are also glib liars, willing to say anything to get what they want, and they manipulate their victims' emotions with the same cynicism. Consider the performance of Faro, a seventeen-year-old member of a Los Angeles gang who crippled a mother and her baby in a drive-by shooting, which he described with more pride than remorse. Driving in a car with Leon Bing, who was writing a book about the Los Angeles gangs the Crips and the Bloods, Faro wants to show off. Faro tells Bing he's "gonna look crazy" at the "two dudes" in the next car. As Bing recounts the exchange:

> The driver, sensing that someone is looking at him, glances over at my car. His eyes connect with Faro's, widen for an instant. Then he breaks the contact, looks down, looks away. And there is no mistaking what I saw there in his eyes: It was fear.

Faro demonstrates the look he flashed at the next car for Bing:

> He looks straight at me and everything about his face shifts and changes, as if by some trick of time-lapse photography. It becomes a nightmare face, and it is a scary thing to see. It tells you that if you return his stare, if you challenge this kid, you'd better be able to stand your ground. His look tells you that he doesn't care about anything, not your life and not his.[19]

Of course, in behavior as complex as crime, there are many plausible explanations that do not evoke a biological basis. One might be that a perverse kind of emotional skill—intimidating other people—has survival value in violent neighborhoods, as might turning to crime; in these cases too much empathy might be counterproductive. Indeed, an opportunistic lack of empathy may be a "virtue" in many roles in life, from "bad cop" police interrogator to corporate raider. Men who have been torturers for terrorist states, for example, describe how they learned to dissociate from the feelings of their victims in order to do their "job." There are many routes to manipulativeness.

One of the more ominous ways this absence of empathy may display itself was discovered by accident in a study of the most vicious of wife batterers. The research revealed a physiological anomaly among many of the most violent husbands, who regularly beat up their wives or threaten them with knives or guns: the husbands do so in a cold, calculating state rather than while being carried away by the heat of fury.[20] As their anger mounts, the anomaly emerges: their heart rate *drops,* instead of climbing higher, as is ordinarily the case with mounting fury. This means they are growing physiologically calmer, even as they get more belligerent and abusive. Their violence appears to be a calculated act of terrorism, a method for controlling their wives by instilling fear.

These coolly brutal husbands are a breed apart from most other men who batter their wives. For one, they are far more likely to be violent outside the marriage as well, getting into bar fights and battling with coworkers and other family members. And while most men who become violent with their wives do so impulsively, out of rage after feeling rejected or jealous, or out of fear of abandonment, these calculating batterers will strike out at their wives seemingly for no reason at all—and once they start, nothing she does, including trying to leave, seems to restrain their violence.

Some researchers who study criminal psychopaths suspect their cold manipulativeness, such absence of empathy or caring, can sometimes stem from a neural defect.* A possible physiological basis of heartless psychopathy has been shown in two ways, both of which suggest the involvement of neural pathways to the limbic brain. In one, people's brain waves are measured as they try to decipher words that have been scrambled. The words are flashed very quickly, for just a tenth of a second or so. Most people react differently to emotional words such as *kill* than to neutral words such as *chair:* they can decide more quickly if the emotional word was scrambled, and their brains show a distinctive wave pattern in response to the emotional words, but not the neutral ones. But psychopaths have neither of these responses: their brains do not show the distinctive pattern in response to the emotional words, and they do not respond more quickly to them, suggesting a disruption in circuits between the verbal cortex, which recognizes the word, and the limbic brain, which attaches feeling to it.

---

* A note of caution: If there are biological patterns at play in some kinds of criminality— such as a neural defect in empathy—that does not argue that all criminals are biologically flawed, or that there is some biological marker for crime. A controversy has raged on this issue, and the best consensus is that there is no such biological marker, and certainly no "criminal gene." Even if there is a biological basis for a lack of empathy in some cases, that does not mean all who have it will drift to crime; most will not. A lack of empathy should be factored in with all the other psychological, economic, and social forces that contribute to a vector toward criminality.

Robert Hare, the University of British Columbia psychologist who has done this research, interprets these results as meaning that psychopaths have a shallow understanding of emotional words, a reflection of their more general shallowness in the affective realm. The callousness of psychopaths, Hare believes, is based in part on another physiological pattern he discovered in earlier research, one that also suggests an irregularity in the workings of the amygdala and related circuits: psychopaths about to receive an electrical shock show no sign of the fear response that is normal in people about to experience pain.[21] Because the prospect of pain does not trigger a surge of anxiety, Hare contends that psychopaths lack concern about future punishment for what they do. And because they themselves do not feel fear, they have no empathy—or compassion—for the fear and pain of their victims.

8

The Social Arts

As so often happens to five-year-olds with younger siblings, Len has lost all patience with Jay, his two-and-a-half-year-old brother, who is making a mess of the Lego blocks they've been playing with. Carried away by a wave of rage, Len bites Jay, who breaks into tears. Their mother, hearing Jay's pained yelp, bustles over and scolds Len, ordering him to put away those objects of contention, the Lego blocks. At this—what surely must seem a gross miscarriage of justice—Len bursts out crying. Still peeved, his mother refuses to console him.

But Len is proffered comfort from an unlikely source: Jay, who, although the original injured party, is now so concerned by his older brother's tears that he undertakes a campaign to calm Len down. The exchange goes something like this:[1]

"Len, don't," Jay implores. "Stop crying, mate. Stop it crying."

But Len still cries. His direct plea a failure, Jay beseeches their mother on Len's behalf: "Len crying, Mummy! Len crying. Look. Me show you. Len crying."

And then, turning to Len, Jay adopts a mothering mode, patting his weeping brother as he reassures him in soothing tones, "Look, Len. No go on crying."

Len's sobs continue, despite the comforting. So Jay turns to another tactic, lending a helping hand in putting away the Lego blocks in their bag, with a friendly, "Ah, Len. I put it back for Lennie, hey?"

Even so, the tears continue. The ever-ingenious Jay tries yet another strategy, distraction. Showing his brother a toy car, Jay tries to draw his attention away from the minor tragedy that has just befallen him. "There's this man in here. What's this, Len? What's this, Len?"

Len takes no interest. He's inconsolable; his tears know no end. Losing her patience with him, his mother resorts to that classic parental threat, "Do you want me to smack you?" to which Len responds with a wavering, "No."

"Then just stop it, please," says his mother firmly, if a bit exasperatedly.

Through his sobs, Len manages a pathetic, gasping, "I'm trying to."

Which prompts Jay's final stratagem: borrowing his mother's firmness and voice of authority, he threatens, "Stop crying, Len. Smack your bottom!"

This microdrama reveals the remarkable emotional sophistication that a toddler of just thirty months can bring to bear in trying to manage someone else's emotions. In his urgent attempts to soothe his brother, Jay is able to draw on a large repertoire of tactics, ranging from a simple plea, to seeking an ally in his mother (no help, she), to physically comforting him, to lending a helping hand, to distraction, threats, and direct commands. No doubt Jay relies on an arsenal that has been tried with him in his own moments of distress. No matter. What counts is that he can readily put them to use in a pinch even at this very young age.

Of course, as every parent of young children knows, Jay's display of empathy and soothing is by no means universal. It is perhaps as likely that a child his age will see a sibling's upset as a chance for vengeance, and so do whatever it takes to make the upset even worse. The same skills can be used to tease or torment a sibling. But even that mean-spiritedness bespeaks the emergence of a crucial emotional aptitude: the ability to know another's feelings and to act in a way that further shapes those feelings. Being able to manage emotions in someone else is the core of the art of handling relationships.

To manifest such interpersonal power, toddlers must first reach a benchmark of self-control, the beginnings of the capacity to damp down their own anger and distress, their impulses and excitement—even if that ability usually falters. Attunement to others demands a modicum of calm in oneself. Tentative signs of this ability to manage their own emotions emerge around this same period: toddlers begin to be able to wait without wailing, to argue or cajole to get their way rather than using brute force—even if they don't always choose to use this ability. Patience emerges as an alternative to tantrums, at least occasionally. And signs of empathy emerge by age two; it was Jay's empathy, the root of compassion, that drove him to try so hard to cheer up his sobbing brother, Len. Thus handling emotions in someone else—the fine art of relationships—requires the ripeness of two other emotional skills, self-management and empathy.

With this base, the "people skills" ripen. These are the social competences that make for effectiveness in dealings with others; deficits here lead to ineptness in the social world or repeated interpersonal disasters. Indeed, it is precisely the lack of these skills that can cause even the intellectually brightest to founder in their relationships, coming off as arrogant, obnoxious, or insensitive. These social abilities allow one to shape an encounter, to mobilize and inspire others, to thrive in intimate relationships, to persuade and influence, to put others at ease.

SHOW SOME EMOTION

One key social competence is how well or poorly people express their own feelings. Paul Ekman uses the term *display rules* for the social consensus about which feelings can be properly shown when. Cultures sometimes vary tremendously in this regard. For example, Ekman and colleagues in Japan studied the facial reactions of students to a horrific film about ritual circumcisions of teenage Aborigines. When the Japanese students watched the film with an authority figure present, their faces showed only the slightest hints of reaction. But when they thought they were alone (though they were being taped by a secret camera) their faces twisted into vivid mixes of anguished distress, dread, and disgust.

There are several basic kinds of display rules.[2] One is *minimizing* the show of emotion—this is the Japanese norm for feelings of distress in the presence of someone in authority, which the students were following when they masked their upset with a poker face. Another is *exaggerating* what one feels by magnifying the emotional expression; this is the ploy used by the six-year-old who dramatically twists her face into a pathetic frown, lips quivering, as she runs to complain to her mother about being teased by her older brother. A third is *substituting* one feeling for another; this comes into play in some Asian cultures where it is impolite to say no, and positive (but false) assurances are given instead. How well one employs these strategies, and knows when to do so, is one factor in emotional intelligence.

We learn these display rules very early, partly by explicit instruction. An education in display rules is imparted when we instruct a child not to seem disappointed, but to smile and say thank you instead, when Grandpa has given a dreadful but well-meant birthday present. This education in display rules, though, is more often through modeling: children learn to do what they see done. In educating the sentiments, emotions are both the medium and the message. If a child is told to "smile and say thank you" by a parent who is, at that moment, harsh, demanding, and cold—who hisses the message instead of warmly whispering it—the child is more likely to learn a very different lesson, and in fact respond to Grandpa with a frown and a curt, flat "Thank you." The effect on Grandpa is very different: in the first case he's happy (though misled); in the second he's hurt by the mixed message.

Emotional displays, of course, have immediate consequences in the impact they make on the person who receives them. The rule being learned by the child is something like, "Mask your real feelings when they will hurt someone you love; substitute a phony, but less hurtful feeling instead." Such rules for expressing emotions are more than part of the lexicon of social propriety; they dictate how our own feelings impact on everyone else. To follow these rules well is to have optimal impact; to do so poorly is to foment emotional havoc.

Actors, of course, are artists of the emotional display; their expressiveness is what evokes response in their audience. And, no doubt, some of us come into life as natural actors. But partly because the lessons we learn about display rules vary according to the models we've had, people differ greatly in their adeptness.

EXPRESSIVENESS AND EMOTIONAL CONTAGION

It was early in the Vietnam War, and an American platoon was hunkered down in some rice paddies, in the heat of a firefight with the Vietcong. Suddenly a line of six monks started walking along the elevated berms that separated paddy from paddy. Perfectly calm and poised, the monks walked directly toward the line of fire.

"They didn't look right, they didn't look left. They walked straight through," recalls David Busch, one of the American soldiers. "It was really strange, because nobody shot at 'em. And after they walked over the berm, suddenly all the fight was out of me. It just didn't feel like I wanted to do this anymore, at least not that day. It must have been that way for everybody, because everybody quit. We just stopped fighting."[3]

The power of the monks' quietly courageous calm to pacify soldiers in the heat of battle illustrates a basic principle of social life: Emotions are contagious. To be sure, this tale marks an extreme. Most emotional contagion is far more subtle, part of a tacit exchange that happens in every encounter. We transmit and catch moods from each other in what amounts to a subterranean economy of the psyche in which some encounters are toxic, some nourishing. This emotional exchange is typically at a subtle, almost imperceptible level; the way a salesperson says thank you can leave us feeling ignored, resented, or genuinely welcomed and appreciated. We catch feelings from one another as though they were some kind of social virus.

We send emotional signals in every encounter, and those signals affect those we are with. The more adroit we are socially, the better we control the signals we send; the reserve of polite society is, after all, simply a means to ensure that no disturbing emotional leakage will unsettle the encounter (a social rule that, when brought into the domain of intimate relationships, is stifling). Emotional intelligence includes managing this exchange; "popular" and "charming" are terms we use for people whom we like to be with because their emotional skills make us feel good. People who are able to help others soothe their feelings have an especially valued social commodity; they are the souls others turn to when in greatest emotional need. We are all part of each other's tool kit for emotional change, for better or for worse.

Consider a remarkable demonstration of the subtlety with which emotions pass from one person to another. In a simple experiment two volunteers filled out a checklist about their moods at the moment, then simply sat facing each other quietly while waiting for an experimenter to return to the room. Two minutes later she came back and asked them to fill out a mood checklist again. The pairs were purposely composed of one partner who was highly expressive of emotion and one who was deadpan. Invariably the mood of the one who was more expressive of emotions had been transferred to the more passive partner.[4]

How does this magical transmission occur? The most likely answer is that we unconsciously imitate the emotions we see displayed by someone else, through an out-of-awareness motor mimicry of their facial expression, gestures, tone of voice, and other nonverbal markers of emotion. Through this imitation people re-create in themselves the mood of the other person—a low-key version of the Stanislavsky method, in which actors recall gestures, movements, and other expressions of an emotion they have felt strongly in the past in order to evoke those feelings once again.

The day-to-day imitation of feeling is ordinarily quite subtle. Ulf Dimberg, a Swedish researcher at the University of Uppsala, found that when people view a smiling or angry face, their own faces show evidence of that same mood through slight changes in the facial muscles. The changes are evident through electronic sensors but are typically not visible to the naked eye.

When two people interact, the direction of mood transfer is from the one who is more forceful in expressing feelings to the one who is more passive. But some people are particularly susceptible to emotional contagion; their . innate sensitivity makes their autonomic nervous system (a marker of emotional activity) more easily triggered. This lability seems to make them more impressionable; sentimental commercials can move them to tears, while a quick chat with someone who is feeling cheerful can buoy them (it also may make them more empathic, since they are more readily moved by someone else's feelings).

John Cacioppo, the social psychophysiologist at Ohio State University who has studied this subtle emotional exchange, observes, "Just seeing someone express an emotion can evoke that mood, whether you realize you mimic the facial expression or not. This happens to us all the time—there's a dance, a synchrony, a transmission of emotions. This mood synchrony determines whether you feel an interaction went well or not."

The degree of emotional rapport people feel in an encounter is mirrored by how tightly orchestrated their physical movements are as they talk—an index of closeness that is typically out of awareness. One person nods just as the other makes a point, or both shift in their chairs at the same moment, or one leans forward as the other moves back. The orchestration can be as subtle as both people rocking in swivel chairs at the same rhythm. Just as Daniel Stern found in watching the synchrony between attuned mothers and their infants, the same reciprocity links the movements of people who feel emotional rapport.

This synchrony seems to facilitate the sending and receiving of moods, even if the moods are negative. For example, in one study of physical synchrony, women who were depressed came to a laboratory with their romantic partners, and discussed a problem in their relationship. The more synchrony between the partners at the nonverbal level, the worse the depressed women's partners felt after the discussion—they had caught their girlfriends' bad moods.[5] In short, whether people feel upbeat or down, the more physically attuned their encounter, the more similar their moods will become.

The synchrony between teachers and students indicates how much rapport they feel; studies in classrooms show that the closer the movement coordination between teacher and student, the more they felt friendly, happy, enthused, interested, and easygoing while interacting. In general, a high level of synchrony in an interaction means the people involved like each other. Frank Bernieri, the Oregon State University psychologist who did these studies, told me, "How awkward or comfortable you feel with someone is at some level physical. You need to have compatible timing, to coordinate your movements, to feel comfortable. Synchrony reflects the depth of engagement between the partners; if you're highly engaged, your moods begin to mesh, whether positive or negative."

In short, coordination of moods is the essence of rapport, the adult version of the attunement a mother has with her infant. One determinant of interpersonal effectiveness, Cacioppo proposes, is how deftly people carry out this emotional synchrony. If they are adept at attuning to people's moods, or can easily bring others under the sway of their own, then their interactions will go more smoothly at the emotional level. The mark of a powerful leader or performer is being able to move an audience of thousands in this way. By the same token, Cacioppo points out that people who are poor at receiving and sending emotions are prone to problems in their relationships, since people often feel uncomfortable with them, even if they can't articulate just why this is so.

Setting the emotional tone of an interaction is, in a sense, a sign of dominance at a deep and intimate level: it means driving the emotional state of the other person. This power to determine emotion is akin to what is called in biology a *zeitgeber* (literally, "time-grabber"), a process (such as the day-night cycle or the monthly phases of the moon) that entrains biological rhythms. For a couple dancing, the music is a bodily zeitgeber. When it comes to personal encounters, the person who has the more forceful expressivity—or the most power—is typically the one whose emotions entrain the other. Dominant partners talk more, while the subordinate partner watches the other's face more—a setup for the transmission of affect. By the same token, the forcefulness of a good speaker—a politician or an evangelist, say—works to entrain the emotions of the audience.[6] That is what we mean by, "He had them in the palm of his hand." Emotional entrainment is the heart of influence.

THE RUDIMENTS OF SOCIAL INTELLIGENCE

It's recess at a preschool, and a band of boys is running across the grass. Reggie trips, hurts his knee, and starts crying, but the other boys keep right on running—save for Roger, who stops. As Reggie's sobs subside Roger reaches down and rubs his own knee, calling out, "I hurt my knee, too!"

Roger is cited as having exemplary interpersonal intelligence by Thomas Hatch, a colleague of Howard Gardner at Spectrum, the school based on the concept of multiple intelligences.[7] Roger, it seems, is unusually adept at recognizing the feelings of his playmates and making rapid, smooth connections with them. It was only Roger who noticed Reggie's plight and pain, and only Roger who tried to provide some solace, even if all he could offer was rubbing his own knee. This small gesture bespeaks a talent for rapport, an emotional skill essential for the preservation of close relationships, whether in a marriage, a friendship, or a business partnership. Such skills in preschoolers are the buds of talents that ripen through life.

Roger's talent represents one of four separate abilities that Hatch and Gardner identify as components of interpersonal intelligence:

• *Organizing groups*—the essential skill of the leader, this involves initiating and coordinating the efforts of a network of people. This is the talent seen in theater directors or producers, in military officers, and in effective heads of organizations and units of all kinds. On the playground, this is the child who takes the lead in deciding what everyone will play, or becomes team captain.

• *Negotiating solutions*—the talent of the mediator, preventing conflicts or resolving those that flare up. People who have this ability excel in deal-making, in arbitrating or mediating disputes; they might have a career in diplomacy, in arbitration or law, or as middlemen or managers of takeovers. These are the kids who settle arguments on the playing field.

• *Personal connection*—Roger's talent, that of empathy and connecting. This makes it easy to enter into an encounter or to recognize and respond fittingly to people's feelings and concerns—the art of relationship. Such people make good "team players," dependable spouses, good friends or business partners; in the business world they do well as salespeople or managers, or can be excellent teachers. Children like Roger get along well with virtually everyone else, easily enter into playing with them, and are happy doing so. These children tend to be best at reading emotions from facial expressions and are most liked by their classmates.

• *Social analysis*—being able to detect and have insights about people's feelings, motives, and concerns. This knowledge of how others feel can lead to an easy intimacy or sense of rapport. At its best, this ability makes one a competent therapist or counselor—or, if combined with some literary talent, a gifted novelist or dramatist.

Taken together, these skills are the stuff of interpersonal polish, the necessary ingredients for charm, social success, even charisma. Those who are adept in social intelligence can connect with people quite smoothly, be astute in reading their reactions and feelings, lead and organize, and handle the disputes that are bound to flare up in any human activity. They are the natural leaders, the people who can express the unspoken collective sentiment and articulate it so as to guide a group toward its goals. They are the kind of people others like to be with because they are emotionally nourishing—they leave other people in a good mood, and evoke the comment, "What a pleasure to be around someone like that."

These interpersonal abilities build on other emotional intelligences. People who make an excellent social impression, for example, are adept at monitoring their own expression of emotion, are keenly attuned to the ways others are reacting, and so are able to continually fine-tune their social performance, adjusting it to make sure they are having the desired effect. In that sense, they are like skilled actors.

However, if these interpersonal abilities are not balanced by an astute sense of one's own needs and feelings and how to fulfill them, they can lead to a hollow social success—a popularity won at the cost of one's true satisfaction. Such is the argument of Mark Snyder, a University of Minnesota psychologist who has studied people whose social skills make them first-rate social chameleons, champions at making a good impression.[8] Their psychological credo might well be a remark by W. H. Auden, who said that his private image of himself "is very different from the image which I try to create in the minds of others in order that they may love me." That trade-off can be made if social skills outstrip the ability to know and honor one's own feelings: in order to be loved—or at least liked—the social chameleon will seem to be whatever those he is with seem to want. The sign that someone falls into this pattern, Snyder finds, is that they make an excellent impression, yet have few stable or satisfying intimate relationships. A more healthy pattern, of course, is to balance being true to oneself with social skills, using them with integrity.

Social chameleons, though, don't mind in the least saying one thing and doing another, if that will win them social approval. They simply live with the discrepancy between their public face and their private reality. Helena Deutsch, a psychoanalyst, called such people the "as-if personality," shifting personas with remarkable plasticity as they pick up signals from those around them. "For some people," Snyder told me, "the public and private person meshes well, while for others there seems to be only a kaleidoscope of changing appearances. They are like Woody Allen's character Zelig, madly trying to fit in with whomever they are with."

Such people try to scan someone for a hint as to what is wanted from them before they make a response, rather than simply saying what they truly feel. To get along and be liked, they are willing to make people they dislike think they are friendly with them. And they use their social abilities to mold their actions as disparate social situations demand, so that they may act like very different people depending on whom they are with, swinging from bubbly sociability, say, to reserved withdrawal. To be sure, to the extent that these traits lead to effective impression management, they are highly prized in certain professions, notably acting, trial law, sales, diplomacy, and politics.

Another, perhaps more crucial kind of self-monitoring seems to make the difference between those who end up as anchorless social chameleons, trying to impress everyone, and those who can use their social polish more in keeping with their true feelings. That is the capacity to be true, as the saying has it, "to thine own self," which allows acting in accord with one's deepest feelings and values no matter what the social consequences. Such emotional integrity could well lead to, say, deliberately provoking a confrontation in order to cut through duplicity or denial—a clearing of the air that a social chameleon would never attempt.

THE MAKING OF A SOCIAL INCOMPETENT

There was no doubt Cecil was bright; he was a college-trained expert in foreign languages, superb at translating. But there were crucial ways in which he was completely inept. Cecil seemed to lack the simplest social skills. He would muff a casual conversation over coffee, and fumble when having to pass the time of day; in short, he seemed incapable of the most routine social exchange. Because his lack of social grace was most profound when he was around women, Cecil came to therapy wondering if perhaps he had "homosexual tendencies of an underlying nature," as he put it, though he had no such fantasies.

The real problem, Cecil confided to his therapist, was that he feared that nothing he could say would be of any interest to anybody. This underlying fear only compounded a profound paucity of social graces. His nervousness during encounters led him to snicker and laugh at the most awkward moments, even though he failed to laugh when someone said something genuinely funny. Cecil's awkwardness, he confided to his therapist, went back to childhood; all his life he had felt socially at ease only when he was with his older brother, who somehow helped ease things for him. But once he left home, his ineptitude was overwhelming; he was socially paralyzed.

The tale is told by Lakin Phillips, a psychologist at George Washington University, who proposes that Cecil's plight stems from a failure to learn in childhood the most elementary lessons of social interaction:

> What could Cecil have been taught earlier? To speak directly to others when spoken to; to initiate social contact, not always wait for others; to carry on a conversation, not simply fall back on yes or no or other one-word replies; to express gratitude toward others, to let another person walk before one in passing through a door; to wait until one is served something . . . to thank others, to say "please," to share, and all the other elementary interactions we begin to teach children from age 2 onward.[9]

Whether Cecil's deficiency was due to another's failure to teach him such rudiments of social civility or to his own inability to learn is unclear. But whatever its roots, Cecil's story is instructive because it points up the crucial nature of the countless lessons children get in interaction synchrony and the unspoken rules of social harmony. The net effect of failing to follow these rules is to create waves, to make those around us uncomfortable. The function of these rules, of course, is to keep everyone involved in a social exchange at ease; awkwardness spawns anxiety. People who lack these skills are inept not just at social niceties, but at handling the emotions of those they encounter; they inevitably leave disturbance in their wake.

We all have known Cecils, people with an annoying lack of social graces—people who don't seem to know when to end a conversation or phone call and who keep on talking, oblivious to all cues and hints to say good-bye; people whose conversation centers on themselves all the time, without the least interest in anyone else, and who ignore tentative attempts to refocus on another topic; people who intrude or ask "nosy" questions. These derailments of a smooth social trajectory all bespeak a deficit in the rudimentary building blocks of interaction.

Psychologists have coined the term *dyssemia* (from the Greek *dys-* for "difficulty" and *semes* for "signal") for what amounts to a learning disability in the realm of nonverbal messages; about one in ten children has one or more problems in this realm.[10] The problem can be in a poor sense of personal space, so that a child stands too close while talking or spreads their belongings into other people's territory; in interpreting or using body language poorly; in misinterpreting or misusing facial expressions by, say, failing to make eye contact; or in a poor sense of prosody, the emotional quality of speech, so that they talk too shrilly or flatly.

Much research has focused on spotting children who show signs of social deficiency, children whose awkwardness makes them neglected or rejected by their playmates. Apart from children who are spurned because they are bullies, those whom other children avoid are invariably deficient in the rudiments of face-to-face interaction, particularly the unspoken rules that govern encounters. If children do poorly in language, people assume they are not very bright or poorly educated; but when they do poorly in the nonverbal rules of interaction, people—especially playmates—see them as "strange," and avoid them. These are the children who don't know how to join a game gracefully, who touch others in ways that make for discomfort rather than camaraderie—in short, who are "off." They are children who have failed to master the silent language of emotion, and who unwittingly send messages that create uneasiness.

As Stephen Nowicki, an Emory University psychologist who studies children's nonverbal abilities, put it, "Children who can't read or express emotions well constantly feel frustrated. In essence, they don't understand what's going on. This kind of communication is a constant subtext of everything you do; you can't stop showing your facial expression or posture, or hide your tone of voice. If you make mistakes in what emotional messages you send, you constantly experience that people react to you in funny ways—you get rebuffed and don't know why. If you're thinking you're acting happy but actually seem too hyper or angry, you find other kids getting angry at you in turn, and you don't realize why. Such kids end up feeling no sense of control over how other people treat them, that their actions have no impact on what happens to them. It leaves them feeling powerless, depressed, and apathetic."

Apart from becoming social isolates, such children also suffer academically. The classroom, of course, is as much a social situation as an academic one; the socially awkward child is as likely to misread and misrespond to a teacher as to another child. The resulting anxiety and bewilderment can themselves interfere with their ability to learn effectively. Indeed, as tests of children's nonverbal sensitivity have shown, those who misread emotional cues tend to do poorly in school compared to their academic potential as reflected in IQ tests.[11]

"WE HATE YOU": AT THE THRESHOLD

Social ineptitude is perhaps most painful and explicit when it comes to one of the more perilous moments in the life of a young child: being on the edge of a group at play you want to join. It is a moment of peril, one when being liked or hated, belonging or not, is made all too public. For that reason that crucial moment has been the subject of intense scrutiny by students of child development, revealing a stark contrast in approach strategies used by popular children and by social outcasts. The findings highlight just how crucial it is for social competence to notice, interpret, and respond to emotional and interpersonal cues. While it is poignant to see a child hover on the edge of others at play, wanting to join in but being left out, it is a universal predicament. Even the most popular children are sometimes rejected—a study of second and third graders found that 26 percent of the time the most well liked children were rebuffed when they tried to enter a group already at play.

Young children are brutally candid about the emotional judgment implicit in such rejections. Witness the following dialogue from four-year-olds in a preschool.[12] Linda wants to join Barbara, Nancy, and Bill, who are playing with toy animals and building blocks. She watches for a minute, then makes her approach, sitting next to Barbara and starting to play with the animals. Barbara turns to her and says, "You can't play!"

"Yes, I can," Linda counters. "I can have some animals, too."

"No, you can't," Barbara says bluntly. "We don't like you today."

When Bill protests on Linda's behalf, Nancy joins the attack: "We hate her today."

Because of the danger of being told, either explicitly or implicitly, "We hate you," all children are understandably cautious on the threshold of approaching a group. That anxiety, of course, is probably not much different from that felt by a grown-up at a cocktail party with strangers who hangs back from a happily chatting group who seem to be intimate friends. Because this moment at the threshold of a group is so momentous for a child, it is also, as one researcher put it, "highly diagnostic . . . quickly revealing differences in social skillfulness."[13]

Typically, newcomers simply watch for a time, then join in very tentatively at first, being more assertive only in very cautious steps. What matters most for whether a child is accepted or not is how well he or she is able to enter into the group's frame of reference, sensing what kind of play is in flow, what out of place.

The two cardinal sins that almost always lead to rejection are trying to take the lead too soon and being out of synch with the frame of reference. But this is exactly what unpopular children tend to do: they push their way into a group, trying to change the subject too abruptly or too soon, or offering their own opinions, or simply disagreeing with the others right away—all apparent attempts to draw attention to themselves. Paradoxically, this results in their being ignored or rejected. By contrast, popular children spend time observing the group to understand what's going on before entering in, and then do something that shows they accept it; they wait to have their status in the group confirmed before taking initiative in suggesting what the group should do.

Let's return to Roger, the four-year-old whom Thomas Hatch spotted exhibiting a high level of interpersonal intelligence.[14] Roger's tactic for entering a group was first to observe, then to imitate what another child was doing, and finally to talk to the child and fully join the activity—a winning strategy. Roger's skill was shown, for instance, when he and Warren were playing at putting "bombs" (actually pebbles) in their socks. Warren asks Roger if he wants to be in a helicopter or an airplane. Roger asks, before committing himself, "Are you in a helicopter?"

This seemingly innocuous moment reveals sensitivity to others' concerns, and the ability to act on that knowledge in a way that maintains the connection. Hatch comments about Roger, "He 'checks in' with his playmate so that they and their play remain connected. I have watched many other children who simply get in their own helicopters or planes and, literally and figuratively, fly away from each other."

EMOTIONAL BRILLIANCE: A CASE REPORT

If the test of social skill is the ability to calm distressing emotions in others, then handling someone at the peak of rage is perhaps the ultimate measure of mastery. The data on self-regulation of anger and emotional contagion suggest that one effective strategy might be to distract the angry person, empathize with his feelings and perspective, and then draw him into an alternative focus, one that attunes him with a more positive range of feeling—a kind of emotional judo.

Such refined skill in the fine art of emotional influence is perhaps best exemplified by a story told by an old friend, the late Terry Dobson, who in the 1950s was one of the first Americans ever to study the martial art aikido in Japan. One afternoon he was riding home on a suburban Tokyo train when a huge, bellicose, and very drunk and begrimed laborer got on. The man, staggering, began terrorizing the passengers: screaming curses, he took a swing at a woman holding a baby, sending her sprawling in the laps of an elderly couple, who then jumped up and joined a stampede to the other end of the car. The drunk, taking a few other swings (and, in his rage, missing), grabbed the metal pole in the middle of the car with a roar and tried to tear it out of its socket.

At that point Terry, who was in peak physical condition from daily eight-hour aikido workouts, felt called upon to intervene, lest someone get seriously hurt. But he recalled the words of his teacher: "Aikido is the art of reconciliation. Whoever has the mind to fight has broken his connection with the universe. If you try to dominate people you are already defeated. We study how to resolve conflict, not how to start it."

Indeed, Terry had agreed upon beginning lessons with his teacher never to pick a fight, and to use his martial-arts skills only in defense. Now, at last, he saw his chance to test his aikido abilities in real life, in what was clearly a legitimate opportunity. So, as all the other passengers sat frozen in their seats, Terry stood up, slowly and with deliberation.

Seeing him, the drunk roared, "Aha! A foreigner! You need a lesson in Japanese manners!" and began gathering himself to take on Terry.

But just as the drunk was on the verge of making his move, someone gave an earsplitting, oddly joyous shout: "Hey!"

The shout had the cheery tone of someone who has suddenly come upon a fond friend. The drunk, surprised, spun around to see a tiny Japanese man, probably in his seventies, sitting there in a kimono. The old man beamed with delight at the drunk, and beckoned him over with a light wave of his hand and a lilting "C'mere."

The drunk strode over with a belligerent, "Why the hell should I talk to you?" Meanwhile, Terry was ready to fell the drunk in a moment if he made the least violent move.

"What'cha been drinking?" the old man asked, his eyes beaming at the drunken laborer.

"I been drinking sake, and it's none of your business," the drunk bellowed.

"Oh, that's wonderful, absolutely wonderful," the old man replied in a warm tone. "You see, I love sake, too. Every night, me and my wife (she's seventy-six, you know), we warm up a little bottle of sake and take it out into the garden, and we sit on an old wooden bench . . ." He continued on about the persimmon tree in his backyard, the fortunes of his garden, enjoying sake in the evening.

The drunk's face began to soften as he listened to the old man; his fists unclenched. "Yeah . . . I love persimmons, too . . . ," he said, his voice trailing off.

"Yes," the old man replied in a sprightly voice, "and I'm sure you have a wonderful wife."

"No," said the laborer. "My wife died. . . ." Sobbing, he launched into a sad tale of losing his wife, his home, his job, of being ashamed of himself.

Just then the train came to Terry's stop, and as he was getting off he turned to hear the old man invite the drunk to join him and tell him all about it, and to see the drunk sprawl along the seat, his head in the old man's lap.

That is emotional brilliance.

PART THREE

EMOTIONAL INTELLIGENCE APPLIED

9

Intimate Enemies

To love and to work, Sigmund Freud once remarked to his disciple Erik Erikson, are the twin capacities that mark full maturity. If that is the case, then maturity may be an endangered way station in life—and current trends in marriage and divorce make emotional intelligence more crucial than ever.

Consider divorce rates. The rate *per year* of divorces has more or less leveled off. But there is another way of calculating divorce rates, one that suggests a perilous climb: looking at the odds that a given newly married couple will have their marriage *eventually* end in divorce. Although the overall rate of divorce has stopped climbing, the *risk* of divorce has been shifting to newlyweds.

The shift gets clearer in comparing divorce rates for couples wed in a given year. For American marriages that began in 1890, about 10 percent ended in divorce. For those wed in 1920, the rate was about 18 percent; for couples married in 1950, 30 percent. Couples that were newly wed in 1970 had a fifty-fifty chance of splitting up or staying together. And for married couples starting out in 1990, the likelihood that the marriage would end in divorce was projected to be close to a staggering 67 percent![1] If the estimate holds, just three in ten of recent newlyweds can count on staying married to their new partner.

It can be argued that much of this rise is due not so much to a decline in emotional intelligence as to the steady erosion of social pressures—the stigma surrounding divorce, or the economic dependence of wives on their husbands—that used to keep couples together in even the most miserable of matches. But if social pressures are no longer the glue that holds a marriage together, then the emotional forces between wife and husband are that much more crucial if their union is to survive.

These ties between husband and wife—and the emotional fault lines that can break them apart—have been assayed in recent years with a precision never seen before. Perhaps the biggest breakthrough in understanding what holds a marriage together or tears it apart has come from the use of sophisticated physiological measures that allow the moment-to-moment tracking of the emotional nuances of a couple's encounter. Scientists are now able to detect a husband's otherwise invisible adrenaline surges and jumps in blood pressure, and to observe fleeting but telling microemotions as they flit across a wife's face. These physiological measures reveal a hidden biological subtext to a couple's difficulties, a critical level of emotional reality that is typically imperceptible to or disregarded by the couple themselves. These measures lay bare the emotional forces that hold a relationship together or destroy it. The fault lines have their earliest beginnings in the differences between the emotional worlds of girls and boys.

HIS MARRIAGE AND HERS: CHILDHOOD ROOTS

As I was entering a restaurant on a recent evening, a young man stalked out the door, his face set in an expression both stony and sullen. Close on his heels a young woman came running, her fists desperately pummeling his back while she yelled, "Goddamn you! Come back here and be nice to me!" That poignant, impossibly self-contradictory plea aimed at a retreating back epitomizes the pattern most commonly seen in couples whose relationship is distressed: She seeks to engage, he withdraws. Marital therapists have long noted that by the time a couple finds their way to the therapy office they are in this pattern of engage-withdraw, with his complaint about her "unreasonable" demands and outbursts, and her lamenting his indifference to what she is saying.

This marital endgame reflects the fact that there are, in effect, two emotional realities in a couple, his and hers. The roots of these emotional differences, while they may be partly biological, also can be traced back to childhood, and to the separate emotional worlds boys and girls inhabit while growing up. There is a vast amount of research on these separate worlds, their barriers reinforced not just by the different games boys and girls prefer, but by young children's fear of being teased for having a "girlfriend" or "boyfriend."[2] One study of children's friendships found that three-year-olds say about half their friends are of the opposite sex; for five-year-olds it's about 20 percent, and by age seven almost no boys or girls say they have a best friend of the opposite sex.[3] These separate social universes intersect little until teenagers start dating.

Meanwhile, boys and girls are taught very different lessons about handling emotions. Parents, in general, discuss emotions—with the exception of anger—more with their daughters than their sons.[4] Girls are exposed to more information about emotions than are boys: when parents make up stories to tell their preschool children, they use more emotion words when talking to daughters than to sons; when mothers play with their infants, they display a wider range of emotions to daughters than to sons; when mothers talk to daughters about feelings, they discuss in more detail the emotional state itself than they do with their sons—though with the sons they go into more detail about the causes and consequences of emotions like anger (probably as a cautionary tale).

Leslie Brody and Judith Hall, who have summarized the research on differences in emotions between the sexes, propose that because girls develop facility with language more quickly than do boys, this leads them to be more experienced at articulating their feelings and more skilled than boys at using words to explore and substitute for emotional reactions such as physical fights; in contrast, they note, "boys, for whom the verbalization of affects is de-emphasized, may become largely unconscious of their emotional states, both in themselves and in others."[5]

At age ten, roughly the same percent of girls as boys are overtly aggressive, given to open confrontation when angered. But by age thirteen, a telling difference between the sexes emerges: Girls become more adept than boys at artful aggressive tactics like ostracism, vicious gossip, and indirect vendettas. Boys, by and large, simply continue being confrontational when angered, oblivious to these more covert strategies.[6] This is just one of many ways that boys—and later, men—are less sophisticated than the opposite sex in the byways of emotional life.

When girls play together, they do so in small, intimate groups, with an emphasis on minimizing hostility and maximizing cooperation, while boys' games are in larger groups, with an emphasis on competition. One key difference can be seen in what happens when games boys or girls are playing get disrupted by someone getting hurt. If a boy who has gotten hurt gets upset, he is expected to get out of the way and stop crying so the game can go on. If the same happens among a group of girls who are playing, the *game stops* while everyone gathers around to help the girl who is crying. This difference between boys and girls at play epitomizes what Harvard's Carol Gilligan points to as a key disparity between the sexes: boys take pride in a lone, tough-minded independence and autonomy, while girls see themselves as part of a web of connectedness. Thus boys are threatened by anything that might challenge their independence, while girls are more threatened by a rupture in their relationships. And, as Deborah Tannen has pointed out in her book *You Just Don't Understand,* these differing perspectives mean that men and women want and expect very different things out of a conversation, with men content to talk about "things," while women seek emotional connection.

In short, these contrasts in schooling in the emotions foster very different skills, with girls becoming "adept at reading both verbal and nonverbal emotional signals, at expressing and communicating their feelings," and boys becoming adept at "minimizing emotions having to do with vulnerability, guilt, fear and hurt".[7] Evidence for these different stances is very strong in the scientific literature. Hundreds of studies have found, for example, that on average women are more empathic than men, at least as measured by the ability to read someone else's unstated feelings from facial expression, tone of voice, and other nonverbal cues. Likewise, it is generally easier to read feelings from a woman's face than a man's; while there is no difference in facial expressiveness among very young boys and girls, as they go through the elementary-school grades boys become less expressive, girls more so. This may partly reflect another key difference: women, on average, experience the entire range of emotions with greater intensity and more volatility than men—in this sense, women *are* more "emotional" than men.[8]

All of this means that, in general, women come into a marriage groomed for the role of emotional manager, while men arrive with much less appreciation of the importance of this task for helping a relationship survive. Indeed, the most important element for women—but not for men—in satisfaction with their relationship reported in a study of 264 couples was the sense that the couple has "good communication."[9] Ted Huston, a psychologist at the University of Texas who has studied couples in depth, observes, "For the wives, intimacy means talking things over, especially talking about the relationship itself. The men, by and large, don't understand what the wives want from them. They say, 'I want to do things with her, and all she wants to do is talk.' " During courtship, Huston found, men were much more willing to spend time talking in ways that suited the wish for intimacy of their wives-to-be. But once married, as time went on the men—especially in more traditional couples—spent less and less time talking in this way with their wives, finding a sense of closeness simply in doing things like gardening together rather than talking things over.

This growing silence on the part of husbands may be partly due to the fact that, if anything, men are a bit Pollyannaish about the state of their marriage, while their wives are attuned to the trouble spots: in one study of marriages, men had a rosier view than their wives of just about everything in their relationship—lovemaking, finances, ties with in-laws, how well they listened to each other, how much their flaws mattered.[10] Wives, in general, are more vocal about their complaints than are their husbands, particularly among unhappy couples. Combine men's rosy view of marriage with their aversion to emotional confrontations, and it is clear why wives so often complain that their husbands try to wiggle out of discussing the troubling things about their relationship. (Of course this gender difference is a generalization, and is not true in every case; a psychiatrist friend complained that in his marriage his wife is reluctant to discuss emotional matters between them, and he is the one who is left to bring them up.)

The slowness of men to bring up problems in a relationship is no doubt compounded by their relative lack of skill when it comes to reading facial expressions of emotions. Women, for example, are more sensitive to a sad expression on a man's face than are men in detecting sadness from a woman's expression.[11] Thus a woman has to be all the sadder for a man to notice her feelings in the first place, let alone for him to raise the question of what is making her so sad.

Consider the implications of this emotional gender gap for how couples handle the grievances and disagreements that any intimate relationship inevitably spawns. In fact, specific issues such as how often a couple has sex, how to discipline the children, or how much debt and savings a couple feels comfortable with are not what make or break a marriage. Rather, it is *how* a couple discusses such sore points that matters more for the fate of their marriage. Simply having reached an agreement about *how* to disagree is key to marital survival; men and women have to overcome the innate gender differences in approaching rocky emotions. Failing this, couples are vulnerable to emotional rifts that eventually can tear their relationship apart. As we shall see, these rifts are far more likely to develop if one or both partners have certain deficits in emotional intelligence.

MARITAL FAULT LINES

Fred: Did you pick up my dry cleaning?
Ingrid: (In a mocking tone) "Did you pick up my dry cleaning." Pick up your own damn dry cleaning. What am I, your maid?
Fred: Hardly. If you were a maid, at least you'd know how to clean.

If this were dialogue from a sitcom, it might be amusing. But this painfully caustic interchange was between a couple who (perhaps not surprisingly) divorced within the next few years.[12] Their encounter took place in a laboratory run by John Gottman, a University of Washington psychologist who has done perhaps the most detailed analysis ever of the emotional glue that binds couples together and the corrosive feelings that can destroy marriages.[13] In his laboratory, couples' conversations are videotaped and then subjected to hours of microanalysis designed to reveal the subterranean emotional currents at play. This mapping of the fault lines that may lead a couple to divorce makes a convincing case for the crucial role of emotional intelligence in the survival of a marriage.

During the last two decades Gottman has tracked the ups and downs of more than two hundred couples, some just newlyweds, others married for decades. Gottman has charted the emotional ecology of marriage with such precision that, in one study, he was able to predict which couples seen in his lab (like Fred and Ingrid, whose discussion of getting the dry cleaning was so acrimonious) would divorce within three years with *94 percent accuracy,* a precision unheard of in marital studies!

The power of Gottman's analysis comes from his painstaking method and the thoroughness of his probes. While the couples talk, sensors record the slightest flux in their physiology; a second-by-second analysis of their facial expressions (using the system for reading emotions developed by Paul Ekman) detects the most fleeting and subtle nuance of feeling. After their session, each partner comes separately to the lab and watches a videotape of the conversation, and narrates his or her secret thoughts during the heated moments of the exchange. The result is akin to an emotional X-ray of the marriage.

An early warning signal that a marriage is in danger, Gottman finds, is harsh criticism. In a healthy marriage husband and wife feel free to voice a complaint. But too often in the heat of anger complaints are expressed in a destructive fashion, as an attack on the spouse's character. For example, Pamela and her daughter went shoe shopping while her husband, Tom, went to a bookstore. They agreed to meet in front of the post office in an hour, and then go to a matinee. Pamela was prompt, but there was no sign of Tom. "Where is he? The movie starts in ten minutes," Pamela complained to her daughter. "If there's a way for your father to screw something up, he will."

When Tom showed up ten minutes later, happy about having run into a friend and apologizing for being late, Pamela lashed out with sarcasm:

"That's okay—it gave us a chance to discuss your amazing ability to screw up every single plan we make. You're so thoughtless and self-centered!"

Pamela's complaint is more than that: it is a character assassination, a critique of the person, not the deed. In fact, Tom had apologized. But for this lapse Pamela brands him as "thoughtless and self-centered." Most couples have moments like this from time to time, where a complaint about something a partner has done is voiced as an attack against the person rather than the deed. But these harsh personal criticisms have a far more corrosive emotional impact than do more reasoned complaints. And such attacks, perhaps understandably, become more likely the more a husband or wife feels their complaints go unheard or ignored.

The differences between complaints and personal criticisms are simple. In a complaint, a wife states specifically what is upsetting her, and criticizes her husband's *action,* not her husband, saying how it made her feel: "When you forgot to pick up my clothes at the cleaner's it made me feel like you don't care about me." It is an expression of basic emotional intelligence: assertive, not belligerent or passive. But in a personal criticism she uses the specific grievance to launch a global attack on her husband: "You're always so selfish and uncaring. It just proves I can't trust you to do anything right." This kind of criticism leaves the person on the receiving end feeling ashamed, disliked, blamed, and defective—all of which are more likely to lead to a defensive response than to steps to improve things.

All the more so when the criticism comes laden with contempt, a particularly destructive emotion. Contempt comes easily with anger; it is usually expressed not just in the words used, but also in a tone of voice and an angry expression. Its most obvious form, of course, is mockery or insult—"jerk," "bitch," "wimp." But just as hurtful is the body language that conveys contempt, particularly the sneer or curled lip that are the universal facial signals for disgust, or a rolling of the eyes, as if to say, "Oh, brother!"

Contempt's facial signature is a contraction of the "dimpler," the muscle that pulls the corners of the mouth to the side (usually the left) while the eyes roll upward. When one spouse flashes this expression, the other, in a tacit emotional exchange, registers a jump in heart rate of two or three beats per minute. This hidden conversation takes its toll; if a husband shows contempt regularly, Gottman found, his wife will be more prone to a range of health problems, from frequent colds and flus to bladder and yeast infections, as well as gastrointestinal symptoms. And when a wife's face shows disgust, a near cousin of contempt, four or more times within a fifteen-minute conversation, it is a silent sign that the couple is likely to separate within four years.

Of course, an occasional show of contempt or disgust will not undo a marriage. Rather, such emotional volleys are akin to smoking and high cholesterol as risk factors for heart disease—the more intense and prolonged, the greater the danger. On the road to divorce, one of these factors predicts the next, in an escalating scale of misery. Habitual criticism and contempt or disgust are danger signs because they indicate that a husband or wife has made a silent judgment for the worse about their partner. In his or her thoughts, the spouse is the subject of constant condemnation. Such negative and hostile thinking leads naturally to attacks that make the partner on the receiving end defensive—or ready to counterattack in return.

The two arms of the fight-or-flight response each represent ways a spouse can respond to an attack. The most obvious is to fight back, lashing out in anger. That route typically ends in a fruitless shouting match. But the alternative response, fleeing, can be more pernicious, particularly when the "flight" is a retreat into stony silence.

Stonewalling is the ultimate defense. The stonewaller just goes blank, in effect withdrawing from the conversation by responding with a stony expression and silence. Stonewalling sends a powerful, unnerving message, something like a combination of icy distance, superiority, and distaste. Stonewalling showed up mainly in marriages that were heading for trouble; in 85 percent of these cases it was the husband who stonewalled in response to a wife who attacked with criticism and contempt.[14] As a habitual response stonewalling is devastating to the health of a relationship: it cuts off all possibility of working out disagreements.

TOXIC THOUGHTS

The children are being rambunctious, and Martin, their father, is getting annoyed. He turns to his wife, Melanie, and says in a sharp tone, "Dear, don't you think the kids could quiet down?"

His actual thought: "She's too easy on the kids."

Melanie, responding to his ire, feels a surge of anger. Her face grows taut, her brows knit in a frown, and she replies, "The kids are having a good time. Anyhow, they'll be going up to bed soon."

Her thought: "There he goes again, complaining all the time."

Martin now is visibly enraged. He leans forward menacingly, his fists clenched, as he says in an annoyed tone, "Should I put them to bed now?"

His thought: "She opposes me in everything. I'd better take over."

Melanie, suddenly frightened by Martin's wrath, says meekly, "No, I'll put them to bed right away."

Her thought: "He's getting out of control—he could hurt the kids. I'd better give in."

These parallel conversations—the spoken and the silent—are reported by Aaron Beck, the founder of cognitive therapy, as an example of the kinds of thinking that can poison a marriage.[15] The real emotional exchange between Melanie and Martin is shaped by their thoughts, and those thoughts, in turn, are determined by another, deeper layer, which Beck calls "automatic thoughts"—fleeting, background assumptions about oneself and the people in one's life that reflect our deepest emotional attitudes. For Melanie the background thought is something like, "He's always bullying me with his anger." For Martin, the key thought is, "She has no right to treat me like this." Melanie feels like an innocent victim in their marriage, and Martin feels righteous indignation at what he feels is unjust treatment.

Thoughts of being an innocent victim or of righteous indignation are typical of partners in troubled marriages, continually fueling anger and hurt.[16] Once distressing thoughts such as righteous indignation become automatic, they are self-confirming: the partner who feels victimized is constantly scanning everything his partner does that might confirm the view that she is victimizing him, ignoring or discounting any acts of kindness on her part that would question or disconfirm that view.

These thoughts are powerful; they trip the neural alarm system. Once the husband's thought of being victimized triggers an emotional hijacking, he will for the time being easily call to mind and ruminate on a list of grievances that remind him of the ways she victimizes him, while not recalling anything she may have done in their entire relationship that would disconfirm the view that he is an innocent victim. It puts his spouse in a no-win situation: even things she does that are intentionally kind can be reinterpreted when viewed through such a negative lens and dismissed as feeble attempts to deny she is a victimizer.

Partners who are free of such distress-triggering views can entertain a more benign interpretation of what is going on in the same situations, and so are less likely to have such a hijacking, or if they do, tend to recover from it more readily. The general template for thoughts that maintain or alleviate distress follows the pattern outlined in Chapter 6 by psychologist Martin Seligman for pessimistic and optimistic outlooks. The pessimistic view is that the partner is inherently flawed in a way that cannot change and that guarantees misery:

"He's selfish and self-absorbed; that's the way he was brought up and that's the way he will always be; he expects me to wait on him hand and foot and he couldn't care less about how I feel." The contrasting optimistic view would be something like: "He's being demanding now, but he's been thoughtful in the past; maybe he's in a bad mood—I wonder if something's bothering him about his work." This is a view that does not write off the husband (or the marriage) as irredeemably damaged and hopeless. Instead it sees a bad moment as due to circumstances that can change. The first attitude brings continual distress; the second soothes.

Partners who take the pessimistic stance are extremely prone to emotional hijackings; they get angry, hurt, or otherwise distressed by things their spouses do, and they stay disturbed once the episode begins. Their internal distress and pessimistic attitude, of course, makes it far more likely they will resort to criticism and contempt in confronting the partner, which in turn heightens the likelihood of defensiveness and stonewalling.

Perhaps the most virulent of such toxic thoughts are found in husbands who are physically violent to their wives. A study of violent husbands by psychologists at Indiana University found that these men think like schoolyard bullies: they read hostile intent into even neutral actions by their wives, and use this misreading to justify to themselves their own violence (men who are sexually aggressive with dates do something similar, viewing the women with suspicion and so disregarding their objections).[17] As we saw in Chapter 7, such men are particularly threatened by perceived slights, rejection, or public embarrassment by their wives. A typical scenario that triggers thoughts "justifying" violence in wife-batterers: "You are at a social gathering and you notice that for the past half hour your wife has been talking and laughing with the same attractive man. He seems to be flirting with her." When these men perceive their wives as doing something suggesting rejection or abandonment, their reactions run to indignation and outrage. Presumably, automatic thoughts like "She's going to leave me" are triggers for an emotional hijacking in which battering husbands respond impulsively, as the researchers put it, with "incompetent behavioral responses"—they become violent.[18]

FLOODING: THE SWAMPING OF A MARRIAGE

The net effect of these distressing attitudes is to create incessant crisis, since they trigger emotional hijackings more often and make it harder to recover from the resulting hurt and rage. Gottman uses the apt term *flooding* for this susceptibility to frequent emotional distress; flooded husbands or wives are so overwhelmed by their partner's negativity and their own reaction to it that they are swamped by dreadful, out-of-control feelings. People who are flooded cannot hear without distortion or respond with clear-headedness; they find it hard to organize their thinking, and they fall back on primitive reactions. They just want things to stop, or want to run or, sometimes, to strike back. Flooding is a self-perpetuating emotional hijacking.

Some people have high thresholds for flooding, easily enduring anger and contempt, while others may be triggered the moment their spouse makes a mild criticism. The technical description of flooding is in terms of heart rate rise from calm levels.[19] At rest, women's heart rates are about 82 beats per minute, men's about 72 (the specific heart rate varies mainly according to a person's body size). Flooding begins at about 10 beats per minute above a person's resting rate; if the heart rate reaches 100 beats per minute (as it easily can do during moments of rage or tears), then the body is pumping adrenaline and other hormones that keep the distress high for some time. The moment of emotional hijacking is apparent from the heart rate: it can jump 10, 20, or even as many as 30 beats per minute within the space of a single heartbeat. Muscles tense; it can seem hard to breathe. There is a swamp of toxic feelings, an unpleasant wash of fear and anger that seems inescapable and, subjectively, takes "forever" to get over. At this point—full hijacking—a person's emotions are so intense, their perspective so narrow, and their thinking so confused that there is no hope of taking the other's viewpoint or settling things in a reasonable way.

Of course, most husbands and wives have such intense moments from time to time when they fight—it's only natural. The problem for a marriage begins when one or another spouse feels flooded almost continually. Then the partner feels overwhelmed by the other partner, is always on guard for an emotional assault or injustice, becomes hypervigilant for any sign of attack, insult, or grievance, and is sure to overreact to even the least sign. If a husband is in such a state, his wife saying, "Honey, we've got to talk," can elicit the reactive thought, "She's picking a fight again," and so trigger flooding. It becomes harder and harder to recover from the physiological arousal, which in turn makes it easier for innocuous exchanges to be seen in a sinister light, triggering flooding all over again.

This is perhaps the most dangerous turning point for marriage, a catastrophic shift in the relationship. The flooded partner has come to think the worst of the spouse virtually all the time, reading everything she does in a negative light. Small issues become major battles; feelings are hurt continually. With time, the partner who is being flooded starts to see any and all problems in the marriage as severe and impossible to fix, since the flooding itself sabotages any attempt to work things out. As this continues it begins to seem useless to talk things over, and the partners try to soothe their troubled feelings on their own. They start leading parallel lives, essentially living in isolation from each other, and feel alone within the marriage. All too often, Gottman finds, the next step is divorce.

In this trajectory toward divorce the tragic consequences of deficits in emotional competences are self-evident. As a couple gets caught in the reverberating cycle of criticism and contempt, defensiveness and stonewalling, distressing thoughts and emotional flooding, the cycle itself reflects a disintegration of emotional self-awareness and self-control, of empathy and the abilities to soothe each other and oneself.

MEN: THE VULNERABLE SEX

Back to gender differences in emotional life, which prove to be a hidden spur to marital meltdowns. Consider this finding: Even after thirty-five or more years of marriage, there is a basic distinction between husbands and wives in how they regard emotional encounters. Women, on average, do not mind plunging into the unpleasantness of a marital squabble nearly so much as do the men in their lives. That conclusion, reached in a study by Robert Levenson at the University of California at Berkeley, is based on the testimony of 151 couples, all in long-lasting marriages. Levenson found that husbands uniformly found it unpleasant, even aversive, to become upset during a marital disagreement, while their wives did not mind it much.[20]

Husbands are prone to flooding at a lower intensity of negativity than are their wives; more men than women react to their spouse's criticism with flooding. Once flooded, husbands secrete more adrenaline into their bloodstream, and the adrenaline flow is triggered by lower levels of negativity on their wife's part; it takes husbands longer to recover physiologically from flooding.[21] This suggests the possibility that the stoic, Clint Eastwood type of male imperturbability may represent a defense against feeling emotionally overwhelmed.

The reason men are so likely to stonewall, Gottman proposes, is to protect themselves from flooding; his research showed that once they began stonewalling, their heart rates dropped by about ten beats per minute, bringing a subjective sense of relief. But—and here's a paradox—once the men started stonewalling, it was the wives whose heart rate shot up to levels signaling high distress. This limbic tango, with each sex seeking comfort in opposing gambits, leads to a very different stance toward emotional confrontations: men want to avoid them as fervently as their wives feel compelled to seek them.

Just as men are far more likely to be stonewallers, so the women are more likely to criticize their husbands.[22] This asymmetry arises as a result of wives pursuing their role as emotional managers. As they try to bring up and resolve disagreements and grievances, their husbands are more reluctant to engage in what are bound to be heated discussions. As the wife sees her husband withdraw from engagement, she ups the volume and intensity of her complaint, starting to criticize him. As he becomes defensive or stonewalls in return, she feels frustrated and angry, and so adds contempt to underscore the strength of her frustration. As her husband finds himself the object of his wife's criticism and contempt, he begins to fall into the innocent-victim or righteous-indignation thoughts that more and more easily trigger flooding. To protect himself from flooding, he becomes more and more defensive or simply stonewalls altogether. But when husbands stonewall, remember, it triggers flooding in their wives, who feel completely stymied. And as the cycle of marital fights escalates it all too easily can spin out of control.

HIS AND HERS: MARITAL ADVICE

Given the grim potential outcome of the differences in how men and women deal with distressing feelings in their relationship, what can couples do to protect the love and affection they feel for each other—in short, what protects a marriage? On the basis of watching interaction in the couples whose marriages have continued to thrive over the years, marital researchers offer specific advice for men and for women, and some general words for both.

Men and women, in general, need different emotional fine-tuning. For men, the advice is not to sidestep conflict, but to realize that when their wife brings up some grievance or disagreement, she may be doing it as an act of love, trying to keep the relationship healthy and on course (although there may well be other motives for a wife's hostility). When grievances simmer, they build and build in intensity until there's an explosion; when they are aired and worked out, it takes the pressure off. But husbands need to realize that anger or discontent is not synonymous with personal attack—their wives' emotions are often simply underliners, emphasizing the strength of her feelings about the matter.

Men also need to be on guard against short-circuiting the discussion by offering a practical solution too early on—it's typically more important to a wife that she feel her husband hears her complaint and empathizes with her *feelings* about the matter (though he need not agree with her). She may hear his offering advice as a way of dismissing her feelings as inconsequential. Husbands who are able to stay with their wives through the heat of anger, rather than dismissing their complaints as petty, help their wives feel heard and respected. Most especially, wives want to have their feelings acknowledged and respected as valid, even if their husbands disagree. More often than not, when a wife feels her view is heard and her feelings registered, she calms down.

As for women, the advice is quite parallel. Since a major problem for men is that their wives are too intense in voicing complaints, wives need to make a purposeful effort to be careful not to attack their husbands—to complain about what they did, but not criticize them as a person or express contempt. Complaints are not attacks on character, but rather a clear statement that a particular action is distressing. An angry personal attack will almost certainly lead to a husband's getting defensive or stonewalling, which will be all the more frustrating, and only escalate the fight. It helps, too, if a wife's complaints are put in the larger context of reassuring her husband of her love for him.

THE GOOD FIGHT

The morning paper offers an object lesson in how not to resolve differences in a marriage. Marlene Lenick had a dispute with her husband, Michael: he wanted to watch the Dallas Cowboys–Philadelphia Eagles game, she wanted to watch the news. As he settled down to watch the game, Mrs. Lenick told him that she had "had enough of that football," went into the bedroom to fetch a .38 caliber handgun, and shot him twice as he sat watching the game in the den. Mrs. Lenick was charged with aggravated assault and freed on a $50,000 bond; Mr. Lenick was listed in good condition, recovering from the bullets that grazed his abdomen and tunneled through his left shoulder blade and neck.[23]

While few marital fights are that violent—or that costly—they offer a prime chance to bring emotional intelligence to marriage. For example, couples in marriages that last tend to stick to one topic, and to give each partner the chance to state their point of view at the outset.[24] But these couples go one important step further: they show each other that they are being listened to. Since feeling heard is often exactly what the aggrieved partner really is after, emotionally an act of empathy is a masterly tension reducer.

Most notably missing in couples who eventually divorce are attempts by either partner in an argument to de-escalate the tension. The presence or absence of ways to repair a rift is a crucial difference between the fights of couples who have a healthy marriage and those of couples who eventually end up divorcing.[25] The repair mechanisms that keep an argument from escalating into a dire explosion are simple moves such as keeping the discussion on track, empathizing, and tension reduction. These basic moves are like an emotional thermostat, preventing the feelings being expressed from boiling over and overwhelming the partners' ability to focus on the issue at hand.

One overall strategy for making a marriage work is not to concentrate on the specific issues—childrearing, sex, money, housework—that couples fight about, but rather to cultivate a couple's shared emotional intelligence, thereby improving the chances of working things out. A handful of emotional competences—mainly being able to calm down (and calm your partner), empathy, and listening well—can make it more likely a couple will settle their disagreements effectively. These make possible healthy disagreements, the "good fights" that allow a marriage to flourish and which overcome the negativities that, if left to grow, can destroy a marriage.[26]

Of course, none of these emotional habits changes overnight; it takes persistence and vigilance at the very least. Couples will be able to make the key changes in direct proportion to how motivated they are to try. Many or most emotional responses triggered so easily in marriage have been sculpted since childhood, first learned in our most intimate relationships or modeled for us by our parents, and then brought to marriage fully formed. And so we are primed for certain emotional habits—overreacting to perceived slights, say, or shutting down at the first sign of a confrontation—even though we may have sworn that we would not act like our parents.

Calming Down

Every strong emotion has at its root an impulse to action; managing those impulses is basic to emotional intelligence. This can be particularly difficult, though, in love relationships, where we have so much at stake. The reactions triggered here touch on some of our deepest needs—to be loved and feel respected, fears of abandonment or of being emotionally deprived. Small wonder we can act in a marital fight as though our very survival were at stake.

Even so, nothing gets resolved positively when husband or wife is in the midst of an emotional hijacking. One key marital competence is for partners to learn to soothe their own distressed feelings. Essentially, this means mastering the ability to recover quickly from the flooding caused by an emotional hijacking. Because the ability to hear, think, and speak with clarity dissolves during such an emotional peak, calming down is an immensely constructive step, without which there can be no further progress in settling what's at issue.

Ambitious couples can learn to monitor their pulse rates every five minutes or so during a troubling encounter, feeling the pulse at the carotid artery a few inches below the earlobe and jaw (people who do aerobic workouts learn to do this easily).[27] Counting the pulse for fifteen seconds and multiplying by four gives the pulse rate in beats per minute. Doing so while feeling calm gives a baseline; if the pulse rate rises more than, say, ten beats per minute above that level, it signals the beginning of flooding. If the pulse climbs this much, a couple needs a twenty-minute break from each other to cool down before resuming the discussion. Although a five-minute break may feel long enough, the actual physiological recovery time is more gradual. As we saw in Chapter 5, residual anger triggers more anger; the longer wait gives the body more time to recover from the earlier arousal.

For couples who, understandably, find it awkward to monitor heart rate during a fight, it is simpler to have a prestated agreement that allows one or another partner to call the time-out at the first signs of flooding in either partner. During that time-out period, cooling down can be helped along by engaging in a relaxation technique or aerobic exercise (or any of the other methods we explored in Chapter 5) that might help the partners recover from the emotional hijacking.

Detoxifying Self-talk

Because flooding is triggered by negative thoughts about the partner, it helps if a husband or wife who is being upset by such harsh judgments tackles them head-on. Sentiments like "I'm not going to take this anymore" or "I don't deserve this kind of treatment" are innocent-victim or righteous-indignation slogans. As cognitive therapist Aaron Beck points out, by catching these thoughts and challenging them—rather than simply being enraged or hurt by them—a husband or wife can begin to become free of their hold.[28]

This requires monitoring such thoughts, realizing that one does not have to believe them, and making the intentional effort to bring to mind evidence or perspectives that put them in question. For example, a wife who feels in the heat of the moment that "he doesn't care about my needs—he's always so selfish" might challenge the thought by reminding herself of a number of things her husband has done that are, in fact, thoughtful. This allows her to reframe the thought as: "Well, he does show he cares about me sometimes, even though what he just did was thoughtless and upsetting to me." The latter formulation opens the possibility of change and a positive resolution; the former only foments anger and hurt.

Nondefensive Listening and Speaking

He: "You're shouting!"

She: "Of course I'm shouting—you haven't heard a word I'm saying. You just don't listen!"

Listening is a skill that keeps couples together. Even in the heat of an argument, when both are seized by emotional hijackings, one or the other, and sometimes both, can manage to listen past the anger, and hear and respond to a partner's reparative gesture. Couples headed for divorce, though, get absorbed in the anger and fixated on the specifics of the issue at hand, not managing to hear—let alone return—any peace offerings that might be implicit in what their partner is saying. Defensiveness in a listener takes the form of ignoring or immediately rebutting the spouse's complaint, reacting to it as though it were an attack rather than an attempt to change behavior. Of course, in an argument what one spouse says is often in the form of an attack, or is said with such strong negativity that it is hard to hear anything other than an attack.

Even in the worst case, it's possible for a couple to purposely edit what they hear, ignoring the hostile and negative parts of the exchange—the nasty tone, the insult, the contemptuous criticism—to hear the main message. For this feat it helps if partners can remember to see each other's negativity as an implicit statement of how important the issue is to them—a demand for attention to be paid. Then if she yells, "Will you *stop* interrupting me, for crissake!" he might be more able to say, without reacting overtly to her hostility, "Okay, go ahead and finish."

The most powerful form of nondefensive listening, of course, is empathy: actually hearing the feelings *behind* what is being said. As we saw in Chapter 7, for one partner in a couple to truly empathize with the other demands that his own emotional reactions calm down to the point where he is receptive enough for his own physiology to be able to mirror the feelings of his partner. Without this physiological attunement, a partner's sense of what the other is feeling is likely to be entirely off base. Empathy deteriorates when one's own feelings are so strong that they allow no physiological harmonizing, but simply override everything else.

One method for effective emotional listening, called "mirroring," is commonly used in marital therapy. When one partner makes a complaint, the other repeats it back in her own words, trying to capture not just the thought, but also the feelings that go with it. The partner mirroring checks with the other to be sure the restatement is on target, and if not, tries again until it is right—something that seems simple, but is surprisingly tricky in execution.[29] The effect of being mirrored accurately is not just feeling understood, but having the added sense of being in emotional attunement. That in itself can sometimes disarm an imminent attack, and goes far toward keeping discussions of grievances from escalating into fights.

The art of nondefensive speaking for couples centers around keeping what is said to a specific complaint rather than escalating to a personal attack. Psychologist Haim Ginott, the grandfather of effective-communication programs, recommended that the best formula for a complaint is "XYZ": "When you did X, it made me feel Y, and I'd rather you did Z instead." For example: "When you didn't call to tell me you were going to be late for our dinner appointment, I felt unappreciated and angry. I wish you'd call to let me know you'll be late" instead of "You're a thoughtless, self-centered bastard," which is how the issue is all too often put in couples' fights. In short, open communication has no bullying, threats, or insults. Nor does it allow for any of the innumerable forms of defensiveness—excuses, denying responsibility, counterattacking with a criticism, and the like. Here again empathy is a potent tool.

Finally, respect and love disarm hostility in marriage, as elsewhere in life. One powerful way to de-escalate a fight is to let your partner know that you can see things from the other perspective, and that this point of view may have validity, even if you do not agree with it yourself. Another is to take responsibility or even apologize if you see you are in the wrong. At a minimum, validation means at least conveying that you are listening, and can acknowledge the emotions being expressed, even if you can't go along with the argument: "I see you're upset." And at other times, when there is no fight going on, validation takes the form of compliments, finding something you genuinely appreciate and voicing some praise. Validation, of course, is a way to help soothe your spouse, or to build up emotional capital in the form of positive feelings.

Practicing

Because these maneuvers are to be called upon during the heat of confrontation, when emotional arousal is sure to be high, they have to be overlearned if they are to be accessible when needed most. This is because the emotional brain engages those response routines that were learned earliest in life during repeated moments of anger and hurt, and so become dominant. Memory and response being emotion-specific, in such moments reactions associated with calmer times are less easy to remember and act on. If a more productive emotional response is unfamiliar or not well practiced, it is extremely difficult to try it while upset. But if a response is practiced so that it has become automatic, it has a better chance of finding expression during emotional crisis. For these reasons, the above strategies need to be tried out and rehearsed during encounters that are not stressful, as well as in the heat of battle, if they are to have a chance to become an acquired first response (or at least a not-too-belated second response) in the repertoire of the emotional circuitry. In essence, these antidotes to marital disintegration are a small remedial education in emotional intelligence.

10

Managing with Heart

Melburn McBroom was a domineering boss, with a temper that intimidated those who worked with him. That fact might have passed unremarked had McBroom worked in an office or factory. But McBroom was an airline pilot.

One day in 1978 McBroom's plane was approaching Portland, Oregon, when he noticed a problem with the landing gear. So McBroom went into a holding pattern, circling the field at a high altitude while he fiddled with the mechanism.

As McBroom obsessed about the landing gear, the plane's fuel gauges steadily approached the empty level. But his copilots were so fearful of McBroom's wrath that they said nothing, even as disaster loomed. The plane crashed, killing ten people.

Today the story of that crash is told as a cautionary tale in the safety training of airline pilots.[1] In 80 percent of airline crashes, pilots make mistakes that could have been prevented, particularly if the crew worked together more harmoniously. Teamwork, open lines of communication, cooperation, listening, and speaking one's mind—rudiments of social intelligence—are now emphasized in training pilots, along with technical prowess.

The cockpit is a microcosm of any working organization. But lacking the dramatic reality check of an airplane crash, the destructive effects of miserable morale, intimidated workers, or arrogant bosses—or any of the dozens of other permutations of emotional deficiencies in the workplace—can go largely unnoticed by those outside the immediate scene. But the costs can be read in signs such as decreased productivity, an increase in missed deadlines, mistakes and mishaps, and an exodus of employees to more congenial settings. There is, inevitably, a cost to the bottom line from low levels of emotional intelligence on the job. When it is rampant, companies can crash and burn.

The cost-effectiveness of emotional intelligence is a relatively new idea for business, one some managers may find hard to accept. A study of 250 executives found that most felt their work demanded "their heads but not their hearts." Many said they feared that feeling empathy or compassion for those they worked with would put them in conflict with their organizational goals. One felt the idea of sensing the feelings of those who worked for him was absurd—it would, he said, "be impossible to deal with people." Others protested that if they were not emotionally aloof they would be unable to make the "hard" decisions that business requires—although the likelihood is that they would deliver those decisions more humanely.[2]

That study was done in the 1970s, when the business environment was very different. My argument is that such attitudes are outmoded, a luxury of a former day; a new competitive reality is putting emotional intelligence at a premium in the workplace and in the marketplace. As Shoshona Zuboff, a psychologist at Harvard Business School, pointed out to me, "corporations have gone through a radical revolution within this century, and with this has come a corresponding transformation of the emotional landscape. There was a long period of managerial domination of the corporate hierarchy when the manipulative, jungle-fighter boss was rewarded. But that rigid hierarchy started breaking down in the 1980s under the twin pressures of globalization and information technology. The jungle fighter symbolizes where the corporation has been; the virtuoso in interpersonal skills is the corporate future."[3]

Some of the reasons are patently obvious—imagine the consequences for a working group when someone is unable to keep from exploding in anger or has no sensitivity about what the people around him are feeling. All the deleterious effects of agitation on thinking reviewed in Chapter 6 operate in the workplace too: When emotionally upset, people cannot remember, attend, learn, or make decisions clearly. As one management consultant put it, "Stress makes people stupid."

On the positive side, imagine the benefits for work of being skilled in the basic emotional competences—being attuned to the feelings of those we deal with, being able to handle disagreements so they do not escalate, having the ability to get into flow states while doing our work. Leadership is not domination, but the art of persuading people to work toward a common goal. And, in terms of managing our own career, there may be nothing more essential than recognizing our deepest feelings about what we do—and what changes might make us more truly satisfied with our work.

Some of the less obvious reasons emotional aptitudes are moving to the forefront of business skills reflect sweeping changes in the workplace. Let me make my point by tracking the difference three applications of emotional intelligence make: being able to air grievances as helpful critiques, creating an atmosphere in which diversity is valued rather than a source of friction, and networking effectively.

CRITICISM IS JOB ONE

He was a seasoned engineer, heading a software development project, presenting the result of months of work by his team to the company's vice president for product development. The men and women who had worked long days week after week were there with him, proud to present the fruit of their hard labor. But as the engineer finished his presentation, the vice president turned to him and asked sarcastically, "How long have you been out of graduate school? These specifications are ridiculous. They have no chance of getting past my desk."

The engineer, utterly embarrassed and deflated, sat glumly through the rest of the meeting, reduced to silence. The men and women on his team made a few desultory—and some hostile—remarks in defense of their effort. The vice president was then called away and the meeting broke up abruptly, leaving a residue of bitterness and anger.

For the next two weeks the engineer was obsessed by the vice president's remarks. Dispirited and depressed, he was convinced he would never get another assignment of importance at the company, and was thinking of leaving, even though he enjoyed his work there.

Finally the engineer went to see the vice president, reminding him of the meeting, his critical remarks, and their demoralizing effect. Then he made a carefully worded inquiry: "I'm a little confused by what you were trying to accomplish. I assume you were not just trying to embarrass me—did you have some other goal in mind?"

The vice president was astonished—he had no idea that his remark, which he meant as a throwaway line, had been so devastating. In fact, he thought the software plan was promising, but needed more work—he hadn't meant to dismiss it as utterly worthless at all. He simply had not realized, he said, how poorly he had put his reaction, nor that he had hurt anyone's feelings. And, belatedly, he apologized.[4]

It's a question of feedback, really, of people getting the information essential to keep their efforts on track. In its original sense in systems theory, *feedback* meant the exchange of data about how one part of a system is working, with the understanding that one part affects all others in the system, so that any part heading off course could be changed for the better. In a company everyone is part of the system, and so feedback is the lifeblood of the organization—the exchange of information that lets people know if the job they are doing is going well or needs to be fine-tuned, upgraded, or redirected entirely. Without feedback people are in the dark; they have no idea how they stand with their boss, with their peers, or in terms of what is expected of them, and any problems will only get worse as time passes.

In a sense, criticism is one of the most important tasks a manager has. Yet it's also one of the most dreaded and put off. And, like the sarcastic vice president, too many managers have poorly mastered the crucial art of feedback. This deficiency has a great cost: just as the emotional health of a couple depends on how well they air their grievances, so do the effectiveness, satisfaction, and productivity of people at work depend on how they are told about nagging problems. Indeed, how criticisms are given and received goes a long way in determining how satisfied people are with their work, with those they work with, and with those to whom they are responsible.

The Worst Way to Motivate Someone

The emotional vicissitudes at work in marriage also operate in the workplace, where they take similar forms. Criticisms are voiced as personal attacks rather than complaints that can be acted upon; there are ad hominem charges with dollops of disgust, sarcasm, and contempt; both give rise to defensiveness and dodging of responsibility and, finally, to stonewalling or the embittered passive resistance that comes from feeling unfairly treated. Indeed, one of the more common forms of destructive criticism in the workplace, says one business consultant, is a blanket, generalized statement like "You're screwing up," delivered in a harsh, sarcastic, angry tone, providing neither a chance to respond nor any suggestion of how to do things better. It leaves the person receiving it feeling helpless and angry. From the vantage point of emotional intelligence, such criticism displays an ignorance of the feelings it will trigger in those who receive it, and the devastating effect those feelings will have on their motivation, energy, and confidence in doing their work.

This destructive dynamic showed up in a survey of managers who were asked to think back to times they blew up at employees and, in the heat of the moment, made a personal attack.[5] The angry attacks had effects much like they would in a married couple: the employees who received them reacted most often by becoming defensive, making excuses, or evading responsibility. Or they stonewalled—that is, tried to avoid all contact with the manager who blew up at them. If they had been subjected to the same emotional microscope that John Gottman used with married couples, these embittered employees would no doubt have been shown to be thinking the thoughts of innocent victimhood or righteous indignation typical of husbands or wives who feel unfairly attacked. If their physiology were measured, they would probably also display the flooding that reinforces such thoughts. And yet the managers were only further annoyed and provoked by these responses, suggesting the beginning of a cycle that, in the business world, ends in the employee quitting or being fired—the business equivalent of a divorce.

Indeed, in a study of 108 managers and white-collar workers, inept criticism was ahead of mistrust, personality struggles, and disputes over power and pay as a reason for conflict on the job.[6] An experiment done at Rensselaer Polytechnic Institute shows just how damaging to working relationships a cutting criticism can be. In a simulation, volunteers were given the task of creating an ad for a new shampoo. Another volunteer (a confederate) supposedly judged the proposed ads; volunteers actually received one of two prearranged criticisms. One critique was considerate and specific. But the other included threats and blamed the person's innate deficiencies, with remarks like, "Didn't even try; can't seem to do anything right" and "Maybe it's just lack of talent. I'd try to get someone else to do it."

Understandably, those who were attacked became tense and angry and antagonistic, saying they would refuse to collaborate or cooperate on future projects with the person who gave the criticism. Many indicated they would want to avoid contact altogether—in other words, they felt like stonewalling. The harsh criticism made those who received it so demoralized that they no longer tried as hard at their work and, perhaps most damaging, said they no longer felt capable of doing well. The personal attack was devastating to their morale.

Many managers are too willing to criticize, but frugal with praise, leaving their employees feeling that they only hear about how they're doing when they make a mistake. This propensity to criticism is compounded by managers who delay giving any feedback at all for long periods. "Most problems in an employee's performance are not sudden; they develop slowly over time," J. R. Larson, a University of Illinois at Urbana psychologist, notes. "When the boss fails to let his feelings be known promptly, it leads to his frustration building up slowly. Then, one day, he blows up about it. If the criticism had been given earlier on, the employee would have been able to correct the problem. Too often people criticize only when things boil over, when they get too angry to contain themselves. And that's when they give the criticism in the worst way, in a tone of biting sarcasm, calling to mind a long list of grievances they had kept to themselves, or making threats. Such attacks backfire. They are received as an affront, so the recipient becomes angry in return. It's the worst way to motivate someone."

The Artful Critique

Consider the alternative.

An artful critique can be one of the most helpful messages a manager can send. For example, what the contemptuous vice president could have told the software engineer—but did not—was something like: "The main difficulty at this stage is that your plan will take too long and so escalate costs. I'd like you to think more about your proposal, especially the design specifications for software development, to see if you can figure out a way to do the same job more quickly." Such a message has the opposite impact of destructive criticism: instead of creating helplessness, anger, and rebellion, it holds out the hope of doing better and suggests the beginning of a plan for doing so.

An artful critique focuses on what a person has done and can do rather than reading a mark of character into a job poorly done. As Larson observes, "A character attack—calling someone stupid or incompetent—misses the point. You immediately put him on the defensive, so that he's no longer receptive to what you have to tell him about how to do things better." That advice, of course, is precisely the same as for married couples airing their grievances.

And, in terms of motivation, when people believe that their failures are due to some unchangeable deficit in themselves, they lose hope and stop trying. The basic belief that leads to optimism, remember, is that setbacks or failures are due to circumstances that we can do something about to change them for the better.

Harry Levinson, a psychoanalyst turned corporate consultant, gives the following advice on the art of the critique, which is intricately entwined with the art of praise:

• *Be specific.* Pick a significant incident, an event that illustrates a key problem that needs changing or a pattern of deficiency, such as the inability to do certain parts of a job well. It demoralizes people just to hear that they are doing "something" wrong without knowing what the specifics are so they can change. Focus on the specifics, saying what the person did well, what was done poorly, and how it could be changed. Don't beat around the bush or be oblique or evasive; it will muddy the real message. This, of course, is akin to the advice to couples about the "XYZ" statement of a grievance: say exactly what the problem is, what's wrong with it or how it makes you feel, and what could be changed.

"Specificity," Levinson points out, "is just as important for praise as for criticism. I won't say that vague praise has no effect at all, but it doesn't have much, and you can't learn from it."[7]

• *Offer a solution.* The critique, like all useful feedback, should point to a way to fix the problem. Otherwise it leaves the recipient frustrated, demoralized, or demotivated. The critique may open the door to possibilities and alternatives that the person did not realize were there, or simply sensitize her to deficiencies that need attention—but should include suggestions about how to take care of these problems.

• *Be present.* Critiques, like praise, are most effective face to face and in private. People who are uncomfortable giving a criticism—or offering praise—are likely to ease the burden on themselves by doing it at a distance, such as in a memo. But this makes the communication too impersonal, and robs the person receiving it of an opportunity for a response or clarification.

• *Be sensitive.* This is a call for empathy, for being attuned to the impact of what you say and how you say it on the person at the receiving end. Managers who have little empathy, Levinson points out, are most prone to giving feedback in a hurtful fashion, such as the withering put-down. The net effect of such criticism is destructive: instead of opening the way for a corrective, it creates an emotional backlash of resentment, bitterness, defensiveness, and distance.

Levinson also offers some emotional counsel for those at the receiving end of criticism. One is to see the criticism as valuable information about how to do better, not as a personal attack. Another is to watch for the impulse toward defensiveness instead of taking responsibility. And, if it gets too upsetting, ask to resume the meeting later, after a period to absorb the difficult message and cool down a bit. Finally, he advises people to see criticism as an opportunity to work together with the critic to solve the problem, not as an adversarial situation. All this sage advice, of course, directly echoes suggestions for married couples trying to handle their complaints without doing permanent damage to their relationship. As with marriage, so with work.

DEALING WITH DIVERSITY

Sylvia Skeeter, a former army captain in her thirties, was a shift manager at a Denny's restaurant in Columbia, South Carolina. One slow afternoon a group of black customers—a minister, an assistant pastor, and two visiting gospel singers—came in for a meal, and sat and sat while the waitresses ignored them. The waitresses, recalls Skeeter, "would kind of glare, with their hands on their hips, and then they'd go back to talking among themselves, like a black person standing five feet away didn't exist."

Skeeter, indignant, confronted the waitresses, and complained to the manager, who shrugged off their actions, saying, "That's how they were raised, and there's nothing I can do about it." Skeeter quit on the spot; she is black.

If that had been an isolated incident, this moment of blatant prejudice might have passed unnoted. But Sylvia Skeeter was one of hundreds of people who came forward to testify to a widespread pattern of antiblack prejudice throughout the Denny's restaurant chain, a pattern that resulted in a $54 million settlement of a class-action suit on behalf of thousands of black customers who had suffered such indignities.

The plaintiffs included a detail of seven African-American Secret Service agents who sat waiting for an hour for their breakfast while their white colleagues at the next table were served promptly—as they were all on their way to provide security for a visit by President Clinton to the United States Naval Academy at Annapolis. They also included a black girl with paralyzed legs in Tampa, Florida, who sat in her wheelchair for two hours waiting for her food late one night after a prom. The pattern of discrimination, the class-action suit held, was due to the widespread assumption throughout the Denny's chain—particularly at the level of district and branch manager—that black customers were bad for business. Today, largely as a result of the suit and publicity surrounding it, the Denny's chain is making amends to the black community. And every employee, especially managers, must attend sessions on the advantages of a multiracial clientele.

Such seminars have become a staple of in-house training in companies throughout America, with the growing realization by managers that even if people bring prejudices to work with them, they must learn to act as though they have none. The reasons, over and above human decency, are pragmatic. One is the shifting face of the workforce, as white males, who used to be the dominant group, are becoming a minority. A survey of several hundred American companies found that more than three quarters of new employees were nonwhite—a demographic shift that is also reflected to a large extent in the changing pool of customers.[8] Another reason is the increasing need for international companies to have employees who not only put any bias aside to appreciate people from diverse cultures (and markets) but also turn that appreciation to competitive advantage. A third motivation is the potential fruit of diversity, in terms of heightened collective creativity and entrepreneurial energy.

All this means the culture of an organization must change to foster tolerance, even if individual biases remain. But how can a company do this? The sad fact is that the panoply of one-day, one-video, or single-weekend "diversity training" courses do not really seem to budge the biases of those employees who come to them with deep prejudice against one or another group, whether it be whites biased against blacks, blacks against Asians, or Asians resenting Hispanics. Indeed, the net effect of inept diversity courses—those that raise false expectations by promising too much, or simply create an atmosphere of confrontation instead of understanding—can be to heighten the tensions that divide groups in the workplace, calling even greater attention to these differences. To understand what *can* be done, it helps to first understand the nature of prejudice itself.

The Roots of Prejudice

Dr. Vamik Volkan is a psychiatrist at the University of Virginia now, but he remembers what it was like growing up in a Turkish family on the island of Cyprus, then bitterly contested between Turks and Greeks. As a boy Volkan heard rumors that the local Greek priest's cincture had a knot for each Turkish child he had strangled, and remembers the tone of dismay in which he was told how his Greek neighbors ate pigs, whose meat was considered too filthy to eat in his own Turkish culture. Now, as a student of ethnic conflict, Volkan points to such childhood memories to show how hatreds between groups are kept alive over the years, as each new generation is steeped in hostile biases like these.[9] The psychological price of loyalty to one's own group can be antipathy toward another, especially when there is a long history of enmity between the groups.

Prejudices are a kind of emotional learning that occurs early in life, making these reactions especially hard to eradicate entirely, even in people who as adults feel it is wrong to hold them. "The emotions of prejudice are formed in childhood, while the beliefs that are used to justify it come later," explained Thomas Pettigrew, a social psychologist at the University of California at Santa Cruz, who has studied prejudice for decades. "Later in life you may want to change your prejudice, but it is far easier to change your intellectual beliefs than your deep feelings. Many Southerners have confessed to me, for instance, that even though in their minds they no longer feel prejudice against blacks, they feel squeamish when they shake hands with a black. The feelings are left over from what they learned in their families as children."[10]

The power of the stereotypes that buttress prejudice comes in part from a more neutral dynamic in the mind that makes stereotypes of all kinds self-confirming.[11] People remember more readily instances that support the stereotype while tending to discount instances that challenge it. On meeting at a party an emotionally open and warm Englishman who disconfirms the stereotype of the cold, reserved Briton, for example, people can tell themselves that he's just unusual, or "he's been drinking."

The tenacity of subtle biases may explain why, while over the last forty years or so racial attitudes of American whites toward blacks have become increasingly more tolerant, more subtle forms of bias persist: people disavow racist attitudes while still acting with covert bias.[12] When asked, such people say they feel no bigotry, but in ambiguous situations still act in a biased way—though they give a rationale other than prejudice. Such bias can take the form, say, of a white senior manager—who believes he has no prejudices—rejecting a black job applicant, ostensibly not because of his race but because his education and experience "are not quite right" for the job, while hiring a white applicant with about the same background. Or it might take the form of giving a briefing and helpful tips to a white salesman about to make a call, but somehow neglecting to do the same for a black or Hispanic salesman.

Zero Tolerance for Intolerance

If people's long-held biases cannot be so easily weeded out, what *can* be changed is what they *do* about them. At Denny's, for example, waitresses or branch managers who took it upon themselves to discriminate against blacks were seldom, if ever, challenged. Instead, some managers seem to have encouraged them, at least tacitly, to discriminate, even suggesting policies such as demanding payment for meals in advance from black customers only, denying blacks widely advertised free birthday meals, or locking the doors and claiming to be closed if a group of black customers was coming. As John P. Relman, an attorney who sued Denny's on behalf of the black Secret Service agents, put it, "Denny's management closed their eyes to what the field staff was doing. There must have been some message . . . which freed up the inhibitions of local managers to act on their racist impulses."[13]

But everything we know about the roots of prejudice and how to fight it effectively suggests that precisely this attitude—turning a blind eye to acts of bias—allows discrimination to thrive. To do nothing, in this context, is an act of consequence in itself, letting the virus of prejudice spread unopposed. More to the point than diversity training courses—or perhaps essential to their having much effect—is that the norms of a group be decisively changed by taking an active stance against any acts of discrimination, from the top echelons of management on down. Biases may not budge, but acts of prejudice can be quashed, if the climate is changed. As an IBM executive put it, "We don't tolerate slights or insults in any way; respect for the individual is central to IBM's culture."[14]

If research on prejudice has any lesson for making a corporate culture more tolerant, it is to encourage people to speak out against even low-key acts of discrimination or harassment—offensive jokes, say, or the posting of girlie calendars demeaning to women coworkers. One study found that when people in a group heard someone make ethnic slurs, it led others to do the same. The simple act of naming bias as such or objecting to it on the spot establishes a social atmosphere that discourages it; saying nothing serves to condone it.[15] In this endeavor, those in positions of authority play a pivotal role: their failure to condemn acts of bias sends the tacit message that such acts are okay. Following through with action such as a reprimand sends a powerful message that bias is not trivial, but has real—and negative—consequences.

Here too the skills of emotional intelligence are an advantage, especially in having the social knack to know not just when but *how* to speak up productively against bias. Such feedback should be couched with all the finesse of an effective criticism, so it can be heard without defensiveness. If managers and coworkers do this naturally, or learn to do so, bias incidents are more likely to fall away.

The more effective diversity training courses set a new, organizationwide, explicit ground rule that makes bias in any form out-of-bounds, and so encourages people who have been silent witnesses and bystanders to voice their discomforts and objections. Another active ingredient in diversity courses is perspective-taking, a stance that encourages empathy and tolerance. To the degree that people come to understand the pain of those who feel discriminated against, they are more likely to speak out against it.

In short, it is more practical to try to suppress the expression of bias rather than trying to eliminate the attitude itself; stereotypes change very slowly, if at all. Simply putting people of different groups together does little or nothing to lower intolerance, as witness cases of school desegregation in which intergroup hostility rose rather than decreased. For the plethora of diversity training programs that are sweeping through the corporate world, this means a realistic goal is to change the *norms* of a group for showing prejudice or harassing; such programs can do much to raise into the collective awareness the idea that bigotry or harassment are not acceptable and will not be tolerated. But to expect that such a program will uproot deeply held prejudices is unrealistic.

Still, since prejudices are a variety of emotional learning, relearning *is* possible—though it takes time and should not be expected as the outcome of a one-time diversity training workshop. What can make a difference, though, is sustained camaraderie and daily efforts toward a common goal by people of different backgrounds. The lesson here is from school desegregation: when groups fail to mix socially, instead forming hostile cliques, the negative stereotypes intensify. But when students have worked together as equals to attain a common goal, as on sports teams or in bands, their stereotypes break down—as can happen naturally in the workplace, when people work together as peers over the years.[16]

But to stop at battling prejudice in the workplace is to miss a greater opportunity: taking advantage of the creative and entrepreneurial possibilities that a diverse workforce can offer. As we shall see, a working group of varied strengths and perspectives, if it can operate in harmony, is likely to come to better, more creative, and more effective solutions than those same people working in isolation.

ORGANIZATIONAL SAVVY AND THE GROUP IQ

By the end of the century, a third of the American workforce will be "knowledge workers," people whose productivity is marked by adding value to information—whether as market analysts, writers, or computer programmers. Peter Drucker, the eminent business maven who coined the term "knowledge worker," points out that such workers' expertise is highly specialized, and that their productivity depends on their efforts being coordinated as part of an organizational team: writers are not publishers; computer programmers are not software distributors. While people have always worked in tandem, notes Drucker, with knowledge work, "teams become the work unit rather than the individual himself."[17] And that suggests why emotional intelligence, the skills that help people harmonize, should become increasingly valued as a workplace asset in the years to come.

Perhaps the most rudimentary form of organizational teamwork is the meeting, that inescapable part of an executive's lot—in a boardroom, on a conference call, in someone's office. Meetings—bodies in the same room— are but the most obvious, and a somewhat antiquated, example of the sense in which work is shared. Electronic networks, e-mail, teleconferences, work teams, informal networks, and the like are emerging as new functional entities in organizations. To the degree that the explicit hierarchy as mapped on an organizational chart is the skeleton of an organization, these human touchpoints are its central nervous system.

Whenever people come together to collaborate, whether it be in an executive planning meeting or as a team working toward a shared product, there is a very real sense in which they have a group IQ, the sum total of the talents and skills of all those involved. And how well they accomplish their task will be determined by how high that IQ is. The single most important element in group intelligence, it turns out, is not the average IQ in the academic sense, but rather in terms of emotional intelligence. The key to a high group IQ is social harmony. It is this ability to harmonize that, all other things being equal, will make one group especially talented, productive, and successful, and another—with members whose talent and skill are equal in other regards—do poorly.

The idea that there is a group intelligence at all comes from Robert Sternberg, the Yale psychologist, and Wendy Williams, a graduate student, who were seeking to understand why some groups are far more effective than others.[18] After all, when people come together to work as a group, each brings certain talents—say, a high verbal fluency, creativity, empathy, or technical expertise. While a group can be no "smarter" than the sum total of all these specific strengths, it can be much dumber if its internal workings don't allow people to share their talents. This maxim became evident when Sternberg and Williams recruited people to take part in groups that were given the creative challenge of coming up with an effective advertising campaign for a fictitious sweetener that showed promise as a sugar substitute.

One surprise was that people who were *too* eager to take part were a drag on the group, lowering its overall performance; these eager beavers were too controlling or domineering. Such people seemed to lack a basic element of social intelligence, the ability to recognize what is apt and what inappropriate in give-and-take. Another negative was having deadweight, members who did not participate.

The single most important factor in maximizing the excellence of a group's product was the degree to which the members were able to create a state of internal harmony, which lets them take advantage of the full talent of their members. The overall performance of harmonious groups was helped by having a member who was particularly talented; groups with more friction were far less able to capitalize on having members of great ability. In groups where there are high levels of emotional and social static—whether it be from fear or anger, from rivalries or resentments—people cannot offer their best. But harmony allows a group to take maximum advantage of its most creative and talented members' abilities.

While the moral of this tale is quite clear for, say, work teams, it has a more general implication for anyone who works within an organization. Many things people do at work depend on their ability to call on a loose network of fellow workers; different tasks can mean calling on different members of the network. In effect, this creates the chance for ad hoc groups, each with a membership tailored to offer an optimal array of talents, expertise, and placement. Just how well people can "work" a network—in effect, make it into a temporary, ad hoc team—is a crucial factor in on-the-job success.

Consider, for example, a study of star performers at Bell Labs, the world-famous scientific think tank near Princeton. The labs are peopled by engineers and scientists who are all at the top on academic IQ tests. But within this pool of talent, some emerge as stars, while others are only average in their output. What makes the difference between stars and the others is not their academic IQ, but their *emotional* IQ. They are better able to motivate themselves, and better able to work their informal networks into ad hoc teams.

The "stars" were studied in one division at the labs, a unit that creates and designs the electronic switches that control telephone systems—a highly sophisticated and demanding piece of electronic engineering.[19] Because the work is beyond the capacity of any one person to tackle, it is done in teams that can range from just 5 or so engineers to 150. No single engineer knows enough to do the job alone; getting things done demands tapping other people's expertise. To find out what made the difference between those who were highly productive and those who were only average, Robert Kelley and Janet Caplan had managers and peers nominate the 10 to 15 percent of engineers who stood out as stars.

When they compared the stars with everyone else, the most dramatic finding, at first, was the paucity of differences between the two groups. "Based on a wide range of cognitive and social measures, from standard tests for IQ to personality inventories, there's little meaningful difference in innate abilities," Kelley and Caplan wrote in the *Harvard Business Review*. "As it develops, academic talent was not a good predictor of on-the-job productivity," nor was IQ.

But after detailed interviews, the critical differences emerged in the internal and interpersonal strategies "stars" used to get their work done. One of the most important turned out to be a rapport with a network of key people. Things go more smoothly for the standouts because they put time into cultivating good relationships with people whose services might be needed in a crunch as part of an instant ad hoc team to solve a problem or handle a crisis. "A middle performer at Bell Labs talked about being stumped by a technical problem," Kelley and Caplan observed. "He painstakingly called various technical gurus and then waited, wasting valuable time while calls went unreturned and e-mail messages unanswered. Star performers, however, rarely face such situations because they do the work of building reliable networks before they actually need them. When they call someone for advice, stars almost always get a faster answer."

Informal networks are especially critical for handling unanticipated problems. "The formal organization is set up to handle easily anticipated problems," one study of these networks observes. "But when unexpected problems arise, the informal organization kicks in. Its complex web of social ties form every time colleagues communicate, and solidify over time into surprisingly stable networks. Highly adaptive, informal networks move diagonally and elliptically, skipping entire functions to get things done."[20]

The analysis of informal networks shows that just because people work together day to day they will not necessarily trust each other with sensitive information (such as a desire to change jobs, or resentment about how a manager or peer behaves), nor turn to them in crisis. Indeed, a more sophisticated view of informal networks shows that there are at least three varieties: communications webs—who talks to whom; expertise networks, based on which people are turned to for advice; and trust networks. Being a main node in the expertise network means someone will have a reputation for technical excellence, which often leads to a promotion. But there is virtually no relationship between being an expert and being seen as someone people can trust with their secrets, doubts, and vulnerabilities. A petty office tyrant or micromanager may be high on expertise, but will be so low on trust that it will undermine their ability to manage, and effectively exclude them from informal networks. The stars of an organization are often those who have thick connections on all networks, whether communications, expertise, or trust.

Beyond a mastery of these essential networks, other forms of organizational savvy the Bell Labs stars had mastered included effectively coordinating their efforts in teamwork; being leaders in building consensus; being able to see things from the perspective of others, such as customers or others on a work team; persuasiveness; and promoting cooperation while avoiding conflicts. While all of these rely on social skills, the stars also displayed another kind of knack: taking initiative—being self-motivated enough to take on responsibilities above and beyond their stated job—and self-management in the sense of regulating their time and work commitments well. All such skills, of course, are aspects of emotional intelligence.

There are strong signs that what is true at Bell Labs augurs for the future of all corporate life, a tomorrow where the basic skills of emotional intelligence will be ever more important, in teamwork, in cooperation, in helping people learn together how to work more effectively. As knowledge-based services and intellectual capital become more central to corporations, improving the way people work together will be a major way to leverage intellectual capital, making a critical competitive difference. To thrive, if not survive, corporations would do well to boost their collective emotional intelligence.

11

Mind and Medicine

"Who taught you all this, Doctor?"
The reply came promptly:
"Suffering."

—ALBERT CAMUS, *The Plague*

A vague ache in my groin sent me to my doctor. Nothing seemed unusual until he looked at the results of a urine test. I had traces of blood in my urine.

"I want you to go to the hospital and get some tests . . . kidney function, cytology . . . ," he said in a businesslike tone.

I don't know what he said next. My mind seemed to freeze at the word *cytology.* Cancer.

I have a foggy memory of his explaining to me when and where to go for diagnostic tests. It was the simplest instruction, but I had to ask him to repeat it three or four times. *Cytology*—my mind would not leave the word. That one word made me feel as though I had just been mugged at my own front door.

Why should I have reacted so strongly? My doctor was just being thorough and competent, checking the limbs in a diagnostic decision tree. There was a tiny likelihood that cancer was the problem. But this rational analysis was irrelevant at that moment. In the land of the sick, emotions reign supreme; fear is a thought away. We can be so emotionally fragile while we are ailing because our mental well-being is based in part on the illusion of invulnerability. Sickness—especially a severe illness—bursts that illusion, attacking the premise that our private world is safe and secure. Suddenly we feel weak, helpless, and vulnerable.

164

The problem is when medical personnel ignore how patients are reacting *emotionally,* even while attending to their physical condition. This inattention to the emotional reality of illness neglects a growing body of evidence showing that people's emotional states can play a sometimes significant role in their vulnerability to disease and in the course of their recovery. Modern medical care too often lacks emotional intelligence.

For the patient, any encounter with a nurse or physician can be a chance for reassuring information, comfort, and solace—or, if handled unfortunately, an invitation to despair. But too often medical caregivers are rushed or indifferent to patients' distress. To be sure, there are compassionate nurses and physicians who take the time to reassure and inform as well as administer medically. But the trend is toward a professional universe in which institutional imperatives can leave medical staff oblivious to the vulnerabilities of patients, or feeling too pressed to do anything about them. With the hard realities of a medical system increasingly timed by accountants, things seem to be getting worse.

Beyond the humanitarian argument for physicians to offer care along with cure, there are other compelling reasons to consider the psychological and social reality of patients as being within the medical realm rather than separate from it. By now a scientific case can be made that there is a margin of *medical* effectiveness, both in prevention and treatment, that can be gained by treating people's emotional state along with their medical condition. Not in every case or every condition, of course. But looking at data from hundreds and hundreds of cases, there is on average enough increment of medical benefit to suggest that an *emotional* intervention should be a standard part of medical care for the range of serious disease.

Historically, medicine in modern society has defined its mission in terms of curing *disease*—the medical disorder—while overlooking *illness*—the patient's experience of disease. Patients, by going along with this view of their problem, join a quiet conspiracy to ignore how they are reacting emotionally to their medical problems—or to dismiss those reactions as irrelevant to the course of the problem itself. That attitude is reinforced by a medical model that dismisses entirely the idea that mind influences body in any consequential way.

Yet there is an equally unproductive ideology in the other direction: the notion that people can cure themselves of even the most pernicious disease simply by making themselves happy or thinking positive thoughts, or that they are somehow to blame for having gotten sick in the first place. The result of this attitude-will-cure-all rhetoric has been to create widespread confusion and misunderstanding about the extent to which illness can be affected by the mind, and, perhaps worse, sometimes to make people feel guilty for having a disease, as though it were a sign of some moral lapse or spiritual unworthiness.

The truth lies somewhere between these extremes. By sorting through the scientific data, my aim is to clarify the contradictions and replace the nonsense with a clearer understanding of the degree to which our emotions—and emotional intelligence—play a part in health and disease.

THE BODY'S MIND: HOW EMOTIONS MATTER FOR HEALTH

In 1974 a finding in a laboratory at the School of Medicine and Dentistry, University of Rochester, rewrote biology's map of the body: Robert Ader, a psychologist, discovered that the immune system, like the brain, could learn. His result was a shock; the prevailing wisdom in medicine had been that only the brain and central nervous system could respond to experience by changing how they behaved. Ader's finding led to the investigation of what are turning out to be myriad ways the central nervous system and the immune system communicate—biological pathways that make the mind, the emotions, and the body not separate, but intimately entwined.

In his experiment white rats had been given a medication that artificially suppressed the quantity of disease-fighting T cells circulating in their blood. Each time they received the medication, they ate it along with saccharin-laced water. But Ader discovered that giving the rats the saccharin-flavored water alone, without the suppressive medication, still resulted in a lowering of the T-cell count—to the point that some of the rats were getting sick and dying. Their immune system had learned to suppress T cells in response to the flavored water. That just should not have happened, according to the best scientific understanding at the time.

The immune system is the "body's brain," as neuroscientist Francisco Varela, at Paris's Ecole Polytechnique, puts it, defining the body's own sense of self—of what belongs within it and what does not.[1] Immune cells travel in the bloodstream throughout the entire body, contacting virtually every other cell. Those cells they recognize, they leave alone; those they fail to recognize, they attack. The attack either defends us against viruses, bacteria, and cancer or, if the immune cells misidentify some of the body's own cells, creates an autoimmune disease such as allergy or lupus. Until the day Ader made his serendipitous discovery, every anatomist, every physician, and every biologist believed that the brain (along with its extensions throughout the body via the central nervous system) and the immune system were separate entities, neither able to influence the operation of the other. There was no pathway that could connect the brain centers monitoring what the rat tasted with the areas of bone marrow that manufacture T cells. Or so it had been thought for a century.

Over the years since then, Ader's modest discovery has forced a new look at the links between the immune system and the central nervous system. The field that studies this, psychoneuroimmunology, or PNI, is now a leading-edge medical science. Its very name acknowledges the links: *psycho,* or "mind"; *neuro,* for the neuroendocrine system (which subsumes the nervous system and hormone systems); and *immunology,* for the immune system.

A network of researchers is finding that the chemical messengers that operate most extensively in both brain and immune system are those that are most dense in neural areas that regulate emotion.[2] Some of the strongest evidence for a direct physical pathway allowing emotions to impact the immune system has come from David Felten, a colleague of Ader's. Felten began by noting that emotions have a powerful effect on the autonomic nervous system, which regulates everything from how much insulin is secreted to blood-pressure levels. Felten, working with his wife, Suzanne, and other colleagues, then detected a meeting point where the autonomic nervous system directly talks to lymphocytes and macrophages, cells of the immune system.[3]

In electron-microscope studies, they found synapselike contacts where the nerve terminals of the autonomic system have endings that directly abut these immune cells. This physical contact point allows the nerve cells to release neurotransmitters to regulate the immune cells; indeed, they signal back and forth. The finding is revolutionary. No one had suspected that immune cells could be targets of messages from the nerves.

To test how important these nerve endings were in the workings of the immune system, Felten went a step further. In experiments with animals he removed some nerves from lymph nodes and spleen—where immune cells are stored or made—and then used viruses to challenge the immune system. The result: a huge drop in immune response to the virus. His conclusion is that without those nerve endings the immune system simply does not respond as it should to the challenge of an invading virus or bacterium. In short, the nervous system not only connects to the immune system, but is essential for proper immune function.

Another key pathway linking emotions and the immune system is via the influence of the hormones released under stress. The catecholamines (epinephrine and norepinephrine—otherwise known as adrenaline and noradrenaline), cortisol and prolactin, and the natural opiates beta-endorphin and enkephalin are all released during stress arousal. Each has a strong impact on immune cells. While the relationships are complex, the main influence is that while these hormones surge through the body, the immune cells are hampered in their function: stress suppresses immune resistance, at least temporarily, presumably in a conservation of energy that puts a priority on the more immediate emergency, which is more pressing for survival. But if stress is constant and intense, that suppression may become long-lasting.[4]

Microbiologists and other scientists are finding more and more such connections between the brain and the cardiovascular and immune systems—having first had to accept the once-radical notion that they exist at all.[5]

TOXIC EMOTIONS: THE CLINICAL DATA

Despite such evidence, many or most physicians are still skeptical that emotions matter clinically. One reason is that while many studies have found stress and negative emotions to weaken the effectiveness of various immune cells, it is not always clear that the range of these changes is great enough to make a *medical* difference.

Even so, an increasing number of physicians acknowledge the place of emotions in medicine. For instance, Dr. Camran Nezhat, an eminent gynecological laparoscopic surgeon at Stanford University, says, "If someone scheduled for surgery tells me she's panicked that day and does not want to go through with it, I cancel the surgery." Nezhat explains, "Every surgeon knows that people who are extremely scared do terribly in surgery. They bleed too much, they have more infections and complications. They have a harder time recovering. It's much better if they are calm."

The reason is straightforward: panic and anxiety hike blood pressure, and veins distended by pressure bleed more profusely when cut by the surgeon's knife. Excess bleeding is one of the most troublesome surgical complications, one that can sometimes lead to death.

Beyond such medical anecdotes, evidence for the *clinical* importance of emotions has been mounting steadily. Perhaps the most compelling data on the medical significance of emotion come from a mass analysis combining results from 101 smaller studies into a single larger one of several thousand men and women. The study confirms that perturbing emotions are bad for health—to a degree.[6] People who experienced chronic anxiety, long periods of sadness and pessimism, unremitting tension or incessant hostility, relentless cynicism or suspiciousness, were found to have *double* the risk of disease—including asthma, arthritis, headaches, peptic ulcers, and heart disease (each representative of major, broad categories of disease). This order of magnitude makes distressing emotions as toxic a risk factor as, say, smoking or high cholesterol are for heart disease—in other words, a major threat to health.

To be sure, this is a broad statistical link, and by no means indicates that everyone who has such chronic feelings will thus more easily fall prey to a disease. But the evidence for a potent role for emotion in disease is far more extensive than this one study of studies indicates. Taking a more detailed look at the data for specific emotions, especially the big three—anger, anxiety, and depression—makes clearer some specific ways that feelings have medical significance, even if the biological mechanisms by which such emotions have their effect are yet to be fully understood.[7]

When Anger Is Suicidal

A while back, the man said, a bump on the side of his car led to a fruitless and frustrating journey. After endless insurance company red tape and auto body shops that did more damage, he still owed $800. And it wasn't even his fault. He was so fed up that whenever he got into the car he was overcome with disgust. He finally sold the car in frustration. Years later the memories still made the man livid with outrage.

This bitter memory was brought to mind purposely, as part of a study of anger in heart patients at Stanford University Medical School. All the patients in the study had, like this embittered man, suffered a first heart attack, and the question was whether anger might have a significant impact of some kind on their heart function. The effect was striking: while the patients recounted incidents that made them mad, the pumping efficiency of their hearts dropped by five percentage points.[8] Some of the patients showed a drop in pumping efficiency of 7 percent or greater—a range that cardiologists regard as a sign of a myocardial ischemia, a dangerous drop in blood flow to the heart itself.

The drop in pumping efficiency was not seen with other distressing feelings, such as anxiety, nor during physical exertion; anger seems to be the one emotion that does most harm to the heart. While recalling the upsetting incident, the patients said they were only about half as mad as they had been while it was happening, suggesting that their hearts would have been even more greatly hampered during an actual angry encounter.

This finding is part of a larger network of evidence emerging from dozens of studies pointing to the power of anger to damage the heart.[9] The old idea has not held up that a hurried, high-pressure Type-A personality is at great risk from heart disease, but from that failed theory has emerged a new finding: it is hostility that puts people at risk.

Much of the data on hostility has come from research by Dr. Redford Williams at Duke University.[10] For example, Williams found that those physicians who had had the highest scores on a test of hostility while still in medical school were seven times as likely to have died by the age of fifty as were those with low hostility scores—being prone to anger was a stronger predictor of dying young than were other risk factors such as smoking, high blood pressure, and high cholesterol. And findings by a colleague, Dr. John Barefoot at the University of North Carolina, show that in heart patients undergoing angiography, in which a tube is inserted into the coronary artery to measure lesions, scores on a test of hostility correlate with the extent and severity of coronary artery disease.

Of course, no one is saying that anger alone causes coronary artery disease; it is one of several interacting factors. As Peter Kaufman, acting chief of the Behavioral Medicine Branch of the National Heart, Lung, and Blood Institute, explained to me, "We can't yet sort out whether anger and hostility play a causal role in the early development of coronary artery disease, or whether it intensifies the problem once heart disease has begun, or both. But take a twenty-year-old who repeatedly gets angry. Each episode of anger adds an additional stress to the heart by increasing his heart rate and blood pressure. When that is repeated over and over again, it can do damage," especially because the turbulence of blood flowing through the coronary artery with each heartbeat "can cause microtears in the vessel, where plaque develops. If your heart rate is faster and blood pressure is higher because you're habitually angry, then over thirty years that may lead to a faster build-up of plaque, and so lead to coronary artery disease."[11]

Once heart disease develops, the mechanisms triggered by anger affect the very efficiency of the heart as a pump, as was shown in the study of angry memories in heart patients. The net effect is to make anger particularly lethal in those who already have heart disease. For instance, a Stanford University Medical School study of 1,012 men and women who suffered from a first heart attack and then were followed for up to eight years showed that those men who were most aggressive and hostile at the outset suffered the highest rate of second heart attacks.[12] There were similar results in a Yale School of Medicine study of 929 men who had survived heart attacks and were tracked for up to ten years.[13] Those who had been rated as easily roused to anger were three times more likely to die of cardiac arrest than those who were more even-tempered. If they also had high cholesterol levels, the added risk from anger was five times higher.

The Yale researchers point out that it may not be anger alone that heightens the risk of death from heart disease, but rather intense negative emotionality of any kind that regularly sends surges of stress hormones through the body. But overall, the strongest scientific links between emotions and heart disease are to anger: a Harvard Medical School study asked more than fifteen hundred men and women who had suffered heart attacks to describe their emotional state in the hours before the attack. Being angry more than doubled the risk of cardiac arrest in people who already had heart disease; the heightened risk lasted for about two hours after the anger was aroused.[14]

These findings do not mean that people should try to suppress anger when it is appropriate. Indeed, there is evidence that trying to completely suppress such feelings in the heat of the moment actually results in magnifying the body's agitation and may raise blood pressure.[15] On the other hand, as we saw in Chapter 5, the net effect of ventilating anger every time it is felt is simply to feed it, making it a more likely response to any annoying situation. Williams resolves this paradox by concluding that whether anger is expressed or not is less important than whether it is chronic. An occasional display of hostility is not dangerous to health; the problem arises when hostility becomes so constant as to define an antagonistic personal style— one marked by repeated feelings of mistrust and cynicism and the propensity to snide comments and put-downs, as well as more obvious bouts of temper and rage.[16]

The hopeful news is that chronic anger need not be a death sentence: hostility is a habit that can change. One group of heart-attack patients at Stanford University Medical School was enrolled in a program designed to help them soften the attitudes that gave them a short temper. This anger-control training resulted in a second-heart-attack rate 44 percent lower than for those who had not tried to change their hostility.[17] A program designed by Williams has had similar beneficial results.[18] Like the Stanford program, it teaches basic elements of emotional intelligence, particularly mindfulness of anger as it begins to stir, the ability to regulate it once it has begun, and empathy. Patients are asked to jot down cynical or hostile thoughts as they notice them. If the thoughts persist, they try to short-circuit them by saying (or thinking), "Stop!" And they are encouraged to purposely substitute reasonable thoughts for cynical, mistrustful ones during trying situations—for instance, if an elevator is delayed, to search for a benign reason rather than harbor anger against some imagined thoughtless person who may be responsible for the delay. For frustrating encounters, they learn the ability to see things from the other person's perspective—empathy is a balm for anger.

As Williams told me, "The antidote to hostility is to develop a more trusting heart. All it takes is the right motivation. When people see that their hostility can lead to an early grave, they are ready to try."

Stress: Anxiety Out of Proportion and Out of Place

I just feel anxious and tense all the time. It all started in high school. I was a straight-A student, and I worried constantly about my grades, whether the other kids and the teachers liked me, being prompt for classes—things like that. There was a lot of pressure from my parents to do well in school and to be a good role model. . . . I guess I just caved in to all that pressure, because my stomach problems began in my sophomore year of high school. Since that time, I've had to be really careful about drinking caffeine and eating spicy meals. I notice that when I'm feeling worried or tense my stomach will flare up, and since I'm usually worried about something, I'm always nauseous.[19]

Anxiety—the distress evoked by life's pressures—is perhaps the emotion with the greatest weight of scientific evidence connecting it to the onset of sickness and course of recovery. When anxiety helps us prepare to deal with some danger (a presumed utility in evolution), then it has served us well. But in modern life anxiety is more often out of proportion and out of place—distress comes in the face of situations that we must live with or that are conjured by the mind, not real dangers we need to confront. Repeated bouts of anxiety signal high levels of stress. The woman whose constant worrying primes her gastrointestinal trouble is a textbook example of how anxiety and stress exacerbate medical problems.

In a 1993 review in the *Archives of Internal Medicine* of extensive research on the stress-disease link, Yale psychologist Bruce McEwen noted a broad spectrum of effects: compromising immune function to the point that it can speed the metastasis of cancer; increasing vulnerability to viral infections; exacerbating plaque formation leading to atherosclerosis and blood clotting leading to myocardial infarction; accelerating the onset of Type I diabetes and the course of Type II diabetes; and worsening or triggering an asthma attack.[20] Stress can also lead to ulceration of the gastrointestinal tract, triggering symptoms in ulcerative colitis and in inflammatory bowel disease. The brain itself is susceptible to the long-term effects of sustained stress, including damage to the hippocampus, and so to memory. In general, says McEwen, "evidence is mounting that the nervous system is subject to 'wear and tear' as a result of stressful experiences."[21]

Particularly compelling evidence for the medical impact from distress has come from studies with infectious diseases such as colds, the flu, and herpes. We are continually exposed to such viruses, but ordinarily our immune system fights them off—except that under emotional stress those defenses more often fail. In experiments in which the robustness of the immune system has been assayed directly, stress and anxiety have been found to weaken it, but in most such results it is unclear whether the range of immune weakening is of clinical significance—that is, great enough to open the way to disease.[22] For that reason stronger scientific links of stress and anxiety to medical vulnerability come from prospective studies: those that start with healthy people and monitor first a heightening of distress followed by a weakening of the immune system and the onset of illness.

In one of the most scientifically compelling studies, Sheldon Cohen, a psychologist at Carnegie-Mellon University, working with scientists at a specialized colds research unit in Sheffield, England, carefully assessed how much stress people were feeling in their lives, and then systematically exposed them to a cold virus. Not everyone so exposed actually comes down with a cold; a robust immune system can—and constantly does—resist the cold virus. Cohen found that the more stress in their lives, the more likely people were to catch cold. Among those with little stress, 27 percent came down with a cold after being exposed to the virus; among those with the most stressful lives, 47 percent got the cold—direct evidence that stress itself weakens the immune system.[23] (While this may be one of those scientific results that confirms what everyone has observed or suspected all along, it is considered a landmark finding because of its scientific rigor.)

Likewise, married couples who for three months kept daily checklists of hassles and upsetting events such as marital fights showed a strong pattern: three or four days after an especially intense batch of upsets, they came down with a cold or upper-respiratory infection. That lag period is precisely the incubation time for many common cold viruses, suggesting that being exposed while they were most worried and upset made them especially vulnerable.[24]

The same stress-infection pattern holds for the herpes virus—both the type that causes cold sores on the lip and the type that causes genital lesions. Once people have been exposed to the herpes virus, it stays latent in the body, flaring up from time to time. The activity of the herpes virus can be tracked by levels of antibodies to it in the blood. Using this measure, reactivation of the herpes virus has been found in medical students undergoing year-end exams, in recently separated women, and among people under constant pressure from caring for a family member with Alzheimer's disease.[25]

The toll of anxiety is not just that it lowers the immune response; other research is showing adverse effects on the cardiovascular system. While chronic hostility and repeated episodes of anger seem to put men at greatest risk for heart disease, the more deadly emotion in women may be anxiety and fear. In research at Stanford University School of Medicine with more than a thousand men and women who had suffered a first heart attack, those women who went on to suffer a second heart attack were marked by high levels of fearfulness and anxiety. In many cases the fearfulness took the form of crippling phobias: after their first heart attack the patients stopped driving, quit their jobs, or avoided going out.[26]

The insidious physical effects of mental stress and anxiety—the kind produced by high-pressure jobs, or high-pressure lives such as that of a single mother juggling day care and a job—are being pinpointed at an anatomically fine-grained level. For example, Stephen Manuck, a University of Pittsburgh psychologist, put thirty volunteers through a rigorous, anxiety-riddled ordeal in a laboratory while he monitored the men's blood, assaying a substance secreted by blood platelets called adenosine triphosphate, or ATP, which can trigger blood-vessel changes that may lead to heart attacks and strokes. While the volunteers were under the intense stress, their ATP levels rose sharply, as did their heart rate and blood pressure.

Understandably, health risks seem greatest for those whose jobs are high in "strain": having high-pressure performance demands while having little or no control over how to get the job done (a predicament that gives bus drivers, for instance, a high rate of hypertension). For example, in a study of 569 patients with colorectal cancer and a matched comparison group, those who said that in the previous ten years they had experienced severe on-the-job aggravation were five and a half times more likely to have developed the cancer compared to those with no such stress in their lives.[27]

Because the medical toll of distress is so broad, relaxation techniques— which directly counter the physiological arousal of stress—are being used clinically to ease the symptoms of a wide variety of chronic illnesses. These include cardiovascular disease, some types of diabetes, arthritis, asthma, gastrointestinal disorders, and chronic pain, to name a few. To the degree any symptoms are worsened by stress and emotional distress, helping patients become more relaxed and able to handle their turbulent feelings can often offer some reprieve.[28]

The Medical Costs of Depression

She had been diagnosed with metastatic breast cancer, a return and spread of the malignancy several years after what she had thought was successful surgery for the disease. Her doctor could no longer talk of a cure, and the chemotherapy, at best, might offer just a few more months of life. Understandably, she was depressed—so much so that whenever she went to her oncologist, she found herself at some point bursting out into tears. Her oncologist's response each time: asking her to leave the office immediately.

Apart from the hurtfulness of the oncologist's coldness, did it matter medically that he would not deal with his patient's constant sadness? By the time a disease has become so virulent, it would be unlikely that any emotion would have an appreciable effect on its progress. While the woman's depression most certainly dimmed the quality of her final months, the medical evidence that melancholy might affect the course of cancer is as yet mixed.[29] But cancer aside, a smattering of studies suggest a role for depression in many other medical conditions, especially in worsening a sickness once it has begun. The evidence is mounting that for patients with serious disease who are depressed, it would pay medically to treat their depression too.

One complication in treating depression in medical patients is that its symptoms, including loss of appetite and lethargy, are easily mistaken for signs of other diseases, particularly by physicians with little training in psychiatric diagnosis. That inability to diagnose depression may itself add to the problem, since it means that a patient's depression—like that of the weepy breast-cancer patient—goes unnoticed and untreated. And that failure to diagnose and treat may add to the risk of death in severe disease.

For instance, of 100 patients who received bone marrow transplants, 12 of the 13 who had been depressed died within the first year of the transplant, while 34 of the remaining 87 were still alive two years later.[30] And in patients with chronic kidney failure who were receiving dialysis, those who were diagnosed with major depression were most likely to die within the following two years; depression was a stronger predictor of death than any medical sign.[31] Here the route connecting emotion to medical status was not biological but attitudinal: The depressed patients were much worse about complying with their medical regimens—cheating on their diets, for example, which put them at higher risk.

Heart disease too seems to be exacerbated by depression. In a study of 2,832 middle-aged men and women tracked for twelve years, those who felt a sense of nagging despair and hopelessness had a heightened rate of death from heart disease.[32] And for the 3 percent or so who were most severely depressed, the death rate from heart disease, compared to the rate for those with no feelings of depression, was four times greater.

Depression seems to pose a particularly grave medical risk for heart attack survivors.[33] In a study of patients in a Montreal hospital who were discharged after being treated for a first heart attack, depressed patients had a sharply higher risk of dying within the following six months. Among the one in eight patients who were seriously depressed, the death rate was five times higher than for others with comparable disease—an effect as great as that of major medical risks for cardiac death, such as left ventricular dysfunction or a history of previous heart attacks. Among the possible mechanisms that might explain why depression so greatly increases the odds of a later heart attack are its effects on heart rate variability, increasing the risk of fatal arrhythmias.

Depression has also been found to complicate recovery from hip fracture. In a study of elderly women with hip fracture, several thousand were given psychiatric evaluations on their admission to the hospital. Those who were depressed on admission stayed an average of eight days longer than those with comparable injury but no depression, and were only a third as likely ever to walk again. But depressed women who had psychiatric help for their depression along with other medical care needed less physical therapy to walk again and had fewer rehospitalizations over the three months after their return home from the hospital.

Likewise, in a study of patients whose condition was so dire that they were among the top 10 percent of those using medical services—often because of having multiple illnesses, such as both heart disease and diabetes—about one in six had serious depression. When these patients were treated for the problem, the number of days per year that they were disabled dropped from 79 to 51 for those who had major depression, and from 62 days per year to just 18 in those who had been treated for mild depression.[34]

THE MEDICAL BENEFITS OF POSITIVE FEELINGS

The cumulative evidence for adverse medical effects from anger, anxiety, and depression, then, is compelling. Both anger and anxiety, when chronic, can make people more susceptible to a range of disease. And while depression may not make people more vulnerable to becoming ill, it does seem to impede medical recovery and heighten the risk of death, especially with more frail patients with severe conditions.

But if chronic emotional distress in its many forms is toxic, the opposite range of emotion can be tonic—to a degree. This by no means says that positive emotion is curative, or that laughter or happiness alone will turn the course of a serious disease. The edge positive emotions offer seems subtle, but, by using studies with large numbers of people, can be teased out of the mass of complex variables that affect the course of disease.

The Price of Pessimism—and Advantages of Optimism

As with depression, there are medical costs to pessimism—and corresponding benefits from optimism. For example, 122 men who had their first heart attack were evaluated on their degree of optimism or pessimism. Eight years later, of the 25 most pessimistic men, 21 had died; of the 25 most optimistic, just 6 had died. Their mental outlook proved a better predictor of survival than any medical risk factor, including the amount of damage to the heart in the first attack, artery blockage, cholesterol level, or blood pressure. And in other research, patients going into artery bypass surgery who were more optimistic had a much faster recovery and fewer medical complications during and after surgery than did more pessimistic patients.[35]

Like its near cousin optimism, hope has healing power. People who have a great deal of hopefulness are, understandably, better able to bear up under trying circumstances, including medical difficulties. In a study of people paralyzed from spinal injuries, those who had more hope were able to gain greater levels of physical mobility compared to other patients with similar degrees of injury, but who felt less hopeful. Hope is especially telling in paralysis from spinal injury, since this medical tragedy typically involves a man who is paralyzed in his twenties by an accident and will remain so for the rest of his life. How he reacts emotionally will have broad consequences for the degree to which he will make the efforts that might bring him greater physical and social functioning.[36]

Just why an optimistic or pessimistic outlook should have health consequences is open to any of several explanations. One theory proposes that
pessimism leads to depression, which in turn interferes with the resistance of
the immune system to tumors and infection—an unproven speculation at
present. Or it may be that pessimists neglect themselves—some studies have
found that pessimists smoke and drink more, and exercise less, than optimists, and are generally much more careless about their health habits. Or it
may one day turn out that the physiology of hopefulness is itself somehow
helpful biologically to the body's fight against disease.

With a Little Help From My Friends:
The Medical Value of Relationships

Add the sounds of silence to the list of emotional risks to health—and close
emotional ties to the list of protective factors. Studies done over two decades
involving more than thirty-seven thousand people show that social
isolation—the sense that you have nobody with whom you can share your
private feelings or have close contact—doubles the chances of sickness or
death.[37] Isolation itself, a 1987 report in *Science* concluded, "is as significant
to mortality rates as smoking, high blood pressure, high cholesterol, obesity,
and lack of physical exercise." Indeed, smoking increases mortality risk by a
factor of just 1.6, while social isolation does so by a factor of 2.0, making it a
greater health risk.[38]

Isolation is harder on men than on women. Isolated men were two to three
times more likely to die as were men with close social ties; for isolated
women, the risk was one and a half times greater than for more socially
connected women. The difference between men and women in the impact of
isolation may be because women's relationships tend to be emotionally
closer than men's; a few strands of such social ties for a woman may be more
comforting than the same small number of friendships for a man.

Of course, solitude is not the same as isolation; many people who live on
their own or see few friends are content and healthy. Rather, it is the
subjective sense of being cut off from people and having no one to turn to
that is the medical risk. This finding is ominous in light of the increasing
isolation bred by solitary TV-watching and the falling away of social habits
such as clubs and visits in modern urban societies, and suggests an added
value to self-help groups such as Alcoholics Anonymous as surrogate communities.

The power of isolation as a mortality risk factor—and the healing power of close ties—can be seen in the study of one hundred bone marrow transplant patients.[39] Among patients who felt they had strong emotional support from their spouse, family, or friends, 54 percent survived the transplants after two years, versus just 20 percent among those who reported little such support. Similarly, elderly people who suffer heart attacks, but have two or more people in their lives they can rely on for emotional support, are more than twice as likely to survive longer than a year after an attack than are those people with no such support.[40]

Perhaps the most telling testimony to the healing potency of emotional ties is a Swedish study published in 1993.[41] All the men living in the Swedish city of Göteborg who were born in 1933 were offered a free medical exam; seven years later the 752 men who had come for the exam were contacted again. Of these, 41 had died in the intervening years.

Men who had originally reported being under intense emotional stress had a death rate three times greater than those who said their lives were calm and placid. The emotional distress was due to events such as serious financial trouble, feeling insecure at work or being forced out of a job, being the object of a legal action, or going through a divorce. Having had three or more of these troubles within the year before the exam was a stronger predictor of dying within the ensuing seven years than were medical indicators such as high blood pressure, high concentrations of blood triglycerides, or high serum cholesterol levels.

Yet among men who said they had a dependable web of intimacy—a wife, close friends, and the like—*there was no relationship whatever* between high stress levels and death rate. Having people to turn to and talk with, people who could offer solace, help, and suggestions, protected them from the deadly impact of life's rigors and trauma.

The quality of relationships as well as their sheer number seems key to buffering stress. Negative relationships take their own toll. Marital arguments, for example, have a negative impact on the immune system.[42] One study of college roommates found that the more they disliked each other, the more susceptible they were to colds and the flu, and the more frequently they went to doctors. John Cacioppo, the Ohio State University psychologist who did the roommate study, told me, "It's the most important relationships in your life, the people you see day in and day out, that seem to be crucial for your health. And the more significant the relationship is in your life, the more it matters for your health."[43]

The Healing Power of Emotional Support

In *The Merry Adventures of Robin Hood,* Robin advises a young follower: "Tell us thy troubles and speak freely. A flow of words doth ever ease the heart of sorrows; it is like opening the waste where the mill dam is overfull." This bit of folk wisdom has great merit; unburdening a troubled heart appears to be good medicine. The scientific corroboration of Robin's advice comes from James Pennebaker, a Southern Methodist University psychologist, who has shown in a series of experiments that getting people to talk about the thoughts that trouble them most has a beneficial medical effect.[44] His method is remarkably simple: he asks people to write, for fifteen to twenty minutes a day over five or so days, about, for example, "the most traumatic experience of your entire life," or some pressing worry of the moment. What people write can be kept entirely to themselves if they like.

The net effect of this confessional is striking: enhanced immune function, significant drops in health-center visits in the following six months, fewer days missed from work, and even improved liver enzyme function. More-over, those whose writing showed most evidence of turbulent feelings had the greatest improvements in their immune function. A specific pattern emerged as the "healthiest" way to ventilate troubling feelings: at first ex-pressing a high level of sadness, anxiety, anger—whatever troubling feelings the topic brought up; then, over the course of the next several days weaving a narrative, finding some meaning in the trauma or travail.

That process, of course, seems akin to what happens when people explore such troubles in psychotherapy. Indeed, Pennebaker's findings suggest one reason why other studies show medical patients given psychotherapy in addition to surgery or medical treatment often fare better *medically* than do those who receive medical treatment alone.[45]

Perhaps the most powerful demonstration of the clinical power of emo-tional support was in groups at Stanford University Medical School for women with advanced metastatic breast cancer. After an initial treatment, often including surgery, these women's cancer had returned and was spread-ing through their bodies. It was only a matter of time, clinically speaking, until the spreading cancer killed them. Dr. David Spiegel, who conducted the study, was himself stunned by the findings, as was the medical community: women with advanced breast cancer who went to weekly meetings with others survived *twice as long* as did women with the same disease who faced it on their own.[46]

All the women received standard medical care; the only difference was that some also went to the groups, where they were able to unburden themselves with others who understood what they faced and were willing to listen to their fears, their pain, and their anger. Often this was the only place where the women could be open about these emotions, because other people in their lives dreaded talking with them about the cancer and their imminent death. Women who attended the groups lived for thirty-seven additional months, on average, while those with the disease who did not go to the groups died, on average, in nineteen months—a gain in life expectancy for such patients beyond the reach of any medication or other medical treatment. As Dr. Jimmie Holland, the chief psychiatric oncologist at Sloan-Kettering Memorial Hospital, a cancer treatment center in New York City, put it to me, "Every cancer patient should be in a group like this." Indeed, if it had been a new drug that produced the extended life expectancy, pharmaceutical companies would be battling to produce it.

BRINGING EMOTIONAL INTELLIGENCE TO MEDICAL CARE

The day a routine checkup spotted some blood in my urine, my doctor sent me for a diagnostic test in which I was injected with a radioactive dye. I lay on a table while an overhead X-ray machine took successive images of the dye's progression through my kidneys and bladder. I had company for the test: a close friend, a physician himself, happened to be visiting for a few days and offered to come to the hospital with me. He sat in the room while the X-ray machine, on an automated track, rotated for new camera angles, whirred and clicked; rotated, whirred, clicked.

The test took an hour and a half. At the very end a kidney specialist hurried into the room, quickly introduced himself, and disappeared to scan the X-rays. He didn't return to tell me what they showed.

As we were leaving the exam room my friend and I passed the nephrologist. Feeling shaken and somewhat dazed by the test, I did not have the presence of mind to ask the one question that had been on my mind all morning. But my companion, the physician, did: "Doctor," he said, "my friend's father died of bladder cancer. He's anxious to know if you saw any signs of cancer in the X-rays."

"No abnormalities," was the curt reply as the nephrologist hurried on to his next appointment.

My inability to ask the single question I cared about most is repeated a thousand times each day in hospitals and clinics everywhere. A study of patients in physicians' waiting rooms found that each had an average of three or more questions in mind to ask the physician they were about to see. But when the patients left the physician's office, an average of only one and a half of those questions had been answered.[47] This finding speaks to one of the many ways patients' emotional needs are unmet by today's medicine. Unanswered questions feed uncertainty, fear, catastrophizing. And they lead patients to balk at going along with treatment regimes they don't fully understand.

There are many ways medicine can expand its view of health to include the emotional realities of illness. For one, patients could routinely be offered fuller information essential to the decisions they must make about their own medical care; some services now offer any caller a state-of-the-art computer search of the medical literature on what ails them, so that patients can be more equal partners with their physicians in making informed decisions.[48] Another approach is programs that, in a few minutes' time, teach patients to be effective questioners with their physicians, so that when they have three questions in mind as they wait for the doctor, they will come out of the office with three answers.[49]

Moments when patients face surgery or invasive and painful tests are fraught with anxiety—and are a prime opportunity to deal with the emotional dimension. Some hospitals have developed presurgery instruction for patients that help them assuage their fears and handle their discomforts—for example, by teaching patients relaxation techniques, answering their questions well in advance of surgery, and telling them several days ahead of surgery precisely what they are likely to experience during their recovery. The result: patients recover from surgery an average of two to three days sooner.[50]

Being a hospital patient can be a tremendously lonely, helpless experience. But some hospitals have begun to design rooms so that family members can stay with patients, cooking and caring for them as they would at home—a progressive step that, ironically, is routine throughout the Third World.[51]

Relaxation training can help patients deal with some of the distress their symptoms bring, as well as with the emotions that may be triggering or exacerbating their symptoms. An exemplary model is Jon Kabat-Zinn's Stress Reduction Clinic at the University of Massachusetts Medical Center, which offers a ten-week course in mindfulness and yoga to patients; the emphasis is on being mindful of emotional episodes as they are happening, and on cultivating a daily practice that offers deep relaxation. Hospitals have made instructional tapes from the course available over patients' television sets—a far better emotional diet for the bedridden than the usual fare, soap operas.[52]

Relaxation and yoga are also at the core of the innovative program for treating heart disease developed by Dr. Dean Ornish.[53] After a year of this program, which included a low-fat diet, patients whose heart disease was severe enough to warrant a coronary bypass actually reversed the buildup of artery-clogging plaque. Ornish tells me that relaxation training is one of the most important parts of the program. Like Kabat-Zinn's, it takes advantage of what Dr. Herbert Benson calls the "relaxation response," the physiological opposite of the stress arousal that contributes to such a wide spectrum of medical problems.

Finally, there is the added medical value of an empathic physician or nurse, attuned to patients, able to listen and be heard. This means fostering "relationship-centered care," recognizing that the relationship between physician and patient is itself a factor of significance. Such relationships would be fostered more readily if medical education included some basic tools of emotional intelligence, especially self-awareness and the arts of empathy and listening.[54]

TOWARD A MEDICINE THAT CARES

Such steps are a beginning. But for medicine to enlarge its vision to embrace the impact of emotions, two large implications of the scientific findings must be taken to heart:

1. *Helping people better manage their upsetting feelings—anger, anxiety, depression, pessimism, and loneliness—is a form of disease prevention.* Since the data show that the toxicity of these emotions, when chronic, is on a par with smoking cigarettes, helping people handle them better could potentially have a medical payoff as great as getting heavy smokers to quit. One way to do this that could have broad public-health effects would be to impart most basic emotional intelligence skills to children, so that they become lifelong habits. Another high-payoff preventive strategy would be to teach emotion management to people reaching retirement age, since emotional well-being is one factor that determines whether an older person declines rapidly or thrives. A third target group might be so-called at-risk populations—the very poor, single working mothers, residents of high-crime

neighborhoods, and the like—who live under extraordinary pressure day in and day out, and so might do better medically with help in handling the emotional toll of these stresses.

2. *Many patients can benefit measurably when their psychological needs are attended to along with their purely medical ones.* While it is a step toward more humane care when a physician or nurse offers a distressed patient comfort and consolation, more can be done. But emotional care is an opportunity too often lost in the way medicine is practiced today; it is a blind spot for medicine. Despite mounting data on the medical usefulness of attending to emotional needs, as well as supporting evidence for connections between the brain's emotional center and the immune system, many physicians remain skeptical that their patients' emotions matter clinically, dismissing the evidence for this as trivial and anecdotal, as "fringe," or, worse, as the exaggerations of a self-promoting few.

Though more and more patients seek a more humane medicine, it is becoming endangered. Of course, there remain dedicated nurses and physicians who give their patients tender, sensitive care. But the changing culture of medicine itself, as it becomes more responsive to the imperatives of business, is making such care increasingly difficult to find.

On the other hand, there may be a business advantage to humane medicine: treating emotional distress in patients, early evidence suggests, can save money—especially to the extent that it prevents or delays the onset of sickness, or helps patients heal more quickly. In a study of elderly patients with hip fracture at Mt. Sinai School of Medicine in New York City and at Northwestern University, patients who received therapy for depression in addition to normal orthopedic care left the hospital an average of two days earlier; total savings for the hundred or so patients was $97,361 in medical costs.[55]

Such care also makes patients more satisfied with their physicians and medical treatment. In the emerging medical marketplace, where patients often have the option to choose between competing health plans, satisfaction levels will no doubt enter the equation of these very personal decisions—souring experiences can lead patients to go elsewhere for care, while pleasing ones translate into loyalty.

Finally, medical ethics may demand such an approach. An editorial in the *Journal of the American Medical Association,* commenting on a report that depression increases fivefold the likelihood of dying after being treated for a heart attack, notes: "[T]he clear demonstration that psychological factors like depression and social isolation distinguish the coronary heart disease patients at highest risk means it would be unethical not to start trying to treat these factors."[56]

If the findings on emotions and health mean anything, it is that medical care that neglects how people *feel* as they battle a chronic or severe disease is no longer adequate. It is time for medicine to take more methodical advantage of the link between emotion and health. What is now the exception could—and should—be part of the mainstream, so that a more caring medicine is available to us all. At the least it would make medicine more humane. And, for some, it could speed the course of recovery. "Compassion," as one patient put it in an open letter to his surgeon, "is not mere hand holding. It is good medicine."[57]

PART FOUR

WINDOWS
OF
OPPORTUNITY

12

The Family Crucible

It's a low-key family tragedy. Carl and Ann are showing their daughter Leslie, just five, how to play a brand-new video game. But as Leslie starts to play, her parents' overly eager attempts to "help" her just seem to get in the way. Contradictory orders fly in every direction.

"To the right, to the right—stop. Stop. Stop!" Ann, the mother, urges, her voice growing more intent and anxious as Leslie, sucking on her lip and staring wide-eyed at the video screen, struggles to follow these directives.

"See, you're not lined up . . . put it to the left! To the left!" Carl, the girl's father, brusquely orders.

Meanwhile Ann, her eyes rolling upward in frustration, yells over his advice, "Stop! Stop!"

Leslie, unable to please either her father or her mother, contorts her jaw in tension and blinks as her eyes fill with tears.

Her parents start bickering, ignoring Leslie's tears. "She's not moving the stick *that* much!" Ann tells Carl, exasperated.

As the tears start rolling down Leslie's cheeks, neither parent makes any move that indicates they notice or care. As Leslie raises her hand to wipe her eyes, her father snaps, "Okay, put your hand back on the stick . . . you wanna get ready to shoot. Okay, put it over!" And her mother barks, "Okay, move it just a teeny bit!"

But by now Leslie is sobbing softly, alone with her anguish.

At such moments children learn deep lessons. For Leslie one conclusion from this painful exchange might well be that neither her parents, nor anyone else, for that matter, cares about her feelings.[1] When similar moments are repeated countless times over the course of childhood they impart some of the most fundamental emotional messages of a lifetime—lessons that can determine a life course. Family life is our first school for emotional learning; in this intimate cauldron we learn how to feel about ourselves and how others will react to our feelings; how to think about these feelings and what choices we have in reacting; how to read and express hopes and fears. This emotional schooling operates not just through the things that parents say and do directly to children, but also in the models they offer for handling their own feelings and those that pass between husband and wife. Some parents are gifted emotional teachers, others atrocious.

There are hundreds of studies showing that how parents treat their children—whether with harsh discipline or empathic understanding, with indifference or warmth, and so on—has deep and lasting consequences for the child's emotional life. Only recently, though, have there been hard data showing that having emotionally intelligent parents is itself of enormous benefit to a child. The ways a couple handles the feelings between them—in addition to their direct dealings with a child—impart powerful lessons to their children, who are astute learners, attuned to the subtlest emotional exchanges in the family. When research teams led by Carole Hooven and John Gottman at the University of Washington did a microanalysis of interactions in couples on how the partners handled their children, they found that those couples who were more emotionally competent in the marriage were also the most effective in helping their children with their emotional ups and downs.[2]

The families were first seen when one of their children was just five years old, and again when the child had reached nine. In addition to observing the parents talk with each other, the research team also watched families (including Leslie's) as the father or mother tried to show their young child how to operate a new video game—a seemingly innocuous interaction, but quite telling about the emotional currents that run between parent and child.

Some mothers and fathers were like Ann and Carl: overbearing, losing patience with their child's ineptness, raising their voices in disgust or exasperation, some even putting their child down as "stupid"—in short, falling prey to the same tendencies toward contempt and disgust that eat away at a marriage. Others, however, were patient with their child's errors, helping the child figure the game out in his or her own way rather than imposing the parents' will. The video game session was a surprisingly powerful barometer of the parents' emotional style.

The three most common emotionally inept parenting styles proved to be:

• *Ignoring feelings altogether.* Such parents treat a child's emotional upset as trivial or a bother, something they should wait to blow over. They fail to use emotional moments as a chance to get closer to the child or to help the child learn lessons in emotional competence.

• *Being too laissez-faire.* These parents notice how a child feels, but hold that however a child handles the emotional storm is fine—even, say, hitting. Like those who ignore a child's feelings, these parents rarely step in to try to show their child an alternative emotional response. They try to soothe all upsets, and will, for instance, use bargaining and bribes to get their child to stop being sad or angry.

• *Being contemptuous, showing no respect for how the child feels.* Such parents are typically disapproving, harsh in both their criticisms and their punishments. They might, for instance, forbid any display of the child's anger at all, and become punitive at the least sign of irritability. These are the parents who angrily yell at a child who is trying to tell his side of the story, "Don't you talk back to me!"

Finally, there are parents who seize the opportunity of a child's upset to act as what amounts to an emotional coach or mentor. They take their child's feelings seriously enough to try to understand exactly what is upsetting them ("Are you angry because Tommy hurt your feelings?") and to help the child find positive ways to soothe their feelings ("Instead of hitting him, why don't you find a toy to play with on your own until you feel like playing with him again?").

In order for parents to be effective coaches in this way, they must have a fairly good grasp of the rudiments of emotional intelligence themselves. One of the basic emotional lessons for a child, for example, is how to distinguish among feelings; a father who is too tuned out of, say, his own sadness cannot help his son understand the difference between grieving over a loss, feeling sad in a sad movie, and the sadness that arises when something bad happens to someone the child cares about. Beyond this distinction, there are more sophisticated insights, such as that anger is so often prompted by first feeling hurt.

As children grow the specific emotional lessons they are ready for—and in need of—shift. As we saw in Chapter 7 the lessons in empathy begin in infancy, with parents who attune to their baby's feelings. Though some emotional skills are honed with friends through the years, emotionally adept parents can do much to help their children with each of the basics of emotional intelligence: learning how to recognize, manage, and harness their feelings; empathizing; and handling the feelings that arise in their relationships.

The impact on children of such parenting is extraordinarily sweeping.[3] The University of Washington team found that when parents are emotionally adept, compared to those who handle feelings poorly, their children—understandably—get along better with, show more affection toward, and have less tension around their parents. But beyond that, these children also are better at handling their own emotions, are more effective at soothing themselves when upset, and get upset less often. The children are also more relaxed *biologically,* with lower levels of stress hormones and other physiological indicators of emotional arousal (a pattern that, if sustained through life, might well augur better physical health, as we saw in Chapter 11). Other advantages are social: these children are more popular with and are better-liked by their peers, and are seen by their teachers as more socially skilled. Their parents and teachers alike rate these children as having fewer behavioral problems such as rudeness or aggressiveness. Finally, the benefits are cognitive; these children can pay attention better, and so are more effective learners. Holding IQ constant, the five-year-olds whose parents were good coaches had higher achievement scores in math and reading when they reached third grade (a powerful argument for teaching emotional skills to help prepare children for learning as well as life). Thus the payoff for children whose parents are emotionally adept is a surprising—almost astounding—range of advantages across, and beyond, the spectrum of emotional intelligence.

HEART START

The impact of parenting on emotional competence starts in the cradle. Dr. T. Berry Brazelton, the eminent Harvard pediatrician, has a simple diagnostic test of a baby's basic outlook toward life. He offers two blocks to an eight-month-old, and then shows the baby how he wants her to put the two blocks together. A baby who is hopeful about life, who has confidence in her own abilities, says Brazelton,

> will pick up one block, mouth it, rub it in her hair, drop it over the side of the table, watching to see whether you will retrieve it for her. When you do, she finally completes the requested task—place the two blocks together. Then she looks up at you with a bright-eyed look of expectancy that says, "Tell me how great I am!"[4]

Babies like these have gotten a goodly dose of approval and encouragement from the adults in their lives; they expect to succeed in life's little challenges. By contrast, babies who come from homes too bleak, chaotic, or neglectful go about the same small task in a way that signals they already expect to fail. It is not that these babies fail to bring the blocks together; they understand the instruction and have the coordination to comply. But even when they do, reports Brazelton, their demeanor is "hangdog," a look that says, "I'm no good. See, I've failed." Such children are likely to go through life with a defeatist outlook, expecting no encouragement or interest from teachers, finding school joyless, perhaps eventually dropping out.

The difference between the two outlooks—children who are confident and optimistic versus those who expect to fail—starts to take shape in the first few years of life. Parents, says Brazelton, "need to understand how their actions can help generate the confidence, the curiosity, the pleasure in learning and the understanding of limits" that help children succeed in life. His advice is informed by a growing body of evidence showing that success in school depends to a surprising extent on emotional characteristics formed in the years before a child enters school. As we saw in Chapter 6, for example, the ability of four-year-olds to control the impulse to grab for a marshmallow predicted a 210-point advantage in their SAT scores fourteen years later.

The first opportunity for shaping the ingredients of emotional intelligence is in the earliest years, though these capacities continue to form throughout the school years. The emotional abilities children acquire in later life build on those of the earliest years. And these abilities, as we saw in Chapter 6, are the essential foundation for all learning. A report from the National Center for Clinical Infant Programs makes the point that school success is not predicted by a child's fund of facts or a precocious ability to read so much as by emotional and social measures: being self-assured and interested; knowing what kind of behavior is expected and how to rein in the impulse to misbehave; being able to wait, to follow directions, and to turn to teachers for help; and expressing needs while getting along with other children.[5]

Almost all students who do poorly in school, says the report, lack one or more of these elements of emotional intelligence (regardless of whether they also have cognitive difficulties such as learning disabilities). The magnitude of the problem is not minor; in some states close to one in five children have to repeat first grade, and then as the years go on fall further behind their peers, becoming increasingly discouraged, resentful, and disruptive.

A child's readiness for school depends on the most basic of all knowledge, *how* to learn. The report lists the seven key ingredients of this crucial capacity—all related to emotional intelligence:[6]

1. *Confidence.* A sense of control and mastery of one's body, behavior, and world; the child's sense that he is more likely than not to succeed at what he undertakes, and that adults will be helpful.

2. *Curiosity.* The sense that finding out about things is positive and leads to pleasure.

3. *Intentionality.* The wish and capacity to have an impact, and to act upon that with persistence. This is related to a sense of competence, of being effective.

4. *Self-control.* The ability to modulate and control one's own actions in age-appropriate ways; a sense of inner control.

5. *Relatedness.* The ability to engage with others based on the sense of being understood by and understanding others.

6. *Capacity to communicate.* The wish and ability to verbally exchange ideas, feelings, and concepts with others. This is related to a sense of trust in others and of pleasure in engaging with others, including adults.

7. *Cooperativeness.* The ability to balance one's own needs with those of others in group activity.

Whether or not a child arrives at school on the first day of kindergarten with these capabilities depends greatly on how much her parents—and preschool teachers—have given her the kind of care that amounts to a "Heart Start," the emotional equivalent of the Head Start programs.

GETTING THE EMOTIONAL BASICS

Say a two-month-old baby wakes up at 3 A.M. and starts crying. Her mother comes in and, for the next half hour, the baby contentedly nurses in her mother's arms while her mother gazes at her affectionately, telling her that she's happy to see her, even in the middle of the night. The baby, content in her mother's love, drifts back to sleep.

Now say another two-month-old baby, who also awoke crying in the wee hours, is met instead by a mother who is tense and irritable, having fallen asleep just an hour before after a fight with her husband. The baby starts to tense up the moment his mother abruptly picks him up, telling him, "Just be quiet—I can't stand one more thing! Come on, let's get it over with." As the baby nurses his mother stares stonily ahead, not looking at him, reviewing her fight with his father, getting more agitated herself as she mulls it over. The baby, sensing her tension, squirms, stiffens, and stops nursing. "That's all you want?" his mother says. "Then don't eat." With the same abruptness she puts him back in his crib and stalks out, letting him cry until he falls back to sleep, exhausted.

The two scenarios are presented by the report from the National Center for Clinical Infant Programs as examples of the kinds of interaction that, if repeated over and over, instill very different feelings in a toddler about himself and his closest relationships.[7] The first baby is learning that people can be trusted to notice her needs and counted on to help, and that she can be effective in getting help; the second is finding that no one really cares, that people can't be counted on, and that his efforts to get solace will meet with failure. Of course, most babies get at least a taste of both kinds of interaction. But to the degree that one or the other is typical of how parents treat a child over the years, basic emotional lessons will be imparted about how secure a child is in the world, how effective he feels, and how dependable others are. Erik Erikson put it in terms of whether a child comes to feel a "basic trust" or a basic mistrust.

Such emotional learning begins in life's earliest moments, and continues throughout childhood. All the small exchanges between parent and child have an emotional subtext, and in the repetition of these messages over the years children form the core of their emotional outlook and capabilities. A little girl who finds a puzzle frustrating and asks her busy mother to help gets one message if the reply is the mother's clear pleasure at the request, and quite another if it's a curt "Don't bother me—I've got important work to do." When such encounters become typical of child and parent, they mold the child's emotional expectations about relationships, outlooks that will flavor her functioning in all realms of life, for better or worse.

The risks are greatest for those children whose parents are grossly inept—immature, abusing drugs, depressed or chronically angry, or simply aimless and living chaotic lives. Such parents are far less likely to give adequate care, let alone attune to their toddler's emotional needs. Simple neglect, studies find, can be more damaging than outright abuse.[8] A survey of maltreated children found the neglected youngsters doing the worst of all: they were the most anxious, inattentive, and apathetic, alternately aggressive and withdrawn. The rate for having to repeat first grade among them was 65 percent.

The first three or four years of life are a period when the toddler's brain grows to about two thirds its full size, and evolves in complexity at a greater rate than it ever will again. During this period key kinds of learning take place more readily than later in life—emotional learning foremost among them.

During this time severe stress can impair the brain's learning centers (and so be damaging to the intellect). Though as we shall see, this can be remedied to some extent by experiences later in life, the impact of this early learning is profound. As one report sums up the key emotional lesson of life's first four years, the lasting consequences are great:

> A child who cannot focus his attention, who is suspicious rather than trusting, sad or angry rather than optimistic, destructive rather than respectful and one who is overcome with anxiety, preoccupied with frightening fantasy and feels generally unhappy about himself—such a child has little opportunity at all, let alone equal opportunity, to claim the possibilities of the world as his own.[9]

HOW TO RAISE A BULLY

Much can be learned about the lifelong effects of emotionally inept parenting—particularly its role in making children aggressive—from longitudinal studies such as one of 870 children from upstate New York who were followed from the time they were eight until they were thirty.[10] The most belligerent among the children—those quickest to start fights and who habitually used force to get their way—were the most likely to have dropped out of school and, by age thirty, to have a record for crimes of violence. They also seemed to be handing down their propensity to violence: their children were, in grade school, just like the troublemakers their delinquent parent had been.

There is a lesson in how aggressiveness is passed from generation to generation. Any inherited propensities aside, the troublemakers as grownups acted in a way that made family life a school for aggression. As children, the troublemakers had parents who disciplined them with arbitrary, relentless severity; as parents they repeated the pattern. This was true whether it had been the father or the mother who had been identified in childhood as highly aggressive. Aggressive little girls grew up to be just as arbitrary and harshly punitive when they became mothers as the aggressive boys were as fathers. And while they punished their children with special severity, they otherwise took little interest in their children's lives, in effect ignoring them much of the time. At the same time the parents offered these children a vivid—and violent—example of aggressiveness, a model the children took with them to school and to the playground, and followed throughout life. The parents were not necessarily mean-spirited, nor did they fail to wish the best for their children; rather, they seemed to be simply repeating the style of parenting that had been modeled for them by their own parents.

In this model for violence, these children were disciplined capriciously: if their parents were in a bad mood, they would be severely punished; if their parents were in a good mood, they could get away with mayhem at home. Thus punishment came not so much because of what the child had done, but by virtue of how the parent felt. This is a recipe for feelings of worthlessness and helplessness, and for the sense that threats are everywhere and may strike at any time. Seen in light of the home life that spawns it, such children's combative and defiant posture toward the world at large makes a certain sense, unfortunate though it remains. What is disheartening is how early these dispiriting lessons can be learned, and how grim the costs for a child's emotional life can be.

ABUSE: THE EXTINCTION OF EMPATHY

In the rough-and-tumble play of the day-care center, Martin, just two and a half, brushed up against a little girl, who, inexplicably, broke out crying. Martin reached for her hand, but as the sobbing girl moved away, Martin slapped her on the arm.

As her tears continued Martin looked away and yelled, "Cut it out! *Cut it out!*" over and over, each time faster and louder.

When Martin then made another attempt to pat her, again she resisted. This time Martin bared his teeth like a snarling dog, hissing at the sobbing girl.

Once more Martin started patting the crying girl, but the pats on the back quickly turned into pounding, and Martin went on hitting and hitting the poor little girl despite her screams.

That disturbing encounter testifies to how abuse—being beaten repeatedly, at the whim of a parent's moods—warps a child's natural bent toward empathy.[11] Martin's bizarre, almost brutal response to his playmate's distress is typical of children like him, who have themselves been the victims of beatings and other physical abuse since their infancy. The response stands in stark contrast to toddlers' usual sympathetic entreaties and attempts to console a crying playmate, reviewed in Chapter 7. Martin's violent response to distress at the day-care center may well mirror the lessons he learned at home about tears and anguish: crying is met at first with a peremptory consoling gesture, but if it continues, the progression is from nasty looks and shouts, to hitting, to outright beating. Perhaps most troubling, Martin already seems to lack the most primitive sort of empathy, the instinct to stop aggression against someone who is hurt. At two and a half he displays the budding moral impulses of a cruel and sadistic brute.

Martin's meanness in place of empathy is typical of other children like him who are already, at their tender age, scarred by severe physical and emotional abuse at home. Martin was part of a group of nine such toddlers, ages one to three, witnessed in a two-hour observation at his day-care center. The abused toddlers were compared with nine others at the day-care center from equally impoverished, high-stress homes, but who were not physically abused. The differences in how the two groups of toddlers reacted when another child was hurt or upset were stark. Of twenty-three such incidents, five of the nine nonabused toddlers responded to the distress of a child nearby with concern, sadness, or empathy. But in the twenty-seven instances where the abused children could have done so, not one showed the least concern; instead they reacted to a crying child with expressions of fear, anger, or, like Martin, a physical attack.

One abused little girl, for instance, made a ferocious, threatening face at another who had broken out into tears. One-year-old Thomas, another of the abused children, froze in terror when he heard a child crying across the room; he sat completely still, his face full of fear, back stiffly straight, his tension increasing as the crying continued—as though bracing for an attack himself. And twenty-eight-month-old Kate, also abused, was almost sadistic: picking on Joey, a smaller infant, she knocked him to the ground with her feet, and as he lay there looked tenderly at him and began patting him gently on the back—only to intensify the pats into hitting him harder and harder, ignoring his misery. She kept swinging away at him, leaning in to slug him six or seven times more, until he crawled away.

These children, of course, treat others as they themselves have been treated. And the callousness of these abused children is simply a more extreme version of that seen in children whose parents are critical, threatening, and harsh in their punishments. Such children also tend to lack concern when playmates get hurt or cry; they seem to represent one end of a continuum of coldness that peaks with the brutality of the abused children. As they go on through life, they are, as a group, more likely to have cognitive difficulties in learning, more likely to be aggressive and unpopular with their peers (small wonder, if their preschool toughness is a harbinger of the future), more prone to depression, and, as adults, more likely to get into trouble with the law and commit more crimes of violence.[12]

This failure of empathy is sometimes, if not often, repeated over generations, with brutal parents having themselves been brutalized by their own parents in childhood.[13] It stands in dramatic contrast to the empathy ordinarily displayed by children of parents who are nurturing, encouraging their toddlers to show concern for others and to understand how meanness makes other children feel. Lacking such lessons in empathy, these children seem not to learn it at all.

What is perhaps most troubling about the abused toddlers is how early they seem to have learned to respond like miniature versions of their own abusive parents. But given the physical beatings they received as a sometimes daily diet, the emotional lessons are all too clear. Remember that it is in moments when passions run high or a crisis is upon us that the primitive proclivities of the brain's limbic centers take on a more dominant role. At such moments the habits the emotional brain has learned over and over will dominate, for better or worse.

Seeing how the brain itself is shaped by brutality—or by love—suggests that childhood represents a special window of opportunity for emotional lessons. These battered children have had an early and steady diet of trauma. Perhaps the most instructive paradigm for understanding the emotional learning such abused children have undergone is in seeing how trauma can leave a lasting imprint on the brain—and how even these savage imprints can be mended.

13

Trauma and Emotional Relearning

Som Chit, a Cambodian refugee, balked when her three sons asked her to buy them toy AK-47 machine guns. Her sons—ages six, nine, and eleven—wanted the toy guns to play the game some of the kids at their school called Purdy. In the game, Purdy, the villain, uses a submachine gun to massacre a group of children, then turns it on himself. Sometimes, though, the children have it end differently: it is they who kill Purdy.

Purdy was the macabre reenactment by some of the survivors of the catastrophic events of February 17, 1989, at Cleveland Elementary School in Stockton, California. There, during the school's late-morning recess for first, second, and third graders, Patrick Purdy—who had himself attended those grades at Cleveland Elementary some twenty years earlier—stood at the playground's edge and fired wave after wave of 7.22 mm bullets at the hundreds of children at play. For seven minutes Purdy sprayed bullets toward the playground, then put a pistol to his head and shot himself. When the police arrived they found five children dying, twenty-nine wounded.

In ensuing months, the Purdy game spontaneously appeared in the play of boys and girls at Cleveland Elementary, one of many signs that those seven minutes and their aftermath were seared into the children's memory. When I visited the school, just a short bike ride from the neighborhood near the University of the Pacific where I myself had grown up, it was five months after Purdy had turned that recess into a nightmare. His presence was still palpable, even though the most horrific of the grisly remnants of the shooting—swarms of bullet holes, pools of blood, bits of flesh, skin, and scalp—were gone by the morning after the shooting, washed away and painted over.

By then the deepest scars at Cleveland Elementary were not to the building but to the psyches of the children and staff there, who were trying to carry on with life as usual.[1] Perhaps most striking was how the memory of those few minutes was revived again and again by any small detail that was similar in the least. A teacher told me, for example, that a wave of fright swept through the school with the announcement that St. Patrick's Day was coming; a number of the children somehow got the idea that the day was to honor the killer, Patrick Purdy.

"Whenever we hear an ambulance on its way to the rest home down the street, everything halts," another teacher told me. "The kids all listen to see if it will stop here or go on." For several weeks many children were terrified of the mirrors in the restrooms; a rumor swept the school that "Bloody Virgin Mary," some kind of fantasied monster, lurked there. Weeks after the shooting a frantic girl came running up to the school's principal, Pat Busher, yelling, "I hear shots! I hear shots!" The sound was from the swinging chain on a tetherball pole.

Many children became hypervigilant, as though continually on guard against a repetition of the terror; some boys and girls would hover at recess next to the classroom doors, not daring to venture out to the playground where the killings had occurred. Others would only play in small groups, posting a designated child as lookout. Many continued for months to avoid the "evil" areas, where children had died.

The memories lived on, too, as disturbing dreams, intruding into the children's unguarded minds as they slept. Apart from nightmares repeating the shooting itself in some way, children were flooded with anxiety dreams that left them apprehensive that they too would die soon. Some children tried to sleep with their eyes open so they wouldn't dream.

All of these reactions are well known to psychiatrists as among the key symptoms of post-traumatic stress disorder, or PTSD. At the core of such trauma, says Dr. Spencer Eth, a child psychiatrist who specializes in PTSD in children, is "the intrusive memory of the central violent action: the final blow with a fist, the plunge of a knife, the blast of a shotgun. The memories are intense perceptual experiences—the sight, sound, and smell of gunfire; the screams or sudden silence of the victim; the splash of blood; the police sirens."

These vivid, terrifying moments, neuroscientists now say, become memories emblazoned in the emotional circuitry. The symptoms are, in effect, signs of an overaroused amygdala impelling the vivid memories of a traumatic moment to continue to intrude on awareness. As such, the traumatic memories become mental hair triggers, ready to sound an alarm at the least hint that the dread moment is about to happen once again. This hair-trigger phenomenon is a hallmark of emotional trauma of all kinds, including suffering repeated physical abuse in childhood.

Any traumatizing event can implant such trigger memories in the amygdala: a fire or an auto accident, being in a natural catastrophe such as an earthquake or a hurricane, being raped or mugged. Hundreds of thousands of people each year endure such disasters, and many or most come away with the kind of emotional wounding that leaves its imprint on the brain.

Violent acts are more pernicious than natural catastrophes such as a hurricane because, unlike victims of a natural disaster, victims of violence feel themselves to have been intentionally selected as the target of malevolence. That fact shatters assumptions about the trustworthiness of people and the safety of the interpersonal world, an assumption natural catastrophes leave untouched. Within an instant, the social world becomes a dangerous place, one in which people are potential threats to your safety.

Human cruelties stamp their victims' memories with a template that regards with fear anything vaguely similar to the assault itself. A man who was struck on the back of his head, never seeing his attacker, was so frightened afterward that he would try to walk down the street directly in front of an old lady to feel safe from being hit on the head again.[2] A woman who was mugged by a man who got on an elevator with her and forced her out at knifepoint to an unoccupied floor was fearful for weeks of going into not just elevators, but also the subway or any other enclosed space where she might feel trapped; she ran from her bank when she saw a man put his hand in his jacket as the mugger had done.

The imprint of horror in memory—and the resulting hypervigilance—can last a lifetime, as a study of Holocaust survivors found. Close to fifty years after they had endured semistarvation, the slaughter of their loved ones, and constant terror in Nazi death camps, the haunting memories were still alive. A third said they felt generally fearful. Nearly three quarters said they still became anxious at reminders of the Nazi persecution, such as the sight of a uniform, a knock at the door, dogs barking, or smoke rising from a chimney. About 60 percent said they thought about the Holocaust almost daily, even after a half century; of those with active symptoms, as many as eight in ten still suffered from repeated nightmares. As one survivor said, "If you've been through Auschwitz and you don't have nightmares, then you're not normal."

HORROR FROZEN IN MEMORY

The words of a forty-eight-year-old Vietnam vet, some twenty-four years after enduring a horrifying moment in a faraway land:

> I can't get the memories out of my mind! The images come flooding back in vivid detail, triggered by the most inconsequential things, like a door slamming, the sight of an Oriental woman, the touch of a bamboo mat, or the smell of stir-fried pork. Last night I went to bed, was having a good sleep for a change. Then in the early morning a storm front passed through and there was a bolt of crackling thunder. I awoke instantly, frozen in fear. I am right back in Vietnam, in the middle of the monsoon season at my guard post. I am sure I'll get hit in the next volley and convinced I will die. My hands are freezing, yet sweat pours from my entire body. I feel each hair on the back of my neck standing on end. I can't catch my breath and my heart is pounding. I smell a damp sulfur smell. Suddenly I see what's left of my buddy Troy . . . on a bamboo platter, sent back to our camp by the Vietcong. . . . The next bolt of lightning and clap of thunder makes me jump so much that I fall to the floor.[3]

This horrible memory, vividly fresh and detailed though more than two decades old, still holds the power to induce the same fear in this ex-soldier that he felt on that fateful day. PTSD represents a perilous lowering of the neural setpoint for alarm, leaving the person to react to life's ordinary moments as though they were emergencies. The hijacking circuit discussed in Chapter 2 seems critical in leaving such a powerful brand on memory: the more brutal, shocking, and horrendous the events that trigger the amygdala hijacking, the more indelible the memory. The neural basis for these memories appears to be a sweeping alteration in the chemistry of the brain set in motion by a single instance of overwhelming terror.[4] While the PTSD findings are typically based on the impact of a single episode, similar results can come from cruelties inflicted over a period of years, as is the case with children who are sexually, physically, or emotionally abused.

The most detailed work on these brain changes is being done at the National Center for Post-Traumatic Stress Disorder, a network of research sites based at Veterans' Administration hospitals where there are large pools of those who suffer from PTSD among the veterans of Vietnam and other wars. It is from studies on vets such as these that most of our knowledge of PTSD has come. But these insights apply as well to children who have suffered severe emotional trauma, such as those at Cleveland Elementary.

"Victims of a devastating trauma may never be the same biologically," Dr. Dennis Charney told me.[5] A Yale psychiatrist, Charney is director of clinical neuroscience at the National Center. "It does not matter if it was the incessant terror of combat, torture, or repeated abuse in childhood, or a one-time experience, like being trapped in a hurricane or nearly dying in an auto accident. All uncontrollable stress can have the same biological impact."

The operative word is *uncontrollable*. If people feel there is something they can do in a catastrophic situation, some control they can exert, no matter how minor, they fare far better emotionally than do those who feel utterly helpless. The element of helplessness is what makes a given event *subjectively* overwhelming. As Dr. John Krystal, director of the center's Laboratory of Clinical Psychopharmacology, told me, "Say someone being attacked with a knife knows how to defend himself and takes action, while another person in the same predicament thinks, 'I'm dead.' The helpless person is the one more susceptible to PTSD afterward. It's the feeling that your life is in danger *and there's nothing you can do to escape it*—that's the moment the brain change begins."

Helplessness as the wild card in triggering PTSD has been shown in dozens of studies on pairs of laboratory rats, each in a different cage, each being given mild—but, to a rat, very stressful—electric shocks of identical severity. Only one rat has a lever in its cage; when the rat pushes the lever, the shock stops for both cages. Over days and weeks, both rats get precisely the same amount of shock. But the rat with the power to turn the shocks off comes through without lasting signs of stress. It is only in the helpless one of the pair that the stress-induced brain changes occur.[6] For a child being shot at on a playground, seeing his playmates bleeding and dying—or for a teacher there, unable to stop the carnage—that helplessness must have been palpable.

PTSD AS A LIMBIC DISORDER

It had been months since a huge earthquake shook her out of bed and sent her yelling in panic through the darkened house to find her four-year-old son. They huddled for hours in the Los Angeles night cold under a protective doorway, pinned there without food, water, or light while wave after wave of aftershocks tumbled the ground beneath them. Now, months later, she had largely recovered from the ready panic that gripped her for the first few days afterward, when a door slamming could start her shivering with fear. The one lingering symptom was her inability to sleep, a problem that struck only on those nights her husband was away—as he had been the night of the quake.

The main symptoms of such learned fearfulness—including the most intense kind, PTSD—can be accounted for by changes in the limbic circuitry focusing on the amygdala.[7] Some of the key changes are in the locus ceruleus, a structure that regulates the brain's secretion of two substances called *catecholamines:* adrenaline and noradrenaline. These neurochemicals mobilize the body for an emergency; the same catecholamine surge stamps memories with special strength. In PTSD this system becomes hyperreactive, secreting extra-large doses of these brain chemicals in response to situations that hold little or no threat but somehow are reminders of the original trauma, like the children at Cleveland Elementary School who panicked when they heard an ambulance siren similar to those they had heard at their school after the shooting.

The locus ceruleus and the amygdala are closely linked, along with other limbic structures such as the hippocampus and hypothalamus; the circuitry for the catecholamines extends into the cortex. Changes in these circuits are thought to underlie PTSD symptoms, which include anxiety, fear, hyper-vigilance, being easily upset and aroused, readiness for fight or flight, and the indelible encoding of intense emotional memories.[8] Vietnam vets with PTSD, one study found, had 40 percent fewer catecholamine-stopping receptors than did men without the symptoms—suggesting that their brains had undergone a lasting change, with their catecholamine secretion poorly controlled.[9]

Other changes occur in the circuit linking the limbic brain with the pituitary gland, which regulates release of CRF, the main stress hormone the body secretes to mobilize the emergency fight-or-flight response. The changes lead this hormone to be oversecreted—particularly in the amygdala, hippocampus, and locus ceruleus—alerting the body for an emergency that is not there in reality.[10]

As Dr. Charles Nemeroff, a Duke University psychiatrist, told me, "Too much CRF makes you overreact. For example, if you're a Vietnam vet with PTSD and a car backfires at the mall parking lot, it is the triggering of CRF that floods you with the same feelings as in the original trauma: you start sweating, you're scared, you have chills and the shakes, you may have flashbacks. In people who hypersecrete CRF, the startle response is overactive. For example, if you sneak up behind most people and suddenly clap your hands, you'll see a startled jump the first time, but not by the third or fourth repetition. But people with too much CRF don't habituate: they'll respond as much to the fourth clap as to the first."[11]

A third set of changes occurs in the brain's opioid system, which secretes endorphins to blunt the feeling of pain. It also becomes hyperactive. This neural circuit again involves the amygdala, this time in concert with a region in the cerebral cortex. The opioids are brain chemicals that are powerful numbing agents, like opium and other narcotics that are chemical cousins. When experiencing high levels of opioids ("the brain's own morphine"), people have a heightened tolerance for pain—an effect that has been noted by battlefield surgeons, who found severely wounded soldiers needed lower doses of narcotics to handle their pain than did civilians with far less serious injuries.

Something similar seems to occur in PTSD.[12] Endorphin changes add a new dimension to the neural mix triggered by reexposure to trauma: a *numbing* of certain feelings. This appears to explain a set of "negative" psychological symptoms long noted in PTSD: anhedonia (the inability to feel pleasure) and a general emotional numbness, a sense of being cut off from life or from concern about others' feelings. Those close to such people may experience this indifference as a lack of empathy. Another possible effect may be dissociation, including the inability to remember crucial minutes, hours, or even days of the traumatic event.

The neural changes of PTSD also seem to make a person more susceptible to further traumatizing. A number of studies with animals have found that when they were exposed even to *mild* stress when young, they were far more vulnerable than unstressed animals to trauma-induced brain changes later in life (suggesting the urgent need to treat children with PTSD). This seems a reason that, exposed to the same catastrophe, one person goes on to develop PTSD and another does not: the amygdala is primed to find danger, and when life presents it once again with real danger, its alarm rises to a higher pitch.

All these neural changes offer short-term advantages for dealing with the grim and dire emergencies that prompt them. Under duress, it is adaptive to be highly vigilant, aroused, ready for anything, impervious to pain, the body primed for sustained physical demands, and—for the moment—indifferent to what might otherwise be intensely disturbing events. These short-term advantages, however, become lasting problems when the brain changes so that they become predispositions, like a car stuck in perpetual high gear. When the amygdala and its connected brain regions take on a new setpoint during a moment of intense trauma, this change in excitability—this heightened readiness to trigger a neural hijacking—means all of life is on the verge of becoming an emergency, and even an innocent moment is susceptible to an explosion of fear run amok.

EMOTIONAL RELEARNING

Such traumatic memories seem to remain as fixtures in brain function because they interfere with subsequent learning—specifically, with relearning a more normal response to those traumatizing events. In acquired fear such as PTSD, the mechanisms of learning and memory have gone awry; again, it is the amygdala that is key among the brain regions involved. But in overcoming the learned fear, the neocortex is critical.

Fear conditioning is the name psychologists use for the process whereby something that is not in the least threatening becomes dreaded as it is associated in someone's mind with something frightening. When such frights are induced in laboratory animals, Charney notes, the fears can last for years.[13] The key region of the brain that learns, retains, and acts on this fearful response is the circuit between the thalamus, amygdala, and prefrontal lobe—the pathway of neural hijacking.

Ordinarily, when someone learns to be frightened by something through fear conditioning, the fear subsides with time. This seems to happen through a natural relearning, as the feared object is encountered again in the absence of anything truly scary. Thus a child who acquires a fear of dogs because of being chased by a snarling German shepherd gradually and naturally loses that fear if, say, she moves next door to someone who owns a friendly shepherd, and spends time playing with the dog.

In PTSD spontaneous relearning fails to occur. Charney proposes that this may be due to the brain changes of PTSD, which are so strong that, in effect, the amygdala hijacking occurs every time something even vaguely reminiscent of the original trauma comes along, strengthening the fear pathway. This means that there is never a time when what is feared is paired with a feeling of calm—the amygdala never relearns a more mild reaction. "Extinction" of the fear, he observes, "appears to involve an active learning process," which is itself impaired in people with PTSD, "leading to the abnormal persistence of emotional memories."[14]

But given the right experiences, even PTSD can lift; strong emotional memories, and the patterns of thought and reaction that they trigger, *can* change with time. This relearning, Charney proposes, is cortical. The original fear ingrained in the amygdala does not go away completely; rather, the prefrontal cortex actively suppresses the amygdala's command to the rest of the brain to respond with fear.

"The question is, how quickly do you let go of learned fear?" asks Richard Davidson, the University of Wisconsin psychologist who discovered the role of the left prefrontal cortex as a damper on distress. In a laboratory experiment in which people first learned an aversion to a loud noise—a paradigm for learned fear, and a lower-key parallel of PTSD—Davidson found that people who had more activity in the left prefrontal cortex got over the acquired fear more quickly, again suggesting a cortical role in letting go of learned distress.[15]

REEDUCATING THE EMOTIONAL BRAIN

One of the more encouraging findings about PTSD came from a study of Holocaust survivors, about three quarters of whom were found to have active PTSD symptoms even a half century later. The positive finding was that a quarter of the survivors who once had been troubled by such symptoms no longer had them; somehow the natural events of their lives had counteracted the problem. Those who still had the symptoms showed evidence of the catecholamine-related brain changes typical of PTSD—but those who had recovered had no such changes.[16] This finding, and others like it, hold out the promise that the brain changes in PTSD are not indelible, and that people can recover from even the most dire emotional imprinting—in short, that the emotional circuitry can be reeducated. The good news, then, is that traumas as profound as those causing PTSD can heal, and that the route to such healing is through relearning.

One way this emotional healing seems to occur spontaneously—at least in children—is through such games as Purdy. These games, played over and over again, let children relive a trauma safely, as play. This allows two avenues for healing: on the one hand, the memory repeats in a context of low anxiety, desensitizing it and allowing a nontraumatized set of responses to become associated with it. Another route to healing is that, in their minds, children can magically give the tragedy another, better outcome: sometimes in playing Purdy, the children kill him, boosting their sense of mastery over that traumatic moment of helplessness.

Games like Purdy are predictable in younger children who have been through such overwhelming violence. These macabre games in traumatized children were first noted by Dr. Lenore Terr, a child psychiatrist in San Francisco.[17] She found such games among children in Chowchilla, California—just a little over an hour down the Central Valley from Stockton, where Purdy wreaked such havoc—who in 1973 had been kidnapped as they rode a bus home from a summer day camp. The kidnappers buried the bus, children and all, in an ordeal that lasted twenty-seven hours.

Five years later Terr found the kidnapping still being reenacted in the victims' games. Girls, for example, played symbolic kidnapping games with their Barbie dolls. One girl, who had hated the feeling of other children's urine on her skin as they lay huddled together in terror, washed her Barbie over and over again. Another played Traveling Barbie, in which Barbie travels somewhere—it doesn't matter where—and returns safely, which is the point of the game. A third girl's favorite was a scenario in which the doll is stuck in a hole and suffocates.

While adults who have been through overwhelming trauma can suffer a psychic numbing, blocking out memory of or feeling about the catastrophe, children's psyches often handle it differently. They less often become numb to the trauma, Terr believes, because they use fantasy, play, and daydreams to recall and rethink their ordeals. Such voluntary replays of trauma seem to head off the need for damming them up in potent memories that can later burst through as flashbacks. If the trauma is minor, such as going to the dentist for a filling, just once or twice may be enough. But if it's overwhelming, a child needs endless repetitions, replaying the trauma over and over again in a grim, monotonous ritual.

One way to get at the picture frozen in the amygdala is through art, which itself is a medium of the unconscious. The emotional brain is highly attuned to symbolic meanings and to the mode Freud called the "primary process": the messages of metaphor, story, myth, the arts. This avenue is often used in treating traumatized children. Sometimes art can open the way for children to talk about a moment of horror that they would not dare speak of otherwise.

Spencer Eth, the Los Angeles child psychiatrist who specializes in treating such children, tells of a five-year-old boy who had been kidnapped with his mother by her ex-lover. The man brought them to a motel room, where he ordered the boy to hide under a blanket while he beat the mother to death. The boy was, understandably, reluctant to talk with Eth about the mayhem he had heard and seen while underneath the blanket. So Eth asked him to draw a picture—any picture.

The drawing was of a race-car driver who had a strikingly large pair of eyes, Eth recalls. The huge eyes Eth took to refer to the boy's own daring in peeking at the killer. Such hidden references to the traumatic scene almost always appear in the artwork of traumatized children; Eth has made having such children draw a picture the opening gambit in therapy. The potent memories that preoccupy them intrude in their art just as in their thoughts. Beyond that, the act of drawing is itself therapeutic, beginning the process of mastering the trauma.

EMOTIONAL RELEARNING AND RECOVERY FROM TRAUMA

Irene had gone on a date that ended in attempted rape. Though she had fought off the attacker, he continued to plague her: harassing her with obscene phone calls, making threats of violence, calling in the middle of the night, stalking her and watching her every move. Once, when she tried to get the police to help, they dismissed her problem as trivial, since "nothing had really happened." By the time she came for therapy Irene had symptoms of PTSD, had given up socializing at all, and felt a prisoner in her own house.

Irene's case is cited by Dr. Judith Lewis Herman, a Harvard psychiatrist whose groundbreaking work outlines the steps to recovery from trauma. Herman sees three stages: attaining a sense of safety, remembering the details of the trauma and mourning the loss it has brought, and finally reestablishing a normal life. There is a biological logic to the ordering of these steps, as we shall see: this sequence seems to reflect how the emotional brain learns once again that life need not be regarded as an emergency about to happen.

The first step, regaining a sense of safety, presumably translates to finding ways to calm the too-fearful, too easily triggered emotional circuits enough to allow relearning.[18] Often this begins with helping patients understand that their jumpiness and nightmares, hypervigilance and panics, are part of the symptoms of PTSD. This understanding makes the symptoms themselves less frightening.

Another early step is to help patients regain some sense of control over what is happening to them, a direct unlearning of the lesson of helplessness that the trauma itself imparted. Irene, for example, mobilized her friends and family to form a buffer between her and her stalker, and was able to get the police to intervene.

The sense in which PTSD patients feel "unsafe" goes beyond fears that dangers lurk around them; their insecurity begins more intimately, in the feeling that they have no control over what is happening in their body and to their emotions. This is understandable, given the hair trigger for emotional hijacking that PTSD creates by hypersensitizing the amygdala circuitry.

Medication offers one way to restore patients' sense that they need not be so at the mercy of the emotional alarms that flood them with inexplicable anxiety, keep them sleepless, or pepper their sleep with nightmares. Pharmacologists are hoping one day to tailor medications that will target precisely the effects of PTSD on the amygdala and connected neurotransmitter circuits. For now, though, there are medications that counter only some of these changes, notably the antidepressants that act on the serotonin system, and beta-blockers like propranolol, which block the activation of the sympathetic nervous system. Patients also may learn relaxation techniques that give them the ability to counter their edginess and nervousness. A physiological calm opens a window for helping the brutalized emotional circuitry rediscover that life is not a threat and for giving back to patients some of the sense of security they had in their lives before the trauma happened.

Another step in healing involves retelling and reconstructing the story of the trauma in the harbor of that safety, allowing the emotional circuitry to acquire a new, more realistic understanding of and response to the traumatic memory and its triggers. As patients retell the horrific details of the trauma, the memory starts to be transformed, both in its emotional meaning and in its effects on the emotional brain. The pace of this retelling is delicate; ideally it mimics the pace that occurs naturally in those people who are able to recover from trauma without suffering PTSD. In these cases there often seems to be an inner clock that "doses" people with intrusive memories that relive the trauma, intercut with weeks or months when they remember hardly anything of the horrible events.[19]

This alternation of reimmersion and respite seems to allow for a spontaneous review of the trauma and relearning of emotional response to it. For those whose PTSD is more intractable, says Herman, retelling their tale can sometimes trigger overwhelming fears, in which case the therapist should ease the pace to keep the patient's reactions within a bearable range, one that will not disrupt the relearning.

The therapist encourages the patient to retell the traumatic events as vividly as possible, like a horror home video, retrieving every sordid detail. This includes not just the specifics of what they saw, heard, smelled, and felt, but also their reactions—the dread, disgust, nausea. The goal here is to put the entire memory into words, which means capturing parts of the memory that may have been dissociated and so are absent from conscious recall. By putting sensory details and feelings into words, presumably memories are brought more under control of the neocortex, where the reactions they kindle can be rendered more understandable and so more manageable. The emotional relearning at this point is largely accomplished through reliving the events and their emotions, but this time in surroundings of safety and security, in the company of a trusted therapist. This begins to impart a telling lesson to the emotional circuitry—that security, rather than unremitting terror, can be experienced in tandem with the trauma memories.

The five-year-old who drew the picture of the giant eyes after he witnessed the grisly murder of his mother did not make any more drawings after that first one; instead he and his therapist, Spencer Eth, played games, creating a bond of rapport. Only slowly did he begin to retell the story of the murder, at first in a stereotyped way, reciting each detail exactly the same in each telling. Gradually, though, his narrative became more open and free-flowing, his body less tense as he told it. At the same time his nightmares of the scene came less often, an indication, says Eth, of some "trauma mastery." Gradually their talk moved away from the fears left by the trauma to more of what was happening in the boy's day-to-day life as he adjusted to a new home with his father. And finally the boy was able to talk just about his daily life as the hold of the trauma faded.

Finally, Herman finds that patients need to mourn the loss the trauma brought—whether an injury, the death of a loved one or a rupture in a relationship, regret over some step not taken to save someone, or just the shattering of confidence that people can be trusted. The mourning that ensues while retelling such painful events serves a crucial purpose: it marks the ability to let go of the trauma itself to some degree. It means that instead of being perpetually captured by this moment in the past, patients can start to look ahead, even to hope, and to rebuild a new life free of the trauma's grip. It is as if the constant recycling and reliving of the trauma's terror by the emotional circuitry were a spell that could finally be lifted. Every siren need not bring a flood of fear; every sound in the night need not compel a flashback to terror.

Aftereffects or occasional recurrences of symptoms often persist, says Herman, but there are specific signs that the trauma has largely been overcome. These include reducing the physiological symptoms to a manageable level, and being able to bear the feelings associated with memories of the trauma. Especially significant is no longer having trauma memories erupt at uncontrollable moments, but rather being able to revisit them voluntarily, like any other memory—and, perhaps more important, to put them aside like any other memory. Finally, it means rebuilding a new life, with strong, trusting relationships and a belief system that finds meaning even in a world where such injustice can happen.[20] All of these together are markers of success in reeducating the emotional brain.

PSYCHOTHERAPY AS AN EMOTIONAL TUTORIAL

Fortunately, the catastrophic moments in which traumatic memories are emblazoned are rare during the course of life for most of us. But the same circuitry that can be seen so boldly imprinting traumatic memories is presumably at work in life's quieter moments, too. The more ordinary travails of childhood, such as being chronically ignored and deprived of attention or tenderness by one's parents, abandonment or loss, or social rejection may never reach the fever pitch of trauma, but they surely leave their imprint on the emotional brain, creating distortions—and tears and rages—in intimate relationships later in life. If PTSD can be healed, so can the more muted emotional scars that so many of us bear; that is the task of psychotherapy. And, in general, it is in learning to deal skillfully with these loaded reactions that emotional intelligence comes into play.

The dynamic between the amygdala and the more fully informed reactions of the prefrontal cortex may offer a neuroanatomical model for how psychotherapy reshapes deep, maladaptive emotional patterns. As Joseph LeDoux, the neuroscientist who discovered the amygdala's hair-trigger role in emotional outbursts, conjectures, "Once your emotional system learns something, it seems you never let it go. What therapy does is teach you to control it—it teaches your neocortex how to inhibit your amygdala. The propensity to act is suppressed, while your basic emotion about it remains in a subdued form."

Given the brain architecture that underlies emotional relearning, what seems to remain, even after successful psychotherapy, is a vestigial reaction, a remnant of the original sensitivity or fear at the root of a troubling emotional pattern.[21] The prefrontal cortex can refine or put the brakes on the amygdala's impulse to rampage, but cannot keep it from reacting in the first place. Thus while we cannot decide *when* we have our emotional outbursts, we have more control over *how long* they last. A quicker recovery time from such outbursts may well be one mark of emotional maturity.

Over the course of therapy, what seems to change in the main are the *responses* that people make once an emotional reaction is triggered—but the tendency for the reaction to be triggered in the first place does not disappear entirely. Evidence for this comes from a series of studies of psychotherapy conducted by Lester Luborsky and his colleagues at the University of Pennsylvania.[22] They analyzed the main relationship conflicts that brought dozens of patients into psychotherapy—issues such as a deep craving to be accepted or find intimacy, or a fear of being a failure or being overly dependent. They then carefully analyzed the typical (always self-defeating) responses the patients made when these wishes and fears were activated in their relationships—responses such as being too demanding, which created a backlash of anger or coldness in the other person, or withdrawing in self-defense from an anticipated slight, leaving the other person miffed by the seeming rebuff. During such ill-fated encounters, the patients, understandably, felt flooded by upsetting feelings—hopelessness and sadness, resentment and anger, tension and fear, guilt and self-blame, and so on. Whatever the specific pattern of the patient, it seemed to show up in most every important relationship, whether with a spouse or lover, a child or parent, or peers and bosses at work.

Over the course of long-term therapy, however, these patients made two kinds of changes: their emotional reaction to the triggering events became less distressing, even calm or bemused, and their overt responses became more effective in getting what they truly wanted from the relationship. What did not change, however, was their underlying wish or fear, and the initial twinge of feeling. By the time the patients had but a few sessions left in therapy, the encounters they told about showed they had only half as many negative emotional reactions compared to when they first started therapy, and were twice as likely to get the positive response they deeply desired from the other person. But what did not change at all was the particular sensitivity at the root of these needs.

In brain terms, we can speculate, the limbic circuitry would send alarm signals in response to cues of a feared event, but the prefrontal cortex and related zones would have learned a new, more healthy response. In short, emotional lessons—even the most deeply implanted habits of the heart learned in childhood—can be reshaped. Emotional learning is lifelong.

14

Temperament Is Not Destiny

So much for altering emotional patterns that have been learned. But what about those responses that are givens of our genetic endowment—what of changing the habitual reactions of people who by nature are, say, highly volatile, or painfully shy? This range of the emotional compass falls under the sweep of temperament, the background murmur of feelings that mark our basic disposition. Temperament can be defined in terms of the moods that typify our emotional life. To some degree we each have such a favored emotional range; temperament is a given at birth, part of the genetic lottery that has compelling force in the unfolding of life. Every parent has seen this: from birth a child will be calm and placid or testy and difficult. The question is whether such a biologically determined emotional set can be changed by experience. Does our biology fix our emotional destiny, or can even an innately shy child grow into a more confident adult?

The clearest answer to this question comes from the work of Jerome Kagan, the eminent developmental psychologist at Harvard University.[1] Kagan posits that there are at least four temperamental types—timid, bold, upbeat, and melancholy—and that each is due to a different pattern of brain activity. There are likely innumerable differences in temperamental endowment, each based in innate differences in emotional circuitry; for any given emotion people can differ in how easily it triggers, how long it lasts, how intense it becomes. Kagan's work concentrates on one of these patterns: the dimension of temperament that runs from boldness to timidity.

For decades mothers have been bringing their infants and toddlers to Kagan's Laboratory for Child Development on the fourteenth floor of

Harvard's William James Hall to take part in his studies of child development. It was there that Kagan and his coresearchers noticed early signs of shyness in a group of twenty-one-month-old toddlers brought for experimental observations. In free play with other toddlers, some were bubbly and spontaneous, playing with other babies without the least hesitation. Others, though, were uncertain and hesitant, hanging back, clinging to their mothers, quietly watching the others at play. Almost four years later, when these same children were in kindergarten, Kagan's group observed them again. Over the intervening years none of the outgoing children had become timid, while two thirds of the timid ones were still reticent.

Kagan finds that children who are overly sensitive and fearful grow into shy and timorous adults; from birth about 15 to 20 percent of children are "behaviorally inhibited," as he calls them. As infants, these children are timid about anything unfamiliar. This makes them finicky about eating new foods, reluctant to approach new animals or places, and shy around strangers. It also renders them sensitive in other ways—for example, prone to guilt and self-reproach. These are the children who become paralyzingly anxious in social situations: in class and on the playground, when meeting new people, whenever the social spotlight shines on them. As adults, they are prone to be wallflowers, and morbidly afraid of having to give a speech or perform in public.

Tom, one of the boys in Kagan's study, is typical of the shy type. At every measurement through childhood—two, five, and seven years of age—Tom was among the most timid children. When interviewed at thirteen, Tom was tense and stiff, biting his lip and wringing his hands, his face impassive, breaking into a tight smile only when talking about his girlfriend; his answers were short, his manner subdued.[2] Throughout the middle years of childhood, until about age eleven, Tom remembers being painfully shy, breaking into a sweat whenever he had to approach playmates. He was also troubled by intense fears: of his house burning down, of diving into a swimming pool, of being alone in the dark. In frequent nightmares, he was attacked by monsters. Though he has felt less shy in the last two years or so, he still feels some anxiety around other children, and his worries now center on doing well at school, even though he is in the top 5 percent of his class. The son of a scientist, Tom finds a career in that field appealing, since its relative solitude fits his introverted inclinations.

By contrast, Ralph was one of the boldest and most outgoing children at every age. Always relaxed and talkative, at thirteen he sat back at ease in his chair, had no nervous mannerisms, and spoke in a confident, friendly tone, as though the interviewer were a peer—though the difference in their ages was twenty-five years. During childhood he had only two short-lived fears—one of dogs, after a big dog jumped on him at age three, and another of flying, when he heard about plane crashes at age seven. Sociable and popular, Ralph has never thought of himself as shy.

The timid children seem to come into life with a neural circuitry that makes them more reactive to even mild stress—from birth, their hearts beat faster than other infants' in response to strange or novel situations. At twenty-one months, when the reticent toddlers were holding back from playing, heart rate monitors showed that their hearts were racing with anxiety. That easily aroused anxiety seems to underlie their lifelong timidity: they treat any new person or situation as though it were a potential threat. Perhaps as a result, middle-aged women who remember having been especially shy in childhood, when compared with their more outgoing peers, tend to go through life with more fears, worries, and guilt, and to suffer more from stress-related problems such as migraine headaches, irritable bowel, and other stomach problems.[3]

THE NEUROCHEMISTRY OF TIMIDITY

The difference between cautious Tom and bold Ralph, Kagan believes, lies in the excitability of a neural circuit centered on the amygdala. Kagan proposes that people like Tom, who are prone to fearfulness, are born with a neurochemistry that makes this circuit easily aroused, and so they avoid the unfamiliar, shy away from uncertainty, and suffer anxiety. Those who, like Ralph, have a nervous system calibrated with a much higher threshold for amygdala arousal, are less easily frightened, more naturally outgoing, and eager to explore new places and meet new people.

An early clue to which pattern a child has inherited is how difficult and irritable she is as an infant, and how distressed she becomes when confronted with something or someone unfamiliar. While about one in five infants falls into the timid category, about two in five have the bold temperament—at least at birth.

Part of Kagan's evidence comes from observations of cats that are unusually timid. About one in seven housecats has a pattern of fearfulness akin to the timid children's: they draw away from novelty (instead of exhibiting a cat's legendary curiosity), they are reluctant to explore new territory, and they attack only the smallest rodents, being too timid to take on larger ones that their more courageous feline peers would pursue with gusto. Direct brain probes have found that portions of the amygdala are unusually excitable in these timid cats, especially when, for instance, they hear a threatening howl from another cat.

The cats' timidity blossoms at about one month of age, which is the point when their amygdala matures enough to take control of the brain circuitry to approach or avoid. One month in kitten brain maturation is akin to eight months in a human infant; it is at eight or nine months, Kagan notes, that "stranger" fear appears in babies—if the baby's mother leaves a room and there is a stranger present, the result is tears. Timid children, Kagan postulates, may have inherited chronically high levels of norepinephrine or other brain chemicals that activate the amygdala and so create a low threshold of excitability, making the amygdala more easily triggered.

One sign of this heightened sensitivity is that, for example, when young men and women who were quite shy in childhood are measured in a laboratory while exposed to stresses such as harsh smells, their heart rate stays elevated much longer than for their more outgoing peers—a sign that surging norepinephrine is keeping their amygdala excited and, through connected neural circuits, their sympathetic nervous system aroused.[4] Kagan finds that timid children have higher levels of reactivity across the range of sympathetic nervous system indices, from higher resting blood pressure and greater dilation of the pupils, to higher levels of norepinephrine markers in their urine.

Silence is another barometer of timidity. Whenever Kagan's team observed shy and bold children in a natural setting—in their kindergarten classes, with other children they did not know, or talking with an interviewer—the timid children talked less. One timid kindergartener would say nothing when other children spoke to her, and spent most of her day just watching the others play. Kagan speculates that a timid silence in the face of novelty or a perceived threat is a sign of the activity of a neural circuit running between the forebrain, the amygdala, and nearby limbic structures that control the ability to vocalize (these same circuits make us "choke up" under stress).

These sensitive children are at high risk for developing an anxiety disorder such as panic attacks, starting as early as sixth or seventh grade. In one study of 754 boys and girls in those grades, 44 were found to have already suffered at least one episode of panic, or to have had several preliminary symptoms. These anxiety episodes were usually triggered by the ordinary alarms of early adolescence, such as a first date or a big exam—alarms that most children handle without developing more serious problems. But teenagers who were timid by temperament and who had been unusually frightened by new situations got panic symptoms such as heart palpitations, shortness of breath, or a choking feeling, along with the feeling that something horrible was going to happen to them, like going crazy or dying. The researchers believe that while the episodes were not significant enough to rate the psychiatric diagnosis "panic disorder," they signal that these teenagers would be at greater risk for developing the disorder as the years went on; many adults who suffer panic attacks say the attacks began during their teen years.[5]

The onset of the anxiety attacks was closely tied to puberty. Girls with few signs of puberty reported no such attacks, but of those who had gone through puberty about 8 percent said they had experienced panic. Once they have had such an attack, they are prone to developing the dread of a recurrence that leads people with panic disorder to shrink from life.

NOTHING BOTHERS ME: THE CHEERFUL TEMPERAMENT

In the 1920s, as a young woman, my aunt June left her home in Kansas City and ventured on her own to Shanghai—a dangerous journey for a solitary woman in those years. There June met and married a British detective in the colonial police force of that international center of commerce and intrigue. When the Japanese captured Shanghai at the outset of World War II, my aunt and her husband were interned in the prison camp depicted in the book and movie *Empire of the Sun*. After surviving five horrific years in the prison camp, she and her husband had, literally, lost everything. Penniless, they were repatriated to British Columbia.

I remember as a child first meeting June, an ebullient elderly woman whose life had followed a remarkable course. In her later years she suffered a stroke that left her partly paralyzed; after a slow and arduous recovery she was able to walk again, but with a limp. In those years I remember going for an outing with June, then in her seventies. Somehow she wandered off, and after several minutes I heard a feeble yell—June crying for help. She had fallen and could not get up on her own. I rushed to help her up, and as I did so, instead of complaining or lamenting she laughed at her predicament. Her only comment was a lighthearted "Well, at least I can walk again."

By nature, some people's emotions seem, like my aunt's, to gravitate toward the positive pole; these people are naturally upbeat and easygoing, while others are dour and melancholy. This dimension of temperament—

ebullience at one end, melancholy at the other—seems linked to the relative activity of the right and left prefrontal areas, the upper poles of the emotional brain. That insight has emerged largely from the work of Richard Davidson, a University of Wisconsin psychologist. He discovered that people who have greater activity in the left frontal lobe, compared to the right, are by temperament cheerful; they typically take delight in people and in what life presents them with, bouncing back from setbacks as my aunt June did. But those with relatively greater activity on the right side are given to negativity and sour moods, and are easily fazed by life's difficulties; in a sense, they seem to suffer because they cannot turn off their worries and depressions.

In one of Davidson's experiments volunteers with the most pronounced activity in the left frontal areas were compared with the fifteen who showed most activity on the right. Those with marked right frontal activity showed a distinctive pattern of negativity on a personality test: they fit the caricature portrayed by Woody Allen's comedy roles, the alarmist who sees catastrophe in the smallest thing—prone to funks and moodiness, and suspicious of a world they saw as fraught with overwhelming difficulties and lurking dangers. By contrast to their melancholy counterparts, those with stronger left frontal activity saw the world very differently. Sociable and cheerful, they typically felt a sense of enjoyment, were frequently in good moods, had a strong sense of self-confidence, and felt rewardingly engaged in life. Their scores on psychological tests suggested a lower lifetime risk for depression and other emotional disorders.[6]

People who have a history of clinical depression, Davidson found, had lower levels of brain activity in the left frontal lobe, and more on the right, than did people who had never been depressed. He found the same pattern in patients newly diagnosed with depression. Davidson speculates that people who overcome depression have learned to increase the level of activity in their left prefrontal lobe—a speculation awaiting experimental testing.

Though his research is on the 30 percent or so of people at the extremes, just about anyone can be classified by their brain wave patterns as tending toward one or the other type, says Davidson. The contrast in temperament between the morose and the cheerful shows up in many ways, large and small. For example, in one experiment volunteers watched short film clips. Some were amusing—a gorilla taking a bath, a puppy at play. Others, like an instructional film for nurses featuring grisly details of surgery, were quite distressing. The right-hemisphere, somber folks found the happy movies only mildly amusing, but they felt extreme fear and disgust in reaction to the surgical blood and gore. The cheerful group had minimal reactions to the surgery; their strongest reactions were of delight when they saw the up-beat films.

Thus we seem by temperament primed to respond to life in either a negative or a positive emotional register. The tendency toward a melancholy or upbeat temperament—like that toward timidity or boldness—emerges within the first year of life, a fact that strongly suggests it too is genetically determined. Like most of the brain, the frontal lobes are still maturing in the first few months of life, and so their activity cannot be reliably measured until the age of ten months or so. But in infants that young, Davidson found that the activity level of the frontal lobes predicted whether they would cry when their mothers left the room. The correlation was virtually 100 percent: of dozens of infants tested this way, every infant who cried had more brain activity on the right side, while those who did not had more activity on the left.

Still, even if this basic dimension of temperament is laid down from birth, or very nearly from birth, those of us who have the morose pattern are not necessarily doomed to go through life brooding and crotchety. The emotional lessons of childhood can have a profound impact on temperament, either amplifying or muting an innate predisposition. The great plasticity of the brain in childhood means that experiences during those years can have a lasting impact on the sculpting of neural pathways for the rest of life. Perhaps the best illustration of the kinds of experiences that can alter temperament for the better is in an observation that emerged from Kagan's research with timid children.

TAMING THE OVEREXCITABLE AMYGDALA

The encouraging news from Kagan's studies is that not all fearful infants grow up hanging back from life—temperament is not destiny. The overexcitable amygdala can be tamed, with the right experiences. What makes the difference are the emotional lessons and responses children learn as they grow. For the timid child, what matters at the outset is how they are treated by their parents, and so how they learn to handle their natural timidness. Those parents who engineer gradual emboldening experiences for their children offer them what may be a lifelong corrective to their fearfulness.

About one in three infants who come into the world with all the signs of an overexcitable amygdala have lost their timidity by the time they reach kindergarten.[7] From observations of these once-fearful children at home, it is clear that parents, and especially mothers, play a major role in whether an innately timid child grows bolder with time or continues to shy away from novelty and become upset by challenge. Kagan's research team found that some of the mothers held to the philosophy that they should protect their timid toddlers from whatever was upsetting; others felt that it was more important to help their timid child learn how to cope with these upsetting moments, and so adapt to life's small struggles. The protective belief seems to have abetted the fearfulness, probably by depriving the youngsters of opportunities for learning how to overcome their fears. The "learn to adapt" philosophy of childrearing seems to have helped fearful children become braver.

Observations in the homes when the babies were about six months old found that the protective mothers, trying to soothe their infants, picked them up and held them when they fretted or cried, and did so longer than those mothers who tried to help their infants learn to master these moments of upset. The ratio of times the infants were held when calm and when upset showed that the protective mothers held their infants much longer during the upsets than the calm periods.

Another difference emerged when the infants were around one year old: the protective mothers were more lenient and indirect in setting limits for their toddlers when they were doing something that might be harmful, such as mouthing an object they might swallow. The other mothers, by contrast, were emphatic, setting firm limits, giving direct commands, blocking the child's actions, insisting on obedience.

Why should firmness lead to a reduction in fearfulness? Kagan speculates that there is something learned when a baby has his steady crawl toward what seems to him an intriguing object (but to his mother a dangerous one) interrupted by her warning, "Get away from that!" The infant is suddenly forced to deal with a mild uncertainty. The repetition of this challenge hundreds and hundreds of times during the first year of life gives the infant continual rehearsals, in small doses, of meeting the unexpected in life. For fearful children that is precisely the encounter that has to be mastered, and manageable doses are just right for learning the lesson. When the encounter takes place with parents who, though loving, do not rush to pick up and soothe the toddler over every little upset, he gradually learns to manage such moments on his own. By age two, when these formerly fearful toddlers are brought back to Kagan's laboratory, they are far less likely to break out into tears when a stranger frowns at them, or an experimenter puts a blood-pressure cuff around their arm.

Kagan's conclusion: "It appears that mothers who protect their high[ly] reactive infants from frustration and anxiety in the hope of effecting a benevolent outcome seem to exacerbate the infant's uncertainty and produce the opposite effect."[8] In other words, the protective strategy backfires by depriving timid toddlers of the very opportunity to learn to calm themselves in the face of the unfamiliar, and so gain some small mastery of their fears. At the neurological level, presumably, this means their prefrontal circuits missed the chance to learn alternate responses to knee-jerk fear; instead, their tendency for unbridled fearfulness may have been strengthened simply through repetition.

In contrast, as Kagan told me, "Those children who had become less timid by kindergarten seem to have had parents who put gentle pressure on them to be more outgoing. Although this temperamental trait seems slightly harder than others to change—probably because of its physiological basis—no human quality is beyond change."

Throughout childhood some timid children grow bolder as experience continues to mold the key neural circuitry. One of the signs that a timid child will be more likely to overcome this natural inhibition is having a higher level of social competence: being cooperative and getting along with other children; being empathic, prone to giving and sharing, and considerate; and being able to develop close friendships. These traits marked a group of children first identified as having a timid temperament at age four, who shook it off by the time they were ten years old.[9]

By contrast, those timid four-year-olds whose temperament changed little over the same six years tended to be less able emotionally: crying and falling apart under stress more easily; being emotionally inappropriate; being fearful, sulky, or whiny; overreacting to minor frustration with anger; having trouble delaying gratification; being overly sensitive to criticism, or mistrustful. These emotional lapses are, of course, likely to mean their relationships with other children will be troubled, should they be able to overcome their initial reluctance to engage.

By contrast, it is easy to see why the more emotionally competent—though shy by temperament—children spontaneously outgrew their timidity. Being more socially skilled, they were far more likely to have a succession of positive experiences with other children. Even if they were tentative about, say, speaking to a new playmate, once the ice was broken they were able to shine socially. The regular repetition of such social success over many years would naturally tend to make the timid more sure of themselves.

These advances toward boldness are encouraging; they suggest that even innate emotional patterns can change to some degree. A child who comes into the world easily frightened can learn to be calmer, or even outgoing, in the face of the unfamiliar. Fearfulness—or any other temperament—may be part of the biological givens of our emotional lives, but we are not necessarily limited to a specific emotional menu by our inherited traits. There is a range of possibility even within genetic constraints. As behavioral geneticists observe, genes alone do not determine behavior; our environment, especially what we experience and learn as we grow, shapes how a temperamental predisposition expresses itself as life unfolds. Our emotional capacities are not a given; with the right learning, they can be improved. The reasons for this lie in how the human brain matures.

CHILDHOOD: A WINDOW OF OPPORTUNITY

The human brain is by no means fully formed at birth. It continues to shape itself through life, with the most intense growth occurring during childhood. Children are born with many more neurons than their mature brain will retain; through a process known as "pruning" the brain actually loses the neuronal connections that are less used, and forms strong connections in those synaptic circuits that have been utilized the most. Pruning, by doing away with extraneous synapses, improves the signal-to-noise ratio in the brain by removing the cause of the "noise." This process is constant and quick; synaptic connections can form in a matter of hours or days. Experience, particularly in childhood, sculpts the brain.

The classic demonstration of the impact of experience on brain growth was by Nobel Prize–winners Thorsten Wiesel and David Hubel, both neuroscientists.[10] They showed that in cats and monkeys, there was a critical period during the first few months of life for the development of the synapses that carry signals from the eye to the visual cortex, where those signals are interpreted. If one eye was kept closed during that period, the number of synapses from that eye to the visual cortex dwindled away, while those from the open eye multiplied. If after the critical period ended the closed eye was reopened, the animal was functionally blind in that eye. Although nothing was wrong with the eye itself, there were too few circuits to the visual cortex for signals from that eye to be interpreted.

In humans the corresponding critical period for vision lasts for the first six years of life. During this time normal seeing stimulates the formation of increasingly complex neural circuitry for vision that begins in the eye and ends in the visual cortex. If a child's eye is taped closed for even a few weeks, it can produce a measurable deficit in the visual capacity of that eye. If a child has had one eye closed for several months during this period, and later has it restored, that eye's vision for detail will be impaired.

A vivid demonstration of the impact of experience on the developing brain is in studies of "rich" and "poor" rats.[11] The "rich" rats lived in small groups in cages with plenty of rat diversions such as ladders and treadmills. The "poor" rats lived in cages that were similar but barren and lacking diversions. Over a period of months the neocortices of the rich rats developed far more complex networks of synaptic circuits interconnecting the neurons; the poor rats' neuronal circuitry was sparse by comparison. The difference was so great that the rich rats' brains were heavier, and, perhaps not surprisingly, they were far smarter at solving mazes than the poor rats. Similar experiments with monkeys show these differences between those "rich" and "poor" in experience, and the same effect is sure to occur in humans.

Psychotherapy—that is, systematic emotional relearning—stands as a case in point for the way experience can both change emotional patterns and shape the brain. The most dramatic demonstration comes from a study of people being treated for obsessive-compulsive disorder.[12] One of the more common compulsions is hand washing, which can be done so often, even hundreds of times in a day, that the person's skin cracks. PET scan studies show that obsessive-compulsives have greater than normal activity in the prefrontal lobes.[13]

Half of the patients in the study received the standard drug treatment, fluoxetine (better known by the brand name Prozac), and half got behavior therapy. During the therapy they were systematically exposed to the object of their obsession or compulsion without performing it; patients with hand-washing compulsions were put at a sink, but not allowed to wash. At the same time they learned to question the fears and dreads that spurred them on—for example, that failure to wash would mean they would get a disease and die. Gradually, through months of such sessions, the compulsions faded, just as they did with the medication.

The remarkable finding, though, was a PET scan test showing that the behavior therapy patients had as significant a decrease in the activity of a key part of the emotional brain, the caudate nucleus, as did the patients successfully treated with the drug fluoxetine. Their experience had changed brain function—and relieved symptoms—as effectively as the medication!

CRUCIAL WINDOWS

Of all species we humans take the longest for our brains to fully mature. While each area of the brain develops at a different rate during childhood, the onset of puberty marks one of the most sweeping periods of pruning throughout the brain. Several brain areas critical for emotional life are among the slowest to mature. While the sensory areas mature during early childhood, and the limbic system by puberty, the frontal lobes—seat of emotional self-control, understanding, and artful response—continue to develop into late adolescence, until somewhere between sixteen and eighteen years of age.[14]

The habits of emotional management that are repeated over and over again during childhood and the teenage years will themselves help mold this circuitry. This makes childhood a crucial window of opportunity for shaping lifelong emotional propensities; habits acquired in childhood become set in the basic synaptic wiring of neural architecture, and are harder to change later in life. Given the importance of the prefrontal lobes for managing emotion, the very long window for synaptic sculpting in this brain region may well mean that, in the grand design of the brain, a child's experiences over the years can mold lasting connections in the regulatory circuitry of the emotional brain. As we have seen, critical experiences include how dependable and responsive to the child's needs parents are, the opportunities and guidance a child has in learning to handle her own distress and control impulse, and practice in empathy. By the same token, neglect or abuse, the misattunement of a self-absorbed or indifferent parent, or brutal discipline can leave their imprint on the emotional circuitry.[15]

One of the most essential emotional lessons, first learned in infancy and refined throughout childhood, is how to soothe oneself when upset. For very young infants, soothing comes from caretakers: a mother hears her infant crying, picks him up, holds and rocks him until he calms down. This biological attunement, some theorists propose, helps the child begin to learn how to do the same for himself.[16] During a critical period between ten and eighteen months, the orbitofrontal area of the prefrontal cortex is rapidly forming the connections with the limbic brain that will make it a key on/off switch for distress. The infant who through countless episodes of being soothed is helped along in learning how to calm down, the speculation goes, will have stronger connections in this circuit for controlling distress, and so throughout life will be better at soothing himself when upset.

To be sure, the art of soothing oneself is mastered over many years, and with new means, as brain maturation offers a child progressively more sophisticated emotional tools. Remember, the frontal lobes, so important for regulating limbic impulse, mature into adolescence.[17] Another key circuit that continues to shape itself through childhood centers on the vagus nerve, which at one end regulates the heart and other parts of the body, and at the other sends signals to the amygdala via other circuits, prompting it to secrete the catecholamines, which prime the fight-or-flight response. A University of Washington team that assessed the impact of childrearing discovered that emotionally adept parenting led to a change for the better in vagus-nerve function.

As John Gottman, the psychologist who led the research, explained, "Parents modify their children's vagal tone"—a measure of how easily triggered the vagus nerve is—"by coaching them emotionally: talking to children about their feelings and how to understand them, not being critical and judgmental, problem-solving about emotional predicaments, coaching them on what to do, like alternatives to hitting, or to withdrawing when you're sad." When parents did this well, children were better able to suppress the vagal activity that keeps the amygdala priming the body with fight-or-flight hormones—and so were better behaved.

It stands to reason that the key skills of emotional intelligence each have critical periods extending over several years in childhood. Each period represents a window for helping that child instill beneficial emotional habits or, if missed, to make it that much harder to offer corrective lessons later in life. The massive sculpting and pruning of neural circuits in childhood may be an underlying reason why early emotional hardships and trauma have such enduring and pervasive effects in adulthood. It may explain, too, why psychotherapy can often take so long to affect some of these patterns—and why, as we've seen, even after therapy those patterns tend to remain as underlying propensities, though with an overlay of new insights and relearned responses.

To be sure, the brain remains plastic throughout life, though not to the spectacular extent seen in childhood. All learning implies a change in the brain, a strengthening of synaptic connection. The brain changes in the patients with obsessive-compulsive disorder show that emotional habits are malleable throughout life, with some sustained effort, even at the neural level. What happens with the brain in PTSD (or in therapy, for that matter) is an analog of the effects all repeated or intense emotional experiences bring, for better or for worse.

Some of the most telling of such lessons come from parent to child. There are very different emotional habits instilled by parents whose attunement means an infant's emotional needs are acknowledged and met or whose discipline includes empathy, on the one hand, or self-absorbed parents who ignore a child's distress or who discipline capriciously by yelling and hitting. Much psychotherapy is, in a sense, a remedial tutorial for what was skewed or missed completely earlier in life. But why not do what we can to prevent that need, by giving children the nurturing and guidance that cultivates the essential emotional skills in the first place?

PART FIVE

EMOTIONAL
LITERACY

15

The Cost of Emotional Illiteracy

It began as a small dispute, but had escalated. Ian Moore, a senior at Thomas Jefferson High School in Brooklyn, and Tyrone Sinkler, a junior, had had a falling-out with a buddy, fifteen-year-old Khalil Sumpter. Then they had started picking on him and making threats. Now it exploded.

Khalil, scared that Ian and Tyrone were going to beat him up, brought a .38 caliber pistol to school one morning, and, fifteen feet from a school guard, shot both boys to death at point-blank range in the school's hallway.

The incident, chilling as it is, can be read as yet another sign of a desperate need for lessons in handling emotions, settling disagreements peaceably, and just plain getting along. Educators, long disturbed by schoolchildren's lagging scores in math and reading, are realizing there is a different and more alarming deficiency: emotional illiteracy.[1] And while laudable efforts are being made to raise academic standards, this new and troubling deficiency is not being addressed in the standard school curriculum. As one Brooklyn teacher put it, the present emphasis in schools suggests that "we care more about how well schoolchildren can read and write than whether they'll be alive next week."

Signs of the deficiency can be seen in violent incidents such as the shooting of Ian and Tyrone, growing ever more common in American schools. But these are more than isolated events; the heightening of the turmoil of adolescence and troubles of childhood can be read for the United States—a bellwether of world trends—in statistics such as these:[2]

In 1990, compared to the previous two decades, the United States saw the highest juvenile arrest rate for violent crimes ever; teen arrests for forcible rape had doubled; teen murder rates quadrupled, mostly due to an increase in shootings.[3] During those same two decades, the suicide rate for teenagers tripled, as did the number of children under fourteen who are murder victims.[4]

More, and younger, teenage girls are getting pregnant. As of 1993 the birthrate among girls ten to fourteen has risen steadily for five years in a row—some call it "babies having babies"—as has the proportion of unwanted teen pregnancies and peer pressure to have sex. Rates of venereal disease among teenagers have tripled over the last three decades.[5]

While these figures are discouraging, if the focus is on African-American youth, especially in the inner city, they are utterly bleak—all the rates are higher by far, sometimes doubled, sometimes tripled or higher. For example, heroin and cocaine use among white youth climbed about 300 percent over the two decades before the 1990s; for African-American youth it jumped to a staggering *13 times* the rate of twenty years before.[6]

The most common cause of disability among teenagers is mental illness. Symptoms of depression, whether major or minor, affect up to one third of teenagers; for girls, the incidence of depression doubles at puberty. The frequency of eating disorders in teenage girls has skyrocketed.[7]

Finally, unless things change, the long-term prospects for today's children marrying and having a fruitful, stable life together are growing more dismal with each generation. As we saw in Chapter 9, while during the 1970s and 1980s the divorce rate was around 50 percent, as we entered the 1990s the rate among newlyweds predicted that two out of three marriages of young people would end in divorce.

AN EMOTIONAL MALAISE

These alarming statistics are like the canary in the coal miner's tunnel whose death warns of too little oxygen. Beyond such sobering numbers, the plight of today's children can be seen at more subtle levels, in day-to-day problems that have not yet blossomed into outright crises. Perhaps the most telling data of all—a direct barometer of dropping levels of emotional competence—are from a national sample of American children, ages seven to sixteen, comparing their emotional condition in the mid-1970s and at the end of the 1980s.[8] Based on parents' and teachers' assessments, there was a steady worsening. No one problem stood out; all indicators simply crept steadily in the wrong direction. Children, on average, were doing more poorly in these specific ways:

• *Withdrawal or social problems:* preferring to be alone; being secretive; sulking a lot; lacking energy; feeling unhappy; being overly dependent

• *Anxious and depressed:* being lonely; having many fears and worries; needing to be perfect; feeling unloved; feeling nervous or sad and depressed

• *Attention or thinking problems:* unable to pay attention or sit still; daydreaming; acting without thinking; being too nervous to concentrate; doing poorly on schoolwork; unable to get mind off thoughts

• *Delinquent or aggressive:* hanging around kids who get in trouble; lying and cheating; arguing a lot; being mean to other people; demanding attention; destroying other people's things; disobeying at home and at school; being stubborn and moody; talking too much; teasing a lot; having a hot temper

While any of these problems in isolation raises no eyebrows, taken as a group they are barometers of a sea change, a new kind of toxicity seeping into and poisoning the very experience of childhood, signifying sweeping deficits in emotional competences. This emotional malaise seems to be a universal price of modern life for children. While Americans often decry their problems as particularly bad compared to other cultures', studies around the world have found rates on a par with or worse than in the United States. For example, in the 1980s teachers and parents in the Netherlands, China, and Germany rated children at about the same level of problems as were found for American children in 1976. And some countries had children in worse shape than current U.S. levels, including Australia, France, and Thailand. But this may not remain true for long. The larger forces that propel the downward spiral in emotional competence seem to be picking up speed in the United States relative to many other developed nations.[9]

No children, rich or poor, are exempt from risk; these problems are universal, occurring in all ethnic, racial, and income groups. Thus while children in poverty have the worst record on indices of emotional skills, their *rate* of deterioration over the decades was no worse than for middle-class children or for wealthy children: all show the same steady slide. There has also been a corresponding threefold rise in the number of children who have gotten psychological help (perhaps a good sign, signaling that help is more available), as well as a near doubling of the number of children who have enough emotional problems that they *should* get such help but have not (a bad sign)—from about 9 percent in 1976 to 18 percent in 1989.

Urie Bronfenbrenner, the eminent Cornell University developmental psychologist who did an international comparison of children's well-being, says:

"In the absence of good support systems, external stresses have become so great that even strong families are falling apart. The hecticness, instability, and inconsistency of daily family life are rampant in all segments of our society, including the well-educated and well-to-do. What is at stake is nothing less than the next generation, particularly males, who in growing up are especially vulnerable to such disruptive forces as the devastating effects of divorce, poverty, and unemployment. The status of American children and families is as desperate as ever. . . . We are depriving millions of children of their competence and moral character."[10]

This is not just an American phenomenon but a global one, with worldwide competition to drive down labor costs creating economic forces that press on the family. These are times of financially besieged families in which both parents work long hours, so that children are left to their own devices or the TV baby-sits; when more children than ever grow up in poverty; when the one-parent family is becoming ever more commonplace; when more infants and toddlers are left in day care so poorly run that it amounts to neglect. All this means, even for well-intentioned parents, the erosion of the countless small, nourishing exchanges between parent and child that build emotional competences.

If families no longer function effectively to put all our children on a firm footing for life, what are we to do? A more careful look at the mechanics of specific problems suggests how given deficits in emotional or social competences lay the foundation for grave problems—and how well-aimed correctives or preventives could keep more children on track.

TAMING AGGRESSION

In my elementary school the tough kid was Jimmy, a fourth grader when I was in first grade. He was the kid who would steal your lunch money, take your bike, slug you as soon as talk to you. Jimmy was the classic bully, starting fights with the least provocation, or none at all. We all stood in awe of Jimmy—and we all stood at a distance. Everyone hated and feared Jimmy; no one would play with him. It was as though everywhere he went on the playground an invisible bodyguard cleared kids out of his way.

Kids like Jimmy are clearly troubled. But what may be less obvious is that being so flagrantly aggressive in childhood is a mark of emotional and other troubles to come. Jimmy was in jail for assault by the time he reached sixteen.

The lifelong legacy of childhood aggressiveness in kids like Jimmy has emerged from many studies.[11] As we have seen, the family life of such aggressive children typically includes parents who alternate neglect with harsh and capricious punishments, a pattern that, perhaps understandably, makes the children a bit paranoid or combative.

Not all angry children are bullies; some are withdrawn social outcasts who overreact to being teased or to what they perceive as slights or unfairness. But the one perceptual flaw that unites such children is that they perceive slights where none were intended, imagining their peers to be more hostile toward them than they actually are. This leads them to misperceive neutral acts as threatening ones—an innocent bump is seen as a vendetta—and to attack in return. That, of course, leads other children to shun them, isolating them further. Such angry, isolated children are highly sensitive to injustices and being treated unfairly. They typically see themselves as victims and can recite a list of instances when, say, teachers blamed them for doing something when in fact they were innocent. Another trait of such children is that once they are in the heat of anger they can think of only one way to react: by lashing out.

These perceptual biases can be seen at work in an experiment in which bullies are paired with a more peaceable child to watch videos. In one video, a boy drops his books when another knocks into him, and children standing nearby laugh; the boy who dropped the books gets angry and tries to hit one of those who laughed. When the boys who watched the video talk about it afterward, the bully always sees the boy who struck out as justified. Even more telling, when they have to rate how aggressive the boys were during their discussion of the video, the bullies see the boy who knocked into the other as more combative, and the anger of the boy who struck out as justified.[12]

This jump to judgment testifies to a deep perceptual bias in people who are unusually aggressive: they act on the basis of the assumption of hostility or threat, paying too little attention to what is actually going on. Once they assume threat, they leapfrog to action. For instance, if an aggressive boy is playing checkers with another who moves a piece out of turn, he'll interpret the move as "cheating" without pausing to find out if it had been an innocent mistake. His presumption is of malevolence rather than innocence; his reaction is automatic hostility. Along with the knee-jerk perception of a hostile act is entwined an equally automatic aggression; instead of, say, pointing out to the other boy that he made a mistake, he will jump to accusation, yelling, hitting. And the more such children do this, the more automatic aggression becomes for them, and the more the repertoire of alternatives—politeness, joking—shrinks.

Such children are emotionally vulnerable in the sense that they have a low threshold for upset, getting peeved more often by more things; once upset, their thinking is muddled, so that they see benign acts as hostile and fall back on their overlearned habit of striking out.[13]

These perceptual biases toward hostility are already in place by the early grades. While most children, and especially boys, are rambunctious in kindergarten and first grade, the more aggressive children fail to learn a modicum of self-control by second grade. Where other children have started to learn negotiation and compromise for playground disagreements, the bullies rely more and more on force and bluster. They pay a social price: within two or three hours of a first playground contact with a bully, other children already say they dislike him.[14]

But studies that have followed children from the preschool years into the teenage ones find that up to half of first graders who are disruptive, unable to get along with other kids, disobedient with their parents, and resistant with teachers will become delinquents in their teen years.[15] Of course, not all such aggressive children are on the trajectory that leads to violence and criminality in later life. But of all children, these are the ones most at risk for eventually committing violent crimes.

The drift toward crime shows up surprisingly early in these children's lives. When children in a Montreal kindergarten were rated for hostility and troublemaking, those highest at age five already had far greater evidence of delinquency just five to eight years later, in their early teens. They were about three times as likely as other children to admit they had beaten up someone who had not done anything to them, to have shoplifted, to have used a weapon in a fight, to have broken into or stolen parts from a car, and to have been drunk—and all this before they reached fourteen years of age.[16]

The prototypical pathway to violence and criminality starts with children who are aggressive and hard to handle in first and second grade.[17] Typically, from the earliest school years their poor impulse control also contributes to their being poor students, seen as, and seeing themselves as, "dumb"—a judgment confirmed by their being shunted to special-education classes (and though such children may have a higher rate of "hyperactivity" or learning disorders, by no means all do). Children who on entering school already have learned in their homes a "coercive" style—that is, bullying—are also written off by their teachers, who have to spend too much time keeping the children in line. The defiance of classroom rules that comes naturally to these children means that they waste time that would otherwise be used in learning; their destined academic failure is usually obvious by about third grade. While boys on a trajectory toward delinquency tend to have lower IQ scores than their peers, their impulsivity is more directly at cause: impulsivity in ten-year-old boys is almost three times as powerful a predictor of their later delinquency as is their IQ.[18]

By fourth or fifth grade these kids—by now seen as bullies or just "difficult"—are rejected by their peers and are unable to make friends easily, if at all, and have become academic failures. Feeling themselves friendless, they gravitate to other social outcasts. Between grade four and grade nine they commit themselves to their outcast group and a life of defying the law: they show a fivefold increase in their truancy, drinking, and drug taking, with the biggest boost between seventh and eighth grade. By the middle-school years, they are joined by another type of "late starters," who are attracted to their defiant style; these late starters are often youngsters who are completely unsupervised at home and have started roaming the streets on their own in grade school. In the high-school years this outcast group typically drops out of school in a drift toward delinquency, engaging in petty crimes such as shoplifting, theft, and drug dealing.

(A telling difference emerges in this trajectory between boys and girls. A study of fourth-grade girls who were "bad"—getting in trouble with teachers and breaking rules, but not unpopular with their peers—found that 40 percent had a child by the time they finished the high-school years.[19] That was three times the average pregnancy rate for girls in their schools. In other words, antisocial teenage girls don't get violent—they get pregnant.)

There is, of course, no single pathway to violence and criminality, and many other factors can put a child at risk: being born in a high-crime neighborhood where they are exposed to more temptations to crime and violence, coming from a family under high levels of stress, or living in poverty. But none of these factors makes a life of violent crime inevitable. All things being equal, the psychological forces at work in aggressive children greatly intensify the likelihood of their ending up as violent criminals. As Gerald Patterson, a psychologist who has closely followed the careers of hundreds of boys into young adulthood, puts it, "the anti-social acts of a five-year-old may be prototypic of the acts of the delinquent adolescent."[20]

SCHOOL FOR BULLIES

The bent of mind that aggressive children take with them through life is one that almost ensures they will end up in trouble. A study of juvenile offenders convicted of violent crimes and of aggressive high-school students found a

common mind-set: When they have difficulties with someone, they immediately see the other person in an antagonistic way, jumping to conclusions
about the other person's hostility toward them without seeking any further
information or trying to think of a peaceful way to settle their differences. At
the same time, the negative consequence of a violent solution—a fight,
typically—never crosses their mind. Their aggressive bent is justified in
their mind by beliefs like, "It's okay to hit someone if you just go crazy from
anger"; "If you back down from a fight everyone will think you're a
coward"; and "People who get beaten up badly don't really suffer that
much."[21]

But timely help can change these attitudes and stop a child's trajectory
toward delinquency; several experimental programs have had some success
in helping such aggressive kids learn to control their antisocial bent before it
leads to more serious trouble. One, at Duke University, worked with anger-
ridden grade-school troublemakers in training sessions for forty minutes
twice a week for six to twelve weeks. The boys were taught, for example, to
see how some of the social cues they interpreted as hostile were in fact
neutral or friendly. They learned to take the perspective of other children, to
get a sense of how they were being seen and of what other children might be
thinking and feeling in the encounters that had gotten them so angry. They
also got direct training in anger control through enacting scenes, such as
being teased, that might lead them to lose their temper. One of the key skills
for anger control was monitoring their feelings—becoming aware of their
body's sensations, such as flushing or muscle tensing, as they were getting
angry, and to take those feelings as a cue to stop and consider what to do next
rather than strike out impulsively.

John Lochman, a Duke University psychologist who was one of the
designers of the program, told me, "They'll discuss situations they've been
in recently, like being bumped in the hallway when they think it was on
purpose. The kids will talk about how they might have handled it. One kid
said, for example, that he just stared at the boy who bumped him and told
him not to do it again, and walked away. That put him in the position of
exerting some control and keeping his self-esteem, without starting a fight."

This appeals; many such aggressive boys are unhappy that they lose their
temper so easily, and so are receptive to learning to control it. In the heat of
the moment, of course, such cool-headed responses as walking away or
counting to ten so the impulse to hit will pass before reacting are not
automatic; the boys practice such alternatives in role-playing scenes such as
getting on a bus where other kids are taunting them. That way they can try

out friendly responses that preserve their dignity while giving them an alternative to hitting, crying, or running away in shame.

Three years after the boys had been through the training, Lochman compared these boys with others who had been just as aggressive, but did not have the benefit of the anger-control sessions. He found that, in adolescence, the boys who graduated from the program were much less disruptive in class, had more positive feelings about themselves, and were less likely to drink or take drugs. And the longer they had been in the program, the less aggressive they were as teenagers.

PREVENTING DEPRESSION

Dana, sixteen, had always seemed to get along. But now, suddenly, she just could not relate with other girls, and, more troubling for her, she could not find a way to hold on to boyfriends, even though she slept with them. Morose and constantly fatigued, Dana lost interest in eating, in having fun of any kind; she said she felt hopeless and helpless to do anything to escape her mood, and was thinking of suicide.

The drop into depression had been triggered by her most recent breakup. She said she didn't know how to go out with a boy without getting sexually involved right away—even if she was uncomfortable about it—and that she did not know how to end a relationship even if it was unsatisfying. She went to bed with boys, she said, when all she really wanted to do was get to know them better.

She had just moved to a new school, and felt shy and anxious about making friends with girls there. For instance, she held back from starting conversations, only talking once someone spoke to her. She felt unable to let them know what she was like, and didn't even feel she knew what to say after "Hello, how are you?"[22]

Dana went for therapy to an experimental program for depressed adolescents at Columbia University. Her treatment focused on helping her learn how to handle her relationships better: how to develop a friendship, how to feel more confident with other teens, how to assert limits on sexual closeness, how to be intimate, how to express her feelings. In essence, it was a remedial tutorial in some of the most basic emotional skills. And it worked; her depression lifted.

Particularly in young people, problems in relationships are a trigger for depression. The difficulty is as often in children's relationships with their parents as it is with their peers. Depressed children and teenagers are frequently unable or unwilling to talk about their sadness. They seem unable to label their feelings accurately, showing instead a sullen irritability, impatience, crankiness, and anger—especially toward their parents. This, in turn, makes it harder for their parents to offer the emotional support and guidance the depressed child actually needs, setting in motion a downward spiral that typically ends in constant arguments and alienation.

A new look at the causes of depression in the young pinpoints deficits in two areas of emotional competence: relationship skills, on the one hand, and a depression-promoting way of interpreting setbacks, on the other. While some of the tendency to depression almost certainly is due to genetic destiny, some of that tendency seems due to reversible, pessimistic habits of thought that predispose children to react to life's small defeats—a bad grade, arguments with parents, a social rejection—by becoming depressed. And there is evidence to suggest that the predisposition to depression, whatever its basis, is becoming ever more widespread among the young.

A COST OF MODERNITY: RISING RATES OF DEPRESSION

These millennial years are ushering in an Age of Melancholy, just as the twentieth century became an Age of Anxiety. International data show what seems to be a modern epidemic of depression, one that is spreading side by side with the adoption throughout the world of modern ways. Each successive generation worldwide since the opening of the century has lived with a higher risk than their parents of suffering a major depression—not just sadness, but a paralyzing listlessness, dejection, and self-pity, and an overwhelming hopelessness—over the course of life.[23] And those episodes are beginning at earlier and earlier ages. Childhood depression, once virtually unknown (or, at least, unrecognized) is emerging as a fixture of the modern scene.

Although the likelihood of becoming depressed rises with age, the greatest increases are among young people. For those born after 1955 the likelihood they will suffer a major depression at some point in life is, in many countries, three times or more greater than for their grandparents. Among Americans born before 1905, the rate of those having a major depression over a lifetime was just 1 percent; for those born since 1955, by age twenty-four about 6 percent had become depressed. For those born between 1945 and 1954, the chances of having had a major depression before age thirty-four are ten times greater than for those born between 1905 and 1914.[24] And for each generation the onset of a person's first episode of depression has tended to occur at an ever-earlier age.

A worldwide study of more than thirty-nine thousand people found the same trend in Puerto Rico, Canada, Italy, Germany, France, Taiwan, Lebanon, and New Zealand. In Beirut, the rise of depression tracked political events closely, the upward trends rocketing during periods of civil war. In Germany, for those born before 1914 the rate of depression by age thirty-five is 4 percent; for those born in the decade before 1944 it is 14 percent at age thirty-five. Worldwide, generations that came of age during politically troubled times had higher rates of depression, though the overall upward trend holds apart from any political events.

The lowering into childhood of the age when people first experience depression also seems to hold worldwide. When I asked experts to hazard a guess as to why, there were several theories.

Dr. Frederick Goodwin, then director of the National Institute of Mental Health, speculated, "There's been a tremendous erosion of the nuclear family—a doubling of the divorce rate, a drop in parents' time available to children, and an increase in mobility. You don't grow up knowing your extended family much anymore. The losses of these stable sources of self-identification mean a greater susceptibility to depression."

Dr. David Kupfer, chairman of psychiatry at the University of Pittsburgh medical school, pointed to another trend: "With the spread of industrialization after World War II, in a sense nobody was home anymore. In more and more families there has been growing parental indifference to children's needs as they grow up. This is not a direct cause of depression, but it sets up a vulnerability. Early emotional stressors may affect neuron development, which can lead to a depression when you are under great stress even decades later."

Martin Seligman, the University of Pennsylvania psychologist, proposed: "For the last thirty or forty years we've seen the ascendance of individualism and a waning of larger beliefs in religion, and in supports from the community and extended family. That means a loss of resources that can buffer you against setbacks and failures. To the extent you see a failure as something that is lasting and which you magnify to taint everything in your life, you are prone to let a momentary defeat become a lasting source of hopelessness. But if you have a larger perspective, like a belief in God and an afterlife, and you lose your job, it's just a temporary defeat."

Whatever the cause, depression in the young is a pressing problem. In the United States, estimates vary widely for how many children and teens are depressed in any given year, as opposed to vulnerability over their lifetime. Some epidemiological studies using strict criteria—the official diagnostic symptoms for depression—have found that for boys and girls between ten and thirteen the rate of major depression over the course of a year is as high as 8 or 9 percent, though other studies place it at about half that rate (and some as low as about 2 percent). At puberty, some data suggest, the rate nearly doubles for girls; up to 16 percent of girls between fourteen and sixteen suffer a bout of depression, while the rate is unchanged for boys.[25]

THE COURSE OF DEPRESSION IN THE YOUNG

That depression should not just be treated, but *prevented,* in children is clear from an alarming discovery: Even mild episodes of depression in a child can augur more severe episodes later in life.[26] This challenges the old assumption that depression in childhood does not matter in the long run, since children supposedly "grow out of it." Of course, every child gets sad from time to time; childhood and adolescence are, like adulthood, times of occasional disappointments and losses large and small with the attendant grief. The need for prevention is not for these times, but for those children for whom sadness spirals downward into a gloom that leaves them despairing, irritable, and withdrawn—a far more severe melancholy.

Among children whose depression was severe enough that they were referred for treatment, three quarters had a subsequent episode of severe depression, according to data collected by Maria Kovacs, a psychologist at Western Psychiatric Institute and Clinic in Pittsburgh.[27] Kovacs studied children diagnosed with depression when they were as young as eight years old, assessing them every few years until some were as old as twenty-four.

The children with major depression had episodes lasting about eleven months on average, though in one in six of them it persisted for as long as eighteen months. Mild depression, which began as early as age five in some children, was less incapacitating but lasted far longer—an average of about four years. And, Kovacs found, children who have a minor depression are more likely to have it intensify into major depression—a so-called double depression. Those who develop double depression are much more prone to suffer recurring episodes as the years go on. As children who had an episode of depression grew into adolescence and early adulthood, they suffered from depression or manic-depressive disorder, on average, one year in three.

The cost to children goes beyond the suffering caused by depression itself. Kovacs told me, "Kids learn social skills in their peer relations—for example, what to do if you want something and aren't getting it, seeing how other children handle the situation and then trying it yourself. But depressed kids are likely to be among the neglected children in a school, the ones other kids don't play with much."[28]

The sullenness or sadness such children feel leads them to avoid initiating social contacts, or to look away when another child is trying to engage them—a social signal the other child only takes as a rebuff; the end result is that depressed children end up rejected or neglected on the playground. This lacuna in their interpersonal experience means they miss out on what they would normally learn in the rough-and-tumble of play, and so can leave them social and emotional laggards, with much catching up to do after the depression lifts.[29] Indeed, when depressed children have been compared to those without depression, they have been found to be more socially inept, to have fewer friends, to be less preferred than others as playmates, to be less liked, and to have more troubled relationships with other children.

Another cost to these children is doing poorly in school; depression interferes with their memory and concentration, making it harder to pay attention in class and retain what is taught. A child who feels no joy in anything will find it hard to marshal the energy to master challenging lessons, let alone experience flow in learning. Understandably, the longer children in Kovacs's study were depressed, the more their grades dropped and the poorer they did on achievement tests, so that they were more likely to be held back in school. In fact, there was a direct correlation between the length of time a child had been depressed and his grade-point average, with a steady plummet over the course of the episode. All of this academic rough going, of course, compounds the depression. As Kovacs observes, "Imagine you're already feeling depressed, and you start flunking out of school, and you sit home by yourself instead of playing with other kids."

DEPRESSIONOGENIC WAYS OF THOUGHT

Just as with adults, pessimistic ways of interpreting life's defeats seem to feed the sense of helplessness and hopelessness at the heart of children's depression. That people who are *already* depressed think in these ways has long been known. What has only recently emerged, though, is that children who are most prone to melancholy tend toward this pessimistic outlook *before* they become depressed. This insight suggests a window of opportunity for inoculating them against depression before it strikes.

One line of evidence comes from studies of children's beliefs about their own ability to control what happens in their lives—for example, being able to change things for the better. This is assessed by children's ratings of themselves in such terms as "When I have problems at home I'm better than most kids at helping to solve the problems" and "When I work hard I get good grades." Children who say none of these positive descriptions fits them have little sense that they can do anything to change things; this sense of helplessness is highest in those children who are most depressed.[30]

A telling study looked at fifth and sixth graders in the few days after they received report cards. As we all remember, report cards are one of the greatest sources of elation and despair in childhood. But researchers find a marked consequence in how children assess their role when they get a worse grade than they expected. Those who see a bad grade as due to some personal flaw ("I'm stupid") feel more depressed than those who explain it away in terms of something they could change ("If I work harder on my math homework I'll get a better grade").[31]

Researchers identified a group of third, fourth, and fifth graders whom classmates had rejected, and tracked which ones continued to be social outcasts in their new classes the following year. How the children explained the rejection to themselves seemed crucial to whether they became depressed. Those who saw their rejection as due to some flaw in themselves grew more depressed. But the optimists, who felt that they could do something to change things for the better, were not especially depressed despite the continuing rejection.[32] And in a study of children making the notoriously stressful transition to seventh grade, those who had the pessimistic attitude responded to high levels of hassles at school and to any additional stress at home by becoming depressed.[33]

The most direct evidence that a pessimistic outlook makes children highly susceptible to depression comes from a five-year study of children beginning when they were in third grade.[34] Among the younger children, the strongest predictor that they would become depressed was a pessimistic outlook coupled with a major blow such as parents divorcing or a death in the family, which left the child upset, unsettled, and, presumably, with parents less able to offer a nurturing buffer. As the children grew through the elementary-school years, there was a telling shift in their thinking about the good and bad events of their lives, with the children increasingly ascribing them to their own traits: "I'm getting good grades because I'm smart"; "I don't have many friends because I'm no fun." This shift seems to set in gradually over the third to fifth grades. As this happens those children who develop a pessimistic outlook—attributing the setbacks in their lives to some dire flaw in themselves—begin to fall prey to depressed moods in reaction to setbacks. What's more, the experience of depression itself seems to reinforce these pessimistic ways of thinking, so that even after the depression lifts, the child is left with what amounts to an emotional scar, a set of convictions fed by the depression and solidified in the mind: that he can't do well in school, is unlikable, and can do nothing to escape his own brooding moods. These fixed ideas can make the child all the more vulnerable to another depression down the road.

SHORT-CIRCUITING DEPRESSION

The good news: there is every sign that teaching children more productive ways of looking at their difficulties lowers their risk of depression.* In a study of one Oregon high school, about one in four students had what psychologists call a "low-level depression," not severe enough to say it was beyond ordinary unhappiness as yet.[35] Some may have been in the early weeks or months of what was to become a depression.

In a special after-school class seventy-five of the mildly depressed students learned to challenge the thinking patterns associated with depression, to become more adept at making friends, to get along better with their parents, and to engage in more social activities they found pleasant. By the end of the eight-week program, 55 percent of the students had recovered from their mild depression, while only about a quarter of equally depressed students who were not in the program had begun to pull out of their depression. A year later a quarter of those in the comparison group had gone on to fall into a major depression, as opposed to only 14 percent of students in the depression-prevention program. Though they lasted just eight sessions, the classes seemed to have cut the risk of depression in half.[36]

---

* In children, unlike adults, medication is not a clear alternative to therapy or preventive education for treating depression; children metabolize medications differently than do adults. Tricyclic antidepressants, often successful with adults, have failed in controlled studies with children to prove better than an inactive placebo drug. Newer depression medications, including Prozac, are as yet untested for use in children. And desipramine, one of the most common (and safest) tricyclics used with adults, has, at this writing, become the focus of FDA scrutiny as a possible cause of death in children.

Similarly promising findings came from a special once-a-week class given to ten- to thirteen-year-old youngsters at odds with their parents and showing some signs of depression. In after-school sessions they learned some basic emotional skills, including handling disagreements, thinking before acting, and, perhaps most important, challenging the pessimistic beliefs associated with depression—for example, resolving to study harder after doing poorly on an exam instead of thinking, "I'm just not smart enough."

"What a child learns in these classes is that moods like anxiety, sadness, and anger don't just descend on you without your having any control over them, but that you can change the way you feel by what you think," points out psychologist Martin Seligman, one of the developers of the twelve-week program. Because disputing the depressing thoughts vanquishes the gathering mood of gloom, Seligman added, "it's an instant reinforcer that becomes a habit."

Again the special sessions lowered depression rates by one half—and did so as long as two years later. A year after the classes ended, just 8 percent of those who participated scored at a moderate-to-severe level on a test of depression, versus 29 percent of children in a comparison group. And after two years, about 20 percent of those in the course were showing some signs of at least mild depression, compared to 44 percent of those in the comparison group.

Learning these emotional skills at the cusp of adolescence may be especially helpful. Seligman observes, "These kids seem to be better at handling the routine teenage agonies of rejection. They seem to have learned this at a crucial window for risk of depression, just as they enter the teen years. And the lesson seems to persist and grow a bit stronger over the course of the years after they learn it, suggesting the kids are actually using it in their day-to-day lives."

Other experts on childhood depression applaud the new programs. "If you want to make a real difference for psychiatric illness like depression, you have to do something before the kids get sick in the first place," Kovacs commented. "The real solution is a psychological inoculation."

EATING DISORDERS

During my days as a graduate student in clinical psychology in the late 1960s, I knew two women who suffered from eating disorders, though I realized this only after many years had passed. One was a brilliant graduate student in mathematics at Harvard, a friend from my undergraduate days; the other was on the staff at M.I.T. The mathematician, though skeletally thin, simply could not bring herself to eat; food, she said, repulsed her. The librarian had an ample figure and was given to bingeing on ice cream, Sara Lee carrot cake, and other desserts; then—as she once confided with some embarrassment—she would secretly go off to the bathroom and make herself vomit. Today the mathematician would be diagnosed with anorexia nervosa, the librarian with bulimia.

In those years there were no such labels. Clinicians were just beginning to comment on the problem; Hilda Bruch, the pioneer in this movement, published her seminal article on eating disorders in 1969.[37] Bruch, puzzled by women who were starving themselves to death, proposed that one of the several underlying causes lay in an inability to label and respond appropriately to bodily urges—notably, of course, hunger. Since then the clinical literature on eating disorders has mushroomed, with a multitude of hypotheses about the causes, ranging from ever-younger girls feeling compelled to compete with unattainably high standards of female beauty, to intrusive mothers who enmesh their daughters in a controlling web of guilt and blame.

Most of these hypotheses suffered from one great drawback: they were extrapolations from observations made during therapy. Far more desirable, from a scientific viewpoint, are studies of large groups of people over a period of several years, to see who among them eventually comes down with the problem. That kind of study allows a clean comparison that can tell, for example, if having controlling parents predisposes a girl to eating disorders. Beyond that, it can identify the cluster of conditions that leads to the problem, and distinguish them from conditions that might seem to be a cause, but which actually are found as often in people without the problem as in those who come for treatment.

When just such a study was done with more than nine hundred girls in the seventh through tenth grades, emotional deficits—particularly a failure to tell distressing feelings from one another and to control them—were found to be key among the factors leading to eating disorders.[38] Even by tenth grade, there were sixty-one girls in this affluent, suburban Minneapolis high school who already had serious symptoms of anorexia or bulimia. The greater the problem, the more the girls reacted to setbacks, difficulties, and minor annoyances with intense negative feelings that they could not soothe, and the less their awareness of what, exactly, they were feeling. When these two emotional tendencies were coupled with being highly dissatisfied with their body, then the outcome was anorexia or bulimia. Overly controlling parents were found not to play a prime role in causing eating disorders. (As Bruch herself had warned, theories based on hindsight were unlikely to be accurate; for example, parents can easily become intensely controlling *in response* to their daughter's eating disorder, out of desperation to help her.) Also judged irrelevant were such popular explanations as fear of sexuality, early onset of puberty, and low self-esteem.

Instead, the causal chain this prospective study revealed began with the effects on young girls of growing up in a society preoccupied with unnatural thinness as a sign of female beauty. Well in advance of adolescence, girls are already self-conscious about their weight. One six-year-old, for example, broke into tears when her mother asked her to go for a swim, saying she'd look fat in a swimsuit. In fact, says her pediatrician, who tells the story, her weight was normal for her height.[39] In one study of 271 young teenagers, half the girls thought they were too fat, even though the vast majority of them were normal in weight. But the Minneapolis study showed that an obsession with being overweight is not in and of itself sufficient to explain why some girls go on to develop eating disorders.

Some obese people are unable to tell the difference between being scared, angry, and hungry, and so lump all those feelings together as signifying hunger, which leads them to overeat whenever they feel upset.[40] Something similar seems to be happening in these girls. Gloria Leon, the University of Minnesota psychologist who did the study of young girls and eating disorders, observed that these girls "have poor awareness of their feelings and body signals; that was the strongest single predictor that they would go on to develop an eating disorder within the next two years. Most children learn to distinguish among their sensations, to tell if they're feeling bored, angry, depressed, or hungry—it's a basic part of emotional learning. But these girls have trouble distinguishing among their most basic feelings. They may have a problem with their boyfriend, and not be sure whether they're angry, or anxious, or depressed—they just experience a diffuse emotional storm that they do not know how to deal with effectively. Instead they learn to make themselves feel better by eating; that can become a strongly entrenched emotional habit."

But when this habit for soothing themselves interacts with the pressures girls feel to stay thin, the way is paved for eating disorders to develop. "At first she might start with binge eating," Leon observes. "But to stay thin she may turn to vomiting or laxatives, or intense physical exertion to undo the weight gain from overeating. Another avenue this struggle to handle emotional confusion can take is for the girl not to eat at all—it can be a way to feel you have at least some control over these overwhelming feelings."

The combination of poor inner awareness and weak social skills means that these girls, when upset by friends or parents, fail to act effectively to soothe either the relationship or their own distress. Instead their upset triggers the eating disorder, whether it be that of bulimia or anorexia, or simply binge eating. Effective treatments for such girls, Leon believes, need to include some remedial instruction in the emotional skills they lack. "Clinicians find," she told me, "that if you address the deficits therapy works better. These girls need to learn to identify their feelings and learn ways to soothe themselves or handle their relationships better, without turning to their maladaptive eating habits to do the job."

ONLY THE LONELY: DROPOUTS

It's a grade-school drama: Ben, a fourth grader with few friends, has just heard from his one buddy, Jason, that they aren't going to play together this lunch period—Jason wants to play with another boy, Chad, instead. Ben, crushed, hangs his head and cries. After his sobs subside, Ben goes over to the lunch table where Jason and Chad are eating.

"I hate your guts!" Ben yells at Jason.

"Why?" Jason asks.

"Because you lied," Ben says, his tone accusatory. "You said this whole week that you were gonna play with me and you lied."

Ben then stalks off to his empty table, crying quietly. Jason and Chad go over to him and try to talk to him, but Ben puts his fingers in his ears, determinedly ignoring them, and runs out of the lunchroom to hide behind the school Dumpster. A group of girls who have witnessed the exchange try to play a peacemaker role, finding Ben and telling him that Jason is willing to play with him too. But Ben will have none of it, and tells them to leave him alone. He nurses his wounds, sulking and sobbing, defiantly alone.[41]

A poignant moment, to be sure; the feeling of being rejected and friendless is one most everyone goes through at some point in childhood or adolescence. But what is most telling about Ben's reaction is his failure to respond to Jason's efforts to repair their friendship, a stance that extends his plight when it might have ended. Such an inability to seize key cues is typical of children who are unpopular; as we saw in Chapter 8, socially rejected children typically are poor at reading emotional and social signals; even when they do read such signals, they may have limited repertoires for response.

Dropping out of school is a particular risk for children who are social rejects. The dropout rate for children who are rejected by their peers is between two and eight times greater than for children who have friends. One study found, for example, that about 25 percent of children who were unpopular in elementary school had dropped out before completing high school, compared to a general rate of 8 percent.[42] Small wonder: imagine spending thirty hours a week in a place where no one likes you.

Two kinds of emotional proclivities lead children to end up as social outcasts. As we have seen, one is the propensity to angry outbursts and to perceive hostility even where none is intended. The second is being timid, anxious, and socially shy. But over and above these temperamental factors, it is children who are "off"—whose awkwardness repeatedly makes people uncomfortable—who tend to be shunted aside.

One way these children are "off" is in the emotional signals they send. When grade schoolers with few friends were asked to match an emotion such as disgust or anger with faces that displayed a range of emotions, they made far more mismatches than did children who were popular. When kindergarteners were asked to explain ways they might make friends with someone or keep from having a fight, it was the unpopular children—the ones others shied away from playing with—who came up with self-defeating answers ("Punch him" for what to do when both children wanted the same toy, for example), or vague appeals for help from a grown-up. And when teenagers were asked to role-play being sad, angry, or mischievous, the more unpopular among them gave the least convincing performances. It is perhaps no surprise that such children come to feel that they are helpless to do any better at making friends; their social incompetence becomes a self-fulfilling prophecy. Instead of learning new approaches to making friends, they simply keep doing the same things that have not worked for them in the past, or come up with even more inept responses.[43]

In the lottery of liking, these children fall short on key emotional criteria: they are not seen as fun to be with, and they don't know how to make another child feel good. Observations of unpopular children at play show, for example, that they are much more likely than others to cheat, sulk, quit when losing, or show off and brag about winning. Of course, most children want to win at a game—but win or lose, most children are able to contain their emotional reaction so that it does not undermine the relationship with the friend they play games with.

While children who are socially tone-deaf—who continually have trouble reading and responding to emotions—end up as social isolates, this does not apply, of course, to children who go through a temporary period of feeling left out. But for those who are continually excluded and rejected, their painful outcast status clings to them as they continue their school years. The consequences of ending up at the social margins are potentially great as a child continues on into adulthood. For one, it is in the cauldron of close friendships and the tumult of play that children refine the social and emotional skills that they will bring to relationships later in life. Children who are excluded from this realm of learning are, inevitably, disadvantaged.

Understandably, those who are rejected report great anxiety and many worries, as well as being depressed and lonely. In fact, how popular a child was in third grade has been shown to be a better predictor of mental-health problems at age eighteen than anything else—teachers' and nurses' ratings, school performance and IQ, even scores on psychological tests.[44] And, as we have seen, in later stages of life people who have few friends and are chronically lonely are at greater risk for medical diseases and an early death.

As psychoanalyst Harry Stack Sullivan pointed out, we learn how to negotiate intimate relations—to work out differences and share our deepest feelings—in our first close friendships with same-sex chums. But children who are socially rejected are only half as likely as their peers to have a best friend during the crucial years of elementary school, and so miss out on one of the essential chances for emotional growth.[45] One friend can make the difference—even when all others turn their backs (and even when that friendship is not all that solid).

COACHING FOR FRIENDSHIP

There is hope for rejected children, despite their ineptness. Steven Asher, a University of Illinois psychologist, has designed a series of "friendship coaching" sessions for unpopular children that has shown some success.[46] Identifying third and fourth graders who were the least liked in their classes, Asher gave them six sessions in how to "make playing games more fun" through being "friendly, fun, and nice." To avoid stigma, the children were told that they were acting as "consultants" to the coach, who was trying to learn what kinds of things make it more enjoyable to play games.

The children were coached to act in ways Asher had found typical of more popular children. For example, they were encouraged to think of alternative suggestions and compromises (rather than fighting) if they disagree about the rules; to remember to talk with and ask questions about the other child while they play; to listen and look at the other child to see how he's doing; to say something nice when the other person does well; to smile and offer help or suggestions and encouragement. The children also tried out these basic social amenities while playing games such as Pick-up Sticks with a classmate, and were coached afterward on how well they did. This minicourse in getting along had a remarkable effect: a year later the children who were coached— all of whom were selected because they were the least-liked in their class— were now solidly in the middle of classroom popularity. None were social stars, but none were rejects.

Similar results have been found by Stephen Nowicki, an Emory University psychologist.[47] His program trains social outcasts to hone their ability to read and respond appropriately to other children's feelings. The children, for example, are videotaped while practicing expression of feelings such as happiness and sadness, and are coached to improve their emotional expressiveness. They then try out their newly honed skills with a child they want to make friends with.

Such programs have reported a 50 to 60 percent success rate in raising the popularity of rejected children. These programs (at least as presently designed) seem to work best for third and fourth graders rather than children in higher grades, and to be more helpful for socially inept children than for highly aggressive ones. But that is all a matter for fine-tuning; the hopeful sign is that many or most rejected children can be brought into the circle of friendship with some basic emotional coaching.

DRINKING AND DRUGS: ADDICTION AS SELF-MEDICATION

Students at the local campus call it *drinking to black*—bingeing on beer to the point of passing out. One of the techniques: attach a funnel to a garden hose, so that a can of beer can be downed in about ten seconds. The method is not an isolated oddity. One survey found that two fifths of male college students down seven or more drinks at a time, while 11 percent call themselves "heavy drinkers." Another term, of course, might be "alcoholics."[48] About half of college men and almost 40 percent of women have at least two binge-drinking episodes in a month.[49]

While in the United States use of most drugs among young people generally tapered off in the 1980s, there is a steady trend toward more alcohol use at ever-younger ages. A 1993 survey found that 35 percent of college women said they drank to get drunk, while just 10 percent did so in 1977; overall, one in three students drinks to get drunk. That poses other risks: 90 percent of all rapes reported on college campuses happened when either the assailant or the victim—or both—had been drinking.[50] Alcohol-related accidents are the leading cause of death among young people between fifteen and twenty-four.[51]

Experimentation with drugs and alcohol might seem a rite of passage for adolescents, but this first taste can have long-lasting results for some. For most alcoholics and drug abusers, the beginnings of addiction can be traced to their teen years, though few of those who so experiment end up as alcoholics or drug abusers. By the time students leave high school, over 90 percent have tried alcohol, yet only about 14 percent eventually become alcoholics; of the millions of Americans who experimented with cocaine, fewer than 5 percent became addicted.[52] What makes the difference?

To be sure, those living in high-crime neighborhoods, where crack is sold on the corner and the drug dealer is the most prominent local model of economic success, are most at risk for substance abuse. Some may end up addicted through becoming small-time dealers themselves, others simply because of the easy access or a peer culture that glamorizes drugs—a factor that heightens the risk of drug use in any neighborhood, even (and perhaps especially) the most well-off. But still the question remains, of the pool of those exposed to these lures and pressures, and who go on to experiment, which ones are most likely to end up with a lasting habit?

One current scientific theory is that those who stay with the habit, becoming increasingly dependent on alcohol or drugs, are using these substances as a medication of sorts, a way to soothe feelings of anxiety, anger, or depression. Through their early experimentation they hit upon a chemical fix, a way to calm the feelings of anxiety or melancholy that have tormented them. Thus of several hundred seventh- and eighth-grade students tracked for two years, it was those who reported higher levels of emotional distress who subsequently went on to have the highest rates of substance abuse.[53] This may explain why so many young people are able to experiment with drugs and drinking without becoming addicted, while others become dependent almost from the start: those most vulnerable to addiction seem to find in the drug or alcohol an instant way to soothe emotions that have distressed them for years.

As Ralph Tarter, a psychologist at the Western Psychiatric Institute and Clinic in Pittsburgh, put it, "For people who are biologically predisposed, the first drink or dose of a drug is immensely reinforcing, in a way others just don't experience. Many recovering drug abusers tell me, 'The moment I took my first drug, I felt normal for the first time.' It stabilizes them physiologically, at least in the short term."[54] That, of course, is the devil's bargain of addiction: a short-term good feeling in exchange for the steady meltdown of one's life.

Certain emotional patterns seem to make people more likely to find emotional relief in one substance rather than another. For example, there are two emotional pathways to alcoholism. One starts with someone who was high-strung and anxious in childhood, who typically discovers as a teenager that alcohol will calm the anxiety. Very often they are children—usually sons—of alcoholics who themselves have turned to alcohol to soothe their nerves. One biological marker for this pattern is undersecretion of GABA, a neurotransmitter that regulates anxiety—too little GABA is experienced as a high level of tension. One study found that sons of alcoholic fathers had low levels of GABA and were highly anxious, but when they drank alcohol, their GABA levels rose as their anxiety fell.[55] These sons of alcoholics drink to ease their tension, finding in alcohol a relaxation that they could not seem to get otherwise. Such people may be vulnerable to abusing sedatives as well as alcohol for the same anxiety-reduction effect.

A neuropsychological study of sons of alcoholics who at age twelve showed signs of anxiety such as a heightened heart rate in response to stress, as well as impulsivity, found the boys also had poor frontal lobe functioning.[56] Thus the brain areas that might have helped ease their anxiety or control their impulsiveness brought them less help than in other boys. And since the pre-frontal lobes also handle working memory—which holds in mind the consequences of various routes of action while making a decision—their deficit could support a slide into alcoholism by helping them ignore the long-term drawbacks of drinking, even as they found an immediate sedation from anxiety through alcohol.

This craving for calm seems to be an emotional marker of a genetic susceptibility to alcoholism. A study of thirteen hundred relatives of alcoholics found that the children of alcoholics who were most at risk for becoming alcoholics themselves were those who reported having chronically high levels of anxiety. Indeed, the researchers concluded that alcoholism develops in such people as "self-medication of anxiety symptoms."[57]

A second emotional pathway to alcoholism comes from a high level of agitation, impulsivity, and boredom. This pattern shows up in infancy as being restless, cranky, and hard to handle, in grade school as having the "fidgets," hyperactivity, and getting into trouble, a propensity that, as we have seen, can push such children to seek out friends on the fringe—sometimes leading to a criminal career or the diagnosis of "antisocial personality disorder." Such people (and they are mainly men) have as their main emotional complaint agitation; their main weakness is unrestrained impulsivity; their usual reaction to boredom—which they often feel—is an impulsive search for risk and excitement. As adults, people with this pattern (which may be tied to deficiencies in two other neurotransmitters, serotonin and MAO) find that alcohol can soothe their agitation. And the fact that they can't stand monotony makes them ready to try anything; coupled with their general impulsivity, it makes them prone to abusing an almost random list of drugs besides alcohol.[58]

While depression can drive some to drink, the metabolic effects of alcohol often simply worsen the depression after a short lift. People who turn to alcohol as an emotional palliative do so much more often to calm anxiety than for depression; an entirely different class of drugs soothes the feelings of people who are depressed—at least temporarily. Feeling chronically unhappy puts people at greater risk for addiction to stimulants such as cocaine, which provide a direct antidote to feeling depressed. One study found that more than half the patients being treated at a clinic for cocaine addiction would have been diagnosed with severe depression before they started their habit, and the deeper the preceding depression, the stronger the habit.[59]

Chronic anger may lead to still another kind of susceptibility. In a study of four hundred patients being treated for addiction to heroin and other opioids, the most striking emotional pattern was a lifelong difficulty handling anger and a quickness to rage. Some of the patients themselves said that with opiates they finally felt normal and relaxed.[60]

Though the predisposition to substance abuse may, in many cases, be brain-based, the feelings that drive people to "self-medicate" themselves through drink or drugs can be handled without recourse to medication, as Alcoholics Anonymous and other recovery programs have demonstrated for decades. Acquiring the ability to handle those feelings—soothing anxiety, lifting depression, calming rage—removes the impetus to use drugs or alcohol in the first place. These basic emotional skills are taught remedially in treatment programs for drug and alcohol abuse. It would be far better, of course, if they were learned early in life, well before the habit became established.

NO MORE WARS: A FINAL COMMON PREVENTIVE PATHWAY

Over the last decade or so "wars" have been proclaimed, in turn, on teen pregnancy, dropping out, drugs, and most recently violence. The trouble with such campaigns, though, is that they come too late, after the targeted problem has reached epidemic proportions and taken firm root in the lives of the young. They are crisis intervention, the equivalent of solving a problem by sending an ambulance to the rescue rather than giving an inoculation that would ward off the disease in the first place. Instead of more such "wars," what we need is to follow the logic of prevention, offering our children the skills for facing life that will increase their chances of avoiding any and all of these fates.[61]

My focus on the place of emotional and social deficits is not to deny the role of other risk factors, such as growing up in a fragmented, abusive, or chaotic family, or in an impoverished, crime- and drug-ridden neighbor-hood. Poverty itself delivers emotional blows to children: poorer children at age five are already more fearful, anxious, and sad than their better-off peers, and have more behavior problems such as frequent tantrums and destroying things, a trend that continues through the teen years. The press of poverty corrodes family life too: there tend to be fewer expressions of parental warmth, more depression in mothers (who are often single and jobless), and a greater reliance on harsh punishments such as yelling, hitting, and physical threats.[62]

But there is a role that emotional competence plays over and above family and economic forces—it may be decisive in determining the extent to which any given child or teenager is undone by these hardships or finds a core of resilience to survive them. Long-term studies of hundreds of children brought up in poverty, in abusive families, or by a parent with severe mental illness show that those who are resilient even in the face of the most grinding hardships tend to share key emotional skills.[63] These include a winning sociability that draws people to them, self-confidence, an optimistic per-sistence in the face of failure and frustration, the ability to recover quickly from upsets, and an easygoing nature.

But the vast majority of children face such difficulties without these advan-tages. Of course, many of these skills are innate, the luck of genes—but even qualities of temperament can change for the better, as we saw in Chapter 14. One line of intervention, of course, is political and economic, alleviating the poverty and other social conditions that breed these problems. But apart from these tactics (which seem to move ever lower on the social agenda) there is much that can be offered to children to help them grapple better with such debilitating hardships.

Take the case of emotional disorders, afflictions that about one in two Americans experiences over the course of life. A study of a representative sample of 8,098 Americans found that 48 percent suffered from at least one psychiatric problem during their lifetime.[64] Most severely affected were the 14 percent of people who developed three or more psychiatric problems at once. This group was the most troubled, accounting for 60 percent of all psychiatric disorders occurring at any one time, and 90 percent of the most severe and disabling ones. While they need intensive care now, the optimal approach would be, wherever possible, to prevent these problems in the first place. To be sure, not every mental disorder can be prevented—but there are some, and perhaps many, that can. Ronald Kessler, the University of Michigan sociologist who did the study, told me, "We need to intervene early in life. Take a young girl who has a social phobia in the sixth grade, and starts drinking in junior high school to handle her social anxieties. By her late twenties, when she shows up in our study, she's still fearful, has become both an alcohol and drug abuser, and is depressed because her life is so messed up. The big question is, what could we have done early in her life to have headed off the whole downward spiral?"

The same holds, of course, for dropping out or violence, or most of the litany of perils faced by young people today. Educational programs to prevent one or another specific problem such as drug use and violence have proliferated wildly in the last decade or so, creating a mini-industry within the education marketplace. But many of them—including many of the most slickly marketed and most widely used—have proven to be ineffective. A few, to the chagrin of educators, even seemed to increase the likelihood of the problems they were meant to head off, particularly drug abuse and teen sex.

Information Is Not Enough

An instructive case in point is sexual abuse of children. As of 1993, about two hundred thousand substantiated cases were reported annually in the United States, with that number growing by about 10 percent per year. And while estimates vary widely, most experts agree that between 20 and 30 percent of girls and about half that number of boys are victims of some form of sexual abuse by age seventeen (the figures rise or fall depending on how sexual abuse is defined, among other factors).[65] There is no single profile of a child who is particularly vulnerable to sexual abuse, but most feel unprotected, unable to resist on their own, and isolated by what has happened to them.

With these risks in mind, many schools have begun to offer programs to prevent sexual abuse. Most such programs are tightly focused on basic information about sexual abuse, teaching kids, for example, to know the difference between "good" and "bad" touching, alerting them to the dangers, and encouraging them to tell an adult if anything untoward happens to them. But a national survey of two thousand children found that this basic training was little better than nothing—or actually worse than nothing—in helping children do something to prevent being victimized, whether by a school bully or a potential child molester.[66] Worse, the children who had only such basic programs and who had subsequently become victims of sexual assault were actually *half* as likely to report it afterward than were children who had had no programs at all.

By contrast, children given more comprehensive training—including related emotional and social competences—were better able to protect themselves against the threat of being victimized: they were far more likely to demand to be left alone, to yell or fight back, to threaten to tell, and to actually tell if something bad did happen to them. This last benefit—reporting the abuse—is preventive in a telling sense: many child molesters victimize hundreds of children. A study of child molesters in their forties found that, on average, they had one victim a month since their teenage years. A report on a bus driver and a high-school computer teacher reveals they molested about three hundred children each year between them—yet not one of the children reported the sexual abuse; the abuse came to light only after one of the boys who had been abused by the teacher started to sexually abuse his sister.[67]

Those children who got the more comprehensive programs were three times more likely than those in minimal programs to report abuse. What worked so well? These programs were not one-shot topics, but were given at different levels several times over the course of a child's school career, as part of health or sex education. They enlisted parents to deliver the message to the child along with what was taught in school (children whose parents did this were the very best at resisting threats of sexual abuse).

Beyond that, social and emotional competences made the difference. It is not enough for a child simply to know about "good" and "bad" touching; children need the self-awareness to know when a situation *feels* wrong or distressing long before the touching begins. This entails not just self-awareness, but also enough self-confidence and assertiveness to trust and act on those feelings of distress, even in the face of an adult who may be trying to reassure her that "it's okay." And then a child needs a repertoire of ways to disrupt what is about to happen—everything from running away to threatening to tell. For these reasons, the better programs teach children to stand up for what they want, to assert their rights rather than be passive, to know what their boundaries are and defend them.

The most effective programs, then, supplemented the basic sexual-abuse information with essential emotional and social skills. These programs taught children to find ways to solve interpersonal conflicts more positively, to have more self-confidence, not to blame themselves if something happened, and to feel they had a network of support in teachers and parents whom they could turn to. And if something bad did happen to them, they were far more likely to tell.

The Active Ingredients

Such findings have led to a reenvisioning of what the ingredients of an optimal prevention program should be, based on those that impartial evaluations showed to be truly effective. In a five-year project sponsored by the W. T. Grant Foundation, a consortium of researchers studied this landscape and distilled the active ingredients that seemed crucial to the success of those programs that worked.[68] The list of key skills the consortium concluded should be covered, no matter what specific problem it is designed to prevent, reads like the ingredients of emotional intelligence (see Appendix D for the full list).[69]

The emotional skills include self-awareness; identifying, expressing, and managing feelings; impulse control and delaying gratification; and handling stress and anxiety. A key ability in impulse control is knowing the difference between feelings and actions, and learning to make better emotional decisions by first controlling the impulse to act, then identifying alternative actions and their consequences before acting. Many competences are interpersonal: reading social and emotional cues, listening, being able to resist negative influences, taking others' perspectives, and understanding what behavior is acceptable in a situation.

These are among the core emotional and social skills for life, and include at least partial remedies for most, if not all, of the difficulties I have discussed in this chapter. The choice of specific problems these skills might inoculate against is nearly arbitrary—similar cases for the role of emotional and social competences could have been made for, say, unwanted teen pregnancy or teen suicide.

To be sure, the causes of all such problems are complex, interweaving differing ratios of biological destiny, family dynamics, the politics of poverty, and the culture of the streets. No single kind of intervention, including one targeting emotions, can claim to do the whole job. But to the degree emotional deficits add to a child's risk—and we have seen that they add a great deal—attention must be paid to emotional remedies, not to the exclusion of other answers, but along with them. The next question is, what would an education in the emotions look like?

16
Schooling the Emotions

The main hope of a nation lies in the proper education of its youth.

—Erasmus

It's a strange roll call, going around the circle of fifteen fifth graders sitting Indian-style on the floor. As a teacher calls their names the students respond not with the vacant "Here" standard in schools, but instead call out a number that indicates how they feel; one means low spirits, ten high energy.

Today spirits are high:

"Jessica."

"Ten: I'm jazzed, it's Friday."

"Patrick."

"Nine: excited, a little nervous."

"Nicole."

"Ten: peaceful, happy . . ."

It's a class in Self Science at the Nueva School, a school retrofitted into what used to be the grand manse of the Crocker family, the dynasty that founded one of San Francisco's biggest banks. Now the building, which resembles a miniature version of the San Francisco Opera House, houses a private school that offers what may be a model course in emotional intelligence.

The subject in Self Science is feelings—your own and those that erupt in relationships. The topic, by its very nature, demands that teachers and students focus on the emotional fabric of a child's life—a focus that is determinedly ignored in almost every other classroom in America. The strategy here includes using the tensions and traumas of children's lives as the topic of the day. Teachers speak to real issues—hurt over being left out, envy, disagreements that could escalate into a schoolyard battle. As Karen Stone McCown, developer of the Self Science Curriculum and founder of Nueva, put it, "Learning doesn't take place in isolation from kids' feelings. Being emotionally literate is as important for learning as instruction in math and reading."[1]

Self Science is a pioneer, an early harbinger of an idea that is spreading to schools coast to coast.* Names for these classes range from "social development" to "life skills" to "social and emotional learning." Some, referring to Howard Gardner's idea of multiple intelligences, use the term "personal intelligences." The common thread is the goal of raising the level of social and emotional competence in children as a part of their regular education—not just something taught remedially to children who are faltering and identified as "troubled," but a set of skills and understandings essential for every child.

The emotional-literacy courses have some remote roots in the affective-education movement of the 1960s. The thinking then was that psychological and motivational lessons were more deeply learned if they involved an immediate experience of what was being taught conceptually. The emotional-literacy movement, though, turns the term *affective education* inside out—instead of using affect to educate, it educates affect itself.

More immediately, many of these courses and the momentum for their spread come from an ongoing series of school-based prevention programs, each targeting a specific problem: teen smoking, drug abuse, pregnancy, dropping out, and most recently violence. As we saw in the last chapter, the W. T. Grant Consortium's study of prevention programs found they are far more effective when they teach a core of emotional and social competences, such as impulse control, managing anger, and finding creative solutions to social predicaments. From this principle a new generation of interventions has emerged.

As we saw in Chapter 15, interventions designed to target the specific deficits in emotional and social skills that undergird problems such as aggression or depression can be highly effective as buffers for children. But those well-designed interventions, in the main, have been run by research psychol-

---

* For more information on emotional literacy courses: The Collaborative for the Advancement of Social and Emotional Learning (CASEL), Department of Psychology (M/C 285), University of Illinois at Chicago, 1007 West Harrison St., Chicago, IL 60606-7137.

ogists as experiments. The next step is to take the lessons learned from such highly focused programs and generalize them as a preventive measure for the entire school population, taught by ordinary teachers.

This more sophisticated and more effective approach to prevention includes information about problems such as AIDS, drugs, and the like, at the points in youngsters' lives when they are beginning to face them. But its main, ongoing subject is the core competence that is brought to bear on any of these specific dilemmas: emotional intelligence.

This new departure in bringing emotional literacy into schools makes emotions and social life themselves topics, rather than treating these most compelling facets of a child's day as irrelevant intrusions or, when they lead to eruptions, relegating them to occasional disciplinary trips to the guidance counselor or the principal's office.

The classes themselves may at first glance seem uneventful, much less a solution to the dramatic problems they address. But that is largely because, like good childrearing at home, the lessons imparted are small but telling, delivered regularly and over a sustained period of years. That is how emotional learning becomes ingrained; as experiences are repeated over and over, the brain reflects them as strengthened pathways, neural habits to apply in times of duress, frustration, hurt. And while the everyday substance of emotional literacy classes may look mundane, the outcome—decent human beings—is more critical to our future than ever.

A LESSON IN COOPERATION

Compare a moment from a class in Self Science with the classroom experiences you can recall.

A fifth-grade group is about to play the Cooperation Squares game, in which the students team up to put together a series of square-shaped jigsaw puzzles. The catch: their teamwork is all in silence, with no gesturing allowed.

The teacher, Jo-An Vargo, divides the class into three groups, each assigned to a different table. Three observers, each familiar with the game, get an evaluation sheet to assess, for example, who in the group takes the lead in organizing, who is a clown, who disrupts.

The students dump the pieces of the puzzles on the table and go to work. Within a minute or so it's clear that one group is surprisingly efficient as a team; they finish in just a few minutes. A second group of four is engaged in solitary, parallel efforts, each working separately on their own puzzle, but getting nowhere. Then they slowly start to work collectively to assemble their first square, and continue to work as a unit until all the puzzles are solved.

But the third group still struggles, with only one puzzle nearing completion, and even that looking more like a trapezoid than a square. Sean, Fairlie, and Rahman have yet to find the smooth coordination that the other two groups fell into. They are clearly frustrated, frantically scanning the pieces on the table, seizing on likely possibilities and putting them near the partly finished squares, only to be disappointed by the lack of fit.

The tension breaks a bit when Rahman takes two of the pieces and puts them in front of his eyes like a mask; his partners giggle. This will prove to be a pivotal moment in the day's lesson.

Jo-An Vargo, the teacher, offers some encouragement: "Those of you who have finished can give one specific hint to those who are still working."

Dagan moseys over to the still-struggling group, points to two pieces that jut out from the square, and suggests, "You've got to move those two pieces around." Suddenly Rahman, his wide face furrowed in concentration, grasps the new gestalt, and the pieces quickly fall into place on the first puzzle, then the others. There's spontaneous applause as the last piece falls into place on the third group's final puzzle.

A POINT OF CONTENTION

But as the class goes on to mull over the object lessons in teamwork they've received, there is another, more intense interchange. Rahman, tall and with a shock of bushy black hair cut into a longish crew cut, and Tucker, the group's observer, are locked in contentious discussion over the rule that you can't gesture. Tucker, his blond hair neatly combed except for a cowlick, wears a baggy blue T-shirt emblazoned with the motto "Be Responsible," which somehow underscores his official role.

"You can *too* offer a piece—that's *not* gesturing," Tucker says to Rahman in an emphatic, argumentative tone.

"But that *is* gesturing," Rahman insists, vehement.

Vargo notices the heightened volume and increasingly aggressive staccato of the exchange, and gravitates to their table. This is a critical incident, a spontaneous exchange of heated feeling; it is in moments such as this that the lessons already learned will pay off, and new ones can be taught most profitably. And, as every good teacher knows, the lessons applied in such electric moments will last in students' memories.

"This isn't a criticism—you cooperated very well—but Tucker, try to say what you mean in a tone of voice that doesn't sound so critical," Vargo coaches.

Tucker, his voice calmer now, says to Rahman, "You can just put a piece where you think it goes, give someone what you think they need, without gesturing. Just offering."

Rahman responds in an angry tone, "You could have just gone like this"—he scratches his head to illustrate an innocent movement—"and he'd say 'No gesturing!' "

There is clearly more to Rahman's ire than this dispute about what does or does not constitute a gesture. His eyes constantly go to the evaluation sheet Tucker has filled out, which—though it has not yet been mentioned—has actually provoked the tension between Tucker and Rahman. On the evaluation sheet Tucker has listed Rahman's name in the blank for "Who is disruptive?"

Vargo, noticing Rahman looking at the offending form, hazards a guess, saying to Tucker, "He's feeling that you used a negative word—*disruptive*—about him. What did you mean?"

"I didn't mean it was a *bad* kind of disruption," says Tucker, now conciliatory.

Rahman isn't buying it, but his voice is calmer, too: "That's a little far-fetched, if you ask me."

Vargo emphasizes a positive way of seeing it. "Tucker is trying to say that what could be considered disruptive could also be part of lightening things up during a frustrating time."

"But," Rahman protests, now more matter-of-fact, "*disruptive* is like when we're all concentrating hard on something and if I went like this"—he makes a ridiculous, clowning expression, his eyes bulging, cheeks puffed out—"that would be disruptive."

Vargo tries more emotional coaching, telling Tucker, "In trying to help, you didn't mean he was disruptive in a bad way. But you send a different message in how you're talking about it. Rahman is needing you to hear and accept his feelings. Rahman was saying that having negative words like *disruptive* feels unfair. He doesn't like being called that."

Then, to Rahman, she adds, "I appreciate the way you're being assertive in talking with Tucker. You're not attacking. But it's not pleasant to have a label like *disruptive* put on you. When you put those pieces up to your eyes it seems like you were feeling frustrated and wanted to lighten things up. But Tucker called it disruptive because he didn't understand your intent. Is that right?"

Both boys nod assent as the other students finish clearing away the puzzles. This small classroom melodrama is reaching its finale. "Do you feel better?" Vargo asks. "Or is this still distressing?"

"Yeah, I feel okay," says Rahman, his voice softer now that he feels heard and understood. Tucker nods, too, smiling. The boys, noticing that everyone else has already left for the next class, turn in unison and dash out together.

POSTMORTEM: A FIGHT THAT DID NOT BREAK OUT

As a new group starts to find their chairs, Vargo dissects what has just transpired. The heated exchange and its cooling-down draw on what the boys have been learning about conflict resolution. What typically escalates to conflict begins, as Vargo puts it, with "not communicating, making assumptions, and jumping to conclusions, sending a 'hard' message in ways that make it tough for people to hear what you're saying."

Students in Self Science learn that the point is not to avoid conflict completely, but to resolve disagreement and resentment before it spirals into an out-and-out fight. There are signs of these earlier lessons in how Tucker and Rahman handled the dispute. Both, for example, made some effort to express their point of view in a way that would not accelerate the conflict. This assertiveness (as distinct from aggression or passivity) is taught at Nueva from third grade on. It emphasizes expressing feelings forthrightly, but in a way that will not spiral into aggression. While at the beginning of their dispute neither boy was looking at the other, as it went on they began to show signs of "active listening," facing each other, making eye contact, and sending the silent cues that let a speaker know that he is being heard.

By putting these tools into action, helped along by some coaching, "assertiveness" and "active listening" for these boys become more than just empty phrases on a quiz—they become ways of reacting the boys can draw on at those moments when they need them most urgently.

Mastery in the emotional domain is especially difficult because skills need to be acquired when people are usually least able to take in new information and learn new habits of response—when they are upset. Coaching in these moments helps. "Anyone, adult or fifth grader, needs some help being a self-observer when they're so upset," Vargo points out. "Your heart is pounding, your hands are sweaty, you're jittery, and you're trying to listen clearly while keeping your own self-control to get through it without screaming, blaming, or clamming up in defensiveness."

For anyone familiar with the rough-and-tumble of fifth-grade boys, what may be most remarkable is that both Tucker and Rahman tried to assert their views without resorting to blaming, name-calling, or yelling. Neither let their feelings escalate to a contemptuous "f—— you!" or a fistfight, nor cut off the other by stalking out of the room. What could have been the seed of a full-fledged battle instead heightened the boys' mastery of the nuances of conflict resolution. How differently it all could have gone in other circumstances. Youngsters daily come to blows—and even worse—over less.

CONCERNS OF THE DAY

At the traditional circle that opens each class in Self Science, the numbers are not always so high as they were today. When they are low—the ones, twos, or threes that indicate feeling terrible—it opens the way for someone to ask, "Do you want to talk about why you feel that way?" And, if the student wants (no one is pressured to talk about things they don't want to), it allows the airing of whatever is so troubling—and the chance to consider creative options for handling it.

The troubles that emerge vary with the grade level. In the lower grades typical ones are teasing, feeling left out, fears. Around sixth grade a new set of concerns emerges—hurt feelings about not being asked on a date, or being left out; friends who are immature; the painful predicaments of the young ("Big kids are picking on me"; "My friends are smoking, and they're always trying to get me to try, too").

These are the topics of gripping import in a child's life, which are aired on the periphery of school—at lunch, on the bus to school, at a friend's house— if at all. More often than not, these are the troubles that children keep to themselves, obsessing about them alone at night, having no one to mull them over with. In Self Science they can become topics of the day.

Each of these discussions is potential grist for the explicit goal of Self Science, which is illuminating the child's sense of self and relationships with others. While the course has a lesson plan, it is flexible so that when moments such as the conflict between Rahman and Tucker occur they can be capitalized on. The issues that students bring up provide the living examples to which students and teachers alike can apply the skills they are learning, such as the conflict-resolution methods that cooled down the heat between the two boys.

THE ABC'S OF EMOTIONAL INTELLIGENCE

In use for close to twenty years, the Self Science curriculum stands as a model for the teaching of emotional intelligence. The lessons sometimes are surprisingly sophisticated; as Nueva's director, Karen Stone McCown, told me, "When we teach about anger, we help kids understand that it is almost always a secondary reaction and to look for what's underneath—are you hurt? jealous? Our kids learn that you always have choices about how you respond to emotion, and the more ways you know to respond to an emotion, the richer your life can be."

A list of the contents of Self Science is an almost point-for-point match with the ingredients of emotional intelligence—and with the core skills recommended as primary prevention for the range of pitfalls threatening children (see Appendix E for the full list).[2] The topics taught include self-awareness, in the sense of recognizing feelings and building a vocabulary for them, and seeing the links between thoughts, feelings, and reactions; knowing if thoughts or feelings are ruling a decision; seeing the consequences of alternative choices; and applying these insights to decisions about such issues as drugs, smoking, and sex. Self-awareness also takes the form of recognizing your strengths and weaknesses, and seeing yourself in a positive but realistic light (and so avoiding a common pitfall of the self-esteem movement).

Another emphasis is managing emotions: realizing what is behind a feeling (for example, the hurt that triggers anger), and learning ways to handle anxieties, anger, and sadness. Still another emphasis is on taking responsibility for decisions and actions, and following through on commitments.

A key social ability is empathy, understanding others' feelings and taking their perspective, and respecting differences in how people feel about things. Relationships are a major focus, including learning to be a good listener and question-asker; distinguishing between what someone says or does and your own reactions and judgments; being assertive rather than angry or passive; and learning the arts of cooperation, conflict resolution, and negotiating compromise.

There are no grades given in Self Science; life itself is the final exam. But at the end of the eighth grade, as students are about to leave Nueva for high school, each is given a Socratic examination, an oral test in Self Science. One question from a recent final: "Describe an appropriate response to help a friend solve a conflict over someone pressuring them to try drugs, or over a friend who likes to tease." Or, "What are some healthy ways to deal with stress, anger, and fear?"

Were he alive today, Aristotle, so concerned with emotional skillfulness, might well approve.

EMOTIONAL LITERACY IN THE INNER CITY

Skeptics understandably will ask if a course like Self Science could work in a less privileged setting, or if it is only possible in a small private school like Nueva, where every child is, in some respect, gifted. In short, can emotional competence be taught where it may be most urgently needed, in the gritty chaos of an inner-city public school? One answer is to visit the Augusta Lewis Troup Middle School in New Haven, which is as far from the Nueva School socially and economically as it is geographically.

To be sure, the atmosphere at Troup has much of the same excitement about learning—the school is also known as the Troup Magnet Academy of Science and is one of two such schools in the district that are designed to draw fifth- to eighth-grade students from all over New Haven to an enriched science curriculum. Students there can ask questions about the physics of outer space through a satellite-dish hookup to astronauts in Houston or program their computers to play music. But despite these academic amenities, as in many cities, white flight to the New Haven suburbs and to private schools has left Troup's enrollment about 95 percent black and Hispanic.

Just a few short blocks from the Yale campus—and again a distant universe—Troup is in a decaying working-class neighborhood that, in the 1950s, had twenty thousand people employed in nearby factories, from Olin Brass Mills to Winchester Arms. Today that job base has shrunk to under three thousand, shrinking with it the economic horizons of the families who live there. New Haven, like so many other New England manufacturing cities, has sunk into a pit of poverty, drugs, and violence.

It was in response to the urgencies of this urban nightmare that in the 1980s a group of Yale psychologists and educators designed the Social Competence Program, a set of courses that covers virtually the same terrain as the Nueva School's Self Science curriculum. But at Troup the connection to the topics is often more direct and raw. It is no mere academic exercise when, in the eighth-grade sex education class, students learn how personal decision-making can help them avoid diseases such as AIDS. New Haven has the highest proportion of women with AIDS in the United States; a number of the mothers who send their children to Troup have the disease—and so do some of the students there. Despite the enriched curriculum, students at Troup struggle with all the problems of the inner city; many children have home situations so chaotic, if not horrific, they just cannot manage to get to school some days.

As in all New Haven schools, the most prominent sign that greets a visitor is in the familiar form of a yellow diamond-shaped traffic sign, but reads "Drug-Free Zone." At the door is Mary Ellen Collins, the school's facilitator—an all-purpose ombudsman who sees to special problems as they surface, and whose role includes helping teachers with the demands of the social competence curriculum. If a teacher is unsure of how to teach a lesson, Collins will come to the class to show how.

"I taught in this school for twenty years," Collins says, greeting me. "Look at this neighborhood—I can't see only teaching academic skills anymore, with the problems these kids face just in living. Take the kids here who are struggling because they have AIDS themselves or it's in their homes—I'm not sure they'd say it during the discussion on AIDS, but once a kid knows a teacher will listen to an emotional problem, not just academic ones, the avenue is open to have that conversation."

On the third floor of the old brick school Joyce Andrews is leading her fifth graders through the social competence class they get three times a week. Andrews, like all the other fifth-grade teachers, went to a special summer course in how to teach it, but her exuberance suggests the topics in social competence come naturally to her.

Today's lesson is on identifying feelings; being able to name feelings, and so better distinguish between them, is a key emotional skill. Last night's assignment was to bring in pictures of a person's face from a magazine, name which emotion the face displays, and explain how to tell the person has those feelings. After collecting the assignment, Andrews lists the feelings on the board—sadness, worry, excitement, happiness, and so on—and launches into a fast-paced repartee with the eighteen students who managed to get to school that day. Sitting in four-desk clusters, the students excitedly raise their hands high, straining to catch her eye so they can give their answer.

As she adds *frustrated* to the list on the board, Andrews asks, "How many people ever felt frustrated?" Every hand goes up.

"How do you feel when you're frustrated?"

The answers come in a cascade: "Tired." "Confused." "You can't think right." "Anxious."

As *aggravated* is added to the list, Joyce says, "I know that one—when does a teacher feel aggravated?"

"When everyone is talking," a girl offers, smiling.

Without missing a beat, Andrews passes out a mimeographed worksheet. In one column are faces of boys and girls, each displaying one of the six basic emotions—happy, sad, angry, surprised, afraid, disgusted—and a description of the facial muscle activity underlying each, for example:

AFRAID:

- The mouth is open and drawn back.
- The eyes are open and the inner corners go up.
- The eyebrows are raised and drawn together.
- There are wrinkles in the middle of the forehead.[3]

While they read through the sheet, expressions of fear, anger, surprise, or disgust float over the faces of the kids in Andrews's class as they imitate the pictures and follow the facial-muscle recipes for each emotion. This lesson comes straight from Paul Ekman's research on facial expression; as such, it is taught in most every college introductory psychology course—and rarely, if ever, in grade school. This elementary lesson in connecting a name with a feeling, and the feeling with the facial expression that matches it, might seem so obvious that it need not be taught at all. Yet it may serve as an antidote to surprisingly common lapses in emotional literacy. Schoolyard bullies, remember, often strike out in anger because they misinterpret neutral messages and expressions as hostile, and girls who develop eating disorders fail to distinguish anger from anxiety from hunger.

EMOTIONAL LITERACY IN DISGUISE

With the curriculum already besieged by a proliferation of new topics and agendas, some teachers who understandably feel overburdened resist taking extra time from the basics for yet another course. So an emerging strategy in emotional education is not to create a new class, but to blend lessons on feelings and relationships with other topics already taught. Emotional lessons can merge naturally into reading and writing, health, science, social studies, and other standard courses as well. While in the New Haven schools Life Skills is a separate topic in some grades, in other years the social development curriculum blends into courses such as reading or health. Some of the lessons are even taught as part of math class—notably basic study skills such as how to put aside distractions, motivate yourself to study, and manage your impulses so you can attend to learning.

Some programs in emotional and social skills take no curriculum or class time as a separate subject at all, but instead infiltrate their lessons into the very fabric of school life. One model for this approach—essentially, an invisible emotional and social competence course—is the Child Development Project, created by a team directed by psychologist Eric Schaps. The project, based in Oakland, California, is currently being tried in a handful of schools across the nation, most in neighborhoods that share many of the troubles of New Haven's decaying core.[4]

The project offers a prepackaged set of materials that fit into existing courses. Thus first graders in their reading class get a story, "Frog and Toad Are Friends," in which Frog, eager to play with his hibernating friend Toad, plays a trick on him to get him up early. The story is used as a platform for a class discussion about friendship, and issues such as how people feel when someone plays a trick on them. A succession of adventures brings up topics such as self-consciousness, being aware of a friend's needs, what it feels like to be teased, and sharing feelings with friends. A set curriculum plan offers increasingly sophisticated stories as children go through the elementary and middle-school grades, giving teachers entry points to discuss topics such as empathy, perspective-taking, and caring.

Another way emotional lessons are woven into the fabric of existing school life is through helping teachers rethink how to discipline students who misbehave. The assumption in the Child Development program is that such moments are ripe opportunities to teach children skills that are lacking—impulse control, explaining their feelings, resolving conflicts—and that there are better ways to discipline than coercion. A teacher seeing three first graders pushing to be the first in the lunchroom line might suggest that they each guess a number, and let the winner go first. The immediate lesson is that there are impartial, fair ways to settle such pint-size disputes, while the deeper teaching is that disputes can be negotiated. And since that is an approach those children can take with them to settle other similar disputes ("Me first!" is, after all, epidemic in lower grades—if not through much of life, in one form or another) it has a more positive message than the ubiquitous, authoritarian "Stop that!"

THE EMOTIONAL TIMETABLE

"My friends Alice and Lynn won't play with me."

That poignant grievance is from a third-grade girl at John Muir Elementary School in Seattle. The anonymous sender put it in the "mailbox" in her classroom—actually a specially painted cardboard box—where she and her classmates are encouraged to write in their complaints and problems so the whole class can talk about them and try to think of ways to deal with them. The discussion will not mention the names of those involved; instead the teacher points out that all children share such problems from time to time, and they all need to learn how to handle them. As they talk about how it feels to be left out, or what they might do to be included, they have the chance to try out new solutions to these quandaries—a corrective for the one-track thinking that sees conflict as the only route to solving disagreements.

The mailbox allows flexibility as to exactly which crises and issues will become the subject of the class, for a too-rigid agenda can be out of step with the fluid realities of childhood. As children change and grow the preoccupation of the hour changes accordingly. To be most effective, emotional lessons must be pegged to the development of the child, and repeated at different ages in ways that fit a child's changing understanding and challenges.

One question is how early to begin. Some say the first few years of life are none too soon. The Harvard pediatrician T. Berry Brazelton proposes that many parents can benefit from being coached as emotional mentors to their infants and toddlers, as some home-visit programs do. A strong argument can be made for emphasizing social and emotional skills more systematically in preschool programs such as Head Start; as we saw in Chapter 12, children's readiness to learn depends to a large extent on acquiring some of these basic emotional skills. The preschool years are crucial ones for laying foundation skills, and there is some evidence that Head Start, when run well (an important caveat), can have beneficial long-term emotional and social effects on the lives of its graduates even into their early adult years—fewer drug problems and arrests, better marriages, greater earning power.[5]

Such interventions work best when they track the emotional timetable of development.[6] As the wail of newborns testifies, babies have intense feelings from the moment they are born. But the newborn's brain is far from fully mature; as we saw in Chapter 15, only as its nervous system reaches final development—a process that unfolds according to an innate biological clock over the entire course of childhood and into early adolescence—will the child's emotions ripen completely. The newborn's repertoire of feeling is primitive compared to the emotional range of a five-year-old, which, in turn, is lacking when measured against the fullness of feelings of a teenager. Indeed, adults all too readily fall into the trap of expecting children to have reached a maturity far beyond their years, forgetting that each emotion has its preprogrammed moment of appearance in a child's growth. A four-year-old's braggadocio, for example, might bring a parent's reprimand—and yet the self-consciousness that can breed humility typically does not emerge until age five or so.

The timetable for emotional growth is intertwined with allied lines of development, particularly for cognition, on the one hand, and brain and biological maturation, on the other. As we have seen, emotional capacities such as empathy and emotional self-regulation start to build virtually from infancy. The kindergarten year marks a peak ripening of the "social emotions"—feelings such as insecurity and humility, jealousy and envy, pride and confidence—all of which require the capacity for comparing oneself with others. The five-year-old, on entering the wider social world of school, enters too the world of social comparison. It is not just the external shift that elicits these comparisons, but also the emergence of a cognitive skill: being able to compare oneself to others on particular qualities, whether popularity, attractiveness, or skateboarding talents. This is the age when, for example, having an older sister who gets straight A's can make the younger sister start to think of herself as "dumb" by comparison.

Dr. David Hamburg, a psychiatrist and president of the Carnegie Corporation, which has evaluated some pioneering emotional-education programs, sees the years of transition into grade school and then again into junior high or middle school as marking two crucial points in a child's adjustment.[7] From ages six to eleven, says Hamburg, "school is a crucible and a defining experience that will heavily influence children's adolescence and beyond. A child's sense of self-worth depends substantially on his or her ability to achieve in school. A child who fails in school sets in motion the self-defeating attitudes that can dim prospects for an entire lifespan." Among the essentials for profiting from school, Hamburg notes, are an ability "to postpone gratification, to be socially responsible in appropriate ways, to maintain control over their emotions, and to have an optimistic outlook"—in other words, emotional intelligence.[8]

Puberty—because it is a time of extraordinary change in the child's biology, thinking capacities, and brain functioning—is also a crucial time for emotional and social lessons. As for the teen years, Hamburg observes that "most adolescents are ten to fifteen years old when they are exposed to sexuality, alcohol and drugs, smoking," and other temptations.[9]

The transition to middle school or junior high marks an end to childhood, and is itself a formidable emotional challenge. All other problems aside, as they enter this new school arrangement virtually all students have a dip in self-confidence and a jump in self-consciousness; their very notions of themselves are rocky and in tumult. One of the greatest specific blows is in "social self-esteem"—students' confidence that they can make and keep friends. It is at this juncture, Hamburg points out, that it helps immensely to buttress boys' and girls' abilities to build close relationships and navigate crises in friendships, and to nurture their self-confidence.

Hamburg notes that as students are entering middle school, just on the cusp of adolescence, there is something different about those who have had emotional literacy classes: they find the new pressures of peer politics, the upping of academic demands, and the temptations to smoke and use drugs less troubling than do their peers. They have mastered emotional abilities that, at least for the short term, inoculate them against the turmoil and pressures they are about to face.

TIMING IS ALL

As developmental psychologists and others map the growth of emotions, they are able to be more specific about just what lessons children should be learning at each point in the unfolding of emotional intelligence, what the lasting deficits are likely to be for those who fail to master the right competences at the appointed time, and what remedial experiences might make up for what was missed.

In the New Haven program, for example, children in the youngest grades get basic lessons in self-awareness, relationships, and decision-making. In first grade students sit in a circle and roll the "feelings cube," which has words such as *sad* or *excited* on each side. At their turn, they describe a time they had that feeling, an exercise that gives them more certainty in tying feelings to words and helps with empathy as they hear others having the same feelings as themselves.

By fourth and fifth grade, as peer relationships take on an immense importance in their lives, they get lessons that help their friendships work better: empathy, impulse control, and anger management. The Life Skills class on reading emotions from facial expressions that the Troup school fifth graders were trying, for example, is essentially about empathizing. For impulse control, there is a "stoplight" poster displayed prominently, with six steps:

Red light	1. Stop, calm down, and think before you act.
Yellow light	2. Say the problem and how you feel.
	3. Set a positive goal.
	4. Think of lots of solutions.
	5. Think ahead to the consequences.
Green Light	6. Go ahead and try the best plan.

The stoplight notion is regularly invoked when a child, for example, is about to strike out in anger, or withdraw into a huff at some slight, or burst into tears at being teased, and offers a concrete set of steps for dealing with these loaded moments in a more measured way. Beyond the management of feelings, it points a way to more effective action. And, as a habitual way of handling the unruly emotional impulse—to think before acting from feelings—it can evolve into a basic strategy for dealing with the risks of adolescence and beyond.

In sixth grade the lessons relate more directly to the temptations and pressures for sex, drugs, or drinking that begin to enter children's lives. By ninth grade, as teenagers are confronted with more ambiguous social realities, the ability to take multiple perspectives—your own as well as those of others involved—is emphasized. "If a kid is mad because he saw his girlfriend talking with another guy," says one of the New Haven teachers, "he'd be encouraged to consider what might be going on from their point of view, too, rather than just plunge into a confrontation."

EMOTIONAL LITERACY AS PREVENTION

Some of the most effective programs in emotional literacy were developed as a response to a specific problem, notably violence. One of the fastest-growing of these prevention-inspired emotional literacy courses is the Resolving Conflict Creatively Program, in several hundred New York City public schools and schools across the country. The conflict-resolution course focuses on how to settle schoolyard arguments that can escalate into incidents like the hallway shooting of Ian Moore and Tyrone Sinkler by their classmate at Jefferson High School.

Linda Lantieri, the founder of the Resolving Conflict Creatively Program and director of the Manhattan-based national center for the approach, sees it as having a mission far beyond just preventing fights. She says, "The program shows students that they have many choices for dealing with conflict besides passivity or aggression. We show them the futility of violence while replacing it with concrete skills. Kids learn to stand up for their rights without resorting to violence. These are lifelong skills, not just for those most prone to violence."[10]

In one exercise, students think of a single realistic step, no matter how small, that might have helped settle some conflict they have had. In another students enact a scene in which a big sister trying to do her homework gets fed up with her younger sister's loud rap tape. In frustration the older sister turns off the tape despite the younger one's protests. The class brainstorms ways they might work out the problem that would satisfy both sisters.

One key to the success of the conflict-resolution program is extending it beyond the classroom to the playground and cafeteria, where tempers are more likely to explode. To that end, some students are trained as mediators, a role that can begin in the latter years of elementary school. When tension erupts, students can seek out a mediator to help them settle it. The schoolyard mediators learn to handle fights, taunts and threats, interracial incidents, and the other potentially incendiary incidents of school life.

The mediators learn to phrase their statements in ways that make both parties feel the mediator is impartial. Their tactics include sitting down with those involved and getting them to listen to the other person without interruptions or insults. They have each party calm down and state their position, then have each paraphrase what's been said so it's clear they've really heard. Then they all try to think of solutions that both sides can live with; the settlements are often in the form of a signed agreement.

Beyond the mediation of a given dispute, the program teaches students to think differently about disagreements in the first place. As Angel Perez, trained as a mediator while in grade school, put it, the program "changed my way of thinking. I used to think, hey, if somebody picks on me, if somebody does something to me, the only thing was to fight, do something to get back at them. Since I had this program, I've had a more positive way of thinking. If something's done negative to me, I don't try to do the negative thing back—I try to solve the problem." And he has found himself spreading the approach in his community.

While the focus of Resolving Conflict Creatively is on preventing violence, Lantieri sees it as having a wider mission. Her view is that the skills needed to head off violence cannot be separated from the full spectrum of emotional competence—that, for example, knowing what you are feeling or how to handle impulse or grief is as important for violence prevention as is managing anger. Much of the training has to do with emotional basics such as recognizing an expanded range of feelings and being able to put names to them, and empathizing. When she describes the evaluation results of her program's effects, Lantieri points with as much pride to the increase in "caring among the kids" as to the drops in fights, put-downs, and name-calling.

A similar convergence on emotional literacy occurred with a consortium of psychologists trying to find ways to help youngsters on a trajectory toward a life marked by crime and violence. Dozens of studies of such boys—as we saw in Chapter 15—yielded a clear sense of the path most take, starting from impulsiveness and a quickness to anger in their earliest school years, through becoming social rejects by the end of grade school, to bonding with a circle of others like themselves and beginning crime sprees in the middle-school years. By early adulthood, a large portion of these boys have acquired police records and a readiness for violence.

When it came to designing interventions that might help such boys get off this road to violence and crime, the result was, once again, an emotional-literacy program.[11] One of these, developed by Carol Kusche along with Mark Greenberg at the University of Washington, is the PATHS curriculum (PATHS is the acronym for Promoting Alternative Thinking Strategies). While those at risk for a trajectory toward crime and violence are most in need of these lessons, the course is given to all those in a class, avoiding any stigmatizing of a more troubled subgroup.

Still, the lessons are useful for all children. These include, for example, learning in the earliest school years to control their impulses; lacking this ability, children have special trouble paying attention to what is being taught and so fall behind in their learning and grades. Another is recognizing their feelings; the PATHS curriculum has fifty lessons on different emotions, teaching the most basic, such as happiness and anger, to the youngest children, and later touching on more complicated feelings such as jealousy, pride, and guilt. The emotional-awareness lessons include how to monitor what they and those around them are feeling, and—most important for those prone to aggression—how to recognize when someone is actually hostile, as opposed to when the attribution of hostility comes from oneself.

One of the most important lessons, of course, is anger management. The basic premise children learn about anger (and all other emotions as well) is that "all feelings are okay to have," but some reactions are okay and others not. Here one of the tools for teaching self-control is the same "stoplight" exercise used in the New Haven course. Other units help children with their friendships, a counter to the social rejections that can help propel a child toward delinquency.

RETHINKING SCHOOLS: TEACHING BY BEING, COMMUNITIES THAT CARE

As family life no longer offers growing numbers of children a sure footing in life, schools are left as the one place communities can turn to for correctives to children's deficiencies in emotional and social competence. That is not to say that schools alone can stand in for all the social institutions that too often are in or nearing collapse. But since virtually every child goes to school (at least at the outset), it offers a place to reach children with basic lessons for living that they may never get otherwise. Emotional literacy implies an expanded mandate for schools, taking up the slack for failing families in socializing children. This daunting task requires two major changes: that teachers go beyond their traditional mission and that people in the community become more involved with schools.

Whether or not there is a class explicitly devoted to emotional literacy may matter far less than *how* these lessons are taught. There is perhaps no subject where the quality of the teacher matters so much, since how a teacher handles her class is in itself a model, a de facto lesson in emotional competence—or the lack thereof. Whenever a teacher responds to one student, twenty or thirty others learn a lesson.

There is a self-selection in the kind of teacher who gravitates to courses such as these, because not everyone is suited by temperament. To begin with, teachers need to be comfortable talking about feelings; not every teacher is at ease doing so or wants to be. There is little or nothing in the standard education of teachers that prepares them for this kind of teaching. For these reasons, emotional literacy programs typically give prospective teachers several weeks of special training in the approach.

While many teachers may be reluctant at the outset to tackle a topic that seems so foreign to their training and routines, there is evidence that once they are willing to try it, most will be pleased rather than put off. In the New Haven schools, when teachers first learned that they would be trained to teach the new emotional literacy courses, 31 percent said they were reluctant to do so. After a year of teaching the courses, more than 90 percent said they were pleased by them, and wanted to teach them again the following year.

AN EXPANDED MISSION FOR SCHOOLS

Beyond teacher training, emotional literacy expands our vision of the task of schools themselves, making them more explicitly society's agent for seeing that children learn these essential lessons for life—a return to a classic role for education. This larger design requires, apart from any specifics of curriculum, using opportunities in and out of class to help students turn moments of personal crisis into lessons in emotional competence. It also works best when the lessons at school are coordinated with what goes on in children's homes. Many emotional literacy programs include special classes for parents to teach them about what their children are learning, not just to complement what is imparted at school, but to help parents who feel the need to deal more effectively with their children's emotional life.

That way, children get consistent messages about emotional competence in all parts of their lives. In the New Haven schools, says Tim Shriver, director of the Social Competence Program, "if kids get into a beef in the cafeteria, they'll be sent to a peer mediator, who sits down with them and works through their conflict with the same perspective-taking technique they learned in class. Coaches will use the technique to handle conflicts on the playing field. We hold classes for parents in using these methods with kids at home."

Such parallel lines of reinforcement of these emotional lessons—not just in the classroom, but also on the playground; not just in the school, but also in the home—is optimal. That means weaving the school, the parents, and the community together more tightly. It increases the likelihood that what children learned in emotional literacy classes will not stay behind at school, but will be tested, practiced, and sharpened in the actual challenges of life.

Another way in which this focus reshapes schools is in building a campus culture that makes it a "caring community," a place where students feel respected, cared about, and bonded to classmates, teachers, and the school itself.[12] For example, schools in areas such as New Haven, where families are disintegrating at a high rate, offer a range of programs that recruit caring people in the community to get engaged with students whose home life is shaky at best. In the New Haven schools, responsible adults volunteer as mentors, regular companions for students who are foundering and who have few, if any, stable and nurturing adults in their home life.

In short, the optimal design of emotional literacy programs is to begin early, be age-appropriate, run throughout the school years, and intertwine efforts at school, at home, and in the community.

Even though much of this fits neatly into existing parts of the school day, these programs are a major change in any curriculum. It would be naive not to anticipate hurdles in getting such programs into schools. Many parents may feel that the topic itself is too personal a domain for the schools, that such things are best left to parents (an argument that gains credibility to the extent that parents actually *do* address these topics—and is less convincing when they fail to). Teachers may be reluctant to yield yet another part of the school day to topics that seem so unrelated to the academic basics; some teachers may be too uncomfortable with the topics to teach them, and all will need special training to do so. Some children, too, will resist, especially to the extent that these classes are out of synch with their actual concerns, or feel like intrusive impositions on their privacy. And then there is the dilemma of maintaining high quality, and ensuring that slick education marketers do not peddle ineptly designed emotional-competence programs that repeat the disasters of, say, ill-conceived courses on drugs or teen pregnancy.

Given all this, why should we bother to try?

DOES EMOTIONAL LITERACY MAKE A DIFFERENCE?

It's every teacher's nightmare: one day Tim Shriver opened the local paper to read that Lamont, one of his favorite former students, had been shot nine times on a New Haven street, and was in critical condition. "Lamont had been one of the school leaders, a huge—six foot two—and hugely popular linebacker, always smiling," recalls Shriver. "Back then Lamont had enjoyed coming to a leadership club I led, where we would toss around ideas in a problem-solving model known as SOCS."

The acronym is for Situation, Options, Consequence, Solutions—a four-step method: say what the situation is and how it makes you feel; think about your options for solving the problem and what their consequences might be; pick a solution and execute it—a grown-up version of the stoplight method. Lamont, Shriver added, loved brainstorming imaginative but potentially effective ways to handle the pressing dilemmas of high-school life, such as problems with girlfriends and how to avoid fights.

But those few lessons seemed to have failed him after high school. Drifting on the streets in a sea of poverty, drugs, and guns, Lamont at twenty-six lay in a hospital bed, shrouded in bandages, his body riddled with bullet holes. Rushing to the hospital, Shriver found Lamont barely able to talk, his mother and girlfriend huddled over him. Seeing his former teacher, Lamont motioned him to the bedside, and as Shriver leaned over to hear, whispered, "Shrive, when I get out of here, I'm gonna use the SOCS method."

Lamont went through Hillhouse High in the years before the social-development course was given there. Would his life have turned out differently had he benefited from such an education throughout his school years, as children in New Haven public schools do now? The signs point to a possible yes, though no one can ever say for sure.

As Tim Shriver put it, "One thing is clear: the proving ground for social problem-solving is not just the classroom, but the cafeteria, the streets, home." Consider testimony from teachers in the New Haven program. One recounts how a former student, still single, visited and said that she almost certainly would have been an unwed mother by now "if she hadn't learned to stand up for her rights during our Social Development classes."[13] Another teacher recalls how a student's relationship with her mother was so poor that their talks continually ended up as screaming matches; after the girl learned about calming down and thinking before reacting, the mother told her teacher that they could now talk without going "off the deep end." At the Troup school, a sixth grader passed a note to the teacher of her Social Development class; her best friend, the note said, was pregnant, had no one to talk to about what to do, and was planning suicide—but she knew the teacher would care.

A revealing moment came when I was observing a seventh-grade class in social development in the New Haven Schools, and the teacher asked for "someone to tell me about a disagreement they've had recently that ended in a good way."

A plumpish twelve-year-old girl shot up her hand: "This girl was supposed to be my friend and someone said she wanted to fight me. They told me she was going to get me in a corner after school."

But instead of confronting the other girl in anger, she applied an approach encouraged in the class—finding out what is going on before jumping to conclusions: "So I went to the girl and I asked why she said that stuff. And she said she never did. So we never had a fight."

The story seems innocuous enough. Except that the girl who tells the tale had already been expelled from another school for fighting. In the past she attacked first, asked questions later—or not at all. For her to engage a seeming adversary in a constructive way rather than immediately wading into an angry confrontal is a small but real victory.

Perhaps the most telling sign of the impact of such emotional literacy classes are the data shared with me by the principal of this twelve-year-old's school. An unbendable rule there is that children caught fighting are suspended. But as the emotional literacy classes have been phased in over the years there has been a steady drop in the number of suspensions. "Last year," says the principal, "there were 106 suspensions. So far this year—we're up to March—there have been only 26."

These are concrete benefits. But apart from such anecdotes of lives bettered or saved, there is the empirical question of how much emotional literacy classes really matter to those who go through them. The data suggest that although such courses do not change anyone overnight, as children advance through the curriculum from grade to grade, there are discernible improvements in the tone of a school and the outlook—and level of emotional competence—of the girls and boys who take them.

There have been a handful of objective evaluations, the best of which compare students in these courses with equivalent students not taking them, with independent observers rating the children's behavior. Another method is to track changes in the same students before and after the courses based on objective measures of their behavior, such as the number of schoolyard fights or suspensions. Pooling such assessments reveals a widespread benefit for children's emotional and social competence, for their behavior in and out of the classroom, and for their ability to learn (see Appendix F for details):

EMOTIONAL SELF-AWARENESS

- Improvement in recognizing and naming own emotions
- Better able to understand the causes of feelings
- Recognizing the difference between feelings and actions

MANAGING EMOTIONS

- Better frustration tolerance and anger management
- Fewer verbal put-downs, fights, and classroom disruptions
- Better able to express anger appropriately, without fighting
- Fewer suspensions and expulsions
- Less aggressive or self-destructive behavior
- More positive feelings about self, school, and family

- Better at handling stress
- Less loneliness and social anxiety

HARNESSING EMOTIONS PRODUCTIVELY

- More responsible
- Better able to focus on the task at hand and pay attention
- Less impulsive; more self-control
- Improved scores on achievement tests

EMPATHY: READING EMOTIONS

- Better able to take another person's perspective
- Improved empathy and sensitivity to others' feelings
- Better at listening to others

HANDLING RELATIONSHIPS

- Increased ability to analyze and understand relationships
- Better at resolving conflicts and negotiating disagreements
- Better at solving problems in relationships
- More assertive and skilled at communicating
- More popular and outgoing; friendly and involved with peers
- More sought out by peers
- More concerned and considerate
- More "pro-social" and harmonious in groups
- More sharing, cooperation, and helpfulness
- More democratic in dealing with others

One item on this list demands special attention: emotional literacy programs improve children's *academic* achievement scores and school performance. This is not an isolated finding; it recurs again and again in such studies. In a time when too many children lack the capacity to handle their upsets, to listen or focus, to rein in impulse, to feel responsible for their work or care about learning, anything that will buttress these skills will help in their education. In this sense, emotional literacy enhances schools' ability to teach. Even in a time of back-to-basics and budget cuts, there is an argument to be made that these programs help reverse a tide of educational decline and strengthen schools in accomplishing their main mission, and so are well worth the investment.

Beyond these educational advantages, the courses seem to help children better fulfill their roles in life, becoming better friends, students, sons and daughters—and in the future are more likely to be better husbands and wives, workers and bosses, parents, and citizens. While not every boy and girl will acquire these skills with equal sureness, to the degree they do we are all the better for it. "A rising tide lifts all boats," as Tim Shriver put it. "It's not just the kids with problems, but all kids who can benefit from these skills; these are an inoculation for life."

CHARACTER, MORALITY, AND THE ARTS OF DEMOCRACY

There is an old-fashioned word for the body of skills that emotional intelligence represents: *character*. Character, writes Amitai Etzioni, the George Washington University social theorist, is "the psychological muscle that moral conduct requires."[14] And philosopher John Dewey saw that a moral education is most potent when lessons are taught to children in the course of real events, not just as abstract lessons—the mode of emotional literacy.[15]

If character development is a foundation of democratic societies, consider some of the ways emotional intelligence buttresses this foundation. The bedrock of character is self-discipline; the virtuous life, as philosophers since Aristotle have observed, is based on self-control. A related keystone of character is being able to motivate and guide oneself, whether in doing homework, finishing a job, or getting up in the morning. And, as we have seen, the ability to defer gratification and to control and channel one's urges to act is a basic emotional skill, one that in a former day was called will. "We need to be in control of ourselves—our appetites, our passions—to do right by others," notes Thomas Lickona, writing about character education.[16] "It takes will to keep emotion under the control of reason."

Being able to put aside one's self-centered focus and impulses has social benefits: it opens the way to empathy, to real listening, to taking another person's perspective. Empathy, as we have seen, leads to caring, altruism, and compassion. Seeing things from another's perspective breaks down biased stereotypes, and so breeds tolerance and acceptance of differences. These capacities are ever more called on in our increasingly pluralistic society, allowing people to live together in mutual respect and creating the possibility of productive public discourse. These are basic arts of democracy.[17]

Schools, notes Etzioni, have a central role in cultivating character by inculcating self-discipline and empathy, which in turn enable true commitment to civic and moral values.[18] In doing so, it is not enough to lecture children about values: they need to practice them, which happens as children build the essential emotional and social skills. In this sense, emotional literacy goes hand in hand with education for character, for moral development, and for citizenship.

A LAST WORD

As I complete this book some troubling newspaper items catch my eye. One announces that guns have become the number-one cause of death in America, edging out auto accidents. The second says that last year murder rates rose by 3 percent.[19] Particularly disturbing is the prediction in that second article, by a criminologist, that we are in a lull before a "crime storm" to come in the next decade. The reason he gives is that murders by teenagers as young as fourteen and fifteen are on the rise, and that age group represents the crest of a mini baby boom. In the next decade this group will become eighteen- to twenty-four-year-olds, the age at which violent crimes peak in the course of a criminal career. The harbingers are on the horizon: A third article says that in the four years between 1988 and 1992 Justice Department figures show a 68 percent jump in the number of juveniles charged with murder, aggravated assault, robbery, and forcible rape, with aggravated assault alone up 80 percent.[20]

These teenagers are the first generation to have not just guns but automatic weaponry easily available to them, just as their parents' generation was the first to have wide access to drugs. The toting of guns by teenagers means that disagreements that in a former day would have led to fistfights can readily lead to shootings instead. And, as another expert points out, these teenagers "just aren't very good at avoiding disputes."

One reason they are so poor at this basic life skill, of course, is that as a society we have not bothered to make sure every child is taught the essentials of handling anger or resolving conflicts positively—nor have we bothered to teach empathy, impulse control, or any of the other fundamentals of emotional competence. By leaving the emotional lessons children learn to chance, we risk largely wasting the window of opportunity presented by the slow maturation of the brain to help children cultivate a healthy emotional repertoire.

Despite high interest in emotional literacy among some educators, these courses are as yet rare; most teachers, principals, and parents simply do not know they exist. The best models are largely outside the education mainstream, in a handful of private schools and a few hundred public schools. Of course no program, including this one, is an answer to every problem. But given the crises we find ourselves and our children facing, and given the quantum of hope held out by courses in emotional literacy, we must ask ourselves: Shouldn't we be teaching these most essential skills for life to every child—now more than ever?

And if not now, when?

APPENDIX A

What Is Emotion?

A word about what I refer to under the rubric *emotion,* a term whose precise meaning psychologists and philosophers have quibbled over for more than a century. In its most literal sense, the *Oxford English Dictionary* defines *emotion* as "any agitation or disturbance of mind, feeling, passion; any vehement or excited mental state." I take *emotion* to refer to a feeling and its distinctive thoughts, psychological and biological states, and range of propensities to act. There are hundreds of emotions, along with their blends, variations, mutations, and nuances. Indeed, there are many more subtleties of emotion than we have words for.

Researchers continue to argue over precisely which emotions can be considered primary—the blue, red, and yellow of feeling from which all blends come—or even if there are such primary emotions at all. Some theorists propose basic families, though not all agree on them. The main candidates and some of the members of their families:

• *Anger:* fury, outrage, resentment, wrath, exasperation, indignation, vexation, acrimony, animosity, annoyance, irritability, hostility, and, perhaps at the extreme, pathological hatred and violence

• *Sadness:* grief, sorrow, cheerlessness, gloom, melancholy, self-pity, loneliness, dejection, despair, and, when pathological, severe depression

• *Fear:* anxiety, apprehension, nervousness, concern, consternation, misgiving, wariness, qualm, edginess, dread, fright, terror; as a psychopathology, phobia and panic

• *Enjoyment:* happiness, joy, relief, contentment, bliss, delight, amusement, pride, sensual pleasure, thrill, rapture, gratification, satisfaction, euphoria, whimsy, ecstasy, and at the far edge, mania

• *Love:* acceptance, friendliness, trust, kindness, affinity, devotion, adoration, infatuation, *agape*

- *Surprise:* shock, astonishment, amazement, wonder
- *Disgust:* contempt, disdain, scorn, abhorrence, aversion, distaste, revulsion
- *Shame:* guilt, embarrassment, chagrin, remorse, humiliation, regret, mortification, and contrition

To be sure, this list does not resolve every question about how to categorize emotion. For example, what about blends such as jealousy, a variant of anger that also melds sadness and fear? And what of the virtues, such as hope and faith, courage and forgiveness, certainty and equanimity? Or some of the classic vices, feelings such as doubt, complacency, sloth, and torpor—or boredom? There are no clear answers; the scientific debate on how to classify emotions continues.

The argument for there being a handful of core emotions hinges to some extent on the discovery by Paul Ekman, at the University of California at San Francisco, that specific facial expressions for four of them (fear, anger, sadness, enjoyment) are recognized by people in cultures around the world, including preliterate peoples presumably untainted by exposure to cinema or television—suggesting their universality. Ekman showed facial photos portraying expressions with technical precision to people in cultures as remote as the Fore of New Guinea, an isolated Stone Age tribe in the remote highlands, and found people everywhere recognized the same basic emotions. This universality of facial expressions for emotion was probably first noted by Darwin, who saw it as evidence the forces of evolution had stamped these signals in our central nervous system.

In seeking basic principles, I follow Ekman and others in thinking of emotions in terms of families or dimensions, taking the main families—anger, sadness, fear, enjoyment, love, shame, and so on—as cases in point for the endless nuances of our emotional life. Each of these families has a basic emotional nucleus at its core, with its relatives rippling out from there in countless mutations. In the outer ripples are *moods*, which, technically speaking, are more muted and last far longer than an emotion (while it's relatively rare to be in the full heat of anger all day, for example, it is not that rare to be in a grumpy, irritable mood, in which shorter bouts of anger are easily triggered). Beyond moods are *temperaments*, the readiness to evoke a given emotion or mood that makes people melancholy, timid, or cheery. And still beyond such emotional dispositions are the outright *disorders* of emotion such as clinical depression or unremitting anxiety, in which someone feels perpetually trapped in a toxic state.

Hallmarks of the Emotional Mind

Only in recent years has there emerged a scientific model of the emotional mind that explains how so much of what we do can be emotionally driven—how we can be so reasonable at one moment and so irrational the next—and the sense in which emotions have their own reasons and their own logic. Perhaps the two best assessments of the emotional mind are offered independently by Paul Ekman, head of the Human Interaction Laboratory at the University of California, San Francisco, and by Seymour Epstein, a clinical psychologist at the University of Massachusetts.[1] While Ekman and Epstein have each weighed different scientific evidence, together they offer a basic list of the qualities that distinguish emotions from the rest of mental life.[2]

A Quick but Sloppy Response

The emotional mind is far quicker than the rational mind, springing into action without pausing even a moment to consider what it is doing. Its quickness precludes the deliberate, analytic reflection that is the hallmark of the thinking mind. In evolution this quickness most likely revolved around that most basic decision, what to pay attention to, and, once vigilant while, say, confronting another animal, making split-second decisions like, Do I eat this, or does it eat me? Those organisms that had to pause too long to reflect on these answers were unlikely to have many progeny to pass on their slower-acting genes.

Actions that spring from the emotional mind carry a particularly strong sense of certainty, a by-product of a streamlined, simplified way of looking at things that can be absolutely bewildering to the rational mind. When the dust settles, or even in mid-response, we find ourselves thinking, "What did I do that for?"—a sign that the rational mind is awakening to the moment, but not with the rapidity of the emotional mind.

Since the interval between what triggers an emotion and its eruption can be virtually instantaneous, the mechanism that appraises perception must be capable of great speed, even in brain time, which is reckoned in thousandths of a second. This appraisal of the need to act needs to be automatic, so rapid that it never enters conscious awareness.[3] This quick-and-dirty variety of emotional response sweeps over us virtually before we quite know what is happening.

This rapid mode of perception sacrifices accuracy for speed, relying on first impressions, reacting to the overall picture or the most striking aspects. It takes things in at once, as a whole, reacting without taking the time for thoughtful analysis. Vivid elements can determine that impression, out-weighing a careful evaluation of the details. The great advantage is that the emotional mind can read an emotional reality (he's angry with me; she's lying; this is making him sad) in an instant, making the intuitive snap judg-ments that tell us who to be wary of, who to trust, who's in distress. The emotional mind is our radar for danger; if we (or our forebears in evolution) waited for the rational mind to make some of these judgments, we might not only be wrong—we might be dead. The drawback is that these impressions and intuitive judgments, because they are made in the snap of a finger, may be mistaken or misguided.

Paul Ekman proposes that this quickness, in which emotions can over-take us before we are quite aware they have started, is essential to their being so highly adaptive: they mobilize us to respond to urgent events without wasting time pondering whether to react or how to respond. Using the system he developed for detecting emotions from subtle changes in facial expression, Ekman can track microemotions that flit across the face in less than a half second. Ekman and his collaborators have discovered that emotional expressions begin to show up in changes in facial musculature within a few thousandths of a second after the event that triggers the reaction, and that the physiological changes typical of a given emotion— like shunting blood flow and increasing heart rate—also take only fractions of a second to begin. This swiftness is particularly true of intense emotion, like fear of a sudden threat.

Ekman argues that, technically speaking, the full heat of emotion is very brief, lasting just seconds rather than minutes, hours, or days. His reasoning is that it would be maladaptive for an emotion to capture the brain and body for a long time regardless of changing circumstance. If the emotions caused by a single event invariably continued to dominate us after it had passed, and regardless of what else was happening around us, then our feelings would be poor guides to action. For emotions to last longer the trigger must be sustained, in effect continually evoking the emotion, as when the loss of a loved one keeps us mourning. When feelings persist for hours, it is usually as moods, a muted form. Moods set an affective tone, but they are not such strong shapers of how we perceive and act as is the high heat of full emotion.

First Feelings, Second Thoughts

Because it takes the rational mind a moment or two longer to register and respond than it does the emotional mind, the "first impulse" in an emotional situation is the heart's, not the head's. There is also a second kind of emotional reaction, slower than the quick-response, which simmers and brews first in our thoughts before it leads to feeling. This second pathway to triggering emotions is more deliberate, and we are typically quite aware of the thoughts that lead to it. In this kind of emotional reaction there is a more extended appraisal; our thoughts—cognition—play the key role in determining what emotions will be roused. Once we make an appraisal—"that taxi driver is cheating me" or "this baby is adorable," a fitting emotional response follows. In this slower sequence, more fully articulated thought precedes feeling. More complicated emotions, like embarrassment or apprehension over an upcoming exam, follow this slower route, taking seconds or minutes to unfold—these are emotions that follow from thoughts.

By contrast, in the fast-response sequence feeling seems to precede or be simultaneous with thought. This rapid-fire emotional reaction takes over in situations that have the urgency of primal survival. This is the power of such rapid decisions: they mobilize us in an instant to rise to an emergency. Our most intense feelings are involuntary reactions; we cannot decide when they will erupt. "Love," wrote Stendhal, "is like a fever that comes and goes independently of the will." Not just love, but our angers and fears, as well, sweep over us, seeming to happen *to* us rather than being our choice. For that reason they can offer an alibi: "It is the fact that *we cannot choose the emotions which we have*," notes Ekman, that allows people to explain away their actions by saying they were in the grip of emotion.[4]

Just as there are quick and slow paths to emotion—one through immediate perception and the other through reflective thought—there are also emotions which come bidden. One example is intentionally manipulated feeling, the actors' stock-in-trade, like the tears that come when sad memories are intentionally milked for their effect. But actors are simply more skilled than the rest of us at the intentional use of the second pathway to emotion, feeling via thinking. While we cannot easily change what specific emotions a certain kind of thought will trigger, we very often can, and do, choose what to think about. Just as a sexual fantasy can lead to sexual feelings, so can happy memories cheer us up, or melancholy thoughts make us reflective.

But the rational mind usually does not decide what emotions we "should" have. Instead, our feelings typically come to us as a fait accompli. What the rational mind can ordinarily control is the *course* of those reactions. A few exceptions aside, we do not decide *when* to be mad, sad, and so on.

A Symbolic, Childlike Reality

The logic of the emotional mind is *associative;* it takes elements that symbolize a reality, or trigger a memory of it, to be the same as that reality. That is why similes, metaphors, and images speak directly to the emotional mind, as do the arts—novels, film, poetry, song, theater, opera. Great spiritual teachers, like Buddha and Jesus, have touched their disciples' hearts by speaking in the language of emotion, teaching in parables, fables, and stories. Indeed, religious symbol and ritual makes little sense from the rational point of view; it is couched in the vernacular of the heart.

This logic of the heart—of the emotional mind—is well-described by Freud in his concept of "primary process" thought; it is the logic of religion and poetry, psychosis and children, dream and myth (as Joseph Campbell put it, "Dreams are private myths; myths are shared dreams"). The primary process is the key that unlocks the meanings of works like James Joyce's *Ulysses:* In primary process thought, loose associations determine the flow of a narrative; one object symbolizes another; one feeling displaces another and stands for it; wholes are condensed into parts. There is no time, no laws of cause-and-effect. Indeed, there is no such thing as "No" in the primary process; anything is possible. The psychoanalytic method is in part the art of deciphering and unraveling these substitutions in meaning.

If the emotional mind follows this logic and its rules, with one element standing for another, things need not necessarily be defined by their objective identity: what matters is how they are *perceived;* things are as they seem. What something reminds us of can be far more important than what it "is." Indeed, in emotional life, identities can be like a hologram in the sense that a single part evokes a whole. As Seymour Epstein points out, while the rational mind makes logical connections between causes and effects, the emotional mind is indiscriminate, connecting things that merely have similar striking features.[5]

There are many ways in which the emotional mind is childlike, the more so the stronger the emotion grows. One way is *categorical* thinking, where everything is in black and white, with no shades of gray; someone who is mortified about a faux pas might have the immediate thought, "I *always* say the wrong thing." Another sign of this childlike mode is *personalized* thinking, with events perceived with a bias centering on oneself, like the driver who, after an accident, explained that "the telephone pole came straight at me."

This childlike mode is *self-confirming,* suppressing or ignoring memories or facts that would undermine its beliefs and seizing on those that support it. The beliefs of the rational mind are tentative; new evidence can disconfirm one belief and replace it with a new one—it reasons by objective evidence. The emotional mind, however, takes its beliefs to be absolutely true, and so discounts any evidence to the contrary. That is why it is so hard to reason with someone who is emotionally upset: no matter the soundness of your argument from a logical point of view, it carries no weight if it is out of keeping with the emotional conviction of the moment. Feelings are self-justifying, with a set of perceptions and "proofs" all their own.

The Past Imposed on the Present

When some feature of an event seems similar to an emotionally charged memory from the past, the emotional mind responds by triggering the feelings that went with the remembered event. The emotional mind reacts to the present *as though it were the past.*[6] The trouble is that, especially when the appraisal is fast and automatic, we may not realize that what was once the case is no longer so. Someone who has learned, through painful childhood beatings, to react to an angry scowl with intense fear and loathing will have that reaction to some degree even as an adult, when the scowl carries no such threat.

If the feelings are strong, then the reaction that is triggered is obvious. But if the feelings are vague or subtle, we may not quite realize the emotional reaction we are having, even though it is subtly coloring how we react to the moment. Thoughts and reactions at this moment will take on the coloration of thoughts and reactions then, even though it may seem that the reaction is due solely to the circumstance of the moment. Our emotional mind will harness the rational mind to its purposes, so we come up with explanations for our feelings and reactions—rationalizations—justifying them in terms of the present moment, without realizing the influence of the emotional memory. In that sense, we can have no idea of what is actually going on, though we may have the conviction of certainty that we know exactly what is happening. At such moments the emotional mind has entrained the rational mind, putting it to its own uses.

State-specific Reality

The working of the emotional mind is to a large degree *state-specific,* dictated by the particular feeling ascendant at a given moment. How we think and act when we are feeling romantic is entirely different from how we behave when enraged or dejected; in the mechanics of emotion, each feeling has its own distinct repertoire of thought, reactions, even memories. These state-specific repertoires become most predominant in moments of intense emotion.

One sign that such a repertoire is active is selective memory. Part of the mind's response to an emotional situation is to reshuffle memory and options for action so that those most relevant are at the top of the hierarchy and so more readily enacted. And, as we have seen, each major emotion has its hallmark biological signature, a pattern of sweeping changes that entrain the body as that emotion becomes ascendant, and a unique set of cues the body automatically sends out when in its grip.[7]

APPENDIX C

The Neural Circuitry of Fear

The amygdala is central to fear. When a rare brain disease destroyed the amygdala (but no other brain structures) in the patient neurologists call "S.M.," fear disappeared from her mental repertoire. She became unable to identify looks of fear on other people's faces, nor to make such an expression herself. As her neurologist put it, "If someone put a gun to S.M.'s head, she would know intellectually to be afraid but she would not feel afraid as you or I would."

Neuroscientists have mapped the circuitry for fear in perhaps finest detail, though at the present state of this art the full circuitry for none of the emotions is completely surveyed. Fear is an apt case in point for understanding the neural dynamics of emotion. Fear, in evolution, has a special prominence: perhaps more than any other emotion it is crucial for survival. Of course in modern times misplaced fears are the bane of daily life, leaving us suffering from frets, angst, and garden variety worries—or at pathological extreme, from panic attacks, phobias, or obsessive-compulsive disorder.

Say you're alone one night at home, reading a book, when suddenly you hear a crash in another room. What happens in your brain over the next moments offers a window into the neural circuitry of fear, and the role of the amygdala as an alarm system. The first brain circuit involved simply takes in that sound as raw physical waves and transforms them into the language of the brain to startle you into alertness. This circuit goes from the ear to the brainstem and then to the thalamus. From there two branches separate: a smaller bundle of projections leads to the amygdala and the nearby hippo-campus; the other, larger pathway leads to the auditory cortex in the tempo-ral lobe, where sounds are sorted out and comprehended.

The hippocampus, a key storage site for memory, quickly sorts that "crash" against other similar sounds you've heard, to see if it is familiar—is this "crash" one that you immediately recognize? Meanwhile the auditory cortex is doing a more sophisticated analysis of the sound to try to understand its source—is it the cat? A shutter banging in the wind? A prowler? The auditory cortex comes up with its hypothesis—it might be the cat knocking a lamp off the table, say, but it might also be a prowler—and sends that message to the amygdala and hippocampus, which quickly compare it to similar memories.

If the conclusion is reassuring (it's only the shutter that bangs whenever it gets too windy) then the general alert does not escalate to the next level. But if you are still unsure, another coil of circuitry reverberating between amygdala, hippocampus, and the prefrontal cortex further heightens your uncertainty and fixates your attention, making you even more concerned about identifying the source of the sound. If no satisfying answer comes from this further keen analysis, the amygdala triggers an alarm, its central area activating the hypothalamus, the brainstem, and the autonomic nervous system.

The superb architecture of the amygdala as a central alarm system for the brain becomes evident in this moment of apprehension and subliminal anxiety. The several bundles of neurons in the amygdala each have a distinct set of projections with receptors primed for different neurotransmitters, something like those home alarm companies where operators stand at the ready to send out calls to the local fire department, police, and a neighbor whenever a home security system signals trouble.

Different parts of the amygdala receive differing information. To the amygdala's lateral nucleus come projections from the thalamus and auditory and visual cortices. Smells, via the olfactory bulb, come to the corticomedial area of the amygdala, and tastes and messages from the viscera go to the central area. These incoming signals make the amygdala a continual sentinel, scrutinizing every sensory experience.

From the amygdala projections extend out to every major part of the brain. From the central and medial areas a branch goes to the areas of the hypothalamus that secrete the body's emergency-response substance, corticotropin-releasing hormone (CRH), which mobilizes the fight-or-flight reaction via a cascade of other hormones. The amygdala's basal area sends out branches to the corpus striatum, linking into the brain's system for movement. And, via the nearby central nucleus, the amygdala sends signals to the autonomic nervous system via the medulla, activating a wide range of far-flung responses in the cardiovascular system, the muscles, and the gut.

From the amygdala's basolateral area, arms go to the cingulate cortex and to the fibers known as the "central gray," cells that regulate the large muscles of the skeleton. It is these cells that make a dog snarl or that arch the back of a cat threatening an interloper on its territory. In humans these same circuits tighten the muscles of the vocal cords, creating the high-pitched voice of fright.

Still another pathway from the amygdala leads to the locus ceruleus in the brainstem, which in turn manufactures norepinephrine (also called "noradrenaline") and disperses it throughout the brain. The net effect of norepinephrine is to heighten the overall reactivity of the brain areas that receive it, making the sensory circuits more sensitive. Norepinephrine suffuses the cortex, the brainstem, and the limbic system itself, in essence setting the brain on edge. Now even the ordinary creaking of the house can send a tremor of fear coursing through you. Most of these changes go on outside awareness, so that you are not yet aware you feel fear.

But as you begin to actually feel fear—that is, as the anxiety that had been unconscious pierces awareness—the amygdala seamlessly commands a wide-ranging response. It signals cells in the brainstem to put a fearful expression on your face, make you edgy and easily startled, freeze unrelated movements your muscles had underway, speed your heart rate and raise your blood pressure, and slow your breathing (you may notice yourself suddenly holding your breath when you first feel fearful, all the better to hear more clearly what it is you are fearful of). That is only one part of a wide, carefully coordinated array of changes the amygdala and connected areas orchestrate as they commandeer the brain in a crisis.

Meanwhile the amygdala, along with the interconnected hippocampus, directs the cells that send key neurotransmitters, for example, to trigger releases of dopamine that lead to the riveting of attention on the source of your fear—the strange sounds—and put your muscles at readiness to react accordingly. At the same time the amygdala signals sensory areas for vision and attention, making sure that the eyes seek out whatever is most relevant to the emergency at hand. Simultaneously cortical memory systems are re-shuffled so that knowledge and memories most relevant to the particular emotional urgency will be most readily recalled, taking precedence over other less relevant strands of thought.

Once these signals have been sent, you are pitched into full-fledged fear: you become aware of the characteristic tightness in your gut, your speeding heart, the tightening of the muscles around your neck and shoulders or the trembling of your limbs; your body freezes in place as you strain your attention to hear any further sounds, and your mind races with possible lurking dangers and ways to respond. This entire sequence—from surprise to uncertainty to apprehension to fear—can be telescoped within a second or so. (For more information, see Jerome Kagan, *Galen's Prophecy*. New York: Basic Books, 1994.)

W. T. Grant Consortium: Active Ingredients of Prevention Programs

Key ingredients of effective programs include:

EMOTIONAL SKILLS

- Identifying and labeling feelings
- Expressing feelings
- Assessing the intensity of feelings
- Managing feelings
- Delaying gratification
- Controlling impulses
- Reducing stress
- Knowing the difference between feelings and actions

COGNITIVE SKILLS

- Self-talk—conducting an "inner dialogue" as a way to cope with a topic or challenge or reinforce one's own behavior
- Reading and interpreting social cues—for example, recognizing social influences on behavior and seeing oneself in the perspective of the larger community
- Using steps for problem-solving and decision-making—for instance, controlling impulses, setting goals, identifying alternative actions, anticipating consequences

- Understanding the perspective of others
- Understanding behavioral norms (what is and is not acceptable behavior)
- A positive attitude toward life
- Self-awareness—for example, developing realistic expectations about oneself

Behavioral Skills

- Nonverbal—communicating through eye contact, facial expressiveness, tone of voice, gestures, and so on
- Verbal—making clear requests, responding effectively to criticism, resisting negative influences, listening to others, helping others, participating in positive peer groups

SOURCE: W. T. Grant Consortium on the School-Based Promotion of Social Competence, "Drug and Alcohol Prevention Curricula," in J. David Hawkins et al., *Communities That Care* (San Francisco: Jossey-Bass, 1992).

The Self Science Curriculum

Main components:

- *Self-awareness:* observing yourself and recognizing your feelings; building a vocabulary for feelings; knowing the relationship between thoughts, feelings, and reactions
- *Personal decision-making:* examining your actions and knowing their consequences; knowing if thought or feeling is ruling a decision; applying these insights to issues such as sex and drugs
- *Managing feelings:* monitoring "self-talk" to catch negative messages such as internal put-downs; realizing what is behind a feeling (e.g., the hurt that underlies anger); finding ways to handle fears and anxieties, anger, and sadness
- *Handling stress:* learning the value of exercise, guided imagery, relaxation methods
- *Empathy:* understanding others' feelings and concerns and taking their perspective; appreciating the differences in how people feel about things
- *Communications:* talking about feelings effectively: becoming a good listener and question-asker; distinguishing between what someone does or says and your own reactions or judgments about it; sending "I" messages instead of blame
- *Self-disclosure:* valuing openness and building trust in a relationship; knowing when it's safe to risk talking about your private feelings
- *Insight:* identifying patterns in your emotional life and reactions; recognizing similar patterns in others
- *Self-acceptance:* feeling pride and seeing yourself in a positive light; recognizing your strengths and weaknesses; being able to laugh at yourself
- *Personal responsibility:* taking responsibility; recognizing the consequences of your decisions and actions, accepting your feelings and moods, following through on commitments (e.g., to studying)

- *Assertiveness:* stating your concerns and feelings without anger or passivity
- *Group dynamics:* cooperation; knowing when and how to lead, when to follow
- *Conflict resolution:* how to fight fair with other kids, with parents, with teachers; the win/win model for negotiating compromise

SOURCE: Karen F. Stone and Harold Q. Dillehunt, *Self Science: The Subject Is Me* (Santa Monica: Goodyear Publishing Co., 1978).

Social and Emotional Learning: Results

Child Development Project

Eric Schaps, Development Studies Center, Oakland, California.

Evaluation in schools in Northern California, grades K–6; rating by independent observers, comparing with control schools.

RESULTS:

- more responsible
- more assertive
- more popular and outgoing
- more pro-social and helpful
- better understanding of others
- more considerate, concerned
- more pro-social strategies for interpersonal problem-solving
- more harmonious
- more "democratic"
- better conflict-resolution skills

SOURCES: E. Schaps and V. Battistich, "Promoting Health Development Through School-Based Prevention: New Approaches," *OSAP Prevention Monograph, no. 8: Preventing Adolescent Drug Use: From Theory to Practice.* Eric Gopelrud (ed.), Rockville, MD: Office of Substance Abuse Prevention, U.S. Dept. of Health and Human Services, 1991.

D. Solomon, M. Watson, V. Battistich, E. Schaps, and K. Delucchi, "Creating a Caring Community: Educational Practices That Promote Children's Prosocial Development," in F. K. Oser, A. Dick, and J.-L. Patry, eds., *Effective and Responsible Teaching: The New Synthesis* (San Francisco: Jossey-Bass, 1992).

Paths

Mark Greenberg, Fast Track Project, University of Washington.

Evaluated in schools in Seattle, grades 1–5; ratings by teachers, comparing matched control students among 1) regular students, 2) deaf students, 3) special-education students.

RESULTS:

- Improvement in social cognitive skills
- Improvement in emotion, recognition, and understanding
- Better self-control
- Better planning for solving cognitive tasks
- More thinking before acting
- More effective conflict resolution
- More positive classroom atmosphere

SPECIAL-NEEDS STUDENTS:

Improved classroom behavior on:

- Frustration tolerance
- Assertive social skills
- Task orientation
- Peer skills
- Sharing
- Sociability
- Self-control

IMPROVED EMOTIONAL UNDERSTANDING:

- Recognition
- Labeling
- Decreases in self-reports of sadness and depression
- Decrease in anxiety and withdrawal

SOURCES: Conduct Problems Research Group, "A Developmental and Clinical Model for the Prevention of Conduct Disorder: The Fast Track Program," *Development and Psychopathology* 4 (1992).

M. T. Greenberg and C. A. Kusche, *Promoting Social and Emotional Development in Deaf Children: The PATHS Project* (Seattle: University of Washington Press, 1993).

M. T. Greenberg, C. A. Kusche, E. T. Cook, and J. P. Quamma, "Promoting Emotional Competence in School-Aged Children: The Effects of the PATHS Curriculum," *Development and Psychopathology* 7 (1995).

Seattle Social Development Project

J. David Hawkins, Social Development Research Group, University of Washington

Evaluated in Seattle elementary and middle schools by independent testing and objective standards, in comparison to nonprogram schools.

RESULTS:

- More positive attachment to family and school
- Boys less aggressive, girls less self-destructive
- Fewer suspensions and expulsions among low-achieving students
- Less drug-use initiation
- Less delinquency
- Better scores on standardized achievement tests

SOURCES: E. Schaps and V. Battistich, "Promoting Health Development Through School-Based Prevention: New Approaches," *OSAP Prevention Monograph, no. 8: Preventing Adolescent Drug Use: From Theory to Practice.* Eric Gopelrud (ed.), Rockville, MD: Office of Substance Abuse Prevention, U.S. Dept. of Health and Human Services, 1991.

J. D. Hawkins et al., "The Seattle Social Development Project," in J. McCord and R. Tremblay, eds., *The Prevention of Antisocial Behavior in Children* (New York: Guilford, 1992).

J. D. Hawkins, E. Von Cleve, and R. F. Catalano, "Reducing Early Childhood Aggression: Results of a Primary Prevention Program," *Journal of the American Academy of Child and Adolescent Psychiatry* 30, 2 (1991), pp. 208–17.

J. A. O'Donnell, J. D. Hawkins, R. F. Catalano, R. D. Abbott, and L. E. Day, "Preventing School Failure, Drug Use, and Delinquency Among Low-Income Children: Effects of a Long-Term Prevention Project in Elementary Schools," *American Journal of Orthopsychiatry* 65 (1994).

Yale–New Haven Social Competence Promotion Program

Roger Weissberg, University of Illinois at Chicago

Evaluated in New Haven Public Schools, grades 5–8, by independent observations and student and teacher reports, compared with control group.

RESULTS:

- Improved problem-solving skills
- More involvement with peers
- Better impulse control
- Improved behavior
- Improved interpersonal effectiveness and popularity

- Enhanced coping skills
- More skill in handling interpersonal problems
- Better coping with anxiety
- Less delinquent behaviors
- Better conflict-resolution skills

SOURCES: M. J. Elias and R. P. Weissberg, "School-Based Social Competence Promotion as a Primary Prevention Strategy: A Tale of Two Projects," *Prevention in Human Services* 7, 1 (1990), pp. 177–200.
   M. Caplan, R. P. Weissberg, J. S. Grober, P. J. Sivo, K. Grady, and C. Jacoby, "Social Competence Promotion with Inner-City and Suburban Young Adolescents: Effects of Social Adjustment and Alcohol Use," *Journal of Consulting and Clinical Psychology* 60, 1 (1992), pp. 56–63.

Resolving Conflict Creatively Program

Linda Lantieri, National Center for Resolving Conflict Creatively Program (an initiative of Educators for Social Responsibility), New York City
   Evaluated in New York City schools, grades K–12, by teachers' ratings, pre- and post-program.

RESULTS:

- Less violence in class
- Fewer verbal put-downs in class
- More-caring atmosphere
- More willingness to cooperate
- More empathy
- Improved communication skills

SOURCE: Metis Associates, Inc., *The Resolving Conflict Creatively Program: 1988–1989. Summary of Significant Findings of RCCP New York Site* (New York: Metis Associates, May 1990).

The Improving Social Awareness–Social Problem Solving Project

Maurice Elias, Rutgers University
   Evaluated in New Jersey schools, grades K–6, by teacher ratings, peer assessments, and school records, compared to nonparticipants.

RESULTS:

- More sensitive to others' feelings
- Better understanding of the consequences of their behavior
- Increased ability to "size up" interpersonal situations and plan appropriate actions
- Higher self-esteem
- More prosocial behavior
- Sought out by peers for help
- Better handled the transition to middle school
- Less antisocial, self-destructive, and socially disordered behavior, even when followed up into high school
- Improved learning-to-learn skills
- Better self-control, social awareness, and social decision-making in and out of the classroom

SOURCES: M. J. Elias, M. A. Gara, T. F. Schuyler, L. R. Branden-Muller, and M. A. Sayette, "The Promotion of Social Competence: Longitudinal Study of a Preventive School-Based Program," *American Journal of Orthopsychiatry* 61 (1991), pp. 409–17.

M. J. Elias and J. Clabby, *Building Social Problem Solving Skills: Guidelines From a School-Based Program* (San Francisco: Jossey-Bass, 1992).

Resources

The first edition of this book could not have had a page like this directing readers who want more information to the best resources—in 1995 there were virtually no resources anywhere on emotional intelligence, while today they seem to be proliferating wildly. The mere existence of this page in itself signifies how much this field has advanced. For more in-depth access to tools and research findings, practical resources, and key people in this field, I recommend the following organizations, websites, and books. (I've tried to include only books I'm familiar with that are based on sound research, but my failure to include a book does not mean it cannot be helpful or may not be sound.)

EDUCATION

The Collaborative for Academic, Social, and Emotional Learning (CASEL), based at the University of Illinois at Chicago, seeks to enhance children's success in school and life by promoting evidence-based social, emotional, and academic learning as an essential part of education from preschool through high school. Website: www.casel.org.

The Center for Social and Emotional Education (CSEE), at Teachers College, Columbia University, is an educational and professional development organization dedicated to supporting effective social emotional learning, teaching, and leadership in schools. Website: www.CSEE.net.

Some Model SEL Programs

> Responsive Classroom: http://responsiveclassroom.org/
> Developmental Studies Center: http://www.devstu.org/

Educators for Social Responsibility:
    http://www.esrnational.org/home.htm
Search Institute: http://www.search-institute.org/
Social Development Research Group:
    http://depts.washington.edu/sdrg/index.html

Learning Standards. For a model statewide policy setting detailed educational standards in social and emotional learning, see the work of the Illinois State Board of Education. This state-of-the-art, developmentally appropriate formulation could be adopted by any educational system seeking to offer SEL to its children. Website: www.isbe.net/ils/social_emotional/standards.htm.

Recommended Books

Bar-On, Reuven, J. G. Maree, and M. J. Elias, eds. *Educating People to Be Emotionally Intelligent*. Portsmouth, NH: Heinemann Educational Publishers, 2005.

Cohen, Jonathan, ed. *Educating Minds and Hearts: Social Emotional Learning and the Passage into Adolescence*. New York: Teachers College Press, 1999.

Collaborative for Academic, Social, and Emotional Learning. *Safe and Sound: An Educational Leader's Guide to Evidence-based Social and Emotional Learning Programs*. Chicago: Collaborative for Academic, Social, and Emotional Learning, 2003.

Elias, Maurice J., A. Arnold, and C. S. Hussey, eds. *EQ + IQ = Best Leadership Practices for Caring and Successful Schools*. Thousand Oaks, CA: Corwin Press, 2003.

Elias, Maurice, et al. *Promoting Social and Emotional Learning: Guidelines for Educators*. Alexandria, VA: Association for Supervision and Curriculum Development, 1997.

Haynes, Norris, Michael Ben-Avie, and Jacque Ensign. *How Social and Emotional Development Add Up: Getting Results in Math and Science Education*. New York: Teachers College Press, 2003.

Lantieri, Linda, and Janet Patti. *Waging Peace in Our Schools*. Boston: Beacon Press, 1996.

Novick, B., J. S. Kress, and Maurice Elias. *Building Learning Communities with Character: How to Integrate Academic, Social, and Emotional Learning*. Alexandria, VA: Association for Supervision and Curriculum Development, 2002.

Patti, Janet, and J. Tobin. *Smart School Leaders: Leading with Emotional Intelligence*. Dubuque, IA: Kendall Hunt, 2003.

Salovey, Peter, and David Sluyter, eds. *Emotional Development and Emotional Intelligence: Educational Implications.* New York: Basic Books, 1997.

Zins, Joseph, Roger Weissberg, Margaret Wang, and Herbert Walberg. *Building Academic Success on Social and Emotional Learning: What Does the Research Say?* New York: Teachers College Press, 2004.

ORGANIZATIONAL LIFE

The Consortium for Research on Emotional Intelligence in Organizations is based in the Graduate School of Applied and Professional Psychology, Rutgers University. Director: Cary Cherniss. Website: www.eiconsortium.org.

Recommended Books

Ashkanasy, Neal, Wilfred Zerbe, and Charmine Hartel. *Managing Emotions in the Workplace.* Armonk, NY: M. E. Sharpe, 2002.

Boyatzis, Richard, and Annie McKee. *Resonant Leadership: Inspiring Yourself and Others Through Mindfulness, Hope, and Compassion.* Boston: Harvard Business School Press, 2005.

Caruso, David R., and Peter Salovey. *The Emotionally Intelligent Manager: How to Develop the Four Key Skills of Leadership.* San Francisco: Jossey-Bass, 2004.

Cherniss, Cary, and Daniel Goleman, eds. *The Emotionally Intelligent Workplace: How to Select For, Measure, and Improve Emotional Intelligence in Individuals, Groups, and Organizations.* San Francisco: Jossey-Bass, 2001.

Druskat, Vanessa, Fabio Sala, and Gerald Mount, eds. *Linking Emotional Intelligence and Performance at Work: Current Research Evidence.* Mahwah, NJ: Lawrence Erlbaum, 2005.

Fineman, Stephen, ed. *Emotion in Organizations,* 2nd ed. London: Sage Publications, 2000.

Frost, Peter J., *Toxic Emotions at Work: How Compassionate Managers Handle Pain and Conflict.* Boston: Harvard Business School Press, 2003.

Riggio, Ronald, Susan E. Murphy, and Francis Pirozzolo. *Multiple Intelligences and Leadership.* Mahwah, NJ: Lawrence Erlbaum, 2002.

PARENTING

Recommended Books

Elias, Maurice, Steven E. Tobias, and Brian S. Friedlander. *Emotionally Intelligent Parenting: How to Raise a Self-disciplined, Responsible, Socially Skilled Child.* New York: Harmony Books, 1999.

Elias, Maurice, Steven E. Tobias, and Brian S. Friedlander. *Raising Emotionally Intelligent Teenagers.* New York: Harmony Books, 2000.

Gottman, John. *Raising an Emotionally Intelligent Child.* New York: Simon and Schuster, 1998.

Schure, Myrna. *Raising a Thinking Child.* New York: Pocket Books, 1994.

GENERAL

6 Seconds is a nonprofit organization that supports emotional intelligence in schools, businesses, and families, with an international scope. It is an excellent source for information on resources, articles, and conferences. Website: www.6seconds.org.

Recommended Books

Bar-On, Reuven, and Parker, James D. A., eds. *Handbook of Emotional Intelligence.* San Francisco: Jossey-Bass, 2000.

Barrett, Lisa Feldman, and Peter Salovey. *The Wisdom of Feeling: Psychological Processes in Emotional Intelligence.* New York: Guilford Press, 2002.

Geher, G., ed. *Measuring Emotional Intelligence: Common Ground and Controversy.* Hauppauge, NY: Nova Science Publishers, 2004.

Salovey, Peter, Marc A. Brackett, and John D. Mayer. *Emotional Intelligence: Key Readings on the Mayer and Salovey Model.* Port Chester, NY: DUDE Publishing, 2004.

Williams, Virginia, and Redford Williams. *Lifeskills.* New York: Times Books, 1997.

A Thoughtful Critique:

Matthews, Gerald, Moshe Zeidner, and Richard D. Roberts. *Emotional Intelligence: Science and Myth*. Cambridge: MIT Press, 2002.

Notes

Introduction

1. J. A. Durlak and R. P. Weissberg, "A Major Meta-analysis of Positive Youth Development Programs," presentation at the annual meeting of the American Psychological Association, Washington, DC, August 2005. See also R. P. Weissberg, "Social and Emotional Learning for School and Life Success," address to the Society for Community Research and Action (APA Division 27), Distinguished Contribution to Theory and Research Award, at the annual meeting of the American Psychological Association, Washington, D.C., August 2005.

2. N. R. Riggs, M. T. Greenberg, C. A. Kusche, and M. A. Pentz, "The Role of Neurocognitive Change in the Behavioral Outcomes of a Social-Emotional Prevention Program in Elementary School Students: Effects of the PATHS Curriculum," 2005, under review.

3. The EI model seems to be emerging as an influential framework within psychology. The span of psychological fields that now are informed by (and inform) the EI model range from neuroscience to health psychology. The areas with strongest connections to EI include: development, education, clinical and counseling, social, and industrial/organizational psychology, among others. Indeed, segments on EI are now routinely included in many college-level and graduate courses in these subjects.

4. J. D. Mayer, P. Salovey, and D. R. Caruso, "Models of Emotional Intelligence," in R. J. Sternberg, ed., *Handbook of Intelligence,* Cambridge, Eng.: Cambridge University Press, 2000.

5. Children rated in 1999: Thomas M. Achenbach et al., "Are American Children's Problems Still Getting Worse? A 23-year Comparison," *Journal of Abnormal Child Psychology,* 31 (2003): 1–11.

PART ONE: THE EMOTIONAL BRAIN

Chapter 1. What Are Emotions For?

1. Associated Press, September 15, 1993.

2. The timelessness of this theme of selfless love is suggested by how pervasive it is in world myth: The Jataka tales, told throughout much of Asia for millennia, all narrate variations on such parables of self-sacrifice.

3. Altruistic love and human survival: The evolutionary theories that posit the adaptive advantages of altruism are well-summarized in Malcolm Slavin and Daniel Kriegman, *The Adaptive Design of the Human Psyche* (New York: Guilford Press, 1992).

4. Much of this discussion is based on Paul Ekman's key essay, "An Argument for Basic Emotions," *Cognition and Emotion,* 6, 1992, pp. 169–200. This point is from P. N. Johnson-Laird and K. Oatley's essay in the same issue of the journal.

5. The shooting of Matilda Crabtree: *The New York Times,* Nov. 11, 1994.

6. Only in adults: An observation by Paul Ekman, University of California at San Francisco.

7. Body changes in emotions and their evolutionary reasons: Some of the changes are documented in Robert W. Levenson, Paul Ekman, and Wallace V. Friesen, "Voluntary Facial Action Generates Emotion-Specific Autonomous Nervous System Activity," *Psychophysi-*

ology, 27, 1990. This list is culled from there and other sources. At this point such a list remains speculative to a degree; there is scientific debate over the precise biological signature of each emotion, with some researchers taking the position that there is far more overlap than difference among emotions, or that our present ability to measure the biological correlates of emotion is too immature to distinguish among them reliably. For this debate see: Paul Ekman and Richard Davidson, eds., *Fundamental Questions About Emotions* (New York: Oxford University Press, 1994).

8. As Paul Ekman puts it, "Anger is the most dangerous emotion; some of the main problems destroying society these days involve anger run amok. It's the least adaptive emotion now because it mobilizes us to fight. Our emotions evolved when we didn't have the technology to act so powerfully on them. In prehistoric times, when you had an instantaneous rage and for a second wanted to kill someone, you couldn't do it very easily—but now you can."

9. Erasmus of Rotterdam, *In Praise of Folly,* trans. Eddie Radice (London: Penguin, 1971), p. 87.

10. Such basic responses defined what might pass for the "emotional life"—more aptly, an "instinct life"—of these species. More important in evolutionary terms, these are the decisions crucial to survival; those animals that could do them well, or well enough, survived to pass on their genes. In these early times, mental life was brutish: the senses and a simple repertoire of reactions to the stimuli they received got a lizard, frog, bird, or fish—and, perhaps, a brontosaurus—through the day. But this runt brain did not yet allow for what we think of as an emotion.

11. The limbic system and emotions: R. Joseph, *The Naked Neuron: Evolution and the Languages of the Brain and Body* (New York: Plenum Publishing, 1993); Paul D. MacLean, *The Triune Brain in Evolution* (New York: Plenum, 1990).

12. Rhesus infants and adaptability: "Aspects of emotion conserved across species," Ned Kalin, M.D., Departments of Psychology and Psychiatry, University of Wisconsin, prepared for the MacArthur Affective Neuroscience Meeting, Nov., 1992.

Chapter 2. Anatomy of an Emotional Hijacking

1. The case of the man with no feelings was described by R. Joseph, op. cit. p. 83. On the other hand, there may be some vestiges of feeling in people who lack an amygdala (see Paul Ekman and Richard Davidson, eds., *Questions About Emotion.* New York: Oxford University Press, 1994). The different findings may hinge on exactly which parts of the amygdala and related circuits were missing; the last word on the detailed neurology of emotion is far from in.

2. Like many neuroscientists, LeDoux works at several levels, studying, for instance, how specific lesions in a rat's brain change its behavior; painstakingly tracing the path of single neurons; setting up elaborate experiments to condition fear in rats whose brains have been surgically altered. His findings, and others reviewed here, are at the frontier of exploration in neuroscience, and so remain somewhat speculative—particularly the implications that seem to flow from the raw data to an understanding of our emotional life. But LeDoux's work is supported by a growing body of converging evidence from a variety of neuroscientists who are steadily laying bare the neural underpinnings of emotions. See, for example, Joseph LeDoux, "Sensory Systems and Emotion," *Integrative Psychiatry,* 4, 1986; Joseph LeDoux, "Emotion and the Limbic System Concept," *Concepts in Neuroscience,* 2, 1992.

3. The idea of the limbic system as the brain's emotional center was introduced by neurologist Paul MacLean more than forty years ago. In recent years discoveries like LeDoux's have refined the limbic system concept, showing that some of its central structures like the hippocampus are less directly involved in emotions, while circuits linking other parts

of the brain—particularly the prefrontal lobes—to the amygdala are more central. Beyond that, there is a growing recognition that each emotion may call on distinct brain areas. The most current thinking is that there is not a neatly defined single "emotional brain," but rather several systems of circuits that disperse the regulation of a given emotion to farflung, but coordinated, parts of the brain. Neuroscientists speculate that when the full brain mapping of the emotions is accomplished, each major emotion will have its own topography, a distinct map of neuronal pathways determining its unique qualities, though many or most of these circuits are likely to be interlinked at key junctures in the limbic system, like the amygdala, and prefrontal cortex. See Joseph LeDoux, "Emotional Memory Systems in the Brain," *Behavioral and Brain Research,* 58, 1993.

4. Brain circuitry of different levels of fear: This analysis is based on the excellent synthesis in Jerome Kagan, *Galen's Prophecy* (New York: Basic Books, 1994).

5. I wrote about Joseph LeDoux's research in *The New York Times* on August 15, 1989. The discussion in this chapter is based on interviews with him, and several of his articles, including Joseph LeDoux, "Emotional Memory Systems in the Brain," *Behavioural Brain Research,* 58, 1993; Joseph LeDoux, "Emotion, Memory and the Brain," *Scientific American,* June, 1994; Joseph LeDoux, "Emotion and the Limbic System Concept," *Concepts in Neuroscience,* 2, 1992.

6. Unconscious preferences: William Raft Kunst-Wilson and R. B. Zajonc, "Affective Discrimination of Stimuli That Cannot Be Recognized," *Science* (Feb. 1, 1980).

7. Unconscious opinion: John A. Bargh, "First Second: The Preconscious in Social Interactions," presented at the meeting of the American Psychological Society, Washington, DC (June 1994).

8. Emotional memory: Larry Cahill et al., "Beta-adrenergic activation and memory for emotional events," *Nature* (Oct. 20, 1994).

9. Psychoanalytic theory and brain maturation: the most detailed discussion of the early years and the emotional consequences of brain development is Allan Schore, *Affect Regulation and the Origin of Self* (Hillsdale, NJ: Lawrence Erlbaum Associates, 1994).

10. Dangerous, even if you don't know what it is: LeDoux, quoted in "How Scary Things Get That Way," *Science* (Nov. 6, 1992), p. 887.

11. Much of this speculation about the fine-tuning of emotional response by the neocortex comes from Ned Kalin, op. cit.

12. A closer look at the neuroanatomy shows how the prefrontal lobes act as emotional managers. Much evidence points to part of the prefrontal cortex as a site where most or all cortical circuits involved in an emotional reaction come together. In humans, the strongest connections between neocortex and amygdala run to the left prefrontal lobe and the temporal lobe below and to the side of the frontal lobe (the temporal lobe is critical in identifying what an object is). Both these connections are made in a single projection, suggesting a rapid and powerful pathway, a virtual neural highway. The single-neuron projection between the amygdala and prefrontal cortex runs to an area called the *orbitofrontal cortex.* This is the area that seems most critical for assessing emotional responses as we are in the midst of them and making mid-course corrections.

    The orbitofrontal cortex both receives signals from the amygdala and has its own intricate, extensive web of projections throughout the limbic brain. Through this web it plays a role in regulating emotional responses—including inhibiting signals from the limbic brain as they reach other areas of the cortex, thus toning down the neural urgency of those signals. The orbitofrontal cortex's connections to the limbic brain are so extensive that some neuroanatomists have called it a kind of "limbic cortex"—the thinking part of the emotional brain. See Ned Kalin, Departments of Psychology and Psychiatry, University of Wisconsin, "Aspects of Emotion Conserved Across Species," an unpublished manuscript prepared for the MacArthur Affective Neuroscience Meeting, November, 1992; and Allan Schore, *Affect Regulation and the Origin of Self* (Hillsdale, NJ: Lawrence Erlbaum Associates, 1994).

There is not only a structural bridge between amygdala and prefrontal cortex, but, as always, a biochemical one: both the ventromedial section of the prefrontal cortex and the amygdala are especially high in concentrations of chemical receptors for the neurotransmitter serotonin. This brain chemical seems, among other things, to prime cooperation: monkeys with extremely high density of receptors for serotonin in the prefrontal-amygdala circuit are "socially well-tuned," while those with low concentrations are hostile and antagonistic. See Antonio Damosio, *Descartes' Error* (New York: Grosset/Putnam, 1994).

13. Animal studies show that when areas of the prefrontal lobes are lesioned, so that they no longer modulate emotional signals from the limbic area, the animals become erratic, impulsively and unpredictably exploding in rage or cringing in fear. A. R. Luria, the brilliant Russian neuropsychologist, proposed as long ago as the 1930s that the prefrontal cortex was key for self-control and constraining emotional outbursts; patients who had damage to this area, he noted, were impulsive and prone to flareups of fear and anger. And a study of two dozen men and women who had been convicted of impulsive, heat-of-passion murders found, using PET scans for brain imaging, that they had a much lower than usual level of activity in these same sections of the prefrontal cortex.

14. Some of the main work on lesioned lobes in rats was done by Victor Dennenberg, a psychologist at the University of Connecticut.

15. Left hemisphere lesions and joviality: G. Gianotti, "Emotional behavior and hemispheric side of lesion," *Cortex*, 8, 1972.

16. The case of the happier stroke patient was reported by Mary K. Morris, of the Department of Neurology at the University of Florida, at the International Neurophysiological Society Meeting, February 13–16, 1991, in San Antonio.

17. Prefrontal cortex and working memory: Lynn D. Selemon et al., "Prefrontal Cortex," *American Journal of Psychiatry*, 152, 1995.

18. Faulty frontal lobes: Philip Harden and Robert Pihl, "Cognitive Function, Cardiovascular Reactivity, and Behavior in Boys at High Risk for Alcoholism," *Journal of Abnormal Psychology*, 104, 1995.

19. Prefrontal cortex: Antonio Damasio, *Descartes' Error: Emotion, Reason and the Human Brain* (New York: Grosset/Putnam, 1994).

PART TWO: THE NATURE OF EMOTIONAL INTELLIGENCE

Chapter 3. When Smart Is Dumb

1. Jason H.'s story was reported in "Warning by a Valedictorian Who Faced Prison," in *The New York Times* (June 23, 1992).

2. One observer notes: Howard Gardner, "Cracking Open the IQ Box," *The American Prospect*, Winter 1995.

3. Richard Herrnstein and Charles Murray, *The Bell Curve: Intelligence and Class Structure in American Life* (New York: Free Press, 1994), p. 66.

4. George Vaillant, *Adaptation to Life* (Boston: Little, Brown, 1977). The average SAT score of the Harvard group was 584, on a scale where 800 is tops. Dr. Vaillant, now at Harvard University Medical School, told me about the relatively poor predictive value of test scores for life success in this group of advantaged men.

5. J. K. Felsman and G. E. Vaillant, "Resilient Children as Adults: A 40-Year Study," in E. J. Anderson and B. J. Cohler, eds., *The Invulnerable Child* (New York: Guilford Press, 1987).

6. Karen Arnold, who did the study of valedictorians with Terry Denny at the University of Illinois, was quoted in *The Chicago Tribune* (May 29, 1992).

7. Project Spectrum: Principal colleagues of Gardner in developing Project Spectrum were Mara Krechevsky and David Feldman.

8. I interviewed Howard Gardner about his theory of multiple intelligences in "Rethinking the Value of Intelligence Tests," in *The New York Times Education Supplement* (Nov. 3, 1986) and several times since.

9. The comparison of IQ tests and Spectrum abilities is reported in a chapter, coauthored with Mara Krechevsky, in Howard Gardner, *Multiple Intelligences: The Theory in Practice* (New York: Basic Books, 1993).

10. The nutshell summary is from Howard Gardner, *Multiple Intelligences*, p. 9.

11. Howard Gardner and Thomas Hatch, "Multiple Intelligences Go to School," *Educational Researcher* 18, 8 (1989).

12. The model of emotional intelligence was first proposed in Peter Salovey and John D. Mayer, "Emotional intelligence," *Imagination, Cognition, and Personality* 9 (1990), pp. 185–211.

13. Practical intelligence and people skills: Robert J. Sternberg, *Beyond I.Q.* (New York: Cambridge University Press, 1985).

14. The basic definition of "emotional intelligence" is in Salovey and Mayer, "Emotional Intelligence," p. 189. Another early model of emotional intelligence is in Reuven Bar-On, "The Development of a Concept of Psychological Well-Being," Ph.D. dissertation, Rhodes University, South Africa, 1988.

15. IQ vs. emotional intelligence: Jack Block, University of California at Berkeley, unpublished manuscript, February, 1995. Block uses the concept "ego resilience" rather than emotional intelligence, but notes that its main components include emotional self-regulation, an adaptive impulse control, a sense of self-efficacy, and social intelligence. Since these are main elements of emotional intelligence, ego resilience can be seen as a surrogate measure for emotional intelligence, much like SAT scores are for IQ. Block analyzed data from a longitudinal study of about a hundred men and women in their teen years and early twenties, and used statistical methods to assess the personality and behavioral correlates of high IQ independent of emotional intelligence, and emotional intelligence apart from IQ. There is, he finds, a modest correlation between IQ and ego resilience, but the two are independent constructs.

Chapter 4. Know Thyself

1. My usage of *self-awareness* refers to a self-reflexive, introspective attention to one's own experience, sometimes called *mindfulness*.

2. See also: Jon Kabat-Zinn, *Wherever You Go, There You Are* (New York: Hyperion, 1994).

3. The observing ego: An insightful comparison of the psychoanalyst's attentional stance and self-awareness appears in Mark Epstein's *Thoughts Without a Thinker* (New York: Basic Books, 1995). Epstein notes that if this ability is cultivated deeply, it can drop the self-consciousness of the observer and become a "more flexible and braver 'developed ego,' capable of embracing all of life."

4. William Styron, *Darkness Visible: A Memoir of Madness* (New York: Random House, 1990), p. 64.

5. John D. Mayer and Alexander Stevens, "An Emerging Understanding of the Reflective (Meta) Experience of Mood," unpublished manuscript (1993).

6. Mayer and Stevens, "An Emerging Understanding." Some of the terms for these emotional self-awareness styles are my own adaptations of their categories.

7. The intensity of emotions: Much of this work was done by or with Randy Larsen, a former graduate student of Diener's now at the University of Michigan.

8. Gary, the emotionally bland surgeon, is described in Hillel I. Swiller, "Alexithymia: Treatment Utilizing Combined Individual and Group Psychotherapy," *International Journal for Group Psychotherapy* 38, 1 (1988), pp. 47–61.

9. *Emotional illiterate* was the term used by M. B. Freedman and B. S. Sweet, "Some Specific Features of Group Psychotherapy," *International Journal for Group Psychotherapy* 4 (1954), pp. 335–68.

10. The clinical features of alexithymia are described in Graeme J. Taylor, "Alexithymia: History of the Concept," paper presented at the annual meeting of the American Psychiatric Association in Washington, DC (May 1986).

11. The description of alexithymia is from Peter Sifneos, "Affect, Emotional Conflict, and Deficit: An Overview," *Psychotherapy-and-Psychosomatics* 56 (1991), pp. 116–22.

12. The woman who did not know why she was crying is reported in H. Warnes, "Alexithymia, Clinical and Therapeutic Aspects," *Psychotherapy-and-Psychosomatics* 46 (1986), pp. 96–104.

13. Role of emotions in reasoning: Damasio, *Descartes' Error*.

14. Unconscious fear: The snake studies are described in Kagan, *Galen's Prophecy*.

Chapter 5. Passion's Slaves

1. For details on the ratio of positive to negative feelings and well-being, see Ed Diener and Randy J. Larsen, "The Experience of Emotional Well-Being," in Michael Lewis and Jeannette Haviland, eds., *Handbook of Emotions* (New York: Guilford Press, 1993).

2. I interviewed Diane Tice about her research on how well people shake off bad moods in December 1992. She published her findings on anger in a chapter she wrote with her husband, Roy Baumeister, in Daniel Wegner and James Pennebaker, eds., *Handbook of Mental Control* v. 5 (Englewood Cliffs, NJ: Prentice-Hall, 1993).

3. Bill collectors: also described in Arlie Hochschild, *The Managed Heart* (New York: Free Press, 1980).

4. The case against anger, and for self-control, is based largely on Diane Tice and Roy F. Baumeister, "Controlling Anger: Self-Induced Emotion Change," in Wegner and Pennebaker, *Handbook of Mental Control*. But see also Carol Tavris, *Anger: The Misunderstood Emotion* (New York: Touchstone, 1989).

5. The research on rage is described in Dolf Zillmann, "Mental Control of Angry Aggression," in Wegner and Pennebaker, *Handbook of Mental Control*.

6. The soothing walk: quoted in Tavris, *Anger: The Misunderstood Emotion,* p. 135.

7. Redford Williams's strategies for controlling hostility are detailed in Redford Williams and Virginia Williams, *Anger Kills* (New York: Times Books, 1993).

8. Venting anger does not dispel it: see, for example, S. K. Mallick and B. R. McCandless, "A Study of Catharsis Aggression," *Journal of Personality and Social Psychology*

4 (1966). For a summary of this research, see Tavris, *Anger: The Misunderstood Emotion*.

9. When lashing out in anger is effective: Tavris, *Anger: The Misunderstood Emotion*.

10. The work of worrying: Lizabeth Roemer and Thomas Borkovec, "Worry: Unwanted Cognitive Activity That Controls Unwanted Somatic Experience," in Wegner and Pennebaker, *Handbook of Mental Control*.

11. Fear of germs: David Riggs and Edna Foa, "Obsessive-Compulsive Disorder," in David Barlow, ed., *Clinical Handbook of Psychological Disorders* (New York: Guilford Press, 1993).

12. The worried patient was quoted in Roemer and Borkovec, "Worry," p. 221.

13. Therapies for anxiety disorder: see, for example, David H. Barlow, ed., *Clinical Handbook of Psychological Disorders* (New York: Guilford Press, 1993).

14. Styron's depression: William Styron, *Darkness Visible: A Memoir of Madness* (New York: Random House, 1990).

15. The worries of the depressed are reported in Susan Nolen-Hoeksma, "Sex Differences in Control of Depression," in Wegner and Pennebaker, *Handbook of Mental Control*, p. 307.

16. Therapy for depression: K. S. Dobson, "A Meta-analysis of the Efficacy of Cognitive Therapy for Depression," *Journal of Consulting and Clinical Psychology* 57 (1989).

17. The study of depressed people's thought patterns is reported in Richard Wenzlaff, "The Mental Control of Depression," in Wegner and Pennebaker, *Handbook of Mental Control*.

18. Shelley Taylor et al., "Maintaining Positive Illusions in the Face of Negative Information," *Journal of Clinical and Social Psychology* 8 (1989).

19. The repressing college student is from Daniel A. Weinberger, "The Construct Validity of the Repressive Coping Style," in J. L. Singer, ed., *Repression and Dissociation* (Chicago: University of Chicago Press, 1990). Weinberger, who developed the concept of repressors in early studies with Gary F. Schwartz and Richard Davidson, has become the leading researcher on the topic.

Chapter 6. The Master Aptitude

1. The terror of the exam: Daniel Goleman, *Vital Lies, Simple Truths: The Psychology of Self-Deception* (New York: Simon and Schuster, 1985).

2. Working memory: Alan Baddeley, *Working Memory* (Oxford: Clarendon Press, 1986).

3. Prefrontal cortex and working memory: Patricia Goldman-Rakic, "Cellular and Circuit Basis of Working Memory in Prefrontal Cortex of Nonhuman Primates," *Progress in Brain Research*, 85, 1990; Daniel Weinberger, "A Connectionist Approach to the Prefrontal Cortex," *Journal of Neuropsychiatry* 5 (1993).

4. Motivation and elite performance: Anders Ericsson, "Expert Performance: Its Structure and Acquisition," *American Psychologist* (Aug. 1994).

5. Asian IQ advantage: Herrnstein and Murray, *The Bell Curve*.

6. IQ and occupation of Asian-Americans: James Flynn, *Asian-American Achievement Beyond IQ* (New Jersey: Lawrence Erlbaum, 1991).

7. The study of delay of gratification in four-year-olds was reported in Yuichi Shoda, Walter Mischel, and Philip K. Peake, "Predicting Adolescent Cognitive and Self-regulatory Competencies From Preschool Delay of Gratification," *Developmental Psychology*, 26, 6 (1990), pp. 978–86.

8. SAT scores of impulsive and self-controlled children: The analysis of SAT data was done by Phil Peake, a psychologist at Smith College.

9. IQ vs. delay as predictors of SAT scores: personal communication from Phil Peake, psychologist at Smith College, who analyzed the SAT data in Walter Mischel's study of delay of gratification.

10. Impulsivity and delinquency: See the discussion in: Jack Block, "On the Relation Between IQ, Impulsivity, and Delinquency," *Journal of Abnormal Psychology* 104 (1995).

11. The worried mother: Timothy A. Brown et al., "Generalized Anxiety Disorder," in David H. Barlow, ed., *Clinical Handbook of Psychological Disorders* (New York: Guilford Press, 1993).

12. Air traffic controllers and anxiety: W. E. Collins et al., "Relationships of Anxiety Scores to Academy and Field Training Performance of Air Traffic Control Specialists," *FAA Office of Aviation Medicine Reports* (May 1989).

13. Anxiety and academic performance: Bettina Seipp, "Anxiety and Academic Performance: A Meta-analysis," *Anxiety Research* 4, 1 (1991).

14. Worriers: Richard Metzger et al., "Worry Changes Decision-making: The Effects of Negative Thoughts on Cognitive Processing," *Journal of Clinical Psychology* (Jan. 1990).

15. Ralph Haber and Richard Alpert, "Test Anxiety," *Journal of Abnormal and Social Psychology* 13 (1958).

16. Anxious students: Theodore Chapin, "The Relationship of Trait Anxiety and Academic Performance to Achievement Anxiety," *Journal of College Student Development* (May 1989).

17. Negative thoughts and test scores: John Hunsley, "Internal Dialogue During Academic Examinations," *Cognitive Therapy and Research* (Dec. 1987).

18. The internists given a gift of candy: Alice Isen et al., "The Influence of Positive Affect on Clinical Problem Solving," *Medical Decision Making* (July–Sept. 1991).

19. Hope and a bad grade: C. R. Snyder et al., "The Will and the Ways: Development and Validation of an Individual-Differences Measure of Hope," *Journal of Personality and Social Psychology* 60, 4 (1991), p. 579.

20. I interviewed C. R. Snyder in *The New York Times* (Dec. 24, 1991).

21. Optimistic swimmers: Martin Seligman, *Learned Optimism* (New York: Knopf, 1991).

22. A realistic vs. naive optimism: see, for example, Carol Whalen et al., "Optimism in Children's Judgments of Health and Environmental Risks," *Health Psychology* 13 (1994).

23. I interviewed Martin Seligman about optimism in *The New York Times* (Feb. 3, 1987).

24. I interviewed Albert Bandura about self-efficacy in *The New York Times* (May 8, 1988).

25. Mihaly Csikszentmihalyi, "Play and Intrinsic Rewards," *Journal of Humanistic Psychology* 15, 3 (1975).

26. Mihaly Csikszentmihalyi, *Flow: The Psychology of Optimal Experience*, 1st ed. (New York: Harper and Row, 1990).

27. "Like a waterfall": *Newsweek* (Feb. 28, 1994).

28. I interviewed Dr. Csikszentmihalyi in *The New York Times* (Mar. 4, 1986).

29. The brain in flow: Jean Hamilton et al., "Intrinsic Enjoyment and Boredom Coping Scales: Validation With Personality, Evoked Potential and Attention Measures," *Personality and Individual Differences* 5, 2 (1984).

30. Cortical activation and fatigue: Ernest Hartmann, *The Functions of Sleep* (New Haven: Yale University Press, 1973).

31. I interviewed Dr. Csikszentmihalyi in *The New York Times* (Mar. 22, 1992).

32. The study of flow and math students: Jeanne Nakamura, "Optimal Experience and the Uses of Talent," in Mihaly Csikszentmihalyi and Isabella Csikszentmihalyi, *Optimal Experience: Psychological Studies of Flow in Consciousness* (Cambridge: Cambridge University Press, 1988).

Chapter 7. The Roots of Empathy

1. Self-awareness and empathy: see, for example, John Mayer and Melissa Kirkpatrick, "Hot Information-Processing Becomes More Accurate With Open Emotional Experience," University of New Hampshire, unpublished manuscript (Oct. 1994); Randy Larsen et al., "Cognitive Operations Associated With Individual Differences in Affect Intensity," *Journal of Personality and Social Psychology* 53 (1987).

2. Robert Rosenthal et al., "The PONS Test: Measuring Sensitivity to Nonverbal Cues," in P. McReynolds, ed., *Advances in Psychological Assessment* (San Francisco: Jossey-Bass, 1977).

3. Stephen Nowicki and Marshall Duke, "A Measure of Nonverbal Social Processing Ability in Children Between the Ages of 6 and 10," paper presented at the American Psychological Society meeting (1989).

4. The mothers who acted as researchers were trained by Marian Radke-Yarrow and Carolyn Zahn-Waxler at the Laboratory of Developmental Psychology, National Institute of Mental Health.

5. I wrote about empathy, its developmental roots, and its neurology in *The New York Times* (Mar. 28, 1989).

6. Instilling empathy in children: Marian Radke-Yarrow and Carolyn Zahn-Waxler, "Roots, Motives and Patterns in Children's Prosocial Behavior," in Ervin Staub et al., eds., *Development and Maintenance of Prosocial Behavior* (New York: Plenum, 1984).

7. Daniel Stern, *The Interpersonal World of the Infant* (New York: Basic Books, 1987), p. 30.

8. Stern, op. cit.

9. The depressed infants are described in Jeffrey Pickens and Tiffany Field, "Facial Expressivity in Infants of Depressed Mothers," *Developmental Psychology* 29, 6 (1993).

10. The study of violent rapists' childhoods was done by Robert Prentky, a psychologist in Philadelphia.

11. Empathy in borderline patients: Lee C. Park et al., "Giftedness and Psychological Abuse in Borderline Personality Disorder: Their Relevance to Genesis and Treatment," *Journal of Personality Disorders* 6 (1992).

12. Leslie Brothers, "A Biological Perspective on Empathy," *American Journal of Psychiatry* 146, 1 (1989).

13. Brothers, "A Biological Perspective," p. 16.

14. Physiology of empathy: Robert Levenson and Anna Ruef, "Empathy: A Physiological Substrate," *Journal of Personality and Social Psychology* 63, 2 (1992).

15. Martin L. Hoffman, "Empathy, Social Cognition, and Moral Action," in W. Kurtines and J. Gerwitz, eds., *Moral Behavior and Development: Advances in Theory, Research, and Applications* (New York: John Wiley and Sons, 1984).

16. Studies of the link between empathy and ethics are in Hoffman, "Empathy, Social Cognition, and Moral Action."

17. I wrote about the emotional cycle that culminates in sex crimes in *The New York Times* (Apr. 14, 1992). The source is William Pithers, a psychologist with the Vermont Department of Corrections.

18. The nature of psychopathy is described in more detail in an article I wrote in *The New York Times* on July 7, 1987. Much of what I write here comes from the work of Robert Hare, a psychologist at the University of British Columbia, an expert on psychopaths.

19. Leon Bing, *Do or Die* (New York: HarperCollins, 1991).

20. Wife batterers: Neil S. Jacobson et al., "Affect, Verbal Content, and Psychophysiology in the Arguments of Couples With a Violent Husband," *Journal of Clinical and Consulting Psychology* (July 1994).

21. Psychopaths have no fear—the effect is seen as criminal psychopaths are about to receive a shock: One of the more recent replications of the effect is Christopher Patrick et al., "Emotion in the Criminal Psychopath: Fear Image Processing," *Journal of Abnormal Psychology* 103 (1994).

Chapter 8. The Social Arts

1. The exchange between Jay and Len was reported by Judy Dunn and Jane Brown in "Relationships, Talk About Feelings, and the Development of Affect Regulation in Early Childhood," Judy Garber and Kenneth A. Dodge, eds., *The Development of Emotion Regulation and Dysregulation* (Cambridge: Cambridge University Press, 1991). The dramatic flourishes are my own.

2. The display rules are in Paul Ekman and Wallace Friesen, *Unmasking the Face* (Englewood Cliffs, NJ: Prentice Hall, 1975).

3. Monks in the heat of battle: the story is told by David Busch in "Culture Cul-de-Sac," *Arizona State University Research* (Spring/Summer 1994).

4. The study of mood transfer was reported by Ellen Sullins in the April 1991 issue of the *Personality and Social Psychology Bulletin*.

5. The studies of mood transmission and synchrony are by Frank Bernieri, a psychologist at Oregon State University; I wrote about his work in *The New York Times*. Much

of his research is reported in Bernieri and Robert Rosenthal, "Interpersonal Coordination, Behavior Matching, and Interpersonal Synchrony," in Robert Feldman and Bernard Rime, eds., *Fundamentals of Nonverbal Behavior* (Cambridge: Cambridge University Press, 1991).

6. The entrainment theory is proposed by Bernieri and Rosenthal, *Fundamentals of Nonverbal Behavior.*

7. Thomas Hatch, "Social Intelligence in Young Children," paper delivered at the annual meeting of the American Psychological Association (1990).

8. Social chameleons: Mark Snyder, "Impression Management: The Self in Social Interaction," in L. S. Wrightsman and K. Deaux, *Social Psychology in the '80s* (Monterey, CA: Brooks/Cole, 1981).

9. E. Lakin Phillips, *The Social Skills Basis of Psychopathology* (New York: Grune and Stratton, 1978), p. 140.

10. Nonverbal learning disorders: Stephen Nowicki and Marshall Duke, *Helping the Child Who Doesn't Fit In* (Atlanta: Peachtree Publishers, 1992). See also Byron Rourke, *Nonverbal Learning Disabilities* (New York: Guilford Press, 1989).

11. Nowicki and Duke, *Helping the Child Who Doesn't Fit In.*

12. This vignette, and the review of research on entering a group, is from Martha Putallaz and Aviva Wasserman, "Children's Entry Behavior," in Steven Asher and John Coie, eds., *Peer Rejection in Childhood* (New York: Cambridge University Press, 1990).

13. Putallaz and Wasserman, "Children's Entry Behavior."

14. Hatch, "Social Intelligence in Young Children."

15. Terry Dobson's tale of the Japanese drunk and the old man is used by permission of Dobson's estate. It is also retold by Ram Dass and Paul Gorman, *How Can I Help?* (New York: Alfred A. Knopf, 1985), pp. 167–71.

PART THREE: EMOTIONAL INTELLIGENCE APPLIED

Chapter 9. Intimate Enemies

1. There are many ways to calculate the divorce rate, and the statistical means used will determine the outcome. Some methods show the divorce rate peaking at around 50 percent and then dipping a bit. When divorces are calculated by the total number in a given year, the rate appears to have peaked in the 1980s. But the statistics I cite here calculate not the number of divorces that occur in a given year, but rather the odds that a couple marrying in a given year will eventually have their marriage end in divorce. That statistic shows a climbing rate of divorce over the last century. For more detail: John Gottman, *What Predicts Divorce: The Relationship Between Marital Processes and Marital Outcomes* (Hillsdale, NJ: Lawrence Erlbaum Associates, Inc., 1993).

2. The separate worlds of boys and girls: Eleanor Maccoby and C. N. Jacklin, "Gender Segregation in Childhood," in H. Reese, ed., *Advances in Child Development and Behavior* (New York: Academic Press, 1987).

3. Same-sex playmates: John Gottman, "Same and Cross Sex Friendship in Young Children," in J. Gottman and J. Parker, eds., *Conversation of Friends* (New York: Cambridge University Press, 1986).

4. This and the following summary of sex differences in socialization of emotions are based on the excellent review in Leslie R. Brody and Judith A. Hall, "Gender and Emotion," in Michael Lewis and Jeannette Haviland, eds., *Handbook of Emotions* (New York: Guilford Press, 1993).

5. Brody and Hall, "Gender and Emotion," p. 456.

6. Girls and the arts of aggression: Robert B. Cairns and Beverley D. Cairns, *Lifelines and Risks* (New York: Cambridge University Press, 1994).

7. Brody and Hall, "Gender and Emotion," p. 454.

8. The findings about gender differences in emotion are reviewed in Brody and Hall, "Gender and Emotion."

9. The importance of good communication for women was reported in Mark H. Davis and H. Alan Oathout, "Maintenance of Satisfaction in Romantic Relationships: Empathy and Relational Competence," *Journal of Personality and Social Psychology* 53, 2 (1987), pp. 397–410.

10. The study of husbands' and wives' complaints: Robert J. Sternberg, "Triangulating Love," in Robert Sternberg and Michael Barnes, eds., *The Psychology of Love* (New Haven: Yale University Press, 1988).

11. Reading sad faces: The research is by Dr. Ruben C. Gur at the University of Pennsylvania School of Medicine.

12. The exchange between Fred and Ingrid is from Gottman, *What Predicts Divorce*, p. 84.

13. The marital research by John Gottman and colleagues at the University of Washington is described in more detail in two books: John Gottman, *Why Marriages Succeed or Fail* (New York: Simon and Schuster, 1994), and *What Predicts Divorce*.

14. Stonewalling: Gottman, *What Predicts Divorce*.

15. Poisonous thoughts: Aaron Beck, *Love Is Never Enough* (New York: Harper and Row, 1988), pp. 145–46.

16. Thoughts in troubled marriages: Gottman, *What Predicts Divorce*.

17. The distorted thinking of violent husbands is described in Amy Holtzworth-Munroe and Glenn Hutchinson, "Attributing Negative Intent to Wife Behavior: The Attributions of Maritally Violent Versus Nonviolent Men," *Journal of Abnormal Psychology* 102, 2 (1993), pp. 206–11. The suspiciousness of sexually aggressive men: Neil Malamuth and Lisa Brown, "Sexually Aggressive Men's Perceptions of Women's Communications," *Journal of Personality and Social Psychology* 67 (1994).

18. Battering husbands: There are three kinds of husbands who become violent: those who rarely do, those who do so impulsively when they get angered, and those who do so in a cool, calculated manner. Therapy seems helpful only with the first two kinds. See Neil Jacobson et al., *Clinical Handbook of Marital Therapy* (New York: Guilford Press, 1994).

19. Flooding: Gottman, *What Predicts Divorce*.

20. Husbands dislike squabbles: Robert Levenson et al., "The Influence of Age and Gender on Affect, Physiology, and Their Interrelations: A Study of Long-term Marriages," *Journal of Personality and Social Psychology* 67 (1994).

21. Flooding in husbands: Gottman, *What Predicts Divorce*.

22. Men stonewall, women criticize: Gottman, *What Predicts Divorce*.

23. "Wife Charged with Shooting Husband Over Football on TV," *The New York Times* (Nov. 3, 1993).

24. Productive marital fights: Gottman, *What Predicts Divorce*.

25. Lack of repair abilities in couples: Gottman, *What Predicts Divorce*.

26. The four steps that lead to "good fights" are from Gottman, *Why Marriages Succeed or Fail*.

27. Monitoring pulse rate: Gottman, Ibid.

28. Catching automatic thoughts: Beck, *Love Is Never Enough*.

29. Mirroring: Harville Hendrix, *Getting the Love You Want* (New York: Henry Holt, 1988).

Chapter 10. Managing With Heart

1. The crash of the intimidating pilot: Carl Lavin, "When Moods Affect Safety: Communications in a Cockpit Mean a Lot a Few Miles Up," *The New York Times* (June 26, 1994).

2. The survey of 250 executives: Michael Maccoby, "The Corporate Climber Has to Find His Heart," *Fortune* (Dec. 1976).

3. Zuboff: in conversation, June 1994. For the impact of information technologies, see her book *In the Age of the Smart Machine* (New York: Basic Books, 1991).

4. The story of the sarcastic vice president was told to me by Hendrie Weisinger, a psychologist at the UCLA Graduate School of Business. His book is *The Critical Edge: How to Criticize Up and Down the Organization and Make It Pay Off* (Boston: Little, Brown, 1989).

5. The survey of times managers blew up was done by Robert Baron, a psychologist at Rensselaer Polytechnic Institute, whom I interviewed for *The New York Times* (Sept. 11, 1990).

6. Criticism as a cause of conflict: Robert Baron, "Countering the Effects of Destructive Criticism: The Relative Efficacy of Four Interventions," *Journal of Applied Psychology* 75, 3 (1990).

7. Specific and vague criticism: Harry Levinson, "Feedback to Subordinates" *Addendum to the Levinson Letter*, Levinson Institute, Waltham, MA (1992).

8. Changing face of workforce: A survey of 645 national companies by Towers Perrin management consultants in Manhattan, reported in *The New York Times* (Aug. 26, 1990).

9. The roots of hatred: Vamik Volkan, *The Need to Have Enemies and Allies* (Northvale, NJ: Jason Aronson, 1988).

10. Thomas Pettigrew: I interviewed Pettigrew in *The New York Times* (May 12, 1987).

11. Stereotypes and subtle bias: Samuel Gaertner and John Davidio, *Prejudice, Discrimination, and Racism* (New York: Academic Press, 1987).

12. Subtle bias: Gaertner and Davidio, *Prejudice, Discrimination, and Racism*.

13. Relman: quoted in Howard Kohn, "Service With a Sneer," *The New York Times Sunday Magazine* (Nov. 11, 1994).

14. IBM: "Responding to a Diverse Work Force," *The New York Times* (Aug. 26, 1990).

15. Power of speaking out: Fletcher Blanchard, "Reducing the Expression of Racial Prejudice," *Psychological Science* (vol. 2, 1991).

16. Stereotypes break down: Gaertner and Davidio, *Prejudice, Discrimination, and Racism.*

17. Teams: Peter Drucker, "The Age of Social Transformation," *The Atlantic Monthly* (Nov. 1994).

18. The concept of group intelligence is set forth in Wendy Williams and Robert Sternberg, "Group Intelligence: Why Some Groups Are Better Than Others," *Intelligence* (1988).

19. The study of the stars at Bell Labs was reported in Robert Kelley and Janet Caplan, "How Bell Labs Creates Star Performers," *Harvard Business Review* (July–Aug. 1993).

20. The usefulness of informal networks is noted by David Krackhardt and Jeffrey R. Hanson, "Informal Networks: The Company Behind the Chart," *Harvard Business Review* (July–Aug. 1993), p. 104.

Chapter 11. Mind and Medicine

1. Immune system as the body's brain: Francisco Varela at the Third Mind and Life meeting, Dharamsala, India (Dec. 1990).

2. Chemical messengers between brain and immune system: see Robert Ader et al., *Psychoneuroimmunology,* 2nd edition (San Diego: Academic Press, 1990).

3. Contact between nerves and immune cells: David Felten et al., "Noradrenergic Sympathetic Innervation of Lymphoid Tissue," *Journal of Immunology* 135 (1985).

4. Hormones and immune function: B. S. Rabin et al., "Bidirectional Interaction Between the Central Nervous System and the Immune System," *Critical Reviews in Immunology* 9 (4), (1989), pp. 279–312.

5. Connections between brain and immune system: see, for example, Steven B. Maier et al., "Psychoneuroimmunology," *American Psychologist* (Dec. 1994).

6. Toxic emotions: Howard Friedman and S. Boothby-Kewley, "The Disease-Prone Personality: A Meta-Analytic View," *American Psychologist* 42 (1987). This broad analysis of studies used "meta-analysis," in which results from many smaller studies can be combined statistically into one immense study. This allows effects that might not show up in any given study to be detected more easily because of the much larger total number of people being studied.

7. Skeptics argue that the emotional picture linked to higher rates of disease is the profile of the quintessential neurotic—an anxious, depressed, and angry emotional wreck—and that the higher rates of disease they report are due not so much to a medical fact as to a propensity to whine and complain about health problems, exaggerating their seriousness. But Friedman and others argue that the weight of evidence for the emotion-disease link is borne by research in which it is physicians' evaluations of observable signs of illness and medical tests, not patients' complaints, that determine the level of sickness—a more objective basis. Of course, there is the possibility that increased distress is the result of a medical condition, as well as precipitating it; for that reason the most convincing data come from prospective studies in which emotional states are evaluated prior to the onset of disease.

8. Gail Ironson et al., "Effects of Anger on Left Ventricular Ejection Fraction in Coronary Artery Disease," *The American Journal of Cardiology* 70 1992. Pumping efficiency, sometimes referred to as the "ejection fraction," quantifies the heart's ability to pump blood out of the left ventricle into the arteries; it measures the percentage of blood pumped out of the ventricles with each beat of the heart. In heart disease the drop in pumping efficiency means a weakening of the heart muscle.

9. Of the dozen or so studies of hostility and death from heart disease, some have failed to find a link. But that failure may be due to differences in method, such as using a poor measure of hostility, and to the relative subtlety of the effect. For instance, the greatest number of deaths from the hostility effect seem to occur in midlife. If a study fails to track down the causes of death for people during this period, it misses the effect.

10. Hostility and heart disease: Redford Williams, *The Trusting Heart* (New York: Times Books/Random House, 1989).

11. Peter Kaufman: I interviewed Dr. Kaufman in *The New York Times* (Sept. 1, 1992).

12. Stanford study of anger and second heart attacks: Carl Thoreson, presented at the International Congress of Behavioral Medicine, Uppsala, Sweden (July 1990).

13. Lynda H. Powell, Emotional Arousal as a Predictor of Long-Term Mortality and Morbidity in Post M.I. Men," *Circulation,* vol. 82, no. 4, Supplement III, Oct. 1990.

14. Murray A. Mittleman, "Triggering of Myocardial Infarction Onset by Episodes of Anger," *Circulation,* vol. 89, no. 2 (1994).

15. Suppressing anger raises blood pressure: Robert Levenson, "Can We Control Our Emotions, and How Does Such Control Change an Emotional Episode?" in Richard Davidson and Paul Ekman, eds., *Fundamental Questions About Emotions* (New York: Oxford University Press, 1995).

16. The angry personal style: I wrote about Redford Williams's research on anger and the heart in *The New York Times Good Health Magazine* (Apr. 16, 1989).

17. A 44 percent reduction in second heart attacks: Thoreson, op. cit.

18. Dr. Williams's program for anger control: Williams, *The Trusting Heart.*

19. The worried woman: Timothy Brown et al., "Generalized Anxiety Disorder," in David H. Barlow, ed., *Clinical Handbook of Psychological Disorders* (New York: Guilford Press, 1993).

20. Stress and metastasis: Bruce McEwen and Eliot Stellar, "Stress and the Individual: Mechanisms Leading to Disease," *Archives of Internal Medicine* 153 (Sept. 27, 1993). The study they are describing is M. Robertson and J. Ritz, "Biology and Clinical Relevance of Human Natural Killer Cells," *Blood* 76 (1990).

21. There may be multiple reasons why people under stress are more vulnerable to sickness, apart from biological pathways. One might be that the ways people try to soothe their anxiety—for example, smoking, drinking, or bingeing on fatty foods—are in themselves unhealthy. Still another is that constant worry and anxiety can make people lose sleep or forget to comply with medical regimens—such as taking medications—and so prolong illnesses they already have. Most likely, all of these work in tandem to link stress and disease.

22. Stress weakens the immune system: For instance, in the study of medical students facing exam stress, the students had not only a lowered immune control of the herpes virus, but also a decline in the ability of their white blood cells to kill infected cells, as well as an increase in levels of a chemical associated with suppression of immune

abilities in lymphocytes, the white blood cells central to the immune response. See Ronald Glaser and Janice Kiecolt-Glaser, "Stress-Associated Depression in Cellular Immunity," *Brain, Behavior, and Immunity* 1 (1987). But in most such studies showing a weakening of immune defenses with stress, it has not been clear that these levels were low enough to lead to medical risk.

23. Stress and colds: Sheldon Cohen et al., "Psychological Stress and Susceptibility to the Common Cold," *New England Journal of Medicine* 325 (1991).

24. Daily upsets and infection: Arthur Stone et al., "Secretory IgA as a Measure of Immunocompetence," *Journal of Human Stress* 13 (1987). In another study, 246 husbands, wives, and children kept daily logs of stresses in their family's life over the course of the flu season. Those who had the most family crises also had the highest rate of flu, as measured both by days with fever and flu antibody levels. See R. D. Clover et al., "Family Functioning and Stress as Predictors of Influenza B Infection," *Journal of Family Practice* 28 (May 1989).

25. Herpes virus flare-up and stress: a series of studies by Ronald Glaser and Janice Kiecolt-Glaser—e.g., "Psychological Influences on Immunity," *American Psychologist* 43 (1988). The relationship between stress and herpes activity is so strong that it has been demonstrated in a study of only ten patients, using the actual breaking-out of herpes sores as a measure; the more anxiety, hassles, and stress reported by the patients, the more likely they were to have herpes outbreaks in the following weeks; placid periods in their lives led to dormancy of the herpes. See H. E. Schmidt et al., "Stress as a Precipitating Factor in Subjects With Recurrent Herpes Labialis," *Journal of Family Practice,* 20 (1985).

26. Anxiety in women and heart disease: Carl Thoreson, presented at the International Congress of Behavioral Medicine, Uppsala, Sweden (July 1990). Anxiety may also play a role in making some men more vulnerable to heart disease. In a study at the University of Alabama medical school, 1,123 men and women between the ages of forty-five and seventy-seven were assessed on their emotional profiles. Those men most prone to anxiety and worry in middle age were far more likely than others to have hypertension when tracked down twenty years later. See Abraham Markowitz et al., *Journal of the American Medical Association* (Nov. 14, 1993).

27. Stress and colorectal cancer: Joseph C. Courtney et al., "Stressful Life Events and the Risk of Colorectal Cancer," *Epidemiology* (Sept. 1993), 4(5).

28. Relaxation to counter stress-based symptoms: See, for example, Daniel Goleman and Joel Gurin, *Mind Body Medicine* (New York: Consumer Reports Books/St. Martin's Press, 1993).

29. Depression and disease: see, e.g., Seymour Reichlin, "Neuroendocrine-Immune Interactions," *New England Journal of Medicine* (Oct. 21, 1993).

30. Bone marrow transplant: cited in James Strain, "Cost Offset From a Psychiatric Consultation-Liaison Intervention With Elderly Hip Fracture Patients," *American Journal of Psychiatry* 148 (1991).

31. Howard Burton et al., "The Relationship of Depression to Survival in Chronic Renal Failure," *Psychosomatic Medicine* (March 1986).

32. Hopelessness and death from heart disease: Robert Anda et al., "Depressed Affect, Hopelessness, and the Risk of Ischemic Heart Disease in a Cohort of U.S. Adults," *Epidemiology* (July 1993).

33. Depression and heart attack: Nancy Frasure-Smith et al., "Depression Following Myocardial Infarction," *Journal of the American Medical Association* (Oct. 20, 1993).

34. Depression in multiple illness: Dr. Michael von Korff, the University of Washington psychiatrist who did the study, pointed out to me that with such patients, who face tremendous challenges just in living from day to day, "If you treat a patient's depression, you see improvements over and above any changes in their medical condition. If you're depressed, your symptoms seem worse to you. Having a chronic physical disease is a major adaptive challenge. If you're depressed, you're less able to learn to take care of your illness. Even with physical impairment, if you're motivated and have energy and feelings of self-worth—all of which are at risk in depression—then people can adapt remarkably even to severe impairments."

35. Optimism and bypass surgery: Chris Peterson et al., *Learned Helplessness: A Theory for the Age of Personal Control* (New York: Oxford University Press, 1993).

36. Spinal injury and hope: Timothy Elliott et al., "Negotiating Reality After Physical Loss: Hope, Depression, and Disability," *Journal of Personality and Social Psychology* 61, 4 (1991).

37. Medical risk of social isolation: James House et al., "Social Relationships and Health," *Science* (July 29, 1988). But also see a mixed finding: Carol Smith et al., "Meta-Analysis of the Associations Between Social Support and Health Outcomes," *Journal of Behavioral Medicine* (1994).

38. Isolation and mortality risk: Other studies suggest a biological mechanism at work. These findings, cited in House, "Social Relationships and Health," have found that the simple presence of another person can reduce anxiety and lessen physiological distress in people in intensive-care units. The comforting effect of another person's presence has been found to lower not just heart rate and blood pressure, but also the secretion of fatty acids that can block arteries. One theory put forward to explain the healing effects of social contact suggests a brain mechanism at work. This theory points to animal data showing a calming effect on the posterior hypothalamic zone, an area of the limbic system with rich connections to the amygdala. The comforting presence of another person, this view holds, inhibits limbic activity, lowering the rate of secretion of acetylcholine, cortisol, and catecholamines, all neurochemicals that trigger more rapid breathing, a quickened heartbeat, and other physiological signs of stress.

39. Strain, "Cost Offset."

40. Heart attack survival and emotional support: Lisa Berkman et al., "Emotional Support and Survival After Myocardial Infarction, A Prospective Population Based Study of the Elderly," *Annals of Internal Medicine* (Dec. 15, 1992).

41. The Swedish study: Annika Rosengren et al., "Stressful Life Events, Social Support, and Mortality in Men Born in 1933," *British Medical Journal* (Oct. 19, 1993).

42. Marital arguments and immune system: Janice Kiecolt-Glaser et al., "Marital Quality, Marital Disruption, and Immune Function," *Psychosomatic Medicine* 49 (1987).

43. I interviewed John Cacioppo for *The New York Times* (Dec. 15, 1992).

44. Talking about troubling thoughts: James Pennebaker, "Putting Stress Into Words: Health, Linguistic and Therapeutic Implications," paper presented at the American Psychological Association meeting, Washington, DC (1992).

45. Psychotherapy and medical improvements: Lester Luborsky et al., "Is Psychotherapy

Good for Your Health?" paper presented at the American Psychological Association meeting, Washington, DC (1993).

46. Cancer support groups: David Spiegel et al., "Effect of Psychosocial Treatment on Survival of Patients with Metastatic Breast Cancer," *Lancet* No. 8668, ii (1989).

47. Patients' questions: The finding was cited by Dr. Steven Cohen-Cole, a psychiatrist at Emory University, when I interviewed him in *The New York Times* (Nov. 13, 1991).

48. Full information: For example, the Planetree program at Pacific Presbyterian Hospital in San Francisco will do searches of medical and lay research on any medical topic for anyone who requests it.

49. Making patients effective: One program has been developed by Dr. Mack Lipkin, Jr., at New York University Medical School.

50. Emotional preparation for surgery: I wrote about this in *The New York Times* (Dec. 10, 1987).

51. Family care in the hospital: Again, Planetree is a model, as are the Ronald McDonald houses that allow parents to stay next door to hospitals where their children are patients.

52. Mindfulness and medicine: See Jon Kabat-Zinn, *Full Catastrophe Living* (New York: Delacorte, 1991).

53. Program for reversing heart disease: See Dean Ornish, *Dr. Dean Ornish's Program for Reversing Heart Disease* (New York: Ballantine, 1991).

54. Relationship-centered medicine: *Health Professions Education and Relationship-Centered Care.* Report of the Pew-Fetzer Task Force on Advancing Psychosocial Health Education, Pew Health Professions Commission and Fetzer Institute at The Center of Health Professions, University of California at San Francisco, San Francisco (Aug. 1994).

55. Left the hospital early: Strain, "Cost Offset."

56. Unethical not to treat depression in heart disease patients: Redford Williams and Margaret Chesney, "Psychosocial Factors and Prognosis in Established Coronary Heart Disease," *Journal of the American Medical Association* (Oct. 20, 1993).

57. An open letter to a surgeon: A. Stanley Kramer, "A Prescription for Healing," *Newsweek* (June 7, 1993).

PART FOUR: WINDOWS OF OPPORTUNITY

Chapter 12. The Family Crucible

1. Leslie and the video game: Beverly Wilson and John Gottman, "Marital Conflict and Parenting: The Role of Negativity in Families," in M. H. Bornstein, ed., *Handbook of Parenting,* vol. 4 (Hillsdale, NJ: Lawrence Erlbaum, 1994).

2. The research on emotions in the family was an extension of John Gottman's marital studies reviewed in Chapter 9. See Carole Hooven, Lynn Katz, and John Gottman, "The Family as a Meta-emotion Culture," *Cognition and Emotion* (Spring 1994).

3. The benefits for children of having emotionally adept parents: Hooven, Katz, and Gottman, "The Family as a Meta-emotion Culture."

4. Optimistic infants: T. Berry Brazelton, in the preface to *Heart Start: The Emotional Foundations of School Readiness* (Arlington, VA: National Center for Clinical Infant Programs, 1992).

5. Emotional predictors of school success: *Heart Start.*

6. Elements of school readiness: *Heart Start*, p. 7.

7. Infants and mothers: *Heart Start*, p. 9.

8. Damage from neglect: M. Erickson et al., "The Relationship Between Quality of Attachment and Behavior Problems in Preschool in a High-Risk Sample," in I. Bether-ton and E. Waters, eds., *Monographs of the Society of Research in Child Development* 50, series no. 209.

9. Lasting lessons of first four years: *Heart Start*, p. 13.

10. The follow-up of aggressive children: L. R. Huesman, Leonard Eron, and Patty Warnicke-Yarmel, "Intellectual Function and Aggression," *The Journal of Personality and Social Psychology* (Jan. 1987). Similar findings were reported by Alexander Thomas and Stella Chess, in the September 1988 issue of *Child Development,* in their study of seventy-five children who were assessed at regular intervals since 1956, when they were between seven and twelve years old. Alexander Thomas et al., "Longitudinal Study of Negative Emotional States and Adjustments From Early Child-hood Through Adolescence," *Child Development* 59 (1988). A decade later the children who parents and teachers had said were the most aggressive in grade school were having the most emotional turmoil in late adolescence. These were children (about twice as many boys as girls) who not only continually picked fights, but who also were belittling or openly hostile toward other children, and even toward their families and teachers. Their hostility was unchanged over the years; as adolescents they were having trouble getting along with classmates and with their families, and were in trouble at school. And, when contacted as adults, their difficulties ranged from tangles with the law to anxiety problems and depression.

11. Lack of empathy in abused children: The day-care observations and findings are reported in Mary Main and Carol George, "Responses of Abused and Disadvantaged Toddlers to Distress in Agemates: A Study in the Day-Care Setting," *Developmental Psychology* 21, 3 (1985). The findings have been repeated with preschoolers as well: Bonnie Klimes-Dougan and Janet Kistner, "Physically Abused Preschoolers' Responses to Peers' Distress," *Developmental Psychology* 26 (1990).

12. Difficulties of abused children: Robert Emery, "Family Violence," *American Psychologist* (Feb. 1989).

13. Abuse over generations: Whether abused children grow up to be abusing parents is a point of scientific debate. See, for example, Cathy Spatz Widom, "Child Abuse, Neglect and Adult Behavior," *American Journal of Orthopsychiatry* (July 1989).

Chapter 13. Trauma and Emotional Relearning

1. I wrote about the lasting trauma of the killings at Cleveland Elementary School in *The New York Times* "Education Life" section (Jan. 7, 1990).

2. The examples of PTSD in crime victims were offered by Dr. Shelly Niederbach, a psychologist at the Victims' Counseling Service, Brooklyn.

3. The Vietnam memory is from M. Davis, "Analysis of Aversive Memories Using the Fear-Potentiated Startle Paradigm," in N. Butters and L. R Squire, eds., *The Neuropsychology of Memory* (New York: Guilford Press, 1992).

4. LeDoux makes the scientific case for these memories being especially enduring in "Indelibility of Subcortical Emotional Memories," *Journal of Cognitive Neuroscience* (1989), vol. 1, 238–43.

5. I interviewed Dr. Charney in *The New York Times* (June 12, 1990).

6. The experiments with paired laboratory animals were described to me by Dr. John Krystal, and have been repeated at several scientific laboratories. The major studies were done by Dr. Jay Weiss at Duke University.

7. The best account of the brain changes underlying PTSD, and the role of the amygdala in them, is in Dennis Charney et al., "Psychobiologic Mechanisms of Posttraumatic Stress Disorder," *Archives of General Psychiatry* 50 (April 1993), 294–305.

8. Some of the evidence for trauma-induced changes in this brain network comes from experiments in which Vietnam vets with PTSD were injected with yohimbine, a drug used on the tips of arrows by South American Indians to render their prey helpless. In tiny doses yohimbine blocks the action of a specific receptor (the point on a neuron that receives a neurotransmitter) that ordinarily acts as a brake on the catecholamines. Yohimbine takes the brakes off, keeping these receptors from sensing the secretion of catecholamines; the result is increasing catecholamine levels. With the neural brakes on anxiety disarmed by the drug injections, the yohimbine triggered panic in 9 of 15 PTSD patients, and lifelike flashbacks in 6. One vet had a hallucination of a helicopter being shot down in a trail of smoke and a bright flash; another saw the explosion by a land mine of a Jeep with his buddies in it—the same scene that had haunted his nightmares and appeared as flashbacks for more than 20 years. The yohimbine study was conducted by Dr. John Krystal, director of the Laboratory of Clinical Psychopharmacology at the National Center for PTSD at the West Haven, Conn., VA Hospital.

9. Fewer alpha-2 receptors in men with PTSD: see Charney, "Psychobiologic Mechanisms."

10. The brain, trying to lower the rate of CRF secretion, compensates by decreasing the number of receptors that release it. One telltale sign that this is what happens in people with PTSD comes from a study in which eight patients being treated for the problem were injected with CRF. Ordinarily, an injection of CRF triggers a flood of ACTH, the hormone that streams through the body to trigger catecholamines. But in the PTSD patients, unlike a comparison group of people without PTSD, there was no discernible change in levels of ACTH—a sign that their brains had cut back on CRF receptors because they already were overloaded with the stress hormone. The research was described to me by Charles Nemeroff, a Duke University psychiatrist.

11. I interviewed Dr. Nemeroff in *The New York Times* (June 12, 1990).

12. Something similar seems to occur in PTSD: For instance, in one experiment Vietnam vets with a PTSD diagnosis were shown a specially edited 15-minute film of graphic combat scenes from the movie *Platoon*. In one group, the vets were injected with naloxone, a substance that blocks endorphins; after watching the movie, these vets showed no change in their sensitivity to pain. But in the group without the endorphin blocker, the men's pain sensitivity decreased 30 percent, indicating an increase in endorphin secretion. The same scene had no such effect on veterans who did not have PTSD, suggesting that in the PTSD victims the nerve pathways that regulate endorphins were overly sensitive or hyperactive—an effect that became apparent

only when they were reexposed to something reminiscent of the original trauma. In this sequence the amygdala first evaluates the emotional importance of what we see. The study was done by Dr. Roger Pitman, a Harvard psychiatrist. As with other symptoms of PTSD, this brain change is not only learned under duress, but can be triggered once again if there is something reminiscent of the original terrible event. For example, Pitman found that when laboratory rats were shocked in a cage, they developed the same endorphin-based analgesia found in the Vietnam vets shown *Platoon*. Weeks later, when the rats were put into the cages where they had been shocked—but without any current being turned on—they once again became insensitive to pain, as they originally had been when shocked. See Roger Pitman, "Naloxone-Reversible Analgesic Response to Combat-Related Stimuli in Posttraumatic Stress Disorder," *Archives of General Medicine* (June 1990). See also Hillel Glover, "Emotional Numbing: A Possible Endorphin-Mediated Phenomenon Associated with Post-Traumatic Stress Disorders and Other Allied Psychopathologic States," *Journal of Traumatic Stress* 5, 4 (1992).

13. The brain evidence reviewed in this section is based on Dennis Charney's excellent article, "Psychobiologic Mechanisms."

14. Charney, "Psychobiologic Mechanisms," 300.

15. Role of prefrontal cortex in unlearning fear: In Richard Davidson's study, volunteers had their sweat response measured (a barometer of anxiety) while they heard a tone followed by a loud, obnoxious noise. The loud noise triggered a rise in sweat. After a time, the tone alone was enough to trigger the same rise, showing that the volunteers had learned an aversion to the tone. As they continued to hear the tone without the obnoxious noise, the learned aversion faded away—the tone sounded without any increase in sweat. The more active the volunteers' left prefrontal cortex, the more quickly they lost the learned fear.

In another experiment showing the prefrontal lobes' role in getting over a fear, lab rats—as is so often the case in these studies—learned to fear a tone paired with an electric shock. The rats then had what amounts to a lobotomy, a surgical lesion in their brain that cut off the prefrontal lobes from the amygdala. For the next several days the rats heard the tone without getting an electric shock. Slowly, over a period of days, rats who have once learned to fear a tone will gradually lose their fear. But for the rats with the disconnected prefrontal lobes, it took nearly twice as long to unlearn the fear—suggesting a crucial role for the prefrontal lobes in managing fear and, more generally, in mastering emotional lessons. This experiment was done by Maria Morgan, a graduate student of Joseph LeDoux's at the Center for Neural Science, New York University.

16. Recovery from PTSD: I was told about this study by Rachel Yehuda, a neurochemist and director of the Traumatic Stress Studies Program at the Mt. Sinai School of Medicine in Manhattan. I reported on the results in *The New York Times* (Oct. 6, 1992).

17. Childhood trauma: Lenore Terr, *Too Scared to Cry* (New York: HarperCollins, 1990).

18. Pathway to recovery from trauma: Judith Lewis Herman, *Trauma and Recovery* (New York: Basic Books, 1992).

19. "Dosing" of trauma: Mardi Horowitz, *Stress Response Syndromes* (Northvale, NJ: Jason Aronson, 1986).

20. Another level at which relearning goes on, at least for adults, is philosophical. The eternal question of the victim—"Why me?"—needs to be addressed. Being the victim of trauma shatters a person's faith that the world is a place that can be trusted, and that what happens to us in life is just—that is, that we can have control over our destiny by

living a righteous life. The answers to the victim's conundrum, of course, need not be philosophical or religious; the task is to rebuild a system of belief or faith that allows living once again as though the world and the people in it can be trusted.

21. That the original fear persists, even if subdued, has been shown in studies where lab rats were conditioned to fear a sound, such as a bell, when it was paired with an electric shock. Afterward, when they heard the bell they reacted with fear, even though no shock accompanied it. Gradually, over the course of a year (a very long time for a rat—about a third of its life), the rats lost their fearfulness of the bell. But the fear was restored in full force when the sound of the bell was once again paired with a shock. The fear came back in a single instant—but took months and months to subside. The parallel in humans, of course, is when a traumatic fear from long ago, dormant for years, floods back in full force with some reminder of the original trauma.

22. Luborsky's therapy research is detailed in Lester Luborsky and Paul Crits-Christoph, *Understanding Transference: The CCRT Method* (New York: Basic Books, 1990).

Chapter 14. Temperament Is Not Destiny

1. See, for example, Jerome Kagan et al., "Initial Reactions to Unfamiliarity," *Current Directions in Psychological Science* (Dec. 1992). The fullest description of the biology of temperament is in Kagan, *Galen's Prophecy.*

2. Tom and Ralph, archetypically timid and bold types, are described in Kagan, *Galen's Prophecy,* pp. 155–57.

3. Lifelong problems of the shy child: Iris Bell, "Increased Prevalence of Stress-related Symptoms in Middle-aged Women Who Report Childhood Shyness," *Annals of Behavior Medicine* 16 (1994).

4. The heightened heart rate: Iris R. Bell et al., "Failure of Heart Rate Habituation During Cognitive and Olfactory Laboratory Stressors in Young Adults With Childhood Shyness," *Annals of Behavior Medicine* 16 (1994).

5. Panic in teenagers: Chris Hayward et al., "Pubertal Stage and Panic Attack History in Sixth- and Seventh-grade Girls," *American Journal of Psychiatry* vol. 149(9) (Sept. 1992), pp. 1239–43; Jerold Rosenbaum et al., "Behavioral Inhibition in Childhood: A Risk Factor for Anxiety Disorders," *Harvard Review of Psychiatry* (May 1993).

6. The research on personality and hemispheric differences was done by Dr. Richard Davidson at the University of Wisconsin, and by Dr. Andrew Tomarken, a psychologist at Vanderbilt University: see Andrew Tomarken and Richard Davidson, "Frontal Brain Activation in Repressors and Nonrepressors," *Journal of Abnormal Psychology* 103 (1994).

7. The observations of how mothers can help timid infants become bolder were done with Doreen Arcus. Details are in Kagan, *Galen's Prophecy.*

8. Kagan, *Galen's Prophecy,* pp. 194–95.

9. Growing less shy: Jens Asendorpf, "The Malleability of Behavioral Inhibition: A Study of Individual Developmental Functions," *Developmental Psychology* 30, 6 (1994).

10. Hubel and Wiesel: David H. Hubel, Thorsten Wiesel, and S. Levay, "Plasticity of Ocular Columns in Monkey Striate Cortex," *Philosophical Transactions of the Royal Society of London* 278 (1977).

11. Experience and the rat's brain: The work of Marian Diamond and others is described in Richard Thompson, *The Brain* (San Francisco: W. H. Freeman, 1985).

12. Brain changes in treating obsessive-compulsive disorder: L. R. Baxter et al., "Caudate Glucose Metabolism Rate Changes With Both Drug and Behavior Therapy for Obsessive-Compulsive Disorder," *Archives of General Psychiatry* 49 (1992).

13. Increased activity in prefrontal lobes: L. R. Baxter et al., "Local Cerebral Glucose Metabolic Rates in Obsessive-Compulsive Disorder," *Archives of General Psychiatry* 44 (1987).

14. Prefrontal lobes maturity: Bryan Kolb, "Brain Development, Plasticity, and Behavior," *American Psychologist* 44 (1989).

15. Childhood experience and prefrontal pruning: Richard Davidson, "Asymmetric Brain Function, Affective Style and Psychopathology: The Role of Early Experience and Plasticity," *Development and Psychopathology* vol. 6 (1994), pp. 741–58.

16. Biological attunement and brain growth: Schore, *Affect Regulation*.

17. M. E. Phelps et al., "PET: A Biochemical Image of the Brain at Work," in N. A. Lassen et al., *Brain Work and Mental Activity: Quantitative Studies with Radioactive Tracers* (Copenhagen: Munksgaard, 1991).

PART FIVE: EMOTIONAL LITERACY

Chapter 15. The Cost of Emotional Illiteracy

1. Emotional literacy: I wrote about such courses in *The New York Times* (March 3, 1992).

2. The statistics on teen crime rates are from the Uniform Crime Reports, *Crime in the U.S., 1991,* published by the Department of Justice.

3. Violent crimes in teenagers: In 1990 the juvenile arrest rate for violent crimes climbed to 430 per 100,000, a 27 percent jump over the 1980 rate. Teen arrest rates for forcible rape rose from 10.9 per 100,000 in 1965 to 21.9 per 100,000 in 1990. Teen murder rates more than quadrupled from 1965 to 1990, from 2.8 per 100,000 to 12.1; by 1990 three of four teenage murders were with guns, a 79 percent increase over the decade. Aggravated assault by teenagers jumped by 64 percent from 1980 to 1990. See, e.g., Ruby Takanashi, "The Opportunities of Adolescence," *American Psychologist* (Feb. 1993).

4. In 1950 the suicide rate for those 15 to 24 was 4.5 per 100,000. By 1989 it was three times higher, 13.3. Suicide rates for children 10 to 14 almost tripled between 1968 and 1985. Figures on suicide, homicide victims, and pregnancies are from *Health, 1991,* U.S. Department of Health and Human Services, and Children's Safety Network, *A Data Book of Child and Adolescent Injury* (Washington, DC: National Center for Education in Maternal and Child Health, 1991).

5. Over the three decades since 1960, rates of gonorrhea jumped to a level four times higher among children 10 to 14, and three times higher among those 15 to 19. By 1990, 20 percent of AIDS patients were in their twenties, many having become infected during their teen years. Pressure to have sex early is getting stronger. A survey in the 1990s found that more than a third of younger women say that pressure from peers made them decide to have sex the first time; a generation earlier just 13

percent of women said so. See Ruby Takanashi, "The Opportunities of Adolescence," and Children's Safety Network, *A Data Book of Child and Adolescent Injury.*

6. Heroin and cocaine use for whites rose from 18 per 100,000 in 1970 to a rate of 68 in 1990—about three times higher. But over the same two decades among blacks, the rise was from a 1970 rate of 53 per 100,000 to a staggering 766 in 1990—close to *13 times* the rate 20 years before. Drug use rates are from *Crime in the U.S., 1991,* U.S. Department of Justice.

7. As many as one in five children have psychological difficulties that impair their lives in some way, according to surveys done in the United States, New Zealand, Canada, and Puerto Rico. Anxiety is the most common problem in children under 11, afflicting 10 percent with phobias severe enough to interfere with normal life, another 5 percent with generalized anxiety and constant worry, and another 4 percent with intense anxiety about being separated from their parents. Binge drinking climbs during the teenage years among boys to a rate of about 20 percent by age 20. I reported much of this data on emotional disorders in children in *The New York Times* (Jan. 10, 1989).

8. The national study of children's emotional problems, and comparison with other countries: Thomas Achenbach and Catherine Howell, "Are America's Children's Problems Getting Worse? A 13-Year Comparison," *Journal of the American Academy of Child and Adolescent Psychiatry* (Nov. 1989).

9. The comparison across nations was by Urie Bronfenbrenner, in Michael Lamb and Kathleen Sternberg, *Child Care in Context: Cross-Cultural Perspectives* (Englewood, NJ: Lawrence Erlbaum, 1992).

10. Urie Bronfenbrenner was speaking at a symposium at Cornell University (Sept. 24, 1993).

11. Longitudinal studies of aggressive and delinquent children: see, for example, Alexander Thomas et al., "Longitudinal Study of Negative Emotional States and Adjustments from Early Childhood Through Adolescence," *Child Development,* vol. 59 (Sept. 1988).

12. The bully experiment: John Lochman, "Social-Cognitive Processes of Severely Violent, Moderately Aggressive, and Nonaggressive Boys," *Journal of Clinical and Consulting Psychology,* 1994.

13. The aggressive boys research: Kenneth A. Dodge, "Emotion and Social Information Processing," in J. Garber and K. Dodge, *The Development of Emotion Regulation and Dysregulation* (New York: Cambridge University Press, 1991).

14. Dislike for bullies within hours: J. D. Coie and J. B. Kupersmidt, "A Behavioral Analysis of Emerging Social Status in Boys' Groups," *Child Development* 54 (1983).

15. Up to half of unruly children: See, for example, Dan Offord et al., "Outcome, Prognosis, and Risk in a Longitudinal Follow-up Study," *Journal of the American Academy of Child and Adolescent Psychiatry* 31 (1992).

16. Aggressive children and crime: Richard Tremblay et al., "Predicting Early Onset of Male Antisocial Behavior from Preschool Behavior," *Archives of General Psychiatry* (Sept. 1994).

17. What happens in a child's family before the child reaches school is, of course, crucial in creating a predisposition to aggression. One study, for example, showed that children whose mothers rejected them at age 1, and whose birth was more complicated, were four times as likely as others to commit a violent crime by age 18. Adriane

Raines et al., "Birth Complications Combined with Early Maternal Rejection at Age One Predispose to Violent Crime at Age 18 Years," *Archives of General Psychiatry* (Dec. 1994).

18. While low verbal IQ has appeared to predict delinquency (one study found an eight-point difference in these scores between delinquents and nondelinquents), there is evidence that impulsivity is more directly and powerfully at cause for both the low IQ scores and delinquency. As for the low scores, impulsive children don't pay attention well enough to learn the language and reasoning skills on which verbal IQ scores are based, and so impulsivity lowers those scores. In the Pittsburgh Youth Study, a well-designed longitudinal project where both IQ and impulsivity were assessed in ten- to twelve-year-olds, impulsivity was almost three times more powerful than verbal IQ in predicting delinquency. See the discussion in: Jack Block, "On the Relation Between IQ, Impulsivity, and Delinquency," *Journal of Abnormal Psychology* 104 (1995).

19. "Bad" girls and pregnancy: Marion Underwood and Melinda Albert, "Fourth-Grade Peer Status as a Predictor of Adolescent Pregnancy," paper presented at the meeting of the Society for Research on Child Development, Kansas City, Missouri (Apr. 1989).

20. The trajectory to delinquency: Gerald R. Patterson, "Orderly Change in a Stable World: The Antisocial Trait as Chimera," *Journal of Clinical and Consulting Psychology* 62 (1993).

21. Mind-set of aggression: Ronald Slaby and Nancy Guerra, "Cognitive Mediators of Aggression in Adolescent Offenders," *Developmental Psychology* 24 (1988).

22. The case of Dana: from Laura Mufson et al., *Interpersonal Psychotherapy for Depressed Adolescents* (New York: Guilford Press, 1993).

23. Rising rates of depression worldwide: Cross-National Collaborative Group, "The Changing Rate of Major Depression: Cross-National Comparisons," *Journal of the American Medical Association* (Dec. 2, 1992).

24. Ten times greater chance of depression: Peter Lewinsohn et al., "Age-Cohort Changes in the Lifetime Occurrence of Depression and Other Mental Disorders," *Journal of Abnormal Psychology* 102 (1993).

25. Epidemiology of depression: Patricia Cohen et al., New York Psychiatric Institute, 1988; Peter Lewinsohn et al., "Adolescent Psychopathology: I. Prevalence and Incidence of Depression in High School Students," *Journal of Abnormal Psychology* 102 (1993). See also Mufson et al., *Interpersonal Psychotherapy*. For a review of lower estimates: E. Costello, "Developments in Child Psychiatric Epidemiology," *Journal of the Academy of Child and Adolescent Psychiatry* 28 (1989).

26. Patterns of depression in youth: Maria Kovacs and Leo Bastiaens, "The Psychotherapeutic Management of Major Depressive and Dysthymic Disorders in Childhood and Adolescence: Issues and Prospects," in I. M. Goodyer, ed., *Mood Disorders in Childhood and Adolescence* (New York: Cambridge University Press, 1994).

27. Depression in children: Kovacs, op. cit.

28. I interviewed Maria Kovacs in *The New York Times* (Jan. 11, 1994).

29. Social and emotional lag in depressed children: Maria Kovacs and David Goldston, "Cognitive and Social Development of Depressed Children and Adolescents," *Journal of the American Academy of Child and Adolescent Psychiatry* (May 1991).

30. Helplessness and depression: John Weiss et al., "Control-related Beliefs and Self-reported Depressive Symptoms in Late Childhood," *Journal of Abnormal Psychology* 102 (1993).

31. Pessimism and depression in children: Judy Garber, Vanderbilt University. See, e.g., Ruth Hilsman and Judy Garber, "A Test of the Cognitive Diathesis Model of Depression in Children: Academic Stressors, Attributional Style, Perceived Competence and Control," *Journal of Personality and Social Psychology* 67 (1994); Judith Garber, "Cognitions, Depressive Symptoms, and Development in Adolescents," *Journal of Abnormal Psychology* 102 (1993).

32. Garber, "Cognitions."

33. Garber, "Cognitions."

34. Susan Nolen-Hoeksema et al., "Predictors and Consequences of Childhood Depressive Symptoms: A Five-Year Longitudinal Study," *Journal of Abnormal Psychology* 101 (1992).

35. Depression rate halved: Gregory Clarke, University of Oregon Health Sciences Center, "Prevention of Depression in At-Risk High School Adolescents," paper delivered at the American Academy of Child and Adolescent Psychiatry (Oct. 1993).

36. Garber, "Cognitions."

37. Hilda Bruch, "Hunger and Instinct," *Journal of Nervous and Mental Disease* 149 (1969). Her seminal book, *The Golden Cage: The Enigma of Anorexia Nervosa* (Cambridge, MA: Harvard University Press) was not published until 1978.

38. The study of eating disorders: Gloria R. Leon et al., "Personality and Behavioral Vulnerabilities Associated with Risk Status for Eating Disorders in Adolescent Girls," *Journal of Abnormal Psychology* 102 (1993).

39. The six-year-old who felt fat was a patient of Dr. William Feldman, a pediatrician at the University of Ottawa.

40. Noted by Sifneos, "Affect, Emotional Conflict, and Deficit."

41. The vignette of Ben's rebuff is from Steven Asher and Sonda Gabriel, "The Social World of Peer-Rejected Children," paper presented at the annual meeting of the American Educational Research Association, San Francisco (Mar. 1989).

42. The dropout rate among socially rejected children: Asher and Gabriel, "The Social World of Peer-Rejected Children."

43. The findings on the poor emotional competence of unpopular children are from Kenneth Dodge and Esther Feldman, "Social Cognition and Sociometric Status," in Steven Asher and John Coie, eds., *Peer Rejection in Childhood* (New York: Cambridge University Press, 1990).

44. Emory Cowen et al., "Longterm Follow-up of Early Detected Vulnerable Children," *Journal of Clinical and Consulting Psychology* 41 (1973).

45. Best friends and the rejected: Jeffrey Parker and Steven Asher, "Friendship Adjustment, Group Acceptance and Social Dissatisfaction in Childhood," paper presented at the annual meeting of the American Educational Research Association, Boston (1990).

46. The coaching for socially rejected children: Steven Asher and Gladys Williams, "Helping Children Without Friends in Home and School Contexts," in *Children's Social Development: Information for Parents and Teachers* (Urbana and Champaign: University of Illinois Press, 1987).

47. Similar results: Stephen Nowicki, "A Remediation Procedure for Nonverbal Processing Deficits," unpublished manuscript, Duke University (1989).

48. Two fifths are heavy drinkers: a survey at the University of Massachusetts by Project Pulse, reported in *The Daily Hampshire Gazette* (Nov. 13, 1993).

49. Binge drinking: Figures are from Harvey Wechsler, director of College Alcohol Studies at the Harvard School of Public Health (Aug. 1994).

50. More women drink to get drunk, and risk of rape: report by the Columbia University Center on Addiction and Substance Abuse (May 1993).

51. Leading cause of death: Alan Marlatt, report at the annual meeting of the American Psychological Association (Aug. 1994).

52. Data on alcoholism and cocaine addiction are from Meyer Glantz, acting chief of the Etiology Research Section of the National Institute for Drug and Alcohol Abuse.

53. Distress and abuse: Jeanne Tschann, "Initiation of Substance Abuse in Early Adolescence," *Health Psychology* 4 (1994).

54. I interviewed Ralph Tarter in *The New York Times* (Apr. 26, 1990).

55. Tension levels in sons of alcoholics: Howard Moss et al., "Plasma GABA-like Activity in Response to Ethanol Challenge in Men at High Risk for Alcoholism" *Biological Psychiatry* 27(6) (Mar. 1990).

56. Frontal lobe deficit in sons of alcoholics: Philip Harden and Robert Pihl, "Cognitive Function, Cardiovascular Reactivity, and Behavior in Boys at High Risk for Alcoholism," *Journal of Abnormal Psychology* 104 (1995).

57. Kathleen Merikangas et al., "Familial Transmission of Depression and Alcoholism," *Archives of General Psychiatry* (Apr. 1985).

58. The restless and impulsive alcoholic: Moss et al.

59. Cocaine and depression: Edward Khantzian, "Psychiatric and Psychodynamic Factors in Cocaine Addiction," in Arnold Washton and Mark Gold, eds., *Cocaine: A Clinician's Handbook* (New York: Guilford Press, 1987).

60. Heroin addiction and anger: Edward Khantzian, Harvard Medical School, in conversation, based on over 200 patients he has treated who were addicted to heroin.

61. No more wars: The phrase was suggested to me by Tim Shriver of the Collaborative for the Advancement of Social and Emotional Learning at the Yale Child Studies Center.

62. Emotional impact of poverty: "Economic Deprivation and Early Childhood Development" and "Poverty Experiences of Young Children and the Quality of Their Home Environments." Greg Duncan and Patricia Garrett each described their research findings in separate articles in *Child Development* (Apr. 1994).

63. Traits of resilient children: Norman Garmezy, *The Invulnerable Child* (New York: Guilford Press, 1987). I wrote about children who thrive despite hardship in *The New York Times* (Oct. 13, 1987).

64. Prevalence of mental disorders: Ronald C. Kessler et al., "Lifetime and 12-month Prevalence of DSM-III-R Psychiatric Disorders in the U.S.," *Archives of General Psychiatry* (Jan. 1994).

65. The figure for boys and girls reporting sexual abuse in the United States are from Malcolm Brown of the Violence and Traumatic Stress Branch of the National Institute of Mental Health; the number of substantiated cases is from the National Committee for the Prevention of Child Abuse and Neglect. A national survey of children found the

rates to be 3.2 percent for girls and 0.6 percent for boys in a given year: David Finkelhor and Jennifer Dziuba-Leatherman, "Children as Victims of Violence: A National Survey," *Pediatrics* (Oct. 1984).

66. The national survey of children about sexual abuse prevention programs was done by David Finkelhor, a sociologist at the University of New Hampshire.

67. The figures on how many victims child molesters have are from an interview with Malcolm Gordon, a psychologist at the Violence and Traumatic Stress Branch of the National Institute of Mental Health.

68. W. T. Grant Consortium on the School-Based Promotion of Social Competence, "Drug and Alcohol Prevention Curricula," in J. David Hawkins et al., *Communities That Care* (San Francisco: Jossey-Bass, 1992).

69. W. T. Grant Consortium, "Drug and Alcohol Prevention Curricula," p. 136.

Chapter 16. Schooling the Emotions

1. I interviewed Karen Stone McCown in *The New York Times* (Nov. 7, 1993).

2. Karen F. Stone and Harold Q. Dillehunt, *Self Science: The Subject Is Me* (Santa Monica: Goodyear Publishing Co., 1978).

3. Committee for Children, "Guide to Feelings," *Second Step 4–5* (1992), p. 84.

4. The Child Development Project: See, e.g., Daniel Solomon et al., "Enhancing Children's Prosocial Behavior in the Classroom," *American Educational Research Journal* (Winter 1988).

5. Benefits from Head Start: Report by High/Scope Educational Research Foundation, Ypsilanti, Michigan (Apr. 1993).

6. The emotional timetable: Carolyn Saarni, "Emotional Competence: How Emotions and Relationships Become Integrated," in R. A. Thompson, ed., *Socioemotional Development/Nebraska Symposium on Motivation* 36 (1990).

7. The transition to grade school and middle school: David Hamburg, *Today's Children: Creating a Future for a Generation in Crisis* (New York: Times Books, 1992).

8. Hamburg, *Today's Children*, pp. 171–72.

9. Hamburg, *Today's Children*, p. 182.

10. I interviewed Linda Lantieri in *The New York Times* (Mar. 3, 1992).

11. Emotional-literacy programs as primary prevention: Hawkins et al., *Communities That Care.*

12. Schools as caring communities: Hawkins et al., *Communities That Care.*

13. The story of the girl who was not pregnant: Roger P. Weisberg et al., "Promoting Positive Social Development and Health Practice in Young Urban Adolescents," in M. J. Elias, ed., *Social Decision-making in the Middle School* (Gaithersburg, MD: Aspen Publishers, 1992).

14. Character-building and moral conduct: Amitai Etzioni, *The Spirit of Community* (New York: Crown, 1993).

15. Moral lessons: Steven C. Rockefeller, *John Dewey: Religious Faith and Democratic Humanism* (New York: Columbia University Press, 1991).

16. Doing right by others: Thomas Lickona, *Educating for Character* (New York: Bantam, 1991).

17. The arts of democracy: Francis Moore Lappe and Paul Martin DuBois, *The Quickening of America* (San Francisco: Jossey-Bass, 1994).

18. Cultivating character: Amitai Etzioni et al., *Character Building for a Democratic, Civil Society* (Washington, DC: The Communitarian Network, 1994).

19. Three percent rise in murder rates: "Murders Across Nation Rise by 3 Percent, but Overall Violent Crime Is Down," *The New York Times* (May 2, 1994).

20. Jump in juvenile crime: "Serious Crimes by Juveniles Soar," Associated Press (July 25, 1994).

Appendix B. Hallmarks of the Emotional Mind

1. I have written about Seymour Epstein's model of the "experiential unconscious" on several occasions in *The New York Times,* and much of this summary of it is based on conversations with him, letters to me, his article, "Integration of the Cognitive and Psychodynamic Unconscious" (*American Psychologist* 44 (1994), and his book with Archie Brodsky, *You're Smarter Than You Think* (New York: Simon & Schuster, 1993). While his model of the experiential mind informs my own about the "emotional mind," I have made my own interpretation.

2. Paul Ekman, "An Argument for the Basic Emotions," *Cognition and Emotion,* 6, 1992, p. 175. The list of traits that distinguish emotions is a bit longer, but these are the traits that will concern us here.

3. Ekman, op cit., p. 187.

4. Ekman, op cit., p. 189.

5. Epstein, 1993, p. 55.

6. J. Toobey and L. Cosmides, "The Past Explains the Present: Emotional Adaptations and the Structure of Ancestral Environments," *Ethology and Sociobiology,* 11, pp. 418–19.

7. While it may seem self-evident that each emotion has its own biological pattern, it has not been so for those studying the psychophysiology of emotion. A highly technical debate continues over whether emotional arousal is basically the same for all emotions, or whether unique patterns can be teased out. Without going into the details of the debate, I have presented the case for those who hold to unique biological profiles for each major emotion.

Acknowledgments

My wife, Tara Bennett-Goleman, a psychotherapist, was a full creative partner in the earliest stages of thinking that led to this book. Her attunement to the emotional currents that move beneath the surface of our thoughts and interactions opened a world to me.

I first heard the phrase "emotional literacy" from Eileen Rockefeller Growald, then the founder and president of the Institute for the Advancement of Health. It was this casual conversation that piqued my interest and framed the investigations that finally became this book.

Support from the Fetzer Institute has allowed me the luxury of time to explore more fully what "emotional literacy" might mean, and I am grateful for the crucial early encouragement of Rob Lehman, president of the Institute, and an ongoing collaboration with David Sluyter, program director there. It was Rob Lehman who, early on in my explorations, urged me to write a book about emotional literacy.

Among my most profound debts is to the hundreds of researchers who over the years have shared their findings with me, and whose efforts are reviewed and synthesized here. To Peter Salovey at Yale I owe the concept of "emotional intelligence." I have also gained much from being privy to the ongoing work of many educators and practitioners of the art of primary prevention, who are at the forefront of the nascent movement in emotional literacy. Their hands-on efforts to bring heightened social and emotional skills to children, and to re-create schools as more humane environments, have been inspiring. Among them are Mark Greenberg and David Hawkins at the University of Washington; Eric Schaps and Catherine Lewis at the Developmental Studies Center in Oakland, California; Tim Shriver at the Yale Child Studies Center; Roger Weissberg at the University of Illinois at Chicago; Maurice Elias at Rutgers; Shelly Kessler of the Goddard Institute on Teaching and Learning in Boulder, Colorado; Chevy Martin and Karen Stone McCown at the Nueva School in Hillsborough, California; Linda Lantieri, director of the National Center for Resolving Conflict Creatively in New York City; and Carol A. Kusche, Developmental Research and Programs, Seattle.

I have a special debt to those who reviewed and commented on parts of this manuscript: Howard Gardner of the Graduate School of Education at Harvard University; Peter Salovey, of the psychology department at Yale University; Paul Ekman, director of the Human Interaction Laboratory at the University of California at San Francisco; Michael Lerner, director of Commonweal in Bolinas, California; Denis Prager, then director of the health program at the John D. and Catherine T. MacArthur Foundation; Mark Gerzon, director of Common Enterprise, Boulder, Colorado; Mary Schwab-Stone, MD, Child Studies Center, Yale University School of Medicine; David Spiegel, MD, Department of Psychiatry, Stanford University Medical School; Mark Greenberg, director of the Fast Track Program, University of Washington; Shoshona Zuboff, Harvard School of Business; Joseph LeDoux, Center for Neural Science, New York University; Richard Davidson, director of the Psychophysiology Laboratory, University of Wisconsin; Paul Kaufman, Mind and Media, Point Reyes, California; Jessica Brackman, Naomi Wolf, and, especially, Fay Goleman.

Helpful scholarly consultations came from Page DuBois, a Greek scholar at the University of Southern California; Matthew Kapstein, a philosopher of ethics and religion at Columbia University; and Steven Rockefeller, intellectual biographer of John Dewey, at Middlebury College. Joy Nolan gathered vignettes of emotional episodes; Margaret Howe and Annette Spychalla prepared the appendix on the effects of emotional literacy curricula. Sam and Susan Harris provided essential equipment.

My editors at *The New York Times* over the last decade have been marvelously supportive of my many enquiries into new findings on the emotions, which first appeared in the pages of that paper and which inform much of this book.

Toni Burbank, my editor at Bantam Books, offered the editorial enthusiasm and acuity that sharpened my resolve and thinking.

And Tara provided the cocoon of warmth, love, and intelligence that nurtured this project along.

Index

Italicized page numbers refer to illustrations.

A

Academic intelligence, 33–34, 36, 38, 97
Acceptingness, as style, 48
Action, impulses to, 5–8
"Active listening," 266
Adenosine triphosphate (ATP), 174
Ader, Robert, 166–67
Ad hoc teams, in workplace, 161–63
Adolescence. *See* Teenagers.
Adrenaline, 140, 168, 205
Adrenals, 227
Adrenocortical arousal, 60
Aerobic exercise, 73–74, 144
"Affective blindness," 15
Affective education, 262
Aggressive children, 196–97, 234–39
Agitation, and alcoholism, 254–55
AIDS, 270
Aikido, 124–25
Alcoholics Anonymous, 178, 255
Alcoholism, 71, 74, 252–55
Alexithymia, 51–52, 75, 96
Allen, Woody, 119, 220
Allergy, 166
Alpert, Richard, 84
Altruism, 104–6
Alzheimer's disease, 174
Amygdala
    and anger, 59–61
    and emergency actions, 22–24
    and emotional memory, 20–22
    as emotional sentinel, 17–20
    and empathy, 102–4
    and hármonizing emotion and
        thought, 27–29
    impulsive reactions of, 24–26
    and neural alarms, out-of-date, 21–22
    as neural tripwire, 16–17
    and passion, 14–16
    taming overexcitable, 221–24

and timidity, 217–19
and traumatic memories, 201–2, 203, 205–9, 211, 213
Andrews, Joyce, 270–71
Anger, 6, 47, 48, 191. *See also* Rage.
    builds on anger, 61–62, 144
    control of, 238–39
    de-escalating, 63–64
    defusing, 62
    different kinds of, 59
    and opiates, 255
    as toxic emotion, 169–72
    ventilating, 64–65
Anhedonia, 206
Anorexia nervosa, 246–49
Antidepressants, 211
    tricyclic, 245n
Antipathy, 105
Antisocial personality disorder, 255
Anxiety, 74, 218. *See also* Stress;
        Worrying.
    and alcoholism, 254–55
    cognitive, 66
    somatic, 66
    soothing, 65–69
    test, 83–84
    as toxic emotion, 172–75
Appropriate emotion, 56
Archives of Internal Medicine, 172
Aristotle, 50, 59, 269, 285
Arnold, Karen, 35–36
Arrhythmias, 176
Artery bypass surgery, 177. *See also*
        Coronary bypass.
Artful critique, in workplace, 153–54
Arthritis, 169, 175
Asher, Steven, 251–52
"As-if personality," 119–20
Assertiveness, 266
Asthma, 169, 173, 175
Atherosclerosis, 172
Attentional stance, toward duress, 49
Attunement, 116–17. *See also*
        Misattunement.

349

Index

About the Author

DANIEL GOLEMAN, Ph.D., is also the author of *Social Intelligence* and the bestseller *Working with Emotional Intelligence* and a coauthor of *Primal Leadership*. He received his Ph.D. from Harvard and reported on the brain and behavioral sciences for the *New York Times* for twelve years. He was awarded the American Psychological Association's Lifetime Achievement Award and is a Fellow of the American Association for the Advancement of Science.